Napoleon's Legacy

Napoleon's Legacy

Problems of Government in Restoration Europe

Edited by
David Laven and Lucy Riall

Oxford • New York

First published in 2000 by
Berg
Editorial offices:
150 Cowley Road, Oxford, OX4 1JJ, UK
838 Broadway, Third Floor, New York, NY 10003-4812, USA

Berg is an imprint of Oxford International Publishers Ltd.

Library of Congress Cataloging-in-Publication Data
A catalogue record for this book is available from the Library of Congress.

British Library Cataloguing-in-Publication Data
A catalogue record for this book is available from the British Library.

ISBN 1 85973 244 5 (Cloth)
1 85973 249 6 (Paper)

Typeset by JS Typesetting, Wellingborough, Northants.
Printed by WBC Book Manufacturers Limited, Bridgend

Contents

Contents

Notes on Contributors

Robert Alexander is an Associate Professor at the University of Victoria. His works include *Bonapartism and Revolutionary Tradition in France* (Cambridge, 1991). He is currently working on a study of the evolution of Napoleon's reputation.

Michael Broers is Reader in History at the University of Aberdeen. His publications include *Europe under Napoleon, 1799–1815* (London, 1997) and *Napoleonic Imperialism and the Savoyard Monarchy, 1773–1821* (Lampeter, 1997). He is currently working on a study of Napoleonic rule in Italy, 1797–1814.

Christopher Clark is a Fellow of St Catherine's College, Cambridge and the author of *Politics of Conversion. Missionary Protestantism and the Jews in Prussia 1728–1941* (Oxford, 1995).

John A. Davis is Professor of History at the University of Connecticut. He has written widely on nineteenth-century Italy; his works include *Conflict and Control, Law and Order in Nineteenth-Century Italy* (Basingstoke, 1988). He is currently editing the Oxford History of Modern Italy and is working on Murat's rule of the Kingdom of Naples.

Charles Esdaile is a Lecturer in the Department of History at the University of Liverpool. Among his publications are: *The Spanish Army in the Peninsular War* (Manchester, 1988), *The Duke of Wellington and the Command of the Spanish Army* (Basingstoke, 1990); *The Wars of Napoleon* (London, 1995). Two further works – *From Constitution to Civil war: Spain in the Liberal Age, 1808–1939* and *The French Wars* are to be published shortly.

Clive Emsley is Professor of History at the Open University. He has published extensively on British and European modern history, and has a particular interest in the history of policing. His most recent work is *Gendarmes and the State* (Oxford, 1999).

Notes on Contributors

Andreas Fahrmeir is a Fellow of the German Historical Institute in London, and an expert on citizenship in nineteenth-century Germany.

Brian Fitzpatrick is a Senior Lecturer in History at the University of Ulster. He has published widely on nineteenth-century French history. His works include *Catholic Royalism in the Department of the Gard, 1814–1852* (Cambridge, 1983).

Michael John is Professor of History at the University of East Anglia. A specialist in nineteenth-century Germany, his most important work is *Politics and the Law in Late Nineteenth-Century Germany* (Oxford, 1989).

David Laven is a Lecturer in History at the University of Reading. He has published a number of articles on Habsburg policy in Italy during the Restoration, and is currently completing a study of Austrian rule in Venetia in the reign of Francis 1.

Marco Meriggi is Professor of the History of Political and Social Institutions at the Federico II University in Naples. His work include: *Amministrazione e classi sociali nel Lombardo-Veneto (1814–1848)*, (Bologna, 1983), *Milano borghese: circoli ed élites nell'800* (Venice, 1992) and *Breve storia dell'Italia settentrionale: dall'800 a oggi* (Rome, 1996).

Andrzej Nieuwazny teaches at the University of Torun in Poland. He has published widely on Poland in the nineteenth century and in particular on the Napoleonic era.

Pamela Pilbeam is Professor of History at Royal Holloway, University of London. Her publications on nineteenth-century France include: *The 1830 Revolution in France* (Basingstoke, 1991); *Republicanism in Ninteenth-Century France* (Basingstoke, 1995); and *Constitutional Monarchy in France, 1814–48* (London, 1999). *Harmony and the New Woman: Early French Socialists* will be published shortly.

Lucy Riall is a Senior Lecturer at Birkbeck College, University of London. Her recent publications include *The Italian Risorgimento. State, Society and National Unification* (London, 1994) and *Sicily and the Unification of Italy. Liberal Policy and Local Power, 1859–1866* (Oxford, 1998).

Notes on Contributors

Brendan Simms is a Fellow of Peterhouse, Cambridge. He is the author of *The Impact of Napoleon. Prussian High Politics, Foreign Policy and the Crisis of the Executive, 1797–1806* (Cambridge, 1997) and *The Struggle for Mastery in Germany, 1780–1850* (Basingstoke, 1998).

Michael Rowe is a Lecturer in the Queen's University, Belfast, and is an expert on the Rhineland in the Napoleonic era.

Preface

The original versions of the chapters collected in this volume were first given as papers at a conference entitled *Napoleon's Legacy: Problems of Government in Restoration Europe,* held in the Institute of Historical Research in London on 18/19 April 1997. The conference, organized by the editors of this volume, sought to address an important but often neglected field of nineteenth-century history from a new perspective. Although studies of the diplomatic problems of Europe abound for the years after the Congress of Vienna, the domestic policies of the Restoration have generally been neglected in favour of either the dramatic events of the Revolutionary and Napoleonic Wars or the great upheavals of 1848–9. Although, as we go on to argue in this volume, this period is a crucial one for understanding the politics and problems of state formation, it is the process of 'state-making' in the later nineteenth century that has captured the interest of more historians. It has been our aim from the outset to encourage students and scholars to view the Restoration as a period worthy of study in its own right, as the era when the complex and often contradictory legacy of the French Revolution and Napoleonic Empire had to be addressed. We hope this book will succeed in helping to restore the Restoration.

Many people have contributed to the production of this work. Without the generosity of the British Academy, the Institute of Historical Research (IHR) and the Association for the Study of Modern Italy, the conference would never have been able to take place. We are greatly indebted to Bridget Taylor at the IHR: her kindness and efficiency guaranteed that the problems usually involved with the practical side of organizing a conference were negligible. Thanks are due too to Berg Publishers, and particularly to Maike Bohn, herself a nineteenth-century specialist, for her help, enthusiasm and advice. We are also grateful to Julian Swann for some cautionary words on the impact of Napoleon when seen from an eighteenth-century perspective. Our greatest debt of gratitude, however, lies with the contributors, not only for their papers and articles but also for their forbearance towards us as (initially) inexperienced editors. Finally, we should like to thank Chiara Cirillo and Fabian Russell-Cobb for their support and tolerance while we completed our editorial labours.

David Laven and Lucy Riall

List of Maps

Restoration Government and the Legacy of Napoleon

David Laven and *Lucy Riall*

I

In the years following the Vienna Settlement of 1815, the rulers of Restoration Europe were faced with the dilemma of what to keep and what to jettison of the Napoleonic system. The apparatus of state erected both in France and its satellites was characterized by an unparalleled level of efficiency, which would have been the envy of most *ancien régime* princes. Throughout the eighteenth century, rulers across Europe had attempted to centralize government, to rationalize adminstrative structures, and to curb the power of the Church, and of privileged orders and provincial estates, while building up ever-bigger military machines. Yet 'absolutist' reformers as diverse as the Habsburg Emperor, Joseph II, the Marquês de Pombal and Louis XVI of France had time and again been forced to temper or abandon their modernizing programmes in the face of resistance. Such resistance took many forms. In *ancien régime* France, for example, it was expressed in the literary sniping of *philosophes* and Grub Street pamphleteers but, perhaps more significantly, in judicial obstruction from the *parlements*, the refusal of the provincial estates to vote new taxes, and, arguably, in the outbreak of the Revolution itself. Elsewhere opposition was not always so dramatic. Nor did it always guarantee the end of reform programmes. But it did mean that every European ruler struggled to establish a 'well-ordered police state', the *état policier* or *Polizeistaat* that was their goal.[1]

Where the centralizing, reform-minded rulers of the 'enlightened' eighteenth century encountered obstacles, Napoleon overcame them. Although the effectiveness and impact of his rationalization has sometimes been exaggerated – by contemporaries just as much as by modern historians – in France, at least, Napoleon built a well-policed, centralized,

bureauratic state, with a powerful executive unchallenged by representative bodies and with well-ordered finances and a vast military
establishment. Of course, Napoleon encountered fierce resistance to
many of his reforms; but within those lands administered directly from
Paris, he managed to outflank or sweep aside opposition. Elsewhere,
more sustained protest and obstruction sometimes prevented the full
imposition of the Napoleonic system, but, as John Davis has written of
Italy, 'what had remained only aspiration in even the most powerful of
the eighteenth-century monarchies was finally put into practice in the
systematic reorganisation of the administrative, bureaucratic and financial
institutions that was carried through in the brief period of French rule'.[2]
Much the same could be said of the other regions of Europe that fell
under Napoleonic sway. For the rulers of Restoration Europe, therefore,
the most obvious and, in Stuart Woolf's words, 'longest-lasting' legacy[3]
of the Napoleonic era was the model of a centrally-controlled, hierarchical
and uniform administration that assumed, as one contemporary put it,
that 'the executive chain descends without interruption from the minister
to the administered and transmits the law and the government's orders to
the furthest ramifications of the social order'.[4] It is this legacy for
government, and its impact on modern political relations, that lies at the
heart of the present study.

This legacy can only be understood within the context of Napoleon's
radical reorganization of central government after the *coup d'état* of 18
Brumaire. He consolidated and increased the size of government ministries
– notably the ministry of the interior, the ministry of police and the
ministry of war. He also reformed the treasury, modernized the accounting
system, stabilized the currency and created a central bank, the Bank of
France. Provincial and local government was similarly restructured along
strictly hierarchical lines. Napoleon established a system of prefectures
in France's provincial departments, giving them a key rôle in a centralized
administrative system. As Geoffrey Ellis has remarked, the prefects were
meant to be 'the crucial agent of the central government'.[5] Directly
responsible to and appointed by Napoleon, the prefects presided over
the bureaucratic structures of local government: they supervised the
arrondissements (run by sub-prefects, also selected by Napoleon), which
were in turn divided into *communes* (under mayors, chosen either by
Napoleon, or, in communities with fewer than 5,000 inhabitants, by the
prefects themselves). Like provincial intendants before them, the prefects
were in charge of the levying of taxation, and played a pivotal rôle in
overseeing education and policing. Moreover, they rapidly came to control
the conscription on which Napoleon's vast army and aggressive foreign

policy depended. In theory at least, the prefects acted as a direct link between the centre and the provinces,[6] and also constituted, albeit indirectly, an essential element in Napoleon's pursuit of his expansionist ambitions.

The growing ambition of Napoleon's centralizing state can also be seen in fundamental changes in the treatment of bureaucratic personnel: all public officials became salaried, trained servants of the state, whose employment and promotion were supposed to be regulated according to 'talent' and seniority within the administration, rather than through the family connections, venality or privileges of class that had characterized the *ancien régime*.[7] A similar approach characterized Napoleon's policy towards the administration of justice, education and the Church. With hindsight, Napoleon was to describe the Civil Code of 1804 (known as the *Code Napoléon* after 1807) as his greatest victory.[8] The work of a special commission closely supervised by Napoleon himself, the code confirmed the revolutionary principle of legal equality and sanctioned legal rights of property, property-acquisition and property-inheritance. Here, as in the other legal codes,[9] and in the judicial structure more generally, uniformity, order and the rule of a single, central authority were the guiding principles. Reforms in education – producing, amongst other innovations, a secondary-school system where the curriculum, examinations, libraries, uniform and, indeed, discipline of each *lycée* were identical and subject to strict government regulation – reflected a similar drive to state control and standardization, even though, in this instance, the actual consequence of such reforms was to drive pupils away from state-controlled schools.[10] Even the Concordat with Rome (described by Christopher Clark as both a 'dramatic departure' from the past and 'among the most durable monuments of the Napoleonic era'),[11] which served in some senses to reinforce Papal authority over the Catholic hierarchy, also helped affirm state control over the French Church.[12]

It is a commonplace that much of Napoleon's energy was expended on enlarging the army and developing the necessary fiscal and administrative machinery to sustain his almost constant campaigning. Sometimes the almost obsessive primacy he afforded matters of military and foreign policy can distract from the way in which he also devised administrative systems for the internal surveillance and control of the population. In this he showed his readiness to draw on different traditions of government, borrowing from and building on the repressive structures he inherited from both the *ancien régime* and the Revolution. Thus, despite his personal reservations about the self-aggrandizing Joseph Fouché, Napoleon had no qualms in confirming him as minister of police, encouraging him to develop his already extensive network of spies and informers, and condoning techniques with 'a ruthless pedigree going back to the old regime'.[13] Meanwhile, the military police force or *gendarmerie*, established in December 1790 (but with its origins in the old, royal *maréchaussée*) was also reorganized and massively enlarged.[14] The machinery for press censorship experienced a similarly dramatic expansion. The activities of the censors reflected the régime's extreme sensitivity to public criticism and its passion for political conformity, but indicated 'relatively little official concern with literature which appeared blasphemous, morally offensive or obscene'.[15] Yet the Napoleonic conception of policing was not limited simply to surveillance and apprehension of criminals, or the identification and repression of potential enemies. Additional mechanisms were developed to provide detailed information on all aspects of economy and society in every department. This was especially evident in the increasingly systematic collection of statistical data, and in the obligation imposed on prefects to make annual tours to guarantee first-hand knowledge of the lands under their jurisdiction.[16]

Arguably, the most innovative aspects of Napoleon's rule lay not with the growth of policing or the trends towards bureaucratization and centralization; indeed, these often represented a continuation of policies introduced by his predecessors. Far more novel was the way in which Napoleon's administrative measures involved a renegotiation of the relations between state and society. Controls on the appointments of judges and teachers, the affirmation in the Civil Code of a 'strongly patriachical bias'[17] in clauses relating to property, inheritance and marriage, and the subordination of the provinces to the central power all pointed to the creation of a more authoritarian (and, in some respects, 'despotic') form of government, as well as to a substantial increase in the penetrative (or 'infrastructural') control by the state.[18] This trend was further confirmed in other areas of the Napoleonic system. Such representative institutions as Napoleon tolerated – from the advisory municipal councils of the *communes* up to the highest national level of the *Corps Législatif*, Tribunate, Senate and *Conseil d'État* – were never permitted to exercise real powers; significantly even the elections to the emasculated national bodies were controlled through an elaborate system of electoral colleges in which only the highest taxpayers could serve.[19]

Yet the illusion of consultation was retained. The Napoleonic state was based famously on 'blocks [*masses*] of granite', on a reconstructed and broadened social 'notability' that combined elements of a new élite (new landowners, professionals, businessmen, government officials and army officers) with a more traditional one (nobles who had 'rallied' to Napoleon). Napoleon tied them to the régime by recognizing their status, by government employment, and through material rewards; later, he also made use of imperial honours.[20] Along with this emphasis on creating a loyal élite, Napoleon made sure, particularly in the early years of his rule, that a façade of popular sovereignty was maintained. If nothing else, plebiscites – votes of popular approval – that legitimized acts of state (the constitution, the life consulate, the hereditary Empire), acknowledged the importance of expressions of public consent for Napoleon.[21] The Concordat with Rome, too, can be seen as a tactic to prevent the emergence of religion as an anti-Napoleonic 'vehicle of protest' and, as Clark argues in this volume, as a new way of thinking about religion in the legitimation of state power.[22] Napoleon supervised a substantial propaganda machine for internal and external consumption, and became himself the centre of an elaborate personality cult.[23] In other words, he created not only a powerful administrative system, but a form of political leadership with its own language, rituals and symbols. Thus, in constructing what Woolf calls a 'unified state identity',[24] based on a programme of administrative modernization and the support of the notables, Napoleon was equally anxious to create a sense of 'national belonging' that tied state and society together.[25]

The importance of nationalism as a legacy of Napoleon has probably been overstated.[26] Still, there is no doubt that greater territorial unity realized in Italy and Germany, and the greater degree of independence granted to those Poles living within the Duchy of Warsaw, played a pivotal part in stimulating national sentiment. At the same time, the opposition to Napoleon also invoked the principle of national struggle in wars of liberation, hoping to foment popular resistance to Napoleonic hegemony. In the German states especially, the struggle to overthrow French domination 'took on the character of a bloodthirsty national crusade',[27] fostered by poets, artists, and political thinkers, and sometimes sponsored by princes (or at least their generals and their ministers). The determination to drive out the French led the governments of some German states to unleash forces that would in the future challenge their very legitimacy.[28] In Portugal, Spain, the Tyrol and parts of Italy, too, a 'patriotic' anti-Napoleonic sentiment flourished and spread, often resulting in bitter fighting against the French oppressor or his collaborators and puppets. Admittedly, insurgents were not always motivated by feelings that would today be recognized as nationalist. Yet a combination of anticlerical legislation, the economic consequences of the Continental Blockade, and the burdens of conscription and heavy taxation generated fierce enmity towards the French. When combined with particularist or dynastic loyalties, such shared resentment of Napoleon could metamorphose into the proto-nationalism that was to prove a major source of instability in Restoration Europe.[29]

When ousted or emasculated rulers promoted popular risings against the French in the hope of winning back lost authority, they played a dangerous game. When they employed national rhetoric, they implicitly recognized that popular will rather than dynastic right was the basis of sovereignty. Moreover, by promising concessions to mobilize support, they ran the risk of mortgaging their political futures. Some rulers were clearly aware of the dangers such a strategy involved. The Habsburg Emperor, Francis I, for example, was reluctant to unleash popular forces in the Tyrol in 1809 against Napoleon's ally, Maximilian Joseph of Bavaria. Francis was almost certainly right. The Tyrolean rebels, led by Andreas Hofer (who had an uneasy relationship with the Austrian government), were notionally loyal to the Habsburgs. Francis I, however, had no wish to endorse any form of popular resistance, even if by doing so he stood to regain lost territories. Other monarchs and their ministers were happier to offer concessions and reforms – including the grant of a constitution – in order to mobilize support against the French, to ensure that their subjects remained loyal in the face of French propaganda, and, in the case of the Bourbons in Sicily, to retain British protection and financial backing.[30] When the French threat disappeared after 1815, many rulers proved reluctant to honour pledges to (re)introduce representative institutions or to make other similar reforms. The effect of this failure to fulfil promises was to contribute significantly to political instability during the Restoration: those who felt cheated of political power would increasingly be found within liberal ranks, critical of the post-Napoleonic order, and, on occasion, ready to force changes through conspiracy and rebellion.

II

Napoleon's success in reforming administrative, fiscal, police and juridical structures, and in constructing a new relationship between state and society based on the appearance of popular consent, could be startling. Significantly, it was achieved at the expense of the rights and privileges of nobility, Church and periphery. It is little surprise, therefore, that, for the princes who came to power in the 'Restoration' of 1815, the prospect of retaining Napoleon's system was immensely seductive. However, for many of the victors of 1814–15, Napoleon's régime was also perceived

– and feared – as the child of Jacobin excess, popular violence and godless revolution. Napoleon's name was itself synonymous with long years of bloody war and the bitter humiliation of defeat and dictated peace. And while the restored rulers of France and Europe often welcomed the limitations imposed on Church and nobility, they were still forced to recognize the necessity of attaching them to the Restoration order to provide both legitimacy and support. The situation was further complicated because the Restoration order faced other awkward legacies of Napoleon. One was the challenge from social groups that had come to prominence under Napoleonic rule: non-noble bureaucrats and army officers, who had risen under the more meritocratic and professionalized French system, had developed a taste for power in the process. Any future attempt to exclude them from their new-found authority involved a double risk: on the one hand, it would mean squandering the services of able technocrats, experienced administrators, and battle-hardened veterans; on the other, their response to exclusion might be to embrace one of the new ideologies – nationalism and liberalism[31] – hostile to the Restoration order. These ideologies were, in turn, largely a product of the Napoleonic years, drawing on traditions of both support for and opposition to the French Emperor.[32]

In the years after 1815, the feelings of the rulers of Europe for the Napoleonic system remained confused. Hence, the policies adopted by Restoration governments were shaped by contradictions: by tensions between admiration for the Napoleonic system, fear of its consequences and the need to inherit – yet somehow distinguish themselves from – its legacy. However, until recently, relatively little has been written on the way in which governments perceived and responded to these tensions. Historians have focused instead on Napoleon's relationship with what came before, on investigating either the underlying continuities between Napoleon's régime and eighteenth-century absolutism or the impact of the French Revolution on Napoleonic policy. Traditional interpretations of the Restoration period have depicted it as rigidly 'reactionary', or as rejecting the Revolutionary and Napoleonic legacies in their entirety. As a result, the experiences of Restoration government have tended to be obscured, either overshadowed as little more than an interlude between two revolutions (1789–1815 and 1848–9) or, perhaps worse, as the embodiment of a doomed attempt to recast *ancien régime* Europe.[33]

The present volume offers a new approach to the Restoration era. It takes as its central theme the way in which Restoration governments sought – and were obliged – to adapt to Napoleon's legacy. Recent research has increasingly stressed the importance of this period as a crucial phase in the emergence of the modern state and of modern political discourse.[34] This suggests that Restoration responses to administrative centralization, foreign policy, relations between Church and state, the creation of 'national' leaderships and the differences between Left and Right in this period merit study, not so much as a case of reaction to modernity, as because the underlying sources of instability – conflict between centre and periphery, tensions between state and civil society and, perhaps most of all, divisions within the political hierarchy and within society – continued to destabilize European states throughout the 'long' nineteenth century, and beyond. At the same time the difficulties encountered in the transition from one régime to the next were immense. The question of establishing the legitimacy of a new ruler had always existed. Hitherto, however, it had usually been seen in terms of dynastic right, military power and the need to satisfy powerful élites. Such considerations, of course, persisted, but the sheer scale of the process after Napoleon's defeat had never previously been encountered in European history. Moreover, emphasis had changed. Restoration rulers were preoccupied with a set of problems that were recognizably modern. The need to emphasize the ideological breach with the past while maintaining administrative stability, the desire to purge the bureaucracy and armed forces yet exploit a *corps* of trained and experienced personnel – these issues that so concerned governments in the years after 1815 find obvious echoes in Europe post-1945 or post-1990.

It should be recognized at the outset, however, that one crucial aspect of Napoleon's legacy for Restoration government was the uneven impact of Napoleonic rule. It is important to remember that the nature of Napoleonic rule changed over the years and, especially after 1804, became more conservative and more authoritarian. Nor was Napoleonic rule always continuous. In some regions of Europe it was regularly interrupted by invasion by Napoleon's enemies or by risings against his domination. Even in France, the chronology of the Empire has to be divided into two very uneven sections, punctuated by the first, short-lived Bourbon restoration of 1814.

Besides distinctions of chronology, it is also important to make distinctions of geography. Outside France itself, the Napoleonic model was not imposed uniformly. The institutions described so far in this introduction were, indeed, exported beyond the frontiers of France to Napoleon's satellite states. However, local requirements, and differences in implementation and adaptation, meant that a uniform system could never have been established for all areas that fell under Napoleonic hegemony. In the most general terms, the impact of the Napoleonic model was greatest in the lands close to the French border and that had been annexed relatively early in Napoleon's rule or even prior to 18 Brumaire: in other words, the former Habsburg Low Countries, the Rhineland, and Piedmont-Liguria.[35] In Holland, in those parts of Italy that were incorporated into metropolitan France at a later stage, and in the satellite and occupied states – the so-called *pays alliés* and *pays conquis* – the influence of the French administrative model was rarely so strong. In these areas Napoleonic control was frequently undermined by popular resistance; it was also handicapped by the need to conciliate and win the support of traditional élites and in some cases by the ability of satellite rulers (perhaps most notably Murat in Naples) to develop independent policies.[36] Thus, among the non-French states, the actual experience of Napoleonic domination, although sharing broadly similar characteristics, could vary quite dramatically in important details.

If the impact of Napoleon on annexed and satellite states varied, it must not be forgotten either that his wars affected every state in Europe. This volume does not include any treatment of Scandinavia, Portugal, Britain or Ireland, Ottoman Turkey, or Russia (outside Congress Poland), and treats the Habsburg Empire only tangentially. However, it would be foolish to deny the impact of Napoleon on the government of even those states he could never dominate directly. Napoleon's constant campaigning forced other states into reform, often in emulation of his style of govern-ment or military organization. In Prussia and Austria, for example, both of which had a history of conflict with Napoleon and were only ever reluctant allies, the influence of Napoleon on domestic and military reform programmes was profound. This was most evident in Prussia after the decisive defeat inflicted by the French at Jena in 1806: the subsequent loss of territories, and the imposition of an indemnity and military limitations forced Prussia's rulers into a programme of radical reform of the Frederician state, society and army.[37] It is true that most of the Prussian reformers preferred to look beyond Napoleon's system for their model. Nevertheless, the changes initiated by the likes of Stein, Hardenberg, Yorck and Scharnhorst – all of whom approached the question of reform from sharply differing ideological perspectives – were a direct response to Napoleon's plans to reduce Prussia to the status of a mere client state. Humiliation by Napoleon also prompted a brief Austrian flirtation with reform, particularly in the army. Significantly, Francis I did his best to keep change to a minimum. Paradoxically, because Austria actually emerged from the conflict with its territories enhanced (in spite of Francis I's obstructive attitude to reform programmes), the Emperor's objection to innovation, at least within the Hereditary Lands of the Habsburg

Empire, actually became more firmly entrenched.[38]

Given that the impact of Napoleon varied greatly from one part of Europe to another, it is little surprise that so did responses to his legacy. Nevertheless, a glance at the policies pursued by differing Restoration governments after 1815 reveals that proximity to France, and the duration and 'penetration' of Revolutionary/Napoleonic rule, were by no means the only factors determining its long-term influence. A crucial factor in the nature of the Restoration régime's response to the Napoleonic legacy was the personal outlook of the Restoration ruler and his close advisers. This is particularly clear in Restoration Italy. Thus the 'almost uninterrupted administrative and institutional continuity' between Napoleonic and Restoration eras, identified in many states by John Davis,[39] was usually a conscious choice of reform-minded princes. Probably the most complete loyalty to the Napoleonic tradition was to be found in the Duchy of Parma, ruled by Napoleon's estranged wife, the Habsburg princess, Marie Louise.[40] Her father, Francis I of Austria, meanwhile retained most of the Kingdom of Italy's administrative institutions that he found in place when he reoccupied Lombardy-Venetia, although Habsburg bankruptcy demanded a drastically reduced personnel. Cosmetic changes (designed to make the apparatus of state appear to conform more closely to that of his Hereditary Lands) and Austrian law were also introduced.[41] More surprisingly, Napoleonic institutions were also retained in the Papal States, where the Secretary of State, Cardinal Consalvi, managed to salvage much that was effective from the Napoleonic régime (including the *gendarmerie*), despite the hostility of reactionary cardinals known as the *zelanti*.[42] In the South, the Restoration actually saw an expansion of Napoleonic practices *after* the defeat of Napoleon. Sicily was never subjected to French rule – the Napoleonic period had seen a reaffirmation of noble 'particularisms', manifest in the reconvening of the Sicilian parliament in 1812. It became, however, a posthumous conquest of Napoleon, when in 1816 the restored Bourbon monarch, Ferdinando I, fused the island with his mainland territories as the Kingdom of the Two Sicilies, imposed a centralized administration and extended to Sicily the social and economic reforms introduced by Murat during the 'French decade' in Naples.[43]

In striking contrast with those Italian states that sought to maintain some degree of continuity with the Napoleonic system were the Duchy of Modena, ruled by Francesco IV d'Este (the model for Stendhal's reactionary monarch, Enrico IV), and the Grand Duchy of Tuscany (where the Habsburg Grand Duke rejected Napoleonic practices to build on the enlightened traditions of eighteenth-century Leopoldine reform).

However, perhaps the most extreme case of 'putting back the clock' was Piedmont. In Piedmont – the region of Italy occupied the longest by the French – there was, in the words of Michael Broers, 'a concerted effort to return to the norms of the *ancien régime*'.[44] Vittorio Emanuele I abolished Napoleonic legislation in a single decree, and – despite the warnings of Metternich – the administration, judiciary and army were purged of those tainted by service under the previous régime.

Outside Italy, the picture varied, but the pivotal rôle of the restored ruler is hard to ignore. It received its most eloquent expression in the case of Poland. As Andrzej Nieuwazny shows, the fate of the French satellite Duchy of Warsaw was dependent almost solely on one man, Tsar Alexander I, who chose to leave its political institutions, legal system and army 'largely intact',[45] ruling it as a separate constitutional monarchy in tandem with his despotic government of Russia. Fernando of Spain also chose to preserve those aspects of Napoleonic rule that he found most useful, particularly in the field of fiscal matters, while rejecting those that he disliked. For example, in his policy towards the army, he tried to abolish the traditional exemptions from military service, and to introduce conscription throughout Spain, but in other respects restored the pre-war status and power of the military authorities. There was probably greater continuity in France itself, where much of the state apparatus was, according to Robert Alexander, 'inherited from the previous régime'.[46] Although Louis XVIII conceded a *Charte* (constitution) in 1814, which introduced formal limitations on royal power, he retained unaltered the centralized and authoritarian administrative-judicial structures of the Napoleonic period.

In Germany the scope for independent action of princes was more constrained. The fundamental reason for this was itself a legacy of Napoleonic hegemony in Germany. Napoleon had radically redrawn the map of Germany, reducing the number of sovereign states through a process of 'mediatization' from over three hundred to around forty. Michael John confirms in this volume that the major beneficiaries of the territorial rearrangement and rationalization were the so-called *Mittelstaaten*.[47] It was quite clear that after the defeat of Napoleon the rulers of these 'medium-sized, relatively well- integrated states'[48] – many of whom had enthusiastically adopted Napoleonic administrative practices during the period of French tutelage – were anxious to safeguard their recent territorial gains. The fusion of administrative zeal and opportunistic, expansionist collaboration that characterized the rulers of states such as Bavaria, Baden and Württemberg, therefore, militated fiercely against their supporting a return to the pre-Napoleonic status quo. To put it simply, a genuine restoration could challenge their very right to exist. In consequence the rulers of the German mediatized states were obliged to collaborate with the Restoration order to protect their newly acquired status. The Austrian Foreign Minister, Metternich, understood this, and was, with rare exception, prepared to trade Habsburg recognition of the new, simplified German map for acceptance of a Habsburg hegemony within the newly formed German Confederation.[49] This latter institution also maintained strong lines of continuity with the Napoleonic past, since its structure was closely modelled on the Confederation of the Rhine, albeit now under Austrian rather than French domination, and with the inclusion of Prussia (carefully excluded by the French Emperor). Most significantly, however, the Confederation guaranteed Austria's ability to impose considerable restrictions on other German states, particularly when it was able to find common cause with the second state of Germany, the greatly expanded Restoration Prussia.

Given the hegemonic position of Francis I's Austria after 1815, Germany's princes found themselves severely restricted in what reforms they could impose. Of course, as Brendan Simms has argued persuasively, the primary function of the Confederation was 'not the maintenance of political illiberalism' but to further foreign policy aims to ensure the security of Germany and the Habsburg Empire from external threats.[50] Nevertheless, it cannot be denied that the Confederation gave Metternich scope to curtail or emasculate the progressive trends emerging in some of Germany's middling and smaller states. When the rulers of Baden, Württemberg and Bavaria experimented with constitutional reform in the early years of the Restoration, largely with a view to giving greater homogeneity to their recently expanded possessions, Metternich viewed the development with apprehension. He responded with the Vienna *Schlussakte* of 1820, which used the Confederation to underscore the principle of princely government, and made it quite clear that Austria would not tolerate the possibility that the new parliaments of southwest Germany might become the focus of agitation. As the conservative thinker Friedrich Gentz remarked, the Confederation's acceptance of the principles contained within the *Schlussakte* was 'a victory more important than the battle of Leipzig'.[51]

In using one Napoleonic inheritance – a German Confederation - to combat another Napoleonic legacy – the reformist tendencies of the south-western German states – Metternich revealed his ambivalent response to the French Emperor. Such ambivalence was by no means exceptional among Restoration statesmen. Restoration reformers in Prussia who had, in Emsley's words, 'little love for Napoleon'[52] engaged in a similar transformation of the state structure, borrowing Napoleonic principles of government. Prussian conservatives may have rejected all things French, but they were unable to do more than reduce the number of Napoleonic-style gendarmes in Prussia. Perhaps the most remarkable example of Prussian 'borrowing' from Napoleon was in the religious sphere, where the king used the 1804 Concordat between Paris and Rome as a model for state control over the Prussian church administration under the control of central government. According to Clark, the type of Church–state 'organism' that was established as a result of Prussian church policy owed much to Napoleon and little, if anything, to restored or neo-absolutism. The newly-created Church of the Prussian Union offered 'romantic deference to history and tradition as the ultimate foundations of legitimacy'; but this was largely a mirage, an invented tradition that accompanied 'the enhancement of the state's supervisory control over the institutions of the church'.[53]

Even in the states that attempted to abolish the legacy of Napoleon there were some surprising continuities. In the most 'reactionary' of the Italian states, Piedmont, the Napoleonic gendarmerie was retained by the returning rulers; meanwhile, in the more reform-minded Two Sicilies and in the Venetian provinces of the Habsburgs' Italian possessions, it was abolished.[54] In religious affairs, the apparently conservative alliance of 'throne and altar' – the concordats between Restoration governments and the Catholic Church that were the central pillar of Restoration legitimacy and order – was not all it seemed either.[55] Charles Esdaile writes that, in Spain, King Fernando was 'unwilling to relinquish the gains made by his eighteenth-century predecessors'.[56] While the Church was undoubtedly the 'chief beneficiary' of the Spanish Restoration, 'here, too, there were limits to what Fernando was prepared to do' to undermine the legacy of Napoleon. Fernando refused to return the ecclesiastical estates that had been sold off during the war and imposed far greater state controls over the Church hierarchy than had existed hitherto.[57] Many *serviles* appointed to high office in the Church found to their dismay 'that they were to be servants of the monarchy rather than its masters'.[58] Similarly, in the Italian states, censorship may have been the expression of an 'alternative ideological, cultural and religious consensus' based on the alliance of throne and altar. However, as John Davis shows us in his chapter, it was controlled and pursued with the political and administrative tools introduced by the French; and it represented a continuation of the system of bureaucratic authority that the French had imposed.[59] In both these cases, an innovatory policy lay behind the conservative image of 'throne and altar' – one that had little to do with restoring the old order, and everything to do with increasing the power of the central authority.

III

A major complication for Restoration rulers was the social and ideological changes that had occurred during the Revolutionary/Napoleonic period. As we have seen, collaboration with Napoleon brought new social groups to prominence in France and elsewhere in Europe. In the aftermath of his defeat, these 'new men' were often 'purged' from their positions in the bureaucracy and army. Such purges could severely threaten the stability of the new state, both by depriving it of experienced men, and by driving the victims into the arms of the opposition. The policies pursued by Charles X (Louis XVIII's successor) in France, designed to place the old aristocracy and the Church at the very centre of French politics, were so unpopular that they eventually brought him and his dynasty down as the first great casualty of the Restoration order. Similarly, in Piedmont, Vittorio Emanuele I helped lay the foundations for the revolution of 1821 by his persecution of servants of the former régime. The appointment of two ministers with Napoleonic connections – Prospero Balbo and San Marzano – was not sufficient to pacify the many thousands who felt rejected by the Restoration order. Napoleonic servants were not always the victims. Paradoxically, in Prussia, the men associated with the Reform Movement (which was in essence anti-Napoleonic) often found themselves marginalized after Napoleon had been defeated. Nor was a compromise solution, balancing servants of the former régime with men without any Napoleonic pedigree, guaranteed to resolve the problem. The situation in the Kingdom of the Two Sicilies highlights the dangers of such a policy of 'amalgamation'. Here the moderate de' Medici tried to combine the most able men from Murat's machinery of state with talented Bourbon loyalists; but, despite his best efforts, he was unable to prevent a rebellion, led in part by disaffected Muratists, from breaking out in 1820.[60]

The Kingdom of Lombardy-Venetia at least escaped without insurrection in the early years after the Vienna Congress. But here too, the issue of personnel generated a series of complex hostilities to the new order. Despite the fact that the purges of masons or 'Jacobins' threatened by Francis I never materialized, the Habsburg administration did not manage to satisfy the aspirations of its Italian subjects. In Lombardy especially, the Restoration was accompanied by widespread optimism among the aristocratic élites – typified by Count Giacomo Mellerio –

that they would be returned to the position of local hegemony that they had enjoyed under the eighteenth- century rule of Maria Theresia. When this did not emerge, many felt aggrieved and gradually drifted towards the liberal camp. At the same time, the Milanese bourgeoisie who had prospered within the Napoleonic system found themselves excluded from the career opportunities they had enjoyed within the more imposing bureaucratic structures of the Napoleonic Kingdom of Italy. During the Restoration they too increasingly looked to the liberal ideas that attracted many of the aristocrats, despite their very different initial perspective.[61] In Venetia, the cause for discontent was rather different. Happy to see the end of a régime that had subjected them to rule from Milan, the Venetian population were at first antagonized by the retention of too many Napoleonic officials, who were often drawn from neighbouring Lombardy. But then this problem was further aggravated by the large numbers of government officers recruited to run the Venetian provinces from the Hereditary Lands of the Habsburg Empire. In short, for the Venetians, one form of foreign rule had simply been exchanged for another, with few opportunities for local talent to rise to prominence.[62]

What these examples highlight is the difficulty faced by the Restoration régimes in reconciling the different interest groups that had evolved during the Revolutionary/Napoleonic era. On the one hand, as the 1820 and 1830 revolutions show clearly, it was not feasible simply to return to the old order. But on the other, an unquestioning acceptance of Napoleonic structures, practices and personnel risked alienating powerful groups who were the most apparently loyal to the Restoration régime. This conflict was made much worse by a real dilemma: the 'loyal' nobility and (in Catholic countries) clergy were in fact those (or the descendants of those) who had been among the most obstructive enemies of reform in the eighteenth century. Matters, therefore, had been complicated by the way in which opposition to Napoleon had forced rulers to reconsider relationships with traditional power-holders. As Michael Broers has pointed out, the experience of counter-revolution during the Revolutionary and Napoleonic period had been played out 'in the name of absent rulers'.[63] It forged a bond between these rulers and traditional élites that replaced the conflicts that had characterized much of the eighteenth century. Such counter-revolutionary alliances could act as a powerful constraint on the ability of Restoration governments to adapt to Napoleon's legacy. Most obviously in France, but also in Spain and much of Italy, the restored monarchies could not simply wash their hands of a Church and nobility anxious to reclaim their old status.

Thus although, as we have seen, the alliance of throne and altar could be used to camouflage an extension of state power over the Church, in other ways it represented a reversal of the secularizing policies of eighteenth-century absolutism. In Spain, Esdaile tells us, resistance to Napoleon had reinforced a group of reactionaries whose programme was 'positively gothic in its mediaevalism', and whose chief aim was 'a return to a semi-mythical golden age in which the Church and nobility would be left to enjoy their privileges free from the attentions of an interfering monarchy'.[64] Reactionaries in Piedmont 'did more to break with the *ancien régime* than any other'; led by the King, Carlo Felice, who came to the throne after Vittorio Emanuele I abdicated in the face of revolution, the Piedmontese absolutist 'tradition' was sacrificed to the 'ideology of reaction'.[65] The Church was given a pre-eminent rôle in political life, and the King took counsel from the *amicizia cattolica*. In a sense, therefore, the struggle against French invasion created a legacy every bit as powerful and distinct as the invasion itself. As a result of alliances made during the wars against Napoleon, Restoration rulers came to be identified with administrative decentralization, and with the restoration of noble prerogatives, clerical privileges and local autonomies. Ironically for them, and most damaging in the long run, Restoration rulers came to be identified with opposition to precisely those aspects of Napoleonic rule that, in reality, they most welcomed.

This tension between what rulers hoped to take from the Napoleonic model, and what their loyalist supporters believed they ought to take was bound to cause problems. Reference has already been made to Lombardy, where the denial of privileges and power to the originally pro-Habsburg nobility turned them into critics of rule from Vienna. The same was true of other parts of Italy, where 'the groups which had historically been privileged' lambasted their returning sovereigns for destroying ancient liberties and corporate rights, in short 'for being no more than replicas of the states which had just been abolished'.[66] Sometimes these groups were successful. Prince Canosa in Naples – so reactionary that both the British and the Austrians brought pressure to bear on Ferdinando to dismiss him – successfully undermined de' Medici's moderate programme of reforms, and was eventually to return to power after 1821. Similarly the *zelanti* were only held at bay by Consalvi while Pius VII lived; under both Leo XII and Gregory XVI the Papal States were plunged once more into reaction and obscurantism. But even reactionaries borrowed from Napoleon. As Brian Fitzpatrick demonstrates, ultra-royalist conspirators in France found aspects of the Napoleonic state 'so useful' that they adopted them shamelessly in their attempt to control the Midi.[67] Similarly, throughout the Restoration period it was not just the French Left that used parliamentary elections to resist the power of the state, as is described in Pamela Pilbeam's essay; the Right, too, whatever its reservations about representative government, was not prepared to shun the chance of power.[68]

If the policies available to Restoration governments were constrained by the alliances and expectations created under Napoleon, and by the attacks they suffered from both Left and Right, they were still further circumscribed by the economic and fiscal consequences of the Napoleonic wars. If Bourbon France managed to pay off the indemnity imposed by the victorious allies after Waterloo (as a punishment for the actions of Napoleon) with remarkable speed, the indemnity imposed on Bourbon Naples (as a punishment for Murat's return to the Napoleonic fold) caused rather greater problems. If one of the great complaints at Napoleonic-style government was the heavy burden imposed by the treasury, de' Medici now found himself unable to cut taxes because of the conduct of the previous régime.[69] Given the post-war economic depression, a government that taxed heavily was unlikely to win many friends. In Austria, too, war and the indemnities imposed by a victorious Napoleon left the treasury coffers permanently empty. This had a number of unfortunate consequences for domestic and foreign policy. Not only did a shortage of cash hamper such plans for reform as were occasionally mooted, but it also impeded Metternich's policies of international intervention. When, for example, he wished to restore the Bourbons in France after the 1830 revolution, he was told quite simply that the Empire was too poor to afford such a military venture.[70] Another consequence of Habsburg bankruptcy was the enormous kudos it gave to anyone who could maintain cheap government, a factor that played into the hands of Metternich's bitter rival, Kolovrat, who in 1830 managed to balance the budget. This might not in itself have been so disastrous a legacy, had it not made Kolovrat as invulnerable to dismissal as Metternich himself. As a result, their personal antipathy generated even greater immobilism at the centre of power in Vienna, with dire consequences for the whole imperial structure.[71]

An equally significant constraint were the territorial readjustments that took place as a consequence of the Napoleonic wars. We have already seen how some of these – the restructuring of Germany, the creation of a semi-independent Polish state – remained largely in place. Elsewhere, Napoleon's defeat enabled the creation of a European order that bore little resemblance to that of the pre-Revolutionary era. Although the discussion of diplomacy in the Restoration years has been treated exhaustively,[72] the effects of shifting frontiers on domestic politics and reform are much less well known. The case of Germany is instructive. In this volume, Brendan Simms shows the way in which the affairs of the German Confederation – as well as its very structures – remained conditioned by the trauma of the Napoleonic Wars, while Michael John argues that the Napoleonic experience in Germany favoured regionalism by giving it 'far stronger institutions to latch onto in the form of internally consolidated sovereign states (the so-called *Mittelstaaten*)'.[73] Michael Rowe points to growing resentment in the Catholic Rhineland, where élites had grown accustomed to French rule, when it was incorporated into the enlarged Prussian state. In the same way Andreas Fahrmeir, in his study of 'national' colours, reveals the difficulties that the rulers of German states faced in trying to create a sense of identity among subjects who had been forced together at the convenience of Napoleon, or in the interests of the victorious great powers.[74]

The redrawing of political frontiers after Napoleon highlights, in turn, another key problem of the Restoration era. The Napoleonic legacy to nationalism has already been discussed. What is sometimes forgotten is that, rather than stimulating unitary nationalism, the recasting of Europe's frontiers in the Restoration caused grave offence to particularist sentiment and, if only indirectly, encouraged movements of national separatism. Napoleon's legacy of administrative centralization further increased the conflict between the centre and those groups henceforth consigned to the 'periphery'. The resentment caused by shifting frontiers and attempts at state formation could be extremely destabilizing, as the problems of the Italian states show all too clearly.[75] Sicilians objected not to a lack of Italian unity, which until 1848 was meaningless to noble and peasant alike, but to oppression from mainland Naples; the main Genoese grievance was rule from Turin. Venetians disliked both French and Austrian rule, not because they were Italian patriots, but because they saw their foreign overlords favouring Lombardy or Trieste. In other words, the political order established after Napoleon also gave rise to, and was undermined by, territorial disintegration and the loss of institutional legitimacy on a wide scale.

IV

The way in which Restoration governments responded to Napoleon's legacy was determined in part by the aims and ideology of individual rulers, in part by the particular alliances and conflicts within different states and in part by the political, social and economic circumstances created by Napoleon's defeat. It is, then, hardly surprising that one of the most striking and, for the historian, difficult aspects of Restoration government is its bewildering variety. Napoleon's impact can only be understood in a pan-European context, yet the character of what came after him depended on factors as diverse as the duration of French rule, confessional differences, socio-economic conditions and the impact of war.

What Restoration rulers shared was a common hostility to what they perceived to be the legacy of the French Revolution. This meant hostility to French expansionism (outside France), to Republican forms of government and to popular representation of any kind. On the whole, these rulers resisted granting constitutions or allowing elected representative assemblies, associating them with executive weakness and popular violence. Where they did grant them – in France, Poland, some German states – their institutional importance was still limited. Thus, while Restoration rulers embraced the authoritarian legacy of Napoleon in terms of building state power, they generally rejected his attempt to legitimize it with expressions of consent.

This brand of conservatism helped to create a gulf between state and society that was the chief source of instability for Restoration governments. Significantly, the rejection of representation frustrated another policy common to most Restoration rulers: the policy of state formation. Without representation, these rulers lacked a basis on which to construct a consensus for strong central government. As we have seen, Napoleon had put together his system by carefully balancing a powerful executive equipped with the tools of repression, the manipulation of popular consent and the fostering of a loyal propertied élite. Although prepared to borrow from this model, Restoration rulers were unable to maintain this balance. In so doing, they risked their own political futures. By underestimating, in particular, the need for at least the appearance of support through public consultation, they tied themselves to the absolutist past: they became associated with traditional power-holders and with reaction, despite the fact that they, and the problems that they faced, were in many ways so modern. It is this fundamental weakness that lies at the root of the problems of government in Restoration Europe.

Notes

1. On the concept of the well-ordered police state see M. Raeff, *The Well-ordered Police State: Social and Institutional Change through Law in the Germanies and Russia, 1600–1800* (New Haven, CT, 1983).

For a useful and wide-ranging introduction to the question of reform in eighteenth-century Europe, see the collection of essays in H. M. Scott (ed.), *Enlightened Absolutism. Reform and Reformers in Later Eighteenth-Century Europe* (Basingstoke, 1990).

2. J. A. Davis, *Conflict and Control. Law and Order in Nineteenth-Century Italy* (Basingstoke, 1988), p.23.

3. S. J. Woolf, 'The Construction of a European World-View in the Revolutionary–Napoleonic Period', *Past and Present*, 137 (1992), p.95.

4. Quoted ibid., p.100.

5. G. Ellis, *The Napoleonic Empire* (London, 1991), p.26.

6. Jacques Godechot has famously, but misleadingly, likened Napoleon's prefects to 'miniature emperors': despite their great authority within the department, prefects were always dependent on orders from above and had little room for manoeuvre. See J. Godechot, *Les institutions de la France sous la Révolution et l'Empire* (3rd revised and expanded edition, Paris, 1985), p.589. See also E. A. Whitcomb's prosopographic analysis, 'Napoleon's Prefects', *American Historical Review*, 79 (1974), pp.1089–118. On the innovatory nature of the prefects see D. M. G. Sutherland, *France 1789–1815. Revolution and Counter-Revolution* (London, 1985), pp.344–5; for the rôle of prefects in conscription see I. Woloch, 'Napoleonic Conscription: State Power and Civil Society', *Past and Present*, 111 (1986), pp.101-29.

7. On Napoleon's reforms of French institutions after the *coup d'état* of 18 Brumaire see J. Tulard, *Napoléon ou le mythe du sauveur* (Paris, 1977), pp.115–29.

8. M. Lyons, *Napoleon Bonaparte and the Legacy of the French Revolution* (London, 1994), p.94.

9. By 1810 Napoleon had also promulgated the Code of Civil Procedure, the Commercial Code, the Criminal Code and the Code on Criminal Procedure. Ellis, *The Napoleonic Empire*, p.46.

10. Ibid., pp.44–8. For the detrimental consequences of Napoleon's educational reforms see Sutherland, *France 1789–1815*, pp.368–9.

11. C. Clark, Ch.13, pp.217–18.

12. Lyons, *Napoleon Bonaparte*, pp.78–93. See also Jean Godel, 'L'Église selon Napoléon', *Revue d'Histoire moderne et contemporaine*, 17 (1970), pp.837-45. For general accounts of the Concordat stressing the Papal perspective, see J. D. Holmes, *The Triumph of the Holy See* (London, 1978), pp.43–50, and E. E. Y. Hales, *Revolution and the Papacy 1769–1846* (London, 1960), pp.139–75. Much of the francophone literature on the Concordat is very dated, but the key

account of its application remains S. Delacroix, *La réorganisation de l'Église de France après le Concordat* (Paris, 1962).

13. G. Ellis, *Napoleon* (London, 1997), p.48. More generally on Fouché see E. A. Arnold, *Fouché, Napoleon and the General Police* (Washington, DC, 1979).
14. C. Emsley, *Policing and its Context 1750–1870* (Basingstoke, 1983), pp.40–1.
15. Lyons, *Napoleon Bonaparte*, pp.120–2. The fullest account of censorship is in A. Cabanais, *La presse sous le Consulat et l'Empire* (Paris, 1975).
16. S. J. Woolf, *Napoleon's Integration of Europe* (London, 1991), pp.87–90.
17. Ellis, *Napoleon*, p.77.
18. For the distinction between despotic power ('the range of actions that state élites can undertake without routine negotiation with civil society groups') and infrastructural power ('the institutional capacity of a central state ... to penetrate its territories and logistically implement decisions') see M. Mann, *The Sources of Social Power, Vol. II: The Rise of Classes and Nation-States, 1760–1914* (Cambridge, 1993), pp.59–63.
19. Ellis, *The Napoleonic Empire*, pp.18–28; I. Collins, *Napoleon and his Parliaments 1800–1815* (London, 1979).
20. Tulard, *Napoléon*, pp.242–54; Ellis, *The Napoleonic Empire*, pp.73–81; Lyons, *Napoleon Bonaparte*, pp.160–77.
21. Ibid., pp.111–17.
22. Clark, Ch.13, p.219.
23. For Napoleonic propaganda and personality cult see Lyons, *Napoleon Bonaparte*, pp.178–94; R. B. Holtman, *Napoleonic Propaganda* (Baton Rouge, LA, 1950); J. Tulard, *Le Mythe de Napoléon* (Paris, 1971), pp.31–44. J. J. Matthews, 'Napoleon's Military Bulletins', *Journal of Modern History*, 22 (1950), pp.137-44 is useful on the way Napoleon fostered a myth of military glory; on painting, see C. Prendegast, *Napoleon and History Painting: Antoine-Jean Gros's La Bataille d'Eylau* (Oxford, 1997). An interesting study on the ambivalent response of contemporary British writers to Napoleon as both heroic champion of liberty and tyranical oppressor is S. Bainbridge, *Napoleon and English Romanticism* (Cambridge, 1995).
24. Woolf, *Napoleon's Integration of Europe*, p.243.
25. For a discussion of this process see G. Mosse, *The Nationalization of the Masses. Political Symbolism and Mass Movements in Germany from the Napoleonic Wars through the Third Reich* (New York, 1975).

26. Woolf, *Napoleon's Integration of Europe*, p.241.
27. B. Simms, *The Struggle for Mastery in Germany, 1779–1850* (Basingstoke, 1998), p.101.
28. There is a vast literature on the question of nationalism in Germany during the Napoleonic period. although much of it is rather outdated. See, for example: H. S. Reiss, *The Political Thought of the German Romantics* (Oxford, 1955); H. Kohn, 'Arndt and the Character of German Nationalism', *American Historical Review*, 54 (1949), pp.787–803; idem, 'Romanticism and the Rise of German Nationalism', *The Review of Politics*, 12 (1950), pp.443–72; W. M. Simon, 'Variations in Nationalism during the Great Reform Period in Prussia', *American Historical Review*, 59 (1954), pp.305–21; G. A. Craig, 'German Intellectuals and Politics: The Case of Heinrich von Kleist', *Central European History*, 2 (1969), pp.3–21; C. Prignitz, *Vaterlandsliebe und Freiheit. Deutscher Patriotismus von 1750–1850* (Wiesbaden, 1981); C. Brinkmann, *Der Nationalismus und die deutschen Universitäten im Zeitalter der deutschen Erhebung* (Heidelberg, 1932); E. N. Anderson, *Nationalism and the Cultural Crisis in Prussia 1806–1815* (New York, 1939); W. C. Langsam, *The Napoleonic Wars and German Nationalism in Austria* (New York, 1930). For a recent survey see H. Schulze, *The Course of German Nationalism: From Frederick the Great to Bismarck, 1763–1867* (Cambridge, 1991), pp.48–55. For cultural developments in Germany, which often revealed a distinctively 'national' outlook, see J. J. Sheehan, *German History, 1770–1866* (Oxford, 1989), pp.324–88.
29. A straightforward account of Portugal under Napoleonic rule is in J. V. Serrão, *História de Portugal. Vol. VII. A Instauração do liberalismo (1807–1832)* (Lisbon, 1983), pp.16–106. On popular insurrection see also A. do Carmo Reis, *As Revoltas do Porto contra Junot* (Lisbon, 1991). On Spain see G. H. Lovett, *Napoleon and the Birth of Modern Spain* (2 vols, New York, 1965), C. Esdaile, *The Spanish Army in the Peninsular War* (Manchester, 1988), and J. R. Aymes, *La guerra de la independencia en España, 1808–14* (Madrid, 1980). For the rising of the Tyrol see F. G. Eyck, *Loyal rebels. Andreas Hofer and the Tyrolean Uprisings of 1809* (New York, 1986). On Napoleonic Italy see C. Zaghi, *L'Italia di Napoleone dalla Cisalpina al Regno* (Turin, 1986), L. Antonielli, *I prefetti dell'Italia napoleonica* (Bologna, 1983) and the special monographic issue of *Quaderni Storici*, 37 (1978), ed. P. Villani, entitled 'Notabili e funzionari nell'Italia napoleonica', pp.5–413. Also useful is A. Grab, 'Army, State and Society: Conscription and Desertion in Napoleonic Italy (1802–1814)', *Journal*

of Modern History, 67 (1995), pp.25–54; and idem, 'State Power, Brigandage and Rural Resistance in Napoleonic Italy', *European History Quarterly*, 25 (1995), pp.39–70.

30. J. Rosselli, *Lord William Bentinck and the British Occupation of Sicily* (Cambridge, 1956).

31. Neither word was widely used in the immediate aftermath of Napoleon's defeat. Liberalism, however, remains a useful umbrella term to cover those elements who were dissatisfied with autocratic rule, and sought some form of representative, constitutional government. For a discussion of the difficulties in using the term see J. J. Sheehan, *German Liberalism in the Nineteenth Century* (Chicago, 1978), pp.5–6. Nationalism is also a problematic term, but can be used with caution to describe those elements who sought autonomy or independence from 'foreign' rule (Poles; Belgians; Italians and Hungarians in the Habsburg Empire), or Germans and Italians who sought closer bonds with co-nationals in 'national' states.

32. On this ideological legacy see M. Broers, *Europe after Napoleon: Revolution, Reaction and Romanticism, 1814–1848* (Manchester, 1996), esp. pp.35–52, 91–105.

33. For a good example of this rather misleading approach see E. Hobsbawm, *The Age of Revolution. Europe 1789–1848* (London, 1962).

34. For a discussion of this problem in the German states, see C. Clark, 'Germany 1815–1848: Restoration or pre-March?', in M. Fulbrook (ed.), *German History since 1800* (London, 1997), pp.38–60, and Sheehan, *German History*. On the Prussian state in the post-1815 period see R. Koselleck, *Preussen zwischen Reform und Revolution: Allgemeines Landrecht, verwaltung und soziale Bewegung von 1791 bis 1848* (Stuttgart, 1981). The latter is usefully discussed in J. Sperber's review article, 'State and Civil Society: Thoughts on a new edition of Reinhart Koselleck's *Preussen zwischen Reform und Revolution*', *Journal of Modern History*, 57 (1985), pp.278–96. For the complex legacy of Napoleon in Italy see, for example, M. Meriggi, *Amministrazione e classi sociali nel Lombardo-Veneto (1814–1848)* (Bologna, 1983); M. Broers, *Napoleonic Imperialism in the Savoyard Monarchy 1773–1821. State-building in Piedmont* (New York, 1997); S. C. Hughes, *Crime, Disorder and the Risorgimento: The Politics of Policing in Bologna* (Cambridge, 1994) pp.14–28; J. A. Davis, 'The Napoleonic Era in Southern Italy: An Ambiguous Legacy?', *Proceedings of the British Academy*, 80 (1993), pp.133–48. For an interesting treatment of Restoration France,

stressing its relationship with the Revolutionary period, see I. Woloch, *Transformations of the French Civic Order, 1789–1820s. The New Regime* (New York, 1994).

35. Broers, *The Savoyard Monarchy*; T. C. W. Blanning, *The French Revolution in Germany: Occupation and Resistance in the Rhineland 1792–1802* (Oxford, 1983); J. M. Diefendorf, *Businessmen and Politics in the Rhineland, 1789–1834* (Princeton, NJ, 1980), pp.50–209; R. Devleeshouwer, 'Le cas de Belgique' in *Occupants–occupés 1792–1815*. Colloque de Bruxelles, 29 et 30 janvier 1968 (Brussels, 1969).

36. Ellis, *Napoleon*, p.236; Woolf, *Napoleon's Integration of Europe*, pp.96–132, 185–96, 226–37. A useful volume on responses to French domination is the collection of essays *Occupants–occupés, 1792–1815*. On the Netherlands see S. Schama, *Patriots and Liberators: Revolution in the Netherlands 1780–1813* (London, 1977). For the Napoleonic Kingdom of Italy, see F. Della Peruta, *Esercito e società nell'Italia napoleonica. Dalla Cisalpina al Regno d'Italia* (Milan, 1988); Zaghi, *L'Italia di Napoleone*, and Antonielli, *I prefetti dell'Italia*.

37. There had, of course, been calls for reform long before the Prussian army was crushed by French forces. For recent discussion of the Prussian reform movement see Simms, *The Struggle for Mastery in Germany*, pp.75–90, and Sheehan, *German History*, pp.291–310. Still the best survey of military reform in English is P. Paret, *Yorck and the Era of Reform in Prussia, 1807–1815* (Princeton, NJ, 1966). For debate on the Constitutional issue see M. Levinger, 'Hardenberg, Wittgenstein, and the Constitutional Question in Prussia, 1815–1822', *German History*, 8 (1990), pp.257–77.

38. C. J. Esdaile, *The Wars of Napoleon* (London, 1995), pp.186–97; G. Rothenberg, *Napoleon's Great Adversaries: The Archduke Charles and the Austrian Army, 1792–1814* (Bloomington, IN, 1982); A. Roider, 'The Habsburg Foreign Ministry and Political Reform, 1801–1805', *Central European History*, 22 (1989), pp.160–82. For a summary of Francis I's self-satisfied position after the Vienna Settlement see C. A. Macartney, *The Habsburg Empire 1790–1918*, (London, 1969), p.206.

39. J. A. Davis, Ch.14, p.244. For general surveys in English of Italy in the Restoration era see M. Meriggi, Ch.3; L. Riall, *The Italian Risorgimento: State, Society and National Unification* (London, 1994), pp.11–28; and D. Laven, 'The Age of Restoration', in John Davis (ed.), *The Oxford History of Modern Italy* (forthcoming).

40. B. Montale, *Parma nel Risorgimento: istituzione e società (1814–1859)* (Milan, 1993).
41. Meriggi, *Amministrazione e classi sociali*; R. J. Rath, *The Provisional Austrian Régime in Lombardy-Venetia, 1814–1815* (Austin, TX, 1969).
42. A. J. Reinerman, *Austria and the Papacy in the Age of Metternich* (2 vols, Washington DC, 1979–89) Vol. 1, pp.36–43; M. Caravale and A. Caracciolo, *Lo stato pontificio da Martino V a Pio X* (Turin, 1978), pp.589–96; Hughes, *Crime, Disorder and the Risorgimento*, pp.29–49, 60–5.
43. A. Spagnoletti, *Storia del Regno delle due Sicilie* (Rome/Bari, 1997), pp.206–19; V. d'Alessandro and G. Giarrizzo, *La Sicilia dal vespro all'unità d'Italia* (Turin, 1989), pp.666–75; R. Romeo, 'Momenti e problemi della restaurazione nel Regno delle Due Sicilie (1815–1820)', in idem, *Mezzogiorno e Sicilia nel Risorgimento* (Naples, 1963), pp.51–69. For a discussion in English, see L. Riall, *Sicily and the Unification of Italy. Liberal Policy and Local Power 1859–1860* (Oxford, 1998), pp.31–3.
44. M. Broers, Ch.9, p.142.
45. A. Nieuwazny, Ch.7, p.120.
46. R. Alexander, Ch.2, p.30.
47. M. John, Ch.5.
48. Sheehan, *German History*, p.249. The most interesting example of how these mediatized states developed is Bavaria. See W. Demel, *Der Bayerische Saatsabsolutismus, 1806/08–1817: Staats- und gesellschaftspolitische Motivationen und Hintergründe der Reformära in der ersten Phase des Königreichs Bayern* (Munich, 1983); K. Aretin, *Bayerns Weg zum souveränen Staat: Landstände und Konstitutionelle Monarchie, 1714–1818* (Munich, 1976). On reform in Bavaria see also A. T. Cronenberg, 'Montgelas and the Reorganization of Napoleonic Bavaria', *Consortium on Revolutionary Europe. Proceedings 1989*, pp.712–19. For other states see the articles in 'Symposium: State Building in the "Third Germany"', in *Central European History*, 24 (1991).
49. E. Kraehe, *Metternich's German Policy* (2 vols, Princeton, NJ, 1963–1984); D. Billinger, *Metternich and the German Question: State Rights and Federal Duties 1820–1834* (London, 1991); F. R. Bridges, *The Habsburg Monarchy among the Great Powers 1815–1918* (Oxford, 1991).
50. Simms, *The Struggle for Mastery*, p.123.
51. Cited in Sheehan, *German History*, p.242.

52. C. Emsley, Ch.15, p.268.
53. Clark, Ch.13, p.229.
54. Emsley, Ch.15; Broers, Ch.9; D. Laven, 'Law and Order in Habsburg Venetia 1814–1835', *The Historical Journal*, 39 (1996), pp.383–403.
55. For a general discussion, see O. Chadwick, *The Popes and European Revolution* (Oxford, 1981).
56. C. Esdaile, Ch.4, p.73.
57. Ibid., p.74.
58. Ibid., p.77.
59. Davis, Ch.14, p.237.
60. G. Cingari, *Mezzogiorno e Risorgimento. La restaurazione a Napoli dal 1821 al 1830* (Bari, 1970)
61. Meriggi, *Amministrazione e classi sociali*, pp.201–15.
62. Ibid., pp.215–28.
63. Broers, *Europe after Napoleon*, p.54.
64. Esdaile, Ch.4, p.71.
65. Broers, Ch.9, pp.158–9.
66. Meriggi, Ch.3, p.52.
67. B. Fitzpatrick, Ch.10, p.167.
68. P. Pilbeam, Ch.11.
69. G. Cingari, 'Gli ultimi Borboni: dalla restaurazione all'unità', *Storia della Sicilia, Vol. 8* (Naples, 1977), pp.10–11.
70. A. Sked, 'The Metternich System', in A. Sked (ed.), *Europe's Balance of Power 1815–48* (London, 1979), pp.98–121, at p.107.
71. Macartney, *The Habsburg Empire*, pp.232–305.
72. The best recent treatment of international relations in this period is in P. W. Schroeder, *The Transformation of European Politics 1763–1848* (Oxford, 1994). See also the same author's *Metternich's Diplomacy at its Zenith 1820–1823* (New York, 1962), and F. R. Bridge and R. Bullen, *The Great Powers and the European States System 1815–1914* (London, 1980). Good examples of earlier treatments of the diplomatic legacy of Napoleon are H. Nicolson, *The Congress of Vienna 1814–1815* (London, 1919); idem, *The Congress of Vienna: A Study in Allied Unity 1812–1822* (London, 1946); and H. G. Schenk, *The Aftermath of the Napoleonic wars. The Concert of Europe – An Experiment* (London, 1947).
73. B. Simms, Ch.6; John, Ch.5, p.83.
74. M. Rowe, Ch.8; A. Fahrmeir, Ch.12.
75. Riall, *The Italian Risorgimento*, pp.22–8.

Part I
The Apparatus of State

–2–

'No, Minister': French Restoration Rejection of Authoritarianism

Robert Alexander

In 1822 the aspiring journalist *cum* politician Adolphe Thiers blasted the government for closing a mutual school at Mont-Fleury, near Grenoble. The council of public instruction had deemed the school neither 'sufficiently monarchical' nor 'sufficiently religious', but closure was based on an imperial decree. Thiers expressed 'surprise' that the order had not been accompanied by cries of 'Long live the Emperor!'; after all, the Emperor had so well provided 'grand-masters, keepers of the seals, prefects with the means to forbid, suspend, close, etc.'.

At one level the fate of Mont-Fleury was a product of partisan politics, a triumph of ultra-royalists over their enemies on the left. Yet Thiers's comments point to a second preoccupation – the authoritarian nature of the state, and association of authoritarianism with Napoleon.[1]

To assess this authoritarian legacy, we need to identify Napoleonic elements within the Restoration constitution, while recognizing that the *Charte* was not written in stone. Very few contemporaries thought the *Charte* was the final word in anything, and whether future change would come by way of reform or revolution was open to question. The one formal division of power was between government and parliament, and even this was clouded by the insistence of Louis XVIII in June 1814 that he granted the *Charte* of his own volition. Whether what was granted could be taken away was anyone's guess, but among many there was expectation that the Crown would in the future be bound by the *Charte*, thereby establishing a rudimentary base for the principle that the state must conform to the rule of law.[2]

Parliament derived its formal legitimation from the *Charte*. It was bicameral, with Chambers of Peers and Deputies. Members of the former were appointed by the Crown; members of the latter were elected. The Chamber of Deputies had significant powers, some of which were expressly stated in the *Charte*, and some of which were a product of evolving convention. Foremost was the right of approval over annual state budgets; and to secure approval, government cabinets needed a majority in both houses. This did not mean that cabinet ministers were responsible to parliament; the executive was appointed by the king, and responsible to him alone. Nevertheless, a convention developed whereby Louis XVIII appointed cabinets capable of gaining a majority when proposing legislation. The cabinet thus to a limited extent bore some relation to electoral results, and elections could lead to the formation of new cabinets capable of taking action against former government ministers and their agents. Elections could, therefore, again to a limited degree, provide a means for disciplining the executive. Moreover, parliament became a public forum wherein abuses could be exposed; revelations of malpractice might lead simply to embarrassment for officials, but could also lead to disciplinary measures.[3]

Napoleon had preserved a façade of representative government; but only the most smitten of Bonapartists would argue that Napoleonic parliaments had any real independent power, or any ability to hold the government to account. Division of power was not the Napoleonic legacy.[4]

Much of the Restoration state apparatus was, however, inherited from the previous régime. Bonaparte's reconstruction of the state had been characterized by extreme centralization, and Louis XVIII was enough of a Bourbon to recognize the utility of this for kings or emperors. All authority flowed from the Crown, and the king appointed the governing executive, composed of cabinet and council of state. The latter body helped in the preparation of legislation and also monitored the administration, giving it a judicial and legislative function. By the standards of the time, the French administration was efficient, and the power of the central government was all the more pronounced in that it appointed all the officials of local government. This held for consultative bodies of notables and those with real decision-making capacity (though only with ministerial approval) – prefects, mayors, police commissioners, and officers of the military and *gendarmerie*.[5]

Thus the division of power hung by a narrow thread. Judges were appointed by the Crown, and while life tenure might encourage a certain spirit of independence, a massive purge conducted in 1816 suggested there were limits as to how far the judiciary could go in opposing the executive. Moreover, by the law of August 1790 judges were prohibited from interfering in, or taking cognizance of, acts of the administration. Similarly, while the peers might at times block government legislation, the origins of their authority lay in crown appointment. One should not be blinded by formal structure: peers and judges did at times act as though they represented the general public, much as *parlementaires* had done under the *ancien régime*. But if choice is an essential ingredient of representation, it was only the deputies who could legitimately claim to represent anything other than the Crown.

Division of power was all the more tenuous in that the state played a major rôle in the process by which deputies were chosen. Qualification for the franchise required documentation of age, nationality, residence and annual tax payment, all of which could be provided only by agents of the Crown. Voter lists were drawn up, revised and published by prefects and their councils. Should dispute arise, adjudication would be conducted by the council of state. Voters assembled in colleges presided over by a crown appointee who commenced proceedings with a speech allegedly expressing the wishes of the king. Also appointed was a provisional bureau of college secretary and scrutineers who watched over voting and counting. The bureau was supposed to prevent irregularities, but was itself well placed to perpetrate them, especially given that the secrecy of the ballot was not firmly established.[6]

Ultimately the capacity of voters to act independently held the key to the division of power. As we shall see, Restoration France witnessed a drive to control elections, and the chief agent of this was the administration. Much of the personnel and ethos of the administration was Napoleonic, and it was basically hostile to the key elements of political liberty: public choice and governmental accountability.

An approach focusing on parliamentary independence may appear distinctly Whiggish, especially when one notes that the Chamber of Deputies was elected by a plutocracy of roughly eighty thousand males. To argue that securing division of power was important rests uncomfortably with any interpretation based on class or gender division, because battle was largely waged within the male socio-economic élite, although groups outside the franchise were hardly disinterested bystanders. Yet among the continental powers France was exceptional because it had an institution capable of at least nibbling the state. If Metternich or the Russian Tsars took note of elections, this was because France remained a source of concern.

Among the leading states, only Britain also had a parliament. Yet France also had the Napoleonic state apparatus and many advocates of a state unbridled by any division of power, especially if that bridle was linked in any way to meaningful representative government. Those who gained control of the state could, of course, use it for their own particular interests. But such groups have long since disappeared, while the dangers of the over-mighty state remain; it was not ultra-royalist nobles who ran Vichy, though the two groups had much in common.

Using the administration as a political tool pivoted on finding compliant agents. Not all officials were willing, but through personnel purges, ministries could replace recalcitrants. Hence the frequent Restoration 'massacres'. Such emetics were not simply partisan, whether in terms of ideology or patronage. The key was to have servants who followed orders regardless of consequence for the political system. It helped if replacements had some ability; but the earlier collapse of the Empire provided a large pool from which to choose.[7]

Moreover, there was an ethos within the Napoleonic corps that made willing agents readily available. The Bonapartist credo of national unity linked politics with factionalism, and was anything but tolerant of public criticism of government. At best politicians brought inefficiency; at worst they brought anarchy. Stuart Woolf has noted the proclivity of civil servants for thinking that the administration, rather than any body of elected individuals, represented the nation. Given the nature of the Empire, this was not entirely illogical; but many officials carried this belief into the Restoration. Baron Pasquier was typical in thinking that inclusion in the dictionary of *girouettes* (political weather vanes) was no great dishonour; the first duty of a civil servant was to serve, regardless of régime. One might see in this a non-partisan civil service; yet those who retained their positions would take the very opposite course. It was not unnatural that many did so; as Spitzer has noted, such men viewed the Chamber of Deputies as 'a consultative body like the *conseil d'état*. Obedience was the essence of government, and a self-limiting monarchy was a self-contradiction'.[8]

In the early Restoration, the noisiest critics of centralization were ultra-royalists. Prior to the proclamation of the *Charte*, Joseph de Villèle had written a pamphlet rejecting representative government in favour of a return to the institutions of the *ancien régime*. Thereafter Villèle knew well where the one potential check to state power lay, and in 1816 he denounced prefect Malouet for interfering in elections in the Pas-de-Calais. He then gave the press a letter in which Malouet advised against voting for ultra-royalists.

Yet all of this was a matter of expediency. When in power in the early 1820s Villèle rejected decentralization because it would lead to 'disorganization'. His right-hand man, Corbière, stated that it was 'impossible to change the administration', having previously lambasted its size, cost and power. Other leading ultra-royalists were no different. When he entered the Polignac cabinet in 1829, La Bourdonnaye happily worked the system, forgetting his earlier calls for reform. Yet, as Villèle himself noted, decentralist arguments had wide appeal, and the opposite end of the political spectrum gained by taking them up.[9]

From the summer of 1816, the leading critics of despotism were to be found on the political Left. This contained republicans, liberals and Bonapartists, who often shared little more than opposition to Bourbon governments, but joined forces in a combination known as 'the liberal opposition'. Their criticism of the unbridled state grew during the White Terror of late 1815 and 1816 – a period of revenge directed against individuals alleged to oppose royalism, especially those who had rallied to Bonaparte during the Hundred Days.[10]

White Terror had legal and illegal components. Initially it was mostly illegal and organized by ultra-royalists; indeed ultra-royalist criticism of central government power in 1816 reflected frustration that the Richelieu cabinet was seeking to substitute State Terror for the more anarchic and vicious form of local reprisal. In this context, when the state could be viewed as a shield, future liberals actually endorsed a government proposal that would have seen the electorate composed largely of government appointees. Ironically, it was ultra-royalists who blocked this proposal.

From late 1815 onwards, however, Terror increasingly became a state monopoly. General elections held in August 1815, when illegal White Terror was rampant, had yielded an overwhelming majority of ultra-royalists in the Chamber. In pursuit of vengeance and hopeful of securing a government to their liking, ultra-royalist parliamentarians passed a series of laws designed to punish non-royalists and then pressured the cabinet into applying the laws rigorously. Because the government resisted their more outrageous demands, it gained an appearance of moderation – yet ultra-royalist initiatives had actually enhanced state power.

Prevotal courts, extraordinary tribunals for the punishment of political 'crimes', only came into operation in the spring of 1816. Because they were not bound by the regulations of ordinary courts, it was easy to associate them with the extraordinary tribunals of the Revolutionary and Napoleonic periods, and hence they were subsequently viewed with much odium. Yet as a rule they were more lenient than the courts of assizes that had judged political 'crimes' up to that point, partly because the judges had themselves been subjected to unofficial ultra-royalist terror in the period leading up to the massive purge of the judiciary in early 1816. But pressure for harsh justice had not come solely from local ultra-royalist organizations.

Ultimately more dangerous for the rule of law (if one considers the state as subject to it) were the extraordinary powers granted to prefects by the sedition laws. Prefects gained authority (subject to ministerial confirmation) to arrest, incarcerate and exile on the basis of suspicion alone. In theory the idea was to strike against enemies of the state before they could endanger it – and in truth the régime was far from secure. Yet setting aside the normal course of justice opened the doors to countless measures based on a mere presumption of opposition rather than any real threat or action. At one level coercion was simply petty – thousands of individuals imprisoned for yelling 'Long live the Emperor!' At another it amounted to vengeance for actions committed in the distant past, in direct contradiction to the *Charte*. But perhaps most lethal was the uncertainty created because there were no means to make prefects accountable for their actions, and the process was anything but transparent. No study has been made of this aspect of the White Terror, but the number of individuals incarcerated without charges ever being laid must have easily been in the tens of thousands. The impact of several months of imprisonment without means to defend oneself should not be underestimated – this was designed to brand and isolate individuals, and it could have disastrous economic consequences for the families involved.

There were several long-term consequences. The inability or unwillingness of the state to punish ultra-royalists for their part in illegal White Terror raised questions about the impartiality of Bourbon justice. Persecuting 'suspects' inevitably gained their enmity, and to this was added the resentment of notables purged from the various wings of the government. Worse still for the régime, however, were doubts about whether it would operate within the rule of law. Repression could be justified as a means to check disorder, but at a certain point the state risked being seen as the agent of disorder.

Concerns over the rule of law lurked behind the publicity given to the Didier Affair of May 1816, notable not so much for the rebellion at Grenoble as for the repression surrounding it. In the course of the Affair, prefect Montlivault and lieutenant-general Donnadieu ran amok, terrorizing the general population and insulting judges whenever they raised concerns about due process. The latter was in fact nothing new; Montlivault had frequently clashed with judges who expressed qualms when no evidence could be found to justify incarceration. What was new was that within the cabinet there was growing recognition that public reaction might jeopardize the prospects of the regime. Both Montlivault and Donnadieu were reprimanded by their respective ministers, while in parliament the Minister of Police, Decazes, sought to play down the significance of the affair. But Louis XVIII, advised by Decazes, realized that 'damage control' necessitated significant change in governmental policies.[11]

The Didier Affair crystallized growing alarm over unregulated state repression, which in turn gave the Left its opportunity to recover from association with Bonaparte during the Hundred Days. When Louis XVIII dissolved parliament in September 1816 he began a phase in which the exceptional powers of the administration would end; but rough justice had alienated many within the legal fraternity, a tendency that the future liberal deputy Bérenger de la Drôme (himself a victim of the White Terror at Grenoble) fostered in his *De la justice criminelle en France*, published in 1818. This author attacked the exceptional laws of 1815 as a violation of the *Charte,* and used the Didier Affair for examples. Echoes of Montesquieu could be heard in pleas for judicial independence of the executive; but Bérenger also urged judges to become versed in politics, so as to be able to constrain the government within legal bounds. Lawyers and judges should guide the development of 'constitutional principles', by such means as the election of administrative officials. While it would be difficult to evaluate the influence of Bérenger's book, its importance lay in the fact that it was part of a stream that would carry lawyers to the forefront of the liberal opposition and make judges unreliable agents of repression. Reaction to the White Terror was not just a call to return to the rule of law; it was a call to remove the rule of law from despotism.[12]

Antagonism towards the administration diminished between 1817 and 1819 as the Richelieu and Decazes ministries embarked on liberal reform. Yet tensions remained, and began to centre on the electoral process. With the support of the King, Decazes concentrated on undermining ultra-royalist influence, and, as part of this, prefects were directed to mobilize support for official candidates. By 1818 Decazes had issued instructions for the compilation of lists classifying voters according to political tendency; initially the task was assigned to departmental commissioners, but thereafter it fell to the prefectoral corps. The lists appear to have taken several years to complete, and under Decazes prefects relied more on persuasion and patronage than coercion and fraud; nevertheless an instrument designed to sabotage voter independence had been forged.

As part of his attack on the extreme Right, Decazes directed officials to act with restraint towards the Left. This was designed to facilitate the formation of a centrist *ministériel* party; but an unexpected result was the rapid development of the liberal opposition. The annual renewal of one-fifth of the Chamber saw the liberals gain twenty seats in 1818 and take thirty-five of fifty-five contests in 1819. While they claimed loyalty to King and constitution, doubts over what this group intended were not unjustified, and royalist fears rose sharply when the former *conventionnel* Grégoire was elected as part of a liberal sweep of the Isère in November 1819. Given that momentum, it could be projected that the liberals would hold a Chamber majority by 1820. Thereafter the 'hands off' approach to elections was dropped.[13]

The drive for state control was typified by the policies of Baron d'Haussez, appointed prefect of the Isère in early 1820. When he arrived, ultra-royalists, liberals and moderate royalists were uncertain of his intentions. He did have a pedigree, being born into a family of the *noblesse de robe*, and having served as Imperial mayor of Neufchâtel in the Seine-Inférieure and Restoration prefect in the Lozère and Gard. But he remained free of obvious political association, which produced confusion. D'Haussez's actions, however, soon removed doubt.[14]

Prefectoral ascendency was the first priority. By describing a mayor as 'useless', reporting that the lieutenant-general was the beneficiary of a subscription by liberals, and raising a ruckus over critical reports from the head of the *gendarmerie*, d'Haussez had local rivals removed. Next came termination of public criticism. Particular targets were the editors and writers of the *Journal libre de l'Isère*, whom the Baron dismissively described as 'all lawyers or law students'. Frequent lawsuits and harsh censorship resulted. Similar treatment was given the *Echo des Alpes*, and by February 1822 the department no longer had an opposition organ.[15]

Few tricks were overlooked in corrupting the electoral process. To break liberal influence among civil servants the prefect threatened the tax receiver-general with sacking if he did not rally prominently to a royalist candidate in April 1820; the receiver-general complied. A more scrupulous councillor at the prefecture was dismissed. Because Grenoble was a liberal bastion, d'Haussez had the electoral college convened at Vienne, and meanwhile trimmed some 260 individuals from voter lists (about one-quarter of the former total). A liberal committee challenged this before the council of state, but their claims were rejected.[16]

Frustration drove liberals to attempt revolt at Grenoble in March 1821, which d'Haussez duly exploited to close two breeding grounds of dissent – the law school and Mont-Fleury. A liberal reading salon was forced to disband and a second, of mixed political hue, was purged. All of which pleased ultra-royalists; but it would be wrong to identify the Baron simply as one of them.[17]

D'Haussez admired the Imperial machine and fretted that Bourbon government might ruin it. In a passage of his memoirs in which he strongly criticized all Restoration Ministers of the Interior, d'Haussez gave what little praise he allotted to Decazes (the leading *bête noire* of ultra-royalists), because the latter had the true administrator's taste for rationalization. Government should be the preserve of technocrats; politicians of any stripe who intervened were simply obstructing efficiency. Elections were an unfortunate necessity; but one could nullify them by rendering the electorate as docile as sheep. In his public pronouncements, the Baron liked to emphasize that while justice would be rendered without discrimination, government favour would be reserved for supporters. By favour he meant public works projects, in particular road- and bridge-building schemes, swamp drainage projects and canal construction. He was candid about his intentions: public works were a means to distract the Dauphinois from politics. During his tenure, d'Haussez oversaw completion of fourteen departmental roads; and, had the central government been more cooperative, he would have achieved more. Indeed, according to the Baron, had the government adopted his 'system' for all of France, the Revolution of 1830 would have been avoided. Sadly politics had intruded, preventing the administrative management France needed.[18]

D'Haussez liked to attribute electoral victories to his 'system'. Certainly the results in 1824 were impressive: royalists swept all six seats in the Isère. Thus the Baron had reason for satisfaction when he was transferred to the Gironde in April 1824. Yet his work was not quite complete. D'Haussez had not been able to purge liberals among the judges, nor had widespread opposition within the bar been overcome. Early in his tenure d'Haussez had attributed the reluctance of the judiciary to cooperate fully to excessive respect for formal procedure. Later, however, his complaints changed. Crown Prosecutor Mallein was accused of protecting liberals and Michoud, president of the court of assizes, was reported to prejudice trials in favour of critics of the régime. By 1824 d'Haussez was certain that officials would not publicly express opposition, but merchants and barristers still maintained a degree of independence which left them impervious to his 'system'.[19]

While d'Haussez could be ruthless, he also exercised discretion. Under a less able successor, articles in the *Journal de Grenoble*, controlled by the prefecture, took on a more aggressive tone. One editorial attacked liberals for constantly referring to public opinion. To consult a people with more imagination than judgement was to invite 'irredeemable stupidities'; during the most fatal moments of the Revolution, it was always public opinion that had been invoked. According to the *Journal*, the Chambers and the courts were 'secondary powers' in relation to the royal will. D'Haussez would have agreed, but he would not have said so in public.[20]

D'Haussez was not an exception. He acted against a backdrop that saw power shift steadily rightward: from Decazes jettisoning reform in late 1819, to formation of the centre-right Richelieu ministry in February 1820, to the Villèle-led cabinet in December 1821, to ultra-royalist triumph in the elections of 1824. Legislation became increasingly reactionary, including the Law of the Double Vote, temporary restrictions on civil liberties similar to the sedition laws of 1815 and a massive clampdown on the free press. Because this ultimately worked to the benefit of ultra-royalists, it is tempting to conclude that the process was simply partisan. But ultra-royalist ascendancy was based not just on gaining control of the state; it also pivoted on making the state an instrument of uncontested domination.

At a time when Richelieu was angling for support from Villèle, it was predictable that despotism would flower in the Haute-Garonne. In 1819 the Chamber had voted for redrawing riding boundaries, and on the surface prefect Saint-Chamans's proposals of 1820 looked reasonable. The *arrondissements* of Muret and Saint-Gaudens would be combined to choose a single deputy and, given the number of qualified voters in the other departmental *arrondissements*, this reduced inequities, although a combination of Villefranche and Muret would have been more appropriate. But in official correspondence Saint-Chamans revealed the real objective: if the electors of Saint-Gaudens were left to their own devices they would choose a deputy devoted to the 'party of democracy'.[21]

Gerrymandering was but one weapon. From 1820 onwards prefects began systematically to corrupt voter lists by eliminating qualified liberals and adding unqualified royalists. Not all were as aggressive as d'Haussez, and the process was gradual; but undoubtedly the lists of voter preference initiated by Decazes were a great boon to his enemies, as fraud and intimidation replaced influence peddling. Administrative engineering was designed to favour candidates who shared the cabinet's complexion, but compromise might be required, and in such cases it was better to err to the right. Thus increased intervention in the Haute-Garonne worked in favour of Villèle, to whom Saint-Chamans turned to facilitate royalist unity. Richelieu endorsed this; moreover there should be no doubt as to official duties: only those who demonstrated 'devotion' would retain their posts and, of course, only 'sane doctrines' could be published.

One of Villèle's proteges, Puymaurin, benefited especially from these arrangements. Escherolles, sub-prefect of Saint-Gaudens, became an agent for Puymaurin, conducting straw polls based on information sent to him by 'men of confidence' in each canton. When the mayor of Muret reported that liberals were wooing supporters of a moderate royalist, Escherolles convinced the 'moderate' to sign a notice instructing supporters to vote instead for Puymaurin. The notice was then distributed in the college assembly, where Escherolles employed 'zealous but prudent' civil servants to influence undecided voters. The victorious Puymaurin duly informed Saint-Chamans of his gratitude.[22]

When in December 1821 Villèle formed his first cabinet the main techniques for subverting elections were already in place. Villèle simply systematized corruption and applied it more expertly. The pressures applied by the cabinet to officials and by officials to voters have become notorious, but what needs to be emphasized is that by 1824 the administration acted, for all intents and purposes, as a political party.[23]

The extent of interference can be illustrated by turning to the Seine-Inférieure, where prefect de Vanssay exercised the most scientific of management. Vanssay had cut his imperial teeth as *auditeur* in the council of state in 1809; his career as prefect commenced in 1810 and lasted until August 1830. When he arrived at Rouen in August 1820 the department was not a *bourg pourri* (rotten borough), having sent mixed deputations of royalists and liberals to the Chamber. But the groundwork for turning local officials into political agents had already been begun. In March Crown Prosecutor Baron Fouquet had responded to a request from Minister of Justice, Portalis (famous for his work on the Napoleonic Codes), for reports on public opinion by complaining that 'espionage' and 'inquisition', were more suited to prefects. Portalis replied that Fouquet had exceeded his purview by commenting on the actions of the ministry. To this dressing down Fouquet responded by asking whether as a magistrate he forfeited the right to express opinions. Whether Portalis responded is unclear, but we can note that Fouquet thereafter was succeeded by Dossier, a man more than willing to follow directions.[24]

In 1824 Vanssay 'wrote off' Rouen centre as unassailable, but this still left nine ridings. For starters, the *Journal de Rouen* became an organ for official candidates and thereby gained 217 subscriptions sent *gratis* to cafés. More remarkable were the efforts of the administration in turning out the royalist vote while discouraging liberals. Vanssay published a preliminary list that included only those who had paid over four hundred francs in taxes. This denied liberals information as to potential voters who had paid between three hundred and four hundred francs and, given that the final count rose to 4,702 from the preliminary list of 2,307, we can deduce that there were many of them. As the lists were posted only on 16 January and the elections scheduled for late February and early March, this constrained liberal efforts to identify potential voters. Meanwhile the administration used agents in each canton to alert qualified royalists and collect and present documents for them. Liberals were allowed to present claims, but when information proved slightly inaccurate, no mention was made until the prefectoral council rejected them, leaving little time for correction.

Stacking registration was combined with directing the vote. 'Men of confidence' in each canton helped royalist voters make travel arrangements and ensured they departed. The agents also sent the prefect and sub-prefects lists of confirmed and lukewarm royalists. Such lists were then collated so that members of the two groups were mixed at banquets hosted by officials during the college assemblies. Fourteen uncertain royalists thus found themselves seated among seven of the confirmed, dining *chez* Dossier. Vanssay himself entertained 109 individuals between 24 and 26 February, and this was but one wave of such occasions.

Stomachs were not always the way to a man's vote, but probabilities were enhanced in the voting halls. For the voters of each canton there was a royalist *surveillant* informed who was susceptible to liberal 'intrigue'. Susceptible voters were paired with a 'mentor' who, if necessary, cast votes for shy rustics. Illiteracy was not, however, the reason for directing a court clerk and barrister to have their votes written by a 'mentor'; Dossier was taking no chances, despite promises. And there was little room for doubt regarding official intentions, given the widespread practice of calling out one's preference while placing the ballot in the urn.

In the end, Vanssay secured the desired result; nine seats went to men backed by the ministry. This, however, had been gained at a price. Vanssay had sent a circular to voters urging them to reject 'our adversaries' and support candidates who 'would be close if necessary to sacrifice all for the defence of the throne'. In the short term, all that remained was to express satisfaction to the vast majority of officials who had shown 'devotion'. There had been a few exceptions, such as a justice of the peace reported to have voted contrary to his promises. A summons by Dossier brought a suitably cringing disavowal. Yet a dangerous legacy had been acquired. Could anyone opposed to cabinet policies view the administration as anything but an enemy?[25]

The years between 1824 and 1830 witnessed an extraordinary reversal, as liberal representation in the Chamber rose from 17 in 1824 to 170 in late 1827 to 274 in July 1830. This was achieved by stopping the executive from controlling elections, which in turn was facilitated by division among royalists. At the constitutional level, divide and rule consisted of enhancing the rôle of the judiciary and driving for decentralization through replacement of appointive officials by elected ones. The former objective was largely achieved in 1827 and 1828, and, while little progress was made in the latter until after the July Revolution, liberals gained support by championing it.[26]

Royalist divisions emerged for a number of reasons. Villèle could not keep all his allies of 1824 happy; patronage could only be stretched so far, and because it went primarily to Villèle's personal supporters, a counter-opposition of the right developed. Attempts to appease the extreme right through legislation favouring nobles and the Catholic Church foundered on the shoals of personal ambition. When the cabinet sought to prevent the counter-opposition from attacking the government, principally through covert attempts to purchase their journals, anger grew, and merged with liberal criticism of Villèle's methods. Muddying waters further were liberal charges that the government was controlled by a conspiratorial Jesuit organization. While most the allegations were inaccurate, ultra-royalism did have theocratic elements that Villèle had to accommodate through initiatives such as the Sacrilege Law of 1825. The spectre of theocracy further alienated members of the judiciary, who carried on the old *parlementaire* tradition of Gallicanism. When the royal courts failed to punish liberal newspapers suitably for allusions to Jesuit conspiracy, the cabinet responded by proposing the draconian Law of Justice and Love, which would have transferred judgement of press offences from the judiciary to the executive.[27]

Because Villèle's answer to criticism was to tighten state control, the backlash against Villèle merged with attempts to limit state power. An early manifestation came in April 1827, when the Peers blocked the press law; but more critical were revisions by both Chambers of a government proposal to revise the process of compiling jury and voter lists. The electoral régime thereby underwent fundamental changes. A series of regulations fixed prefectoral prerogative: lists would be revised annually between 15 August and 30 September, and they would be posted widely. Adjudication of appeals would no longer be monopolized by the executive: questions relating to the *cens* or domicile would continue to go before the council of state, but issues pertaining to civil or political rights would be settled by the royal courts. This was a vague formula, and doubtless the cabinet would have withdrawn the bill had Villèle foreseen the sweeping interpretation the courts would give to their new powers. But Villèle underestimated the resentment against his policies and the desire among judges to play a more decisive constitutional role.[28]

The consequences were apparent in the elections of November 1827. Liberals launched a drive to force revision in the lists, resulting in an increase of some 18,000 voters. In combination with electoral pacts with the counter-opposition of the right, this broke Villèle's majority in the Chamber and paved the way for the centrist Martignac ministry. Below the surface of partisan struggles, several features should be stressed. List revision depended on the willingness of judges to reverse prefectoral decisions. Subsequently the press would rapidly expand; but after the formation of the Polignac Ministry in August 1829, public criticism of government would also depend on judicial defence of freedom of the press. Liberal attempts to force governments to adhere to the rule of law had finally born fruit, and animosity within the legal fraternity towards administrative bullying contributed to this.[29]

Formation of the Martignac cabinet was immediately followed by an attempt in parliament in early 1828 to bring Villèle to trial on charges of treason based principally on his electoral practices. The attempt failed, as the royalists closed ranks; but a commission was established to investigate prefectoral malpractice, and figures such as d'Haussez and Vanssay came under heavy fire. Given the extent of corruption the results were meagre – twelve prefects sacked or effectively demoted to less prestigious prefectures. Yet a point had been made: parliament could hold agents of the executive accountable. Thus officials were informed that simply following cabinet orders might have unpleasant consequences, and the point was grasped by at least some of them. In late 1829 and 1830 the Polignac cabinet was inclined to return to the methods of Villèle, but it found much of the judiciary unwilling to acquiesce in attempts to silence the press. In the electoral campaign of June 1830 the courts ensured that regulations governing the compilation of voters lists were followed, and prefects generally stuck to the letter of the law. Thus the executive and administration were reined in: the very opposite of what had occurred under Bonaparte.[30]

Decentralization proved more elusive, but debate in early 1829 over Martignac's proposal to make local councils elective was highly revealing both of official attitudes and reservations among the élite over state power. Officials voiced alarm over the loss of power in terms of its consequences for royal authority. Esmangart de Feynes, prefect of the Bas-Rhin, warned that the laws of 1790 making local office elective had destroyed the Crown; Napoleon had commenced his rule wisely in Year VIII by restoring central government control. Such sentiments echoed concerns earlier expressed in the Haute-Garonne by prefect de Juiné. Even in 1826 de Juiné had found disrespect on the rise. Eighty inhabitants of Boulogne had 'defamed' their mayor in a pamphlet. The mayor had pursued the matter through the courts, but punishment had been risible. Judges had failed to protect an official 'invested with part of the supreme power' and, in the end, the administration 'could never be certain' of the courts. In consequence authority was losing its force and even appointed municipal councillors wished 'to administer everything'. Thus 'democracy, restrained under the Empire', was spreading.[31]

Critics of centralization saw matters differently. From 1828 onwards, provincial liberal newspapers mushroomed, and dedicated extensive coverage to issues of local government. At Toulouse the *France Méridionale* subjected the departmental budget of 1829 to close analysis, revealing how tax revenues were spent and how this worked to the benefit of certain vested interests. Part of the proposed solution was to make the franchise for council elections broad enough to represent all interests; but a corollary was that prefectoral control over taxation and expenditure would be removed.[32]

At Rouen the *Journal* had fallen under radical liberal ownership and entered into competition with the moderate liberal *Neustrien*. Yet both newspapers saw in Martignac's proposed legislation a means to develop the 'representative principle' embodied in the *Charte*. The *Journal* criticized government proposals because they 'left the Napoleonic system almost entirely intact', leaving prefects with excessive powers. The *Neustrien* specified that local councils should be able to appoint police commissioners and forest guards. Anger was expressed that councils would be limited to advising prefects; those who paid taxes should have the liberty to decide how revenues were spent. The line taken by the *Courier du Bas-Rhin* at Strasburg, which argued that 'all magistrates should be chosen by truly popular elections', was much the same.[33]

From the standpoints of social relations or the advent of democracy, the Revolution of 1830 can appear as a relatively minor affair. While the franchise for electing deputies was widened, and a more generous franchise was accorded to election of local councils (which still held little power), ultimately power simply passed from one narrow élite to another. Yet if we view matters from the perspective of governmental systems, and consider the Revolution to have begun with the election of 1827, '1830' rises in prominence.[34]

Historically, France has lurched between periods when the state was virtually impotent, to phases when state power was largely unchecked by any other institution. In this context, the essential Napoleonic contribution was to enhance the powers of the executive while emasculating all potential rivals. This was possible owing to fear of the anarchy attributed to Revolutionary factionalism; but it was also true that the Napoleonic regime responded to enlightened despotism's desire to secure a better material life for its subjects. Hence the Napoleonic model was a technocrat's paradise, allowing scope for pursuit of prosperity while preventing interference from elected officials. Ultimately the model most appealed to those who wished power untrammelled by public account-ability or, for that matter, public choice.

The Napoleonic legacy was not limited to France, but then again, advances in despotism were nothing new to the Continent in the early 1800s. After the fall of the Empire, restored monarchs happily grafted elements of the Napoleonic model on to their own illiberal regimes. When pushed outside positions of power or traumatized by irrational or inefficient government, even former Napoleonic officials could meta-morphose into champions of liberty. But this was not the true Napoleonic legacy, which lay in state power unchecked by representative bodies.

What made France novel in the Restoration period was that it returned to the liberal Revolutionary heritage by rejecting the Napoleonic model. The achievement was fragile and the arguments of social order, economic prosperity and territorial defence would frequently reappear in justification of enlarging state power. But France had travelled some distance in implementing a system capable of making society master of the state and not the reverse. It was perhaps mostly symbolic that the revised *Charte* was based explicitly on national sovereignty; but a real division of power between government and parliament nevertheless took root. Finding a reasonable balance between the over-mighty and the underachieving state has remained problematic; but clearly rejection of the Napoleonic legacy was a step in the right direction. In the world of the Holy Alliance, this marked a major departure; but in more universal terms it serves as a reminder that any reformulation of the state must include institutions able to limit government and punish those who brush aside such limits. Whether bigger is better is an open question; but whatever the size, members of the state must have reminders that they serve the wishes of their community, not just what they perceive as the interests of that community.

Notes

1. Mutual schools were variants of the Lancastrian system. See A. Thiers, *Les Pyrénées et le Midi de la France pendant les mois de novembre et décembre 1822* (Paris, 1823), pp. 25–30 and R. S. Alexander, 'Restoration Republicanism Reconsidered', *French History*, 8 (1994), pp.456–9. In citing primary sources I have used

the following abbreviations: AN = National Archives, AD = Departmental Archives (of), BM = Municipal Library (of), I = the Isère, HG = the Haute-Garonne, SM = the Seine-Maritime.

2. The Napoleonic legacy was not simply authoritarian. For discussion of the complexities of Bonapartism, see R. S. Alexander, 'Napoleon Bonaparte and the French Revolution', in P. Pilbeam (ed.), *Themes in European History 1780–1830* (London, 1995), pp.40–64.

3. On the *Charte* and electoral régime, see J. H. Stewart, *The Restoration Era in France* (Princeton, NJ, 1968) pp.109–16 and G. de Bertier de Sauvigny, *The Bourbon Restoration* (Philadelphia, 1966), pp.65–72, and P. Bastid, *Les institutions politiques de la monarchie parlementaire française (1814–1848)* (Paris, 1954), pp.211–40.

4. See I. Collins, *Napoleon and his Parliaments, 1800–1815* (New York, 1979).

5. On the Napoleonic state, see R. Holtman, *The Napoleonic Revolution* (Baton Rouge, LA, 1978), S. Woolf, *Napoleon's Integration of Europe* (London, 1991), E. Whitcomb, 'Napoleon's Prefects', *American Historical Review* (1974), pp.1089–118, C. Church, *Revolution and Red Tape: The French Ministerial Bureaucracy, 1770–1850* (Oxford, 1981), pp.254–306, and N. Richardson, *The French Prefectoral Corps 1814–30* (Cambridge, 1966).

6. That officials acted as electoral agents has often been noted, but corruption of voter independence has not been systematically analysed. The present chapter represents a step in the latter direction, but is derived from a broader monograph provisionally entitled *'The Science of Electoral Intrigue': Grass-Roots Liberal Opposition and the Fall of Bourbon Monarchy*. See further B. Chapman, *The Prefects and Provincial France* (London, 1955), pp.32–43, Richardson, *Prefectoral Corps*, pp.37–9, and P. Pilbeam *The 1830 Revolution in France* (Basingstoke, 1991), pp.25–7.

7. J. Vidalenc, 'Note sur les épurations de 1814 et de 1815', in P. Gerbod *et al.*, *Les épurations administratives* (Geneva, 1977), pp.63–8 and Richardson, *Prefectoral Corps*, pp.31–77.

8. Woolf, *Napoleon's Integration of Europe*, pp.8–13, 96–8 and A. Spitzer 'The Ambiguous Heritage of the French Restoration: The Distant Consequences of the Revolution and the Daily Realities of the Empire', in J. Pelenski (ed.), *The American and European Revolutions* (Iowa City, 1980), pp.208–26.

9. Joseph de Villèle, *Mémoires et Correspondance* (Paris, 1888–90) I, pp.218–23, 494, and 499–509, II, pp.65–72, III, pp.15–19. See also V. Schmidt, *Democratizing France* (Cambridge and New York, 1990), pp.26–9 and Richardson, *Prefectoral Corps*, pp.2–3.

10. See G. Lewis, *The Second Vendée* (Oxford, 1978), pp.187–218, B. Fitzpatrick, *Catholic Royalism in the Department of the Gard, 1814–1852* (Cambridge, 1982), pp.28–59, D. Resnick, *The White Terror* (Cambridge, MA, 1966) and R. S. Alexander, *Bonapartism and Revolutionary Tradition in France* (Cambridge, 1991), pp.219–47.

11. H. Dumolard, *La Terreur Blanche dans l'Isère* (Grenoble, 1928). Examples of friction can be found in ADI 52M4, 6 September – 15 November 1815, 52M5, 7 December 1815, 52M9, 31 Dec. 1815, 3 January and 8 April 1816; 52M10, 15–16 March 1816; 52M18, 2 April 1816.

12. M. Bérenger, *De la justice criminelle en France* (Paris, 1818), pp.1–79, 106–40, 220–56, 257–310, and 342–62. See also L. Karpik, 'Lawyers and Politics in France, 1814–1950', *Law and Social Inquiry* (Fall, 1988), pp. 711–16. State Terror was dismantled gradually, beginning with a bill in early 1817 that continued suspension of individual liberty, but reserved orders of arrest and incarceration for government ministers.

13. The *Charte* left much unspecified, but the Lainé Law of February 1817 established that elections would be direct. Men of over thirty years of age who paid three hundred francs or more in annual taxes (the *cens*) would gather in colleges generally held in the departmental *chef lieu*. Each department was assigned a certain number of deputies, the total for France being 258. Each year one-fifth of the Chamber would be renewed in a departmental rotation. By the end of 1819 liberals held roughly ninety seats, making a majority possible for 1820. Hence the electoral regime was changed by the Law of the Double Vote of June 1820. Departmental *arrondissements* would choose their own deputies, and qualification for this franchise would remain at three hundred francs. However, 172 seats would be determined in departmental colleges composed roughly of those who paid one thousand francs or more in taxes annually. Annual renewal was abolished. This régime remained intact until the July Revolution in 1830.

14. See the *Journal libre de l'Isère*, 12 February 1820 and C. Lemercher de Longpré, *Mémoires du Baron D'Haussez* (Paris, 1896), I, pp.321–3.

15. AN, F7 9667, 2 December 1819 – 2 September 1821, F7 3679\6, 30 April and 1 July 1820; *Journal libre*, 4–29 July and 30 November 1820; ADI, 8M5, 28 July 1820.

16. Lemercher de Longpré, *Mémoires*, I, pp.321–3; see also AN, F1c III Isère 4, 17 March 1820.

17. *Journal de Grenoble*, 24 March 1820; *Journal libre*, 22–27 March

1820; AN, F7 9667, 18 December 1822; BM Grenoble, R9513, 8 April 1821 and R7906, 9 April 1821; Lemercher de Longpré, *Mémoires*, pp.354–63.

18. See the introduction to Lemercher de Longpré, *Mémoires*, and I, pp.327–38.

19. AN, F7 6745, 26 March 1820, F7 3679\6, 3 and 6 May 1820, F7 9667, 3–7 December 1820, F7 3794, 22 May 1821.

20. *Journal de Grenoble*, 8 August 1822, 24 January, 26 February and 23 November 1824; AN, F7 9667, 29 April 1820.

21. AN, F1c III Garonne-Haute 6, 6 March, 7–9 August 1820. D'Haussez was more forthright; see AN, F1c III Isère 4, 11 August 1820.

22. ADHG, 2M24, 23 June and 9 August 1820, 15–19 September 1821, 4M24, circulars of 4–30 July 1821 and correspondence of 8 August and 11 September 1821; AN, F1c III Garonne-Haute 6, wherein the completed lists can be found.

23. See A. de Vaulabelle, *Histoire des Deux Restaurations* (Paris, 1858), VII, pp.1–17.

24. AN, BB30 238, 27 March – 5 April 1820.

25. See H. Putz, 'Les élections de 1824 en Seine-Inférieure', *Annales de Normandie* (1955), pp.59–72 and ADSM, 3M158, 17 February and 1 March 1824 and AN, BB30 235, 6–8 May 1824.

26. Such figures are approximate.

27. See G. Cubitt, *The Jesuit Myth* (Oxford, 1993), pp.55–104 and S. Kent, *The Election of 1827 in France* (Cambridge, MA, 1975), pp.9–18.

28. Kent, *1827*, pp.18–31.

29. Ibid., pp.107–29. The jump in voter numbers was roughly from 70,000 to 88,000.

30. For the transitions of this period see Pilbeam, *1830*, pp.27–30. For the onslaught on prefects Calvière and d'Haussez, see the *Pétition* in ADI, 14M5; the travails of Vanssay can be traced in the correspondence of 1828 in ADSM, F1c III Seine-Inférieure 5. See also Villèle, *Mémoires*, V, pp.325–61, Richardson, *Prefectoral Corps*, p.70 and D. L. Rader, *The Journalists and the July Monarchy in France* (The Hague, 1973).

31. Alexander, 'Restoration Republicanism Reconsidered', pp.463–5 and AN, F7 6769, report of March 1826.

32. *France Méridionale*, 19–24 July 1829.

33. *Journal de Rouen*, 10–12 February 1829; *Neustrien*, 13–25 February 1829; *Courier du Bas-Rhin*, 1 March 1829.

34. For discussion of 1830 and the regime it begat, see Pilbeam, *1830*, and H. A. C. Collingham, *The July Monarchy* (London, 1988).

1. Duchy of Parma
2. Duchy of Modena
3. Duchy of Massa and Carrara
4. Duchy of Lucca

Map 1. The Italian States, 1815

–3–

State and Society in Post-Napoleonic Italy
Marco Meriggi

The history of the Italian peninsula in the decades between the fall of Napoleon and 1860 is known principally for the Risorgimento, the struggle to achieve independence and national unity. Figures such as Giuseppe Mazzini, the democrat and republican leader who spent much of his life in exile in London, and Giuseppe Garibaldi, the legendary commander of liberation movements in both Italy and South America, represent key elements in the mosaic of nineteenth-century romantic consciousness, not just in Italy but in the whole of Europe. Equally significant, although for rather different reasons, is Count Camillo Benso di Cavour, the Piedmontese statesman who, in the course of the 1850s, succeeded in steering Italy towards national unification as a liberal monarchy under the House of Savoy, thanks both to his skilful diplomatic strategy on the international front and his successful taming of the democratic republican movement.[1]

Mazzini, Garibaldi and Cavour, and the events in which they assumed so prominent a rôle, belonged to an era that in political, civil and cultural terms is rather remote from the Napoleonic period. At least fifteen years separate their activities from the last days of Napoleon's power. These men began their politically active lives in the 1830s, and never, either in their public pronouncements or their private correspondence, did they evoke the name of Bonaparte except in the most purely incidental way. Their era chose other polemical targets, such as Metternich, General Radetzky or the Habsburg Emperor Francis Joseph, who were identified as responsible for the authoritarian political system that blocked the path to independence and exercised a strong illiberal influence on the domestic affairs of the Italian states. Conversely, if a positive model was sought, the key reference point, particularly for Cavour, was the concrete constitutional experience of liberal countries such as Britain, or, for the likes of Mazzini and Garibaldi, the unrealized dream of a democratic and republican Europe of sovereign peoples.

Yet although barely featured in public discourse during the Risorgimento, the years 1796 to 1814 left an indelible mark on the structures of the states and societies that, in the legitimist spirit of 1815, the Congress of Vienna returned to their *ancien régime* dynasties. Thus both liberals and democrats had to come to terms with Bonaparte's ambiguous legacy during the Risorgimento. Yet even before these groups had to deal with this inheritance, it had to be confronted by those very rulers newly restored to power after Napoleon's defeat.

The aim of this chapter is to cast light on some of the characteristics of the 'hidden' Napoleonic legacy in the Restoration states. I shall also suggest how it was that the aristocratic liberal movement that asserted its influence from the 1830s to the 1850s did not find its major focus of opposition in Austrian despotism. Although this was publicly held up as the object of its polemical attacks, the real target was Bonapartism, or, to be more precise, the specific solution that Napoleon had provided to the conflict between liberty and equality that had emerged during the French Revolution. The democratic movement is only of incidental concern to me here, although it does strike me that it too maintained an intense relationship – in this case a positive one – with the Napoleonic legacy. The democratic movement borrowed the revolutionary idea of equality, which Napoleon had appropriated after his own fashion, but which the liberal movement had great difficulty in accepting, given that it still understood freedom essentially as a privilege.

After the fall of Napoleon the Italian peninsula was divided into eight states. All of these, with the exception of the Papal territory, had dynastic régimes, and all of them, including the Papal territory, had absolutist forms of government. The political and territorial settlement of the Restoration was undoubtedly much more varied than that of the late Napoleonic era, when Italy had been divided into only three units. These had been endowed with institutions that were, if not identical, then certainly very similar, in that they were all based on the French model.[2] However, if we compare the Restoration settlement with the situation under the late *ancien régime*, when oligarchic republics (Genoa, Venice, Lucca) had existed alongside dynastic princedoms, and when there had been a total of ten politico-territorial units, it is clear that in the post-1815 era a considerable simplification had taken place. Thus, on the one hand, the Restoration saw the breaking up of the political geometry established by Napoleon, while on the other, it witnessed a tendency to reduce the plurality of states and institutional forms that had existed in the pre-Revolutionary period. In the years immediately following the Congress of Vienna, despite the strong emphasis on how the *ancien régime* had been 'restored', it was this second tendency that provided the ideological background for public debate and endowed it with such resonance. As I intend to argue, while the Restoration brought with it fragments of two distinct and contrasting legacies, it is the discontinuity with the *ancien régime* that needs to be stressed.

Although the institutional forms imposed by the post-Napoleonic rulers of Italy varied, they were united in invoking the divine right tradition to legitimize their own absolute power. Thus they drew heavily on the ideological resources of the *ancien régime* and its religious, sacred aspects. However, before the French Revolution, this authoritarian and paternalistic model of power, viewed as a temporal version of divine majesty over the earth, had been practised within corporate frameworks, which endowed the privileged ranks in society (the aristocracy and clergy) with the chance to participate actively in public jurisdiction. In some states the reforms of the second half of the eighteenth century had challenged the practice of sharing public authority between privileged bodies and the sovereign, shifting the balance in favour of the latter. However, in the years between the outbreak of the French Revolution and the descent of Bonaparte's army into Italy in 1796, this tendency had been halted throughout the peninsula, and in many instances actively reversed.[3] At the very moment when in France a new social and political model was emerging from the Revolution, based on radical individualism and on the modern institution of state citizenship, throughout Italy the world of nobles and clergy was enjoying a return to prominence. Once again rulers recognized in these groups the most powerful bastions for their thrones, and essential allies in defence of the old corporate order.

Let us turn again to the situation in 1815. Everywhere the nobility recovered official status as a body distinct from the rest of society and endowed with the prerogatives of rank. All of Italy's sovereigns hurriedly proclaimed the renewed alliance between throne and altar, identifying it as the panacea for a society that had long been contaminated by revolutionary heresies and, in particular, by the idea that power was legitimated from below. Twenty years after the Napoleonic invasion, were these the same trends that had blossomed in the years immediately following the outbreak of the French Revolution?

Only apparently. The Restoration monarchs were at pains to cultivate the comfortably nostalgic image of a traditional corporate society distinguished by the exercise of a 'mixed' jurisdiction on the part of the privileged bodies. Yet this was just propaganda, which was quietly but systematically contradicted by the real practices of Restoration governments. All these governments, albeit with varying degrees of self-consciousness and to different extents, adopted significant elements of the Napoleonic legacy. This took place in the Kingdom of Lombardy-Venetia, in the Duchies of Parma and Modena and in the Kingdom of the Two Sicilies, in the Grand Duchy of Tuscany and the principality of Lucca; it even occurred in the Papal States and, within a few years, in the Kingdom of Sardinia-Piedmont, where King Vittorio Emanuele I distinguished himself during the earliest days of the Restoration by the zeal with which he brought back into force both the letter and the spirit of the *ancien régime*. Everywhere the state machine, a centralized administrative system, exercised absolute supremacy over society, without making distinctions between ordinary subjects and those belonging to privileged bodies.[4] Of course, dusted-off noble titles did still retain some of their former value. They could, perhaps, facilitate preferment in public office, and were essential for acceptance at court.[5] But no longer did such titles bring those that bore them, either as individuals or as a group, the immunities and exemptions they had enjoyed under the *ancien régime*. Nor did they bring the jurisdictional powers that had formerly both complemented and challenged those of the state, and that had been the real substance of titles in the pre-Revolutionary era.

After 1815 subjects remained fundamentally equal before uniform legal codes, a Napoleonic innovation not questioned by any of the restored monarchs. No longer did aristocratic title or ecclesiastical status bring with it exemptions or privileges. The old separate jurisdictional institutions possessing a degree of impermeability to state authority (such as feudal estates, city organs of self-government, regional and provincial assemblies based on social rank according to the different social frameworks that existed in different parts of the peninsula) had all disappeared or had their powers drastically reduced. In every state of the peninsula, monarchs now governed in an authoritarian manner through a bureaucratic apparatus to which all subjects – peasant and noble, shopkeeper and landowner, layman and cleric – owed the same form of obedience. Their governments had their own distinct characteristics, but also many common traits, despite the apparent rebirth of the variety and plurality of pre-Revolutionary forms.

So it was that, after a brief interlude during which they gained practical experience of the new power relationships between state and society, the groups that had historically been privileged began to express their unease. In a chorus of protest they accused these new governments, headed by the successors of the late-eighteenth-century rulers, of being no more than replicas of the states that had just been abolished. Just like the Napoleonic states, it seemed that the new governments had endowed the impersonal, bureaucratic mechanisms of administration with a monopoly of power over the public domain. They were, therefore, despotic, and, in the way that they placed all subjects without distinction on the same level before the state, they were depriving society of the ancient freedoms reserved for intermediate bodies. It was because of these freedoms, this mixture of exemptions and privileges, that the *ancien régime* was not a form of despotism or tyranny in the eyes of its defenders, but instead constituted the natural expression of an organic society, organized in hierarchical bodies, and obviously not recognizing any modern notion of equality.

Despotism and tyranny: curiously these same charges were levelled at the Restoration monarchs, albeit from a very different perspective, by those who looked back on the Napoleonic period with nostalgia. These people were for the most part from bourgeois backgrounds, the majority having served as public officials or army officers during the previous decade and a half; at the turn of the century they had often been Jacobins, and they had appreciated the Napoleonic government's reforming drive and its administrative efficiency. To some extent they had come to identify with it, perceiving in the Napoleonic order something more than a mere echo of the Revolutionary era's democratic ideals. Although the Napoleonic régime had conceded very little to the kinds of demands for the citizenry's active participation in power that had propelled the democratic dream of French Revolution, the Napoleonic state did offer a secularized and egalitarian government that aimed to reform society from above and allow the development of modern cultural discourse. For these men, who constituted a not insignificant section of the Italian ruling classes in the early years of the nineteenth century, the Restoration was an unwelcome step. To anyone, for example, interested in gaining access to a modern secular culture, it became apparent from the earliest days of the new order that censorship had become stricter and that the machinery for its implementation was once again usually headed by the clergy. In this sense the despotic alliance between throne and altar was more than a mere declaration of intent; it had become a reality.[6]

Moreover, while the Restoration monarchs had maintained Napoleonic bureaucratic mechanisms, they seemed to favour a debased and run-down version that was unable to continue the modernization of society started under Napoleon in a coherent fashion. Thus it was that, especially in the years immediately after the Congress of Vienna, the task of managing the complex institutional machinery inherited from Napoleon was entrusted to members of the very aristocratic group that so resented the preservation of his system.

In the eyes of the citizenry it seemed as if the new social hierarchies and ideological values established under Bonaparte had been overturned. The myth of a public career open to merit and ability had become a reality in the first decade and a half of the century, and had offered a compensatory basis on which the orphans of the Revolution and Jacobinism could fashion their identity. In Restoration Italy such an idea became no more than a mere memory. Sacked or pensioned off, the men who had been in charge of the administration and the military until 1814 left public offices and the armies of the Restoration monarchies in their droves. In some states – notably the Kingdom of the Two Sicilies – the process was less extensive than in others, but it was nevertheless a defining characteristic of the early Restoration. These men were replaced by thoroughbred aristocrats both young and old, representatives of the pre-Revolutionary ruling class. In the eyes of the former cadres of the Napoleonic army and administration, this substitution constituted incontrovertible proof of the return of the despotic and tyrannical *ancien régime*, founded on the privileges of birth.

The Congress of Vienna installed governments in Italy that were simultaneously anti-reactionary and anti-revolutionary. Although they had markedly different reasons, both those who were nostalgic for the *ancien régime* and the sympathizers of the former government considered the Restoration régimes despotic. This reputation derived from the ambiguous nature of the Restoration governments, or, as I have tried to demonstrate, the double-sided legacy with which they had to deal: the ideological inheritance and the material inheritance.

All Italy's restored monarchies drew on the ideological part of that inheritance to restore their historical legitimacy after replacing someone they considered to be a usurper and the heir of revolutionary heresy. But this appeal to the legitimist spirit and the formal re-establishment of privileges based on social rank lacked a crucial element without which it was wanting in credibility. The definitive and exclusive identifying trait of the aristocracy and the clergy in the pre-Revolutionary era had been their jurisdictional functions. These powers were not returned in the Restoration. Consequently, in almost all cases, the material aspects of the situation inherited by the restored régimes counted for more than the ideological elements.

The material legacy consisted of the range of bureaucratic apparatus through which the Napoleonic public administration had extended its reach. None of the Restoration régimes was eager to forgo certain gains made during the Napoleonic era: the strong bureaucratization of public life; the establishment of a vertical, hierarchical relationship between centre and periphery; the state's ability to determine a simple and profitable relationship with its subjects, permitting a continuous supply of human and fiscal resources from society. The prerequisites for these gains were: that the old society of autonomous bodies be dismantled; that, simultaneously, civil society be reorganized on an equal, individualistic basis; that the state be endowed with a monopoly of public power; and, lastly, that the state's authority be exercised through rigidly bureaucratic, administrative channels. Thus in the majority of Italian states the Restoration monarchs might change the names of the institutions that had typified the Napoleonic era, but at the same time they gave the 'new' administrative structures the same functions as those they had just abolished. Everywhere, for example, the post of prefect, which more than any other office had been the face of the Napoleonic bureaucracy, formally disappeared, often to be replaced by figures with wellnigh identical duties but a different title.

At least in the early years, such changes were not merely cosmetic. As I have already pointed out, there was a mass exodus from the offices of the professional Napoleonic bureaucracy, albeit with differing levels of intensity in different states. Thus in the first instance there was, at least, a change of personnel, as the vacant places were usually filled by members of the nobility. However, over a number of years, the nobles who had taken over administrative rôles tended to stand down and were replaced by a new school of professional bureaucrats, whose very existence was defined by their administrative work.[7]

Rather than an aristocratic *revanche*, what really counted was another phenomenon that ran counter to such a process. In spite of the fact that they were formally resurrected in some of the post-Napoleonic states, the old representative institutions based on social station, which had been so important an expression of noble self-government in the peripheries, soon proved to have been deprived of substantial and effective prerogatives. Once this fact had become clear – and this I feel must be stressed – it also became evident that the nobility's apparent resurgence was, all things considered, of little genuine value. The provincial representative institutions that were reintroduced into, for example, Lombardy-Venetia and the Papal States no longer had the jurisdiction, the active influence in the public sphere, that they had enjoyed under the *ancien régime*. All that they were permitted were auxiliary, technical functions in support of the work of the central bureaucratic administration. It did happen that nobles found themselves at the helm of both state institutions and regional or local representative bodies. Yet, paradoxically, they still could not derive any significant opportunities for self-government from the exercise of either of these rôles.[8] As high-ranking functionaries of the state, holding posts at the summit of public administration, nobles were placed in positions that were new to them, and were asked to carry out tasks that they found fundamentally alien. As during the Napoleonic era, under the Restoration régimes the bureaucratic machine continued to function as an impersonal structure: nobles in government office were now simply cogs in a mechanism over which they had no control. Holding a high post no longer meant wielding significant power that could be used for individual advantage or for the benefit of one's caste. Instead, it involved passively carrying out executive functions, and faithfully and bureaucratically implementing norms and directives issued by the machinery of state.

So, maybe in spite of himself, the noble–functionary of the Restoration era was simply a link in the relationship between state and society, reproducing the way in which that relationship had taken shape during the Napoleonic era. His visible public status did not correspond to his decision-making power: the transitory conquest of the field of administration was a purely illusory victory. Given this, it is not surprising that within ten or fifteen years those very nobles whose presence *en masse* at the head of state institutions in 1815 had seemed to provide testimony to the collapse of the Napoleonic system, and the passing of its values and personnel, spontaneously withdrew in disappointment from their top administrative jobs. There was soon great disappointment in another area: the representative institutions. These were partly rank-based assemblies that the restored sovereigns resurrected and tried to peddle as proof that the spirit of the *ancien régime* had returned and that the monarchic-corporate order had been rebonded. These bodies, the composition of which gave particular weight to the nobility, certainly made the class hierarchies that had been erased by Revolutionary and Napoleonic juridical egalitarianism once again clearly visible. Nevertheless, deprived of jurisdictional functions, they too demonstrated that any apparent return to the *ancien régime* was no more than a charade.

The aristocracy had achieved only Pyrrhic victories in two fields: the state administration, which they had wrenched from the grasp of the Napoleonic bourgeois bureaucrats, and the purely formal resurrection of a social framework based on rank. The machine of state continued to dictate terms. No longer did nobles enjoy the opportunity to exercise authority based on their social status, either as state functionaries or through holding representative office. Yet only such authority could constitute a real measure of the distance that they hoped would be established between the restored monarchies and the Napoleonic régime.

For all that the restored monarchs appealed to a notion of royalty that was deeply ingrained with hierarchical and corporate concepts, the state remained the real arbiter of the public domain, wielding a complete monopoly of bureaucratic power. None of the series of institutions that had been overthrown during the Revolutionary and Napoleonic era was reborn after 1815: the feudal rights and estates, special citizen statutes, fiscal and judicial immunities that had been abolished during the *decennio* were not reintroduced. Essentially the new 'old order' was based on a dominant and authoritarian relationship between state and civil society, analogous to that codified by Napoleon. Notwithstanding the nostalgic rhetoric of the period, Restoration Italy was like the society that preceded it, a society composed of individuals and a public administration that held exclusive sway over all aspects of the public sphere. The Restoration state was just as determined to prevent participation in power by traditional corporate representative institutions as it was anxious to block modern, property-based, individualistic representative bodies.

It was because of this state-centred outlook that the movements that opposed the despotic Restoration régimes drew on three different models of politics and society that were far from easy to disentangle. These were: the corporate and caste-based framework; the liberal, property-based framework; and the democratic framework.[9] The last of these belongs to a tradition that is quite easily identified and that requires no lengthy treatment here. It is enough to recognize that democratic aspirations, typified by Mazzinian opposition, had their origins in the egalitarian and libertarian ideals bequeathed by the French Revolution, albeit adapted to the romantic cultural spirituality of the early nineteenth century. However, the other two models adopted by those demanding change were far more ambiguous in their ideological background. Moreover, they both had points of contact and parallels, which have often not been given sufficient consideration. It for this reason that I shall try in the following pages to identify how the two groups shared hidden connections.[10]

The Restoration states of Italy were characterized by two symptoms: on the one hand, state despotism, and, on the other, the absence of any form of representation of society capable of playing a rôle in the public sphere alongside the state's administration. The former, as we have seen, was an enduring legacy of the Napoleonic period, while the latter was a consequence of the inadequate or illusory legacy of the *ancien régime*. Although those who felt nostalgia for the pre-Revolutionary order put forward rather different solutions from those who defined themselves as liberals, the proposals of both groups derived from the same broad set of motives. In this regard the rôle of the Italian aristocracy is a revealing one. As would be expected, it was the aristocracy that galvanized the ranks of the reactionary opposition, nostalgic for the old order; what is more striking, is that the same social group also lay at the heart of the liberal opposition. This should be qualified with the observation that it was two successive generations of nobles who participated in these two types of opposition. The older generation of aristocrats, those who had experienced the *ancien régime* at first hand, looked to the past, to its minimalist states, to the old corporate structures and institutions that had guaranteed that both privileged classes and sovereign had been able to share in running the public sphere. This had been possible because government had been fundamentally premised on a shared sense of community on both a personal and a class level between the monarch and the aristocracy, coupled with the way in which power over the peripheries was entrusted to the nobility. The younger generation looked elsewhere for its influences, for example to the France of Louis XVIII or to liberal England, countries where representative constitutions guaranteed the élites substantial participation in government, while simultaneously excluding the middle and lower strata of society.

It was above all this modernized version of aristocratic values, displaying a qualified openness towards emerging social groups, that came to the fore during the Restoration and that would eventually become the ideology that united the liberal-moderate movement. The exponents of this political trend were not active in the traditional representative institutions that bore the imprint of old rank-based bodies, but had little real influence. Instead, they frequented the clubs, circles and associations that gave expression to civil society, and that allowed their members to enjoy new forms of social interaction that offered an institutional alternative to the despotism of the state.[11]

Up to a certain point, therefore, reactionaries and liberals alike envisaged following the same path. Both were against the state's authoritarian and bureaucratic character and against its tendency towards levelling society; they were against the hegemony of the administration; they wanted the (re)introduction of constitutions (whether in the modern or old sense of the word).[12] Nor should we be surprised at this, given that they also shared a common foundation in a polemical opposition to the way in which the Napoleonic legacy had maintained the dominance of state over society, a dominance that had been countered by the restored monarchies only in form, not in fact.

Nevertheless, the levelling, despotic tendency of the state had another corollary, derived from its Revolutionary origins: the equality of individuals before the law. At this point, the paths of reaction and liberalism clearly divided, at least in part. For the reactionaries entirely rejected the idea of equality of right. Drawing on ideologies that were of an essentially pre-individualistic stamp, the reactionaries viewed society in terms of autonomous bodies, in which the state dissolved into a plural and strongly class-based society. This state sought to cancel out the epiphany of modern individualism embodied in the 1789 Declaration of Rights. In contrast, liberals accepted individualism and with it the principle of civil equality for all citizens. Yet when they came to the principle of political equality – the right to vote and the opportunity to participate in shaping and regulating legislative authority – their perspective became distinctly oligarchic, or more accurately 'neo-oligarchic'. They accepted the idea of a dialectic between the bureaucratic state and society, in the sense that society should have a more important rôle and that the state should be only a tool in its service. This is why they fought for the full implementation and preservation of civil rights such as freedom of the press and association. It is also why they fought to establish a legislative body besides the executive, in order to shift the balance between authority (embodied by the administration) and the citizenry (represented by parliament) in favour of the latter. Yet at the same time they also envisaged qualifications for political citizenship so exclusive as to make it little more than an updated version of the old privileged corps of nobles.

Reactionaries and liberals: supporters of a society composed of bodies defined by rank, and supporters of an individualistic, property-based society. During the Restoration both of these groups had to deal with the Napoleonic inheritance, and, therefore, with parts of the Revolutionary inheritance. The former group tried to make the inheritance vanish simply by turning their gaze backwards. The latter intended to shape the legacy and counterbalance its authoritarian aspects. Both groups had an antipathy towards the state: the reactionaries for corporatist and traditionalist reasons, the liberals for individualistic and neo-oligarchic reasons. However, it would be wrong to think that these two outlooks were fixed in rigid opposition to one another. Neo-oligarchic liberalism was a close relative of corporatist pluralism. What they had in common was a set of attitudes rooted in Catholic thought, which was both anti-state and anti-individualist at the same time.

Catholic and liberal, but also Catholic and reactionary: these pairs of concepts crop up time and again when analysing the activities of the various strands of opposition to despotism that existed under the post-Napoleonic governments. Indeed, it is not always easy to identify individual figures from the non-democratic political opposition with one pair of concepts rather than the other. Antonio Rosmini is one significant case in point. Although his brand of thought was fiercely anti-individualistic, and, in some respects, embodied a type of late-corporatism, Rosmini also constituted an effective bridge between Catholicism and liberalism. Yet was it really possible to be both Catholic and liberal in the nineteenth century? There is plenty of room for doubt. One need only think of the more concrete aspects of the dream that a very large section of the Italian liberal movement set up in opposition to the central rôle of the administrative state. Many of this group shifted between nostalgia for the old corporate society and cautious acceptance of a more modern society. All the same, they counted on counterbalancing the latter's judicial individualism through the power of the family. Their liberalism was weak, socially exclusive and heavily paternalistic. In fact paternalism is a major theme of Alessandro Manzoni's *The Betrothed* (*I promessi sposi*), the great national novel of the era. Manzoni's work is an apology for divine providence and its corresponding earthly corporate hierarchy. In the novel that hierarchy is guided by a cardinal who is also a member of a great noble family. Yet *The Betrothed* was written at the European peak of the *Bildungsroman*, the very literary genre that was devoted to the modern individual's personal struggle through life.

The Restoration was based on a paradox. For all its authoritarianism, the restored sovereigns' divinely re-legitimated rule ended up by demonstrating elements of continuity with the principle of *égalité* between individuals that had been first proclaimed by the revolutionaries of 1789. Meanwhile, the *liberté* championed by some sections of the opposition bore more than a passing resemblance to the plural liberties, the 'freedoms-as-immunities' that underpinned the corporate society of the *ancien régime*. The Napoleonic legacy was an ambivalent one for the rulers of Restoration Italy, as well as for their subjects. Although they declared their intentions to hark back to an era before the Napoleonic experience, Italy's rulers adopted a considerable portion of its legacy. At the same time, if anyone conducted a dialogue with the *ancien régime* it was definitely not the monarchs, who only evoked it in formal terms; rather it was a substantial sector of those who opposed the monarchs in the name of property-based liberalism, which in turn only expressed the old doctrine of rank-based pluralism in a new vocabulary.

Notes

1. There is a vast literature on Cavour, Garibaldi and Mazzini in both English and Italian. For the English reader the most useful recent

studies of Mazzini are D. Mack Smith, *Mazzini* (New Haven, CT, and London, 1994) and R. Sarti, *Mazzini. A Life for the Religion of Politics* (Westport, CT, 1997). On the democratic movement see F. Della Peruta, *Mazzini e i rivoluzionari italiani. Il partito d'azione 1830–1845* (Milan, 1974) and C. M. Lovett, *The Democratic Movement in Italy 1830–1876* (Cambridge, MA, 1982). For Mazzini's exile in England see E. Morelli, *Mazzini in Inghilterra* (Florence, 1938). D. Mack Smith, *Garibaldi* (London, 1957) remains the best English biography of the Risorgimento's greatest hero, while the same author's *Cavour* (London, 1985) is the standard anglophone work on the Piedmontese Prime Minister; see also H. Hearder, *Cavour* (London, 1994). The most important Italian study of Cavour is R. Romeo, *Cavour e il suo tempo* (3 vols, Bari, 1969–84). For the tensions between republican democrats and moderate monarchists see D. Mack Smith, *Cavour and Garibaldi 1860. A Study in Political Conflict* (Cambridge, 2nd edn, 1985) and R. Grew, *A Sterner Plan for Italian Unity. The Italian National Society in the Risorgimento* (Princeton, NJ, 1963). For the general framework of the problems of the Risorgimento see L. Riall, *The Italian Risorgimento. State, Society and National Unification* (London, 1994).

2. On administrative centralization in Napoleonic Italy and the imposition of Napoleonic institutions see L. Antonielli, *I prefetti dell'Italia napoleonica. Repubblica e Regno d'Italia* (Milan, 1983), A. De Martino, *La nascita delle intendenze* (Naples, 1984), C. Zaghi, *Napoleone e l'Italia* (Naples, 1966) and idem, *L'Italia di Napoleone dalla Cisalpina al Regno* (Turin, 1986).

3. The best example of this process is in eighteenth-century Lombardy, where a high level of local autonomy and extensive patrician privileges had been challenged by Joseph II's abolition of Milan's senate in 1786. In 1791, however, Leopold II had restored Lombardy's traditional privileges. On the reforms in Milan in this period see, for example, D. Sella and C. Capra, *Il ducato di Milano dal 1535 al 1796* (Turin, 1984), S. Cuccia, *La Lombardia alla fine dell'ancien régime* (Florence, 1981) and U. Perronio, *Il senato di Milano. Istituzioni giuridiche ed esercizio del potere nel ducato di Milano da Carlo I a Giuseppe II* (Milan, 1972).

4. For individual studies of states in the post-Napoleonic era see, for example, M. Meriggi, *Il Regno Lombardo-Veneto* (Turin, 1987); R. Romeo, *Dal Piemonte sabaudo all'Italia liberale* (Bari, 1974); B. Montale, *Parma nel Risorgimento. Istituzioni e società (1814–1859)* (Milan, 1993); and A. Spagnoletti, *Storia del Regno delle due Sicilie*

(Bologna, 1997). A useful insight into the debate surrounding continuity with Napoleonic practices is to be found in S. C. Hughes, *Crime, Disorder and the Risorgimento. The Politics of Policing in Bologna* (Cambridge, 1994), pp.1–167.

5. During the Restoration access to court sometimes became more dependent on noble pedigree than it had under the *ancien régime*. This, however, was further proof that real power lay with the centralized state. While, for example, in late eighteenth-century Milan the nobility had been able to co-opt wealthy and powerful bourgeois families into their ranks, members of these families often found themselves excluded by the decisions of the imperial commission on nobility: M. Meriggi, *Amministrazione e classi sociali nel Lombardo-Veneto (1814–1848)* (Bologna, 1983), pp.143–8.

6. See J.A Davis, Ch.14 below.

7. For a fuller discussion of these transformations in Restoration society see M. Meriggi, 'Società, istituzioni e ceti dirigenti', in G. Sabbatucci and V. Vidotto (eds), *Storia d'Italia. Vol. 1. Le premesse dell'unità. Dalla fine del Settecento al 1861* (Bari, 1994), pp.119–228.

8. For a good example of the relationship between élites and central government, see E. Tonetti, *Governo austriaco e notabili sudditi. Congregazioni e municipi nel Veneto della Restaurazione (1816–1848)* (Padua, 1997).

9. It is useful here to give the original Italian: 'costituzione cetual-corporata'; 'costituzione liberal-censitaria'; 'costituzione democratica'. The use of 'costituzione' in the first instance may sound strange to English speakers. However, the notion that the recognition of traditional rights and privileges (including rights of jurisdiction), with or without representative assemblies, represented a constitution was widespread. Indeed, in some senses it could even be applied to the British constitution. Thus, although the word is rendered here as 'framework', it was perfectly possible, for those seeking to limit the power of the state, whether from the point of view of traditional privileges, or from a liberal or democratic perspective, to invoke 'constitutionalism'. Indeed, when dealing with both early-nineteenth-century Italy and German-speaking lands, the idea of a 'constitution' ('costituzione' or 'Verfassung') is often juxtaposed with the notion of an 'administration' ('amministrazione' or 'Verwaltung'), which represented the effective power of the state bureaucratic machine, desired by absolutist monarchs in the eighteenth century, and largely realized in the form of Napoleonic bureaucracy. For a discussion of the debates surrounding these two terms in Germany, see J. J. Sheehan, *German History, 1780–1866* (Oxford, 1989), pp.425–41. [eds].

10. For the ambiguous relationship between liberal aristocrats and those nostalgic for the *ancien régime* see S. La Salvia, 'Il moderatismo in Italia', in U. Corsini and R. Lill (eds), *Istituzioni e ideologie in Italia e in Germania tra le rivoluzioni* (Bologna, 1987), pp.169–310; N. Del Corno (ed.), *Gli 'scritti sani'. Dottrine e propaganda nella pubblicistica reazionaria italiana dalla Restaurazione all'unità* (Milan, 1992); A. de Francesco, 'Ideologie e movimenti politici', in Sabbatucci and Vidotto (eds), *Storia d'Italia*, pp.229–336.

11. M. Meriggi and A. M. Banti (eds) *Elites e associazioni nell'Italia dell'Ottocento*, monographic issue of *Quaderni Storici*, 77 (1991); D. L. Caglioti, *Associazionismo e sociabilità d'élite a Napoli nel XIX secolo* (Naples, 1996); G. Montroni, *Gli uomini del re. La nobiltà napoletana nell'Ottocento* (Catanzaro, 1996).

12. See Note 9.

4

Enlightened Absolutism versus Theocracy in the Spanish Restoration, 1814–1850
Charles Esdaile

The basic point of reference in English for modern Spanish history remains Raymond Carr's *Spain, 1808–1939*. Originally published in 1966, this was superseded by a second edition in 1980. Although this extended the story to the death of General Franco in 1975 (and altered the title accordingly), the author did not take the opportunity to revise the earlier chapters. Stimulating though Carr's remarks remain, this must be regarded as a missed opportunity, for (in large part through his own influence) the period since 1966 has witnessed a dramatic revolution in Spain's historiography. In this particular instance this revolution has led to major changes in the attitude towards the restoration of absolutism in 1814.

At the time that Carr published his book, the scene was dominated by a school of historians who were determined to rehabilitate Fernando VII, or even to argue that he had not been reactionary enough. Within a few years, however, a rival school had emerged that subjected the Spanish Restoration to a critique that was even more damaging than that advanced in traditional works of liberal historiography. Given that the vast majority of English-speaking historians who have chosen to dedicate themselves to the study of modern Spain have concentrated on the late nineteenth, and, *a fortiori*, the twentieth centuries, this process of revision has gone largely unnoticed. The Gallicist or Germanist in search of a comparative perspective is, in consequence, certain to experience considerable frustration. If this chapter does something to alleviate this situation, then it will have served its purpose.[1]

In Spain the Restoration was marked by particularly severe political tensions. Between 1808 and 1814 the country had experienced a liberal revolution that had, at least in theory, transformed government and society. Released from captivity by Napoleon in 1814, Fernando VII had swept the revolution aside and restored absolutism. In this he had the backing of the majority of the army, the clergy, and the *notables* (both noble and non-noble), but there was no agreement as to the form the restoration of absolutism should take. For the so-called *apostólicos* or *renovadores*, the goal was the destruction of not just liberalism, but also the regalism of the eighteenth century. In contrast, for the bureaucrats who formed the bedrock of the administration the aim was a return to the enlightened reform of Carlos III (1759–88), and Carlos IV (1788–1808). At the level of the central government, the result was that the Restoration was marked by an intense debate that a variety of factors rapidly decided in favour of enlightened absolutism.

From all this it follows that, although it would be wrong to imply that there was much advance on the developments of the period from 1808 to 1814, the political and social organization of Spain was by no means simply restored to the state that it had enjoyed prior to the Napoleonic invasion. Before going any further, however, it is clearly necessary to discuss the broad outline of the changes that took place in Spain in the course of the Napoleonic invasion. For, in this respect, Spain's experiences were unique. Thus, many parts of Europe – Holland, Poland, Naples, and the states of the Confederation of the Rhine – were subjected to a dramatic process of political, social and economic reform at the behest of either Napoleon or his satellites. Still others – Prussia, Portugal, Sicily, the Habsburg Empire – experienced reform as a means of responding to the French challenge. In Spain both processes were operative at once. Whilst Joseph Bonaparte sought to impose a classic programme of Napoleonic reform from his capital of Madrid, the rival capital of Cádiz witnessed the elaboration of an even more dramatic political manifesto in the form of the constitution of 1812. There were remarkable similarities between the two models. Given that the rival camps were working towards common goals in accordance with a common agenda, this was not surprising.

Let us look first of all at *josefino* Spain. In addition to giving Spain his brother, Joseph, as king, the emperor also embellished it with a constitution. Very similar to those introduced in other satellite states such as Westphalia, this made provision for the establishment of a cabinet, modern ministries, a council of state, and a bicameral *cortes* of very limited power (chosen in part by royal appointment and in part by indirect election), as well as enshrining such fundamental principles as personal liberty, equality before the law and freedom of occupation. Much of this never materialized; but, for all that, French rule was far from inactive. On the contrary, when Napoleon reoccupied Madrid in December 1808 he immediately abolished feudalism, the Inquisition, the Council of Castile, and all internal customs barriers, suppressed two-thirds of Spain's convents and monasteries, and prohibited the accumulation of the entailed estates known as *mayorazgos*. Thereafter, Joseph's Spanish ministers continued the work by dividing Spain into a network of French-style departments, abolishing the Mesta, the Voto de Santiago, the military orders, and most of the monopolies hitherto enjoyed by the state, suppressing such religious foundations as had been allowed to remain by Napoleon, expropriating known Patriots, selling off the various royal factories, establishing new systems of education and justice, and taking steps towards the introduction of the *Code Napoléon*. By these means, Spain was, in theory, totally transformed. Enormous quantities of urban and landed property were made available for sale; the privileges of the Church and aristocracy were swept away; the way was opened for the rise of the bourgeoisie and the emergence of a capitalist economy; the ideological unity that had underpinned absolute monarchy was undermined; the last of the provincial *fueros* – most notably those of the Basque provinces – disappeared, and Spain was given a modern, centralized administration and a single code of law.[2]

With the establishment of a revolutionary *cortes* in the island stronghold of Cádiz in 1810, the *afrancesados* who surrounded *el rey intruso* no longer constituted the only focus of change. In a series of measures of which the famous constitution promulgated on 19 March 1812 was but the most important, the *cortes* transformed the face of Spain. Although the monarchy was declared sacrosanct, the most severe restrictions were placed on the king. Real power was placed in the hands of the *cortes*, which was to be elected by universal male suffrage, to meet each year for three months, and to enjoy complete control of taxation. With their political freedom further safeguarded by a proviso that no changes in the constitution would be permitted for at least eight years, Spaniards were to enjoy equality before the law, freedom of occupation, employment, and property, equal liability to taxation and military service, and all the basic civil liberties except that of religion.

The corollaries of this programme were manifold: all forms of privilege were swept away, whether it was the rights of the Basque provinces to tax themselves, of army officers always to be tried by military courts, or of the nobility to enjoy a monopoly on direct entry to the officer corps; the power of the guilds and the Mesta was broken; internal customs barriers, torture, the military orders, the Inquisition, and *señorialismo* were all abolished; and a new system of progressive income tax was introduced, this being known as the *contribución único*. Meanwhile, Spain was declared a unitary state, its governance being completely remodelled. The king was to be aided by a council of state, and the network of councils that had stood at the apex of administration and justice was replaced by seven new ministries. In contrast to the confusion that had characterized the *ancien régime*, plans were laid for Spain to be divided into a number of provinces of more or less equal size, each of which would be administered by a centrally-appointed governor – the *jefe político* – assisted by an intendant and an elected *diputación*. At a lower level still, local government would henceforth be in the hands of elected *ayuntamientos* rather than hereditary ones. Last but not least, Spain was also given a unitary system of law courts that envisaged a supreme court in Madrid, an *audiencia* in each province, and a stipendiary magistrate in every municipality.[3]

As if all this were not enough, the *cortes* also applied itself to the problem of disamortization.* Necessary from a financial point of view given the paucity of the resources available to the Patriot cause and the need to liquidate the *vales reales* issued to finance the reforms of the 1790s and early 1800s, this was given further impetus by the determination of the liberals to reduce the power of the Church, create a free market in land, and stimulate Spanish agriculture.

Already reeling from other liberal measures – the destruction of the feudal system, and the abolition of the Inquisition and such levies as the Voto de Santiago (which applied to only one part of the country and, therefore, fell foul of the principle of equality of taxation) – the Church now found that the *cortes* was as keen as Joseph Bonaparte to strip it of its property. Thus a variety of properties were declared available for expropriation and sale, including the lands of the military orders, the Jesuits, the Inquisition and those religious houses that had been abandoned in the course of the war or suppressed by the French. It is clear that only pressures of time prevented the *cortes* from acting upon proposals laid before it for a fundamental reform of the regular clergy that would have increased the Church's losses still further. However, disamortization was not just directed at the Church alone: if the nobility retained its

* Some explanation of this term is perhaps necessary. In brief, in the course of the many centuries that had passed since the *reconquista*, large parts of Spain had been handed over in perpetuity to the Church, the nobility, and other institutions. Known as 'entails', the estates concerned could neither be bought nor sold, and were described as having been 'amortized', or placed in *manos muertas* (dead hands). For a variety of reasons, by the beginning of the nineteenth century a strong belief had begun to emerge that this situation should be abolished, the general intention being that the Church should be stripped of its lands by royal decree and the nobility authorized to dispose of their estates as they wished. Not completed until the 1860s, the process was known as 'disentailment' or 'disamortization'.

mayorazgos, certain crown lands, the properties of those declared as traitors, and half the commons, were all declared *bienes nacionales* and put up for sale.[4]

Increasingly, then, the war in Spain was a struggle between two competing models of political modernization in which the Bourbon monarchy, as represented by the person of the imprisoned Fernando VII, was reduced to the role of a helpless and ill-informed spectator. Thanks to the assistance of the Anglo-Portuguese army of the Duke of Wellington, it was, of course, the *gaditano* version of reform that triumphed. The nominal frontiers of *josefino* rule, which was pretty ephemeral at the best of times, were gradually pushed further and further back, until eventually they became co-terminous with the Pyrenees. At this point, assailed from all sides in central Europe, Napoleon resolved to cut his losses in Spain and Portugal by releasing Fernando VII from the imprisonment in which he had been held ever since the emperor had first intervened in Spain in 1808. Crossing over into Patriot territory on 24 March 1814, the young king discovered to his delight that the political situation was deeply polarized, with large sections of the élites – the Church, the army and the nobility – bitterly at odds with the régime, and the rural population engaged in a savage social conflict that could easily be interpreted as a rejection of liberalism and all its works. Significant elements of the army having rallied to the cause of the restoration of absolutism, he was able to order a substantial force to march on Madrid. On the night of 10 May the city was finally occupied, the revolution collapsing with scarcely a breath of resistance.[5]

So much for the background to the restoration of Spanish absolutism. However, no sooner had Fernando returned to his capital than a new political struggle broke out, this time within the ranks of the régime. Thus, the political backbone of the coup that had brought down the constitution of 1812 had not been provided by *el rey deseado*. Extremely cautious, not to say cowardly, Fernando had returned to Spain with an open mind about whether or not he should swear the oath of loyalty to the new régime, as was expected of him. Indeed, it was the opinion of the British ambassador, Henry Wellesley, that he originally had every intention of doing so 'under a conviction that resistance to it would be unavailing'.[6]

However, no sooner had the king entered Spanish territory than he was joined by a clique of grandees and other aristocrats who immediately began to encourage him to overthrow the constitution. Amongst these men figured the Duque de Infantado, the Conde de Montijo and the war hero, José Palafox, all of whom had been leading figures in the resistance of the privileged orders to the perpetuation of the enlightened absolutism of Carlos III by his successor Carlos IV.[7] The existence of this pre-war opposition to monarchical reform is central to an understanding of the *servilismo* that had sprung up in opposition to the liberals in the course of the war. Ostensibly, the *serviles* – the term originated in liberal jibes that they preferred slavery to liberty – were driven by ferocious hostility to the programme of reform introduced by the *cortes* of Cádiz. The heart of their objection resided in the fact that the latter's measures abolished corporate privilege of all sorts and threatened the immense revenues that the Church and the nobility derived from the amortization of land and the seigneurial system. Made up of conservative ecclesiastics (for there was always a faction in the Church – the so-called 'jansenists' – that favoured reform) and generals, officials, men of letters and even merchants of noble origin, this counter-revolutionary faction was at first able to make little headway in the *cortes*; but a variety of factors gradually strengthened its hand. By the time that the assembly transferred its sessions to Madrid in the winter of 1813 it constituted a substantial force, from whose ranks there emerged the second ideological stimulant for the coup of 1814.[8]

We come here to the famous 'manifesto of the Persians' (so-called because it began with an allusion to the Persian empire of antiquity). In brief, this was a denunciation of the *cortes* and all its works penned by an obscure *sevillano* lawyer named Bernardo Mozo de Rosales who had secured a parliamentary seat in the elections to the ordinary *cortes* that had been held in the summer of 1813. Presented to Fernando VII in the course of his triumphal progress from the French frontier, this was signed by 69 of the new assembly's 184 members, including two generals, fourteen jurists or bureaucrats, and thirty-three members of the clergy (the biographical details of the remaining twenty signatories are unknown).

It is perhaps no surprise that, of the forty-nine signatories whose backgrounds are known, the interests of many had been particularly damaged by the liberal reforms: thus, the two generals had both reached the *generalato* under the *antiguo régimen*, and the jurists and bureaucrats had in many cases served in either the old councils of administration or in the foral governments of such provinces as Alava, whilst the ecclesiastics contained two bishops as well as large numbers of cathedral canons and members of the Inquisition or the regular clergy.[9] At the heart of the manifesto, therefore, lay injured privilege – it was, for example, specifically claimed, that 'to exclude the nobility destroys the juridical order and strips society of its splendour, whilst depriving it of the generous spirits needed for its defence'; in the same vein, the regular clergy had been 'virtually extinguished' and the bishops had been 'banished or forced to emigrate in the style of the worst persecutions of the Church'.[10]

To some extent the underlying character of the manifesto was camouflaged by its general tenor: the central claim of the manifesto was that the *cortes* of Cádiz had been an illegitimate assembly that had abrogated the rights of the throne. But its authors proceeded to give the game away by extending their attack to the eighteenth century and even earlier: 'With the coming of King Charles I, ministerial despotism set in, whilst the constitution which this monarchy enjoyed ceased to be observed, the result being the revolt of the *comuneros* and a decay in the authority of the *cortes*.'[11] For obvious reasons this point was not made explicitly – to convey his message, Mozo de Rosales rather laid out in excruciating detail the laws that established the rights of the traditional *cortes* of Castile and Aragón, knowing full well, of course, that these bodies had hardly met since the seventeenth century – but the implication is very much that from then onwards the history of Spain was marked increasingly by a growth in the power of the monarchy at the expense of its subjects (for which read the privileged corporations).

In short, what was at issue was not just the crimes of the *cortes* of Cádiz, but the whole sweep of Bourbon enlightened absolutism. According to Mozo de Rosales, in fact, monarchy was not absolute at all, but was 'subordinate to divine law, to justice, and to the fundamental laws of the state'.[12] Once Fernando had been restored to the throne, he should, therefore, convoke Spain's traditional *cortes* so that it might 'remedy the faults of ministerial despotism and give expression to whatever concerns . . . the best ordering of the monarchy'.[13] If these vague proposals meant anything – and it is not in fact clear that they did[14] – they essentially constituted a demand that the monarchy should abandon the pretensions that it had acquired from the early-modern era onwards and govern in accordance with the privileges of the Church, the nobility, the provinces and the corporations. This message is driven home all the more when we find not only that many of the liberals' earlier opponents in the *cortes*, including such leading *serviles* as Francisco Javier Borrull, Pedro Inguanzo and the Bishop of Calahorra, had all openly inveighed against such Bourbon actions as the abolition of the *fueros* of Aragón, Catalonia and Valencia in 1715, but that the ideas expressed in the manifesto may also be found in other treatises published at the time of Fernando's return.[15]

Thus, inherent in the coup of 1814 was a programme of reaction that was positively Gothic in its medievalism, the chief object of which was a return to a semi-mythical golden age in which the Church and nobility would be left to enjoy their privileges free from the attentions of an interfering monarchy. To what extent, however, was Fernando VII prepared to go along with such a programme? When the complex manoeuvrings of Montijo and his fellows had brought him briefly to the throne in March 1808, the young king had been too vulnerable to do anything other than to accede to many of his supporters' most significant demands, and thus effectively to turn his back on the enlightened reforms of his father and grandfather. For example, the expropriation and sale of the lands of the Church was immediately halted.[16] Six years later, however, the situation was very different. Rather than owing his position to a clique of grandees who had used their personal influence to whip up an insurrection in the ranks of the royal guard and the population of the towns and villages around Madrid, Fernando knew that his power base was now much stronger. Thus, it was neither Montijo and his fellow grandees, nor Mozo de Rosales and the *persas* who had physically put him back on the throne as absolute ruler of Spain, but rather the army. The crucial factor had been the decision of the commander of the forces stationed in Valencia, General Francisco Elío, to 'pronounce' against the constitution on 17 April 1814. Elío's lead had immediately been followed by almost the entirety of the officer corps. Fernando had, in consequence, been home and dry. What, however, were the implications of this decision for the *renovadores* so admired by Suárez?

In some respects, the fact that Fernando had been restored to power by a military coup should have made very little difference to the military's chances of imposing their prescriptions. In so far as can be ascertained, the War of Independence of 1808–1814 had brought little change to the officer corps, or at least to its higher reaches. Thus, of the 458 new generals appointed in the course of the struggle against Napoleon, at least 174 had already been officers before 1808, whereas only nine had definitely been civilians or members of the rank and file.[17] Moreover, as the majority of these 174 promotions had come from the ranks of men who had been colonels or lieutenant colonels in 1808, it is plain that the *generalato* had also been not much altered in its social composition, the majority of its members, therefore, being men who in one way or another stood to be adversely affected by the abolition of the *señorios* (in 1800 95.5 per cent of captains were of noble origin; as for officers of the rank of Sargento Mayor – roughly-speaking, major – and above, the figure was 100 per cent).[18]

Despite all this, the officer corps did not respond to quite the same triggers as the rest of the privileged orders. For a few officers, certainly, what mattered most were the sort of socio-political factors that had motivated the manifesto of 1814. Thus, not only were two generals – Marimón and Arce – amongst its signatories, but Montijo, Infantado and

Palafox were all regular officers who had held commands in the war against the French. Yet the fact that certain officers were *serviles* proves nothing. As the present author has shown elsewhere, the overwhelming disgust with which the bulk of the army regarded the liberal régime in 1814 stemmed above all from professional issues. The army felt humiliated and betrayed with regard to the war, having ultimately become so decrepit that it had been reduced to the rôle of a virtual spectator during Spain's liberation. In addition, it had been the butt of an ever more virulent anti-militarism whose chief theme was that professional soldiers were slaves and professional armies the tools of despotism.[19] When Elío pronounced against the constitution at Valencia, few officers had much hesitation in following his lead. However, this is a very long way from saying that they were in sympathy with a medievalist *renovación*. For many officers, in fact, nothing could be further from the case. Even more than in other countries, in Spain the army was a vital pillar of enlightened absolutism, in that through the institution of the Captain Generalcy it had been given a major rôle in local government and the administration of justice. As a result, any reduction in the power of the monarchy could not but rebound most heavily on the army. It followed that, for most officers, *renovación* was anything but an attractive prospect. Even less was this the case given the propensity of such *frondeurs* as Montijo to further their schemes by means of riot and mutiny, the war having taught the generals that the people in arms were at best a dangerous ally. In this respect it is worth pointing out, first, that, despite what is commonly supposed, the guerrillas tended to be ferociously hostile to the liberals, and, second, that, with the French gone, many turned immediately to banditry.[20]

Suspicious of even his most devoted followers and determined not to be the prisoner of a faction as he had been in 1808, *el rey deseado* found that he had a powerful ally against which to play off the *renovadores*. Meanwhile, support was also forthcoming in the shape of the many ministers and bureaucrats who had loyally served caroline absolutism prior to 1808 and were now once more offering their services to their court. As a result, whatever the wishes of a Blas Ostolaza or a Duque de Infantado may have been, Fernando was never lacking in alternatives to their suggestions. Even had the king not possessed so much freedom of manoeuvre, the sort of programme that the *renovadores* were proposing was quite out of the question given the financial problems faced by the régime. Fernando was in any case unwilling to relinquish the gains made by his eighteenth-century predecessors. In consequence, although the signatories of the manifesto were for the most part provided with generous rewards, the administration was filled with men who had been associated with the 'ministerial despotism' of the period prior to 1808. Meanwhile, while all the acts of the *cortes* were, in theory, declared null and void, in practice, they were reviewed one by one. The *contribución única* imposed by the liberals was only abandoned with the utmost reluctance, and the judicial attributes of the *señorios* were retained in the hands of the state. Any retreat from the positions reached in 1808 was out of the question, the caroline bureaucrats who filled the machinery of state being most unwilling to let slip successes that the Bourbons had struggled for a century to obtain. Much irritated, elements of the nobility responded with several petitions of protest; but they met with no success whatsoever.[21]

In so far as turning the clock back was concerned, the chief beneficiary of the restoration of absolutism was the Church. A string of decrees permitted those religious communities that had been dissolved to reoccupy their old houses, re-established the Inquisition, and authorized the return of the Jesuits, expelled from Spain by Carlos III. Yet here, too, there were limits to what Fernando was prepared to do. Though he did not actually proceed to any further measures of disentailment, he refused to return even the ecclesiatical estates that had been sold off in the course of the war, let alone the 15 per cent or so of clerical property disamortized between 1798 and 1808. In 1815 he gave serious consideration to a scheme that would have completed the sale of the lands of the Military Orders. On this last issue he was forced to yield; but nothing the *serviles* could do would persuade him to desist from plundering the Church's revenues in other respects; the measures that he introduced included the appropriation of the incomes of all benefices whose incumbents were absentees. At the same time, far from transforming Spain into a theocracy as some of his more extreme supporters desired, he imposed greater controls than ever upon the Church, appointing no fewer than sixty new bishops and blatantly transforming it into a weapon of political control. Although traditionalists were naturally delighted by the favour shown by Fernando to the more reactionary elements of the clergy in his promotions, there was in reality no retreat from the regalism of the eighteenth century.[22]

Fernando's fiscal policy makes it even more apparent that he did not simply turn the clock back to 1808, still less return Spain to the Middle Ages. By 1816 the king had become increasingly aware that the fiscal structure of the *antiguo régimen* was simply incapable of meeting Spain's changed circumstances, not least because revenue had been badly hit by the fact that, since 1810, large parts of Spanish America had been in full-scale revolt. If only because he was determined to reconquer America, he was, therefore, more and more inclined to listen to the numerous servants of caroline absolutism. These urged, first, that the system of taxation should be rationalized, and, second, that greater pressure should be exerted on the Church and nobility. In December 1816 Fernando appointed one of their number Minister of Finance. A senior treasury official of long standing, who had in 1808–10 served as secretary of the Junta Central, the new minister was Martín de Garay. Garay's solution to the problem was to reintroduce a modified form of the system of taxation introduced by the *cortes* of Cádiz. The most important element of the new system was an income tax known as the *contribución general*, although, unlike in 1813, it was decided that this should apply only to the lands of the crowns of Castile and Aragón; the Basque provinces and Navarre were therefore allowed to retain their traditional exemptions. Meanwhile, the large number of indirect taxes paid by the municipalities were unified into a single category known as the *derechas de puertas*. As the manifesto of 1814 had waxed particularly ferocious against the *cortes* in this respect, no clearer proof is necessary that, in reality, Fernando was prepared to adapt the projects of liberalism to his own ends.[23]

For yet another instance of how the *fernandino* régime was not prepared to go along with the precepts of the *persas*, one has only to turn to the question of the *fueros* enjoyed by the Basque *señorios* and the Kingdom of Navarre. Unlike Catalonia and the lands of the crown of Aragón, which had been stripped of their various privileges over the course of the eighteenth century, Vizcaya, Guipúzcoa, Alava, and Navarre had all continued to enjoy a special relationship with the Spanish Crown in that they determined their own levels of taxation, were excluded from the national customs frontier, and were exempt from conscription. As such they had constituted a constant irritant to the Bourbons, although it was not in fact until the very eve of the French invasion that a serious attempt had been made to start homogenizing them with the rest of the Bourbon dominions. Under the French and the liberals alike, of course, the *fueros* had no future – they were ignored by the one, and formally overthrown by the other – the consequence being that the coup of 1814 was greeted with great rejoicing by the oligarchy who monopolized the various foral institutions – indeed, Fernando formally confirmed the Basque provinces and Navarre in all their liberties. All too soon, however, it became apparent that many of the caroline bureaucrats who surrounded Fernando were deeply hostile to the whole concept of provincial particularism. Not only did the small print of the royal decrees that re-established the *fueros* clearly state that the régime intended to review the relationship of the foral provinces with Madrid, but in November

1815 a special commission was established with the specific task of investigating fiscal abuses in the Basque *señorios*.[24]

Over the next few years there duly followed a welter of orders and regulations that severely curtailed the Basques' commercial freedoms. Even more fundamental was the assault that was launched on their exemption from military service. Thus, on 2 January 1818 a new levy of conscripts was announced in terms that made it abundantly clear that no account would be taken of the liberties of the foral provinces. In the event a compromise was reached in that the latter were permitted to redeem their contingents by means of financial payments; but once again it had been shown that the *fueros* would only be allowed to survive where they did not impinge upon the interests of the state.[25]

Important though the extension of the principle of compulsory military service to the Basque provinces was, in other respects the army was one of the few areas where there was indeed a wholesale return to the situation of 1808. In an administrative and juridical sense, this implied the restoration of the power of the military authorities to its pre-war status and the reconstitution of the old *fuero militar*, both of which measures were immediately implemented. However, attention also had to be paid to the size and organization of the army. The basic problem here was that Spain's straitened finances simply did not allow the maintenance of the approximately 184,000 men she had under arms at the end of the war. To make matters worse, the officer corps, which had been thrown open to all classes of society, was grotesquely swollen even by the inflated standards of 1814: the capture of large numbers of officers by the French, the prodigality of the provincial juntas, the creation of too many new regiments, and the demands of the guerrillas having combined to ensure that it had grown much faster than the rank and file. Even as matters stood in May 1814, many officers were effectively unemployed; but there now returned from France the 4,000 officers who had been held there as prisoners-of-war. In short, the régime faced a major crisis.[26]

How this crisis might have been safely defused is by no means clear; but there is no doubt that the problem was handled in a singularly unfortunate manner. As his first War Minister, Fernando appointed Francisco Eguía, a general possessed of a singularly undistinguished record who was so closely identified with the *antiguo régimen* that he continued to wear the periwig and pigtail of the eighteenth century. With such a figure in charge of cutting the army down to size, the chief casualties were inevitably the many officers who had been civilians in 1808, or who had gained vastly accelerated promotion on account of the war. As far as senior posts were concerned, the widespread belief that captain generalcies and the like were given only to gilded courtiers who had sat out the war in safety is unfair; but some of the choices were nonetheless most unfortunate. Perhaps the worst was José Imaz, who was made governor of Santiago despite having in 1811 surrendered Badajoz in circumstances that were near-treasonable. At all events, much offence was caused, and all the more so in view of the imprisonment of such heroes of the struggle against the invaders as Pedro Villacampa and Juan Díaz Porlier. Equally galling was the great partiality displayed in the army's reorganization: the many regiments that disappeared were in almost every instance chosen from those formed during the war, including many whose origins were to be found amongst the guerrillas.[27] Traditionally, these measures have been seen as a move against the liberals, with whom the guerrillas have always tended to be identified. In fact, they suggest another interpretation: namely, that in disarming 'the people', Eguía was disarming popular resistance to enlightened reform, and by extension drawing the teeth of the *renovadores*.[28]

Needless to say, the effect of Eguía's measures was to undermine the anti-liberal consensus of 1814. Deprived of their commands, large numbers of officers were forced to retire, whilst others were attached to other units as supernumeraries, or simply left to fester in miserable provincial towns on half pay. For such men, life was truly desperate: a number are reputed to have died from want. Even for those who managed to remain on the active list, pay was insufficient and constantly in arrears, many of them being forced to rely on the charity of the Church. For the army as a whole, meanwhile, outside the hastily reconstituted royal guard, life continued much as it had under the liberals, with the troops starving, shoeless and in rags.[29]

Thus it was that Spain embarked on the long series of *pronunciamientos* that were to end in the overthrow of the Restoration by means of the revolution of 1820. Yet for all his failure to achieve stability, Fernando had returned to Spain as anything but an apostle of medievalism. Though violently antipathetic towards the liberals, he had little in common with the *serviles*, having no more patience with the notion of a *cortes* of estates than he did with that of a *cortes* of citizens. The result was that the king refused either completely to overturn the work of the *cortes* of Cádiz or to retreat from the achievements of 'ministerial despotism'. In the Church, at least, many prominent *serviles* were rewarded with high office; but to their dismay they discovered that they were to be servants of the monarchy rather than its masters, and, in addition, that nothing was to be done to restore the resources of which the clergy had been stripped. As for the nobility, they discovered that they had in practice lost their judicial powers for all time. Meanwhile, pragmatism forced a revival of reformism in the areas of finance, whilst principle brought a renewed attack on the provincial *fueros*, the result being, of course, that the régime was soon experiencing much internal conflict.

The Restoration régime was not equal to Spain's problems; but, while lacking in the drive and vision that had marked the reigns of Fernando VII's father and grandfather, it was very far from being the period of black reaction of legend. In the words of the Jesuit historian, Suárez Verdeguer, in fact, 'When the revolution of 1820 intervened, not a single step had been taken to extract the country from the "ministerial despotism" against which the choicest elements in the country had risen.'[30] So deep, in fact, were the strains that the reformist dynamic inherited from the years of enlightened absolutism imposed on the *fernandino* régime that already Spain was being set on the road to civil war. Up until 1820, the resistance of the privileged orders who had set so much store by the coup had been confined to more or less respectful petitions of protest; but the renewed disappointment that followed the second restoration of absolutism after the downfall of the revolution of 1820–23 proved too much. Firm links having been forged first in 1808, then in 1813–14, and finally in 1820–23 with the forces of the popular unrest engendered by Spanish enlightened absolutism and liberalism alike, in 1826 Catalonia was rocked by a major *apostólico* revolt. From this, of course, it was but a short step to the Carlist conflict of the 1830s, the latter being in its origins not a struggle between liberalism and legitimism, but rather an extension of the intra-absolutist disputes of 1814–20.[31]

Notes

1. There are, to be fair, a number of thematic studies that are of considerable importance for the study of the Restoration, the two of greatest importance being E. Christiansen, *The Origins of Military Power in Spain, 1800–1854* (Oxford, 1967), and W. Callahan, *Church, Politics and Society in Spain, 1750–1874* (Cambridge, MA, 1984).

2. For Bonaparte policies in Spain, cf. M. Artola Gallego, *La burguesía revolucionaria, 1808–1874* (Madrid, 1990), pp.25–7; O. Connelly, *Napoleon's Satellite Kingdoms* (New York, 1965), pp.237–44; and G. Lovett, *Napoleon and the Birth of Modern Spain* (Princeton, NJ, 1965), pp.516–20.

3. The political and administrative reforms of the *cortes* of Cádiz are discussed at length in M. Artola, *Los origenes de la España contemporánea* (Madrid, 1959), pp.406–32, 457–93, 498–505.

4. Disamortization is discussed ibid., pp.509–36; for a recent study of the *cortes'* relations with the Church, cf. M. Morán Orti, *Revolución y reforma religiosa en las cortes de Cádiz* (Madrid, 1994).

5. Contrasting accounts of the coup of 1814 may be found in J. Fontana Lazaro, *La quiebra de la monarquía absoluta, 1814–1820: la crisis del antiguo régimen en España* (Barcelona, 1979), pp.76–80, and M. C. Pintos Vieites, *La política de Fernando VII entre 1814 y 1820* (Pamplona, 1958), pp.50–94; for two local accounts of the transfer of power, cf. E. González López, *Entre el antiguo y el nuevo régimen: absolutistas y liberales – el reinado de Fernando VII en Galicia* (La Coruña, 1980), pp.24–37, and E. Díaz Lobón, *Granada durante la crisis del antiguo régimen, 1814–1820* (Granada, 1982), pp.134–40.

6. H. Wellesley to Castlereagh, 7 December 1814, quoted in. F. Wellesley, *The Diary and Correspondence of Henry Wellesey, first Lord Cowley* (London, 1930), pp.76–7.

7. For the background to this *fronde*, which culminated in the palace revolution that produced the abdication of Carlos IV in March 1808, cf. M. E. Martínez Quinteiro, 'Descontento y actitudes políticas de la alta nobleza en los origenes de la edad contemporánea', *Hispania*, No. 135 (January, 1977), pp.95–138, and J. Pérez de Guzmán y Gallo, 'El primer conato de rebelión precursor de la revolución de España', *España moderna*, 250–1 (October, 1909), pp.105–24, and ibid., 251 (November, 1909), pp.48–68.

8. The emergence of *servilismo* is discussed in B. Hamnett, *La política española en una época revolucionaria* (Mexico City, 1985), pp.164–73, and B. Hamnett, 'Constitutional Theory and Political Reality: Liberalism, Traditionalism and the Spanish *Cortes*, 1810–1814', *Journal of Modern History*, XLIX (1977), on-demand supplement.

9. M. C. Diz Lois, *El manifiesto de 1814* (Pamplona, 1967), pp.103–30. A full text of the manifesto is contained in pp.193–277.

10. Ibid., pp.206, 211.

11. Ibid., p.255.

12. Ibid., p.265.

13. Ibid., pp.271–2.

14. Cf. Fontana, *Quiebra de la monarquía española*, pp.77–8.

15. Hamnett, *Política española*, pp.106–7; for another example of the traditionalist critique, cf. the anonymous *Observaciones sobre los atentados de las cortes extraordinarias de Cádiz contra las leyes*

fundamentales de la monarquía española, y sobre la nulidad de la constitución que formaron (Madrid, 1814), pp.3–14.

16. F. Marti Gilabert, *El motín de Aranjuez* (Pamplona, 1972), p.244.

17. C. Esdaile, *The Spanish Army in the Peninsular War* (Manchester, 1988), p.177.

18. F. Andújar Castillo, *Los militares en la España del siglo XVIII: un estudio social* (Granada, 1991), p.164.

19. Esdaile, *Spanish Army*, pp.172–82; for the role of the Spanish army in Spain's liberation, cf. idem, *The Duke of Wellington and the Command of the Spanish Army, 1812–1814* (London, 1990), pp.108–73 *passim*.

20. For a discussion of this question, see C. Esdaile, '"Heroes or villains revisited": fresh thoughts on *la guerrilla*', in E. Martínez Ruiz (ed.), *II Seminario Internacional sobre la Guerra de la Independencia: Madrid, 24–26 de octubre de 1994* (Madrid, 1996), pp.191–210.

21. For Fernando's policy with regard to the *señorios*, see Hamnett, *Política española*, pp.229–32.

22. Callahan, *Church, Politics and Society*, pp.112–16; for the fate of the property sold off before 1814, cf. R. Herr, *Rural Change and Royal Finances in Spain at the End of the Old Régime* (Berkeley, CA, 1989), p.716.

23. For Garay's financial reforms, cf. Fontana, *Quiebra de la monarquía absoluta*, pp.135–41; F. Suárez Verdeguer (ed.), *Documentos del reinado de Fernado VII, IV: Martín de Garay y la reforma de la Hacienda, 1817 (i)* (Pamplona, 1967), pp.77–113.

24. R. Barahona, *Vizcaya on the Eve of Carlism: Politics and Society, 1800–1833* (Reno, NV, 1989), pp.38–41.

25. Ibid., p. 41; C. Maqueda Abreu, 'La restauración de Fernando VII y el reclutamiento militar', *Revista de Historia Militar*, 62 (January, 1987), pp.71–92.

26. For the position of the army in 1814, see Esdaile, *Spanish Army*, p. 196; Christiansen, *Origins of Military Power*, pp.18–19.

27. P. Casado Burbano, *Las fuerzas armadas en el inicio del constucionalismo español* (Madrid, 1982), pp.90–1. There is an interesting account of the atmosphere that prevailed in the court at this time in F. Suárez Verdeguer and A. Berazaluce (eds), *Recuerdos de la vida de Don Pedro Agustín Girón* (Pamplona, 1978), II, pp.18–23.

28. Popular hostility to Bourbon reformism is discussed in C. Crowley, '*Luces* and *hispanidad*: nationalism and modernization in eighteenth-century Spain', in M. Palumbo and W. Shanahan, *Nationalism: Essays in Honour of Louis L. Snyder* (Westport, CT, 1981), pp.87–102; the

link between the guerrillas and popular support for *servilismo* in 1814 is admirably substantiated in M. Ardit Lucas, *Revolución liberal y revuelta campesina: un ensayo sobre la desintegración del régimen feudal en el país valenciano* (Barcelona, 1977), pp.213–17.

29. For two contemporary accounts of conditions in the army at this time, see letter of Francisco de Paula Guervos, 17 January 1815, Real Academia de Historia, 11-5-7:9003, no. 60, and S. Whittingham to H. Torrens, 8 August 1815, quoted in F. Whittingham (ed.), *A Memoir of the Services of Lieutenant General Sir Samuel Ford Whittingham* (London, 1868), p.285; a more general discussion is to be found in J. L. Comellas García-Llera, *Los primeros pronunciamientos en España, 1814–1820* (Madrid, 1958), pp.48–52.

30. F. Suárez Verdeguer, *La crisis política del antiguo régimen en España* (Madrid, 1950), p.22.

31. For a helpful study of the manner in which the *renovadores* turned to violence in the wake of the 'second restoration' of 1823, see J. Torras Elías, *La guerra de los agraviados* (Barcelona, 1967).

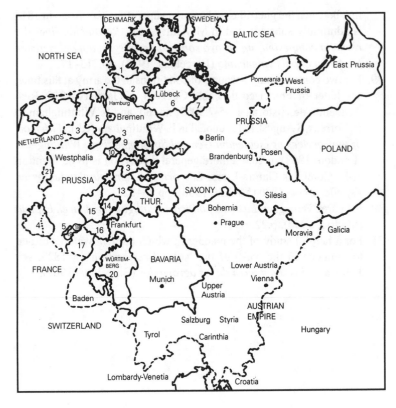

---- Boundary of German Confederation
THUR. Thuringian States

1. Schleswig (Danish)
2. Holstein (Danish)
3. Hanover
4. Luxemburg (Dutch) (Partitioned 1839)
5. Oldenburg
6. Mecklenburg-Schwerin
7. Mecklenburg-Strelitz
8. Brunswick
9. Schaumburg-Lippe
10. Lippe-Detmold
11. Anhalt

12. Waldeck
13. Electoral Hesse (Hesse-Cassel)
14. Hesse
15. Nassau
16. Hesse Darmstadt
17. Bavarian Palatinate
18. Hesse-Homburg
19. Lichtenburg
20. Hohenzollern
21. Limburg (Dutch) (Included within Confederation 1839)

Map 2. The German Confederation

The Napoleonic Legacy and Problems of Restoration in Central Europe: The German Confederation

Michael John

The main aim of this chapter is to re-examine some of the major themes of early nineteenth-century German development in the light of problems posed by the French Revolution in general, and the Napoleonic re-ordering of the area covered by the Holy Roman Empire in particular. At first sight, three broad themes seem to stand out: the sheer scale of the territorial aspects of that re-ordering, which went far beyond anything seen since at least the mid-seventeenth century; the related, unparalleled challenge posed by Napoleonic France to a socio-political system built on varying mixtures of *Herrschaft* (or non-monopolistic exercise of legitimate power by a power-holders or agencies), patrimonial kingship (or at least the quasi-monarchical status enjoyed by the myriad German princes who lacked a formal monarchical title), seigneurialism, and the corporatist (*ständisch*) organization of the state;[1] and the need to place regional, local and confessional dimensions at the centre of any consideration of problems of governance and social and political development after 1815.

A fundamental argument of what follows is that for all the rhetoric of nationalist modernization that emerged in some political and intellectual quarters during this period, the Napoleonic experience in Germany actually fostered tendencies that enhanced regionalism while giving regional perspectives far stronger institutions to latch on to in the form of internally consolidated sovereign states (the so-called *Mittelstaaten*) than had existed before 1801. The boost given to regionalism had profound effects on patterns of political thought and behaviour in Germany. As the research of Heinrich Best on voting patterns within the Frankfurt parliament in 1848/49 has shown, the relevance of the regional divide at the river Main is clear, especially when it came to arguably the most important question of all to be confronted by those who wished to 'solve' the German question – should the future Germany be constructed along the lines of a *Gross-* or a *Kleindeutschland*?[2]

This chapter will not deal with the broader issues of diplomatic and international relations addressed elsewhere in this volume. Instead it will focus on certain themes that have loomed large in the recent historiography of German domestic politics: the delayed and incomplete nature of much-needed social and political reforms; the fact that reforms were stymied by the reformers' perception of the need to compromise with elements of the old order, which were then put in a position to block or subvert aspects of the reform process; the continued strength of 'feudal influences' close to the centre of power; and the inadequate commitment of reformers to pushing through full-scale modernization in the face of these problems. The challenges posed by France provided modernizing reformers with hitherto unprecedented opportunities; but those opportunities were nonetheless constrained by countervailing forces and by the fact that they were, in effect, time-limited.

It has frequently been argued that the reform process enhanced a basic north–south divide in Germany. According to this argument, Prussia underwent a process of socio-economic modernization that was not accompanied by a concomitant political development (normally associated with the growth of recognizably liberal political institutions – state-wide parliaments, written constitutions and the like). In the south, on the other hand, and especially in Baden, there were extensive constitutional innovations by 1820, but these were grafted on to a society in which guild-based, artisanal economies with their attendant restrictions on freedom of movement and domicile, feudal influences in the agrarian economy and so on survived. There is, to be sure, some truth in this characterization; but the dichotomy between north and south is presented too schematically, and relies on a foreshortening of perspective that arguably has its roots in an analysis of the events of 1848/49.[3] Those revolutions, it will be remembered, were finally snuffed out by the use of Prussian military force in liberal Baden.

What is needed is a much more sophisticated awareness of the diversity of German experiences in the early nineteenth century, and this is now increasingly recognized by historians.[4] Such diversity was largely conditioned by the major geographical and territorial factors that were placed in high relief by Napoleonic expansion: the proximity of a given territory to France; the uneven regional distribution of the principal winners and losers in the complex territorial changes between 1801 and 1806/7; whether a given territory was directly incorporated into France (as, for example, was much of the Rhineland or most of the German North Sea coastline); became part of one of those distinctive Napoleonic creations (the Kingdom of Westphalia, the Grand Duchy of Berg) that did not survive the collapse of the empire; was annexed by a neighbour (sometimes several times in this period); or remained under its existing princely house, though often with unfamiliar areas and populations added to that house's possessions. With these features in mind, this chapter will attempt to group widely varying experiences into a limited number of (admittedly crude) categories.

First, it needs to be borne in mind that the major enduring changes arising out of the Napoleonic period were located in the south and west of Germany, an area that certainly played a leading role in liberal politics up to 1848/49 and beyond, but that also contained significant confessional differences. By the Treaty of Lunéville (1801), France gained the left bank of the Rhine and the local secular princes were compensated further east, largely through the secularization of ecclesiastical territories. The *Reichsdeputationshauptschluss* of February 1803 determined that there would be no compensation for such transfers, as a result of which forty-one out of fifty-one imperial cities disappeared and a total of 112 significant units of *Herrschaft* (governance) were lost for ever. A further effect involved the disappearance of around 10,000 square kilometres of clerical territory, with 3.2 million inhabitants changing hands (overwhelmingly in the south and west), the latter figure amounting to approximately one-seventh of the Holy Roman Empire's population.

Strikingly, by 1806 only 2 per cent of the roughly 1,800 units of *Herrschaft* and 10 per cent of the larger ones that had existed in 1789 survived, while 60 per cent of the German population had changed ruler at least once by 1806.[5] The case of a secularized bishopric such as Osnabrück, which changed rulers six times between 1802 and 1814, gives some idea of how traumatic and destabilizing this process was in an age in which loyalties to princely dynasties were still a primary source of political legitimacy for much of the population. Very significant numbers of ordinary Germans were effectively cut adrift from existing dynastic loyalties and forced to come to terms with the imposition of new rulers, sometimes several times within a decade.

Nevertheless the story was not simply one of trauma, important though that was. A key feature of this crucial period was that it manifestly involved winners as well as losers. Baden, for example, saw a 750 per cent increase in its territory and a 950 per cent increase in population, while the comparable figures for neighbouring Württemberg were 450 and 850 per cent. Meanwhile, the princes who ruled these states tended to find their status enhanced (in the case of Bavaria and Württemberg, to that of King, while Baden became a Grand Duchy). To adapt a term more usually applied to the great re-ordering a century later, the process of 'winning' created the framework for the Confederation of the Rhine (1806–15), which was formed around the main 'successor states' in the south and west. The Confederation was undoubtedly a key part of Napoleon's grand strategy for Central Europe; but it also consolidated the position of a bureaucratic, modernizing 'collaborator' class in these states – men such as Sigmund von Reitzenstein in Baden, Ludwig Harscher von Almendingen in Nassau, and Maximilian von Montgelas in Bavaria – who reached unprecedented heights of power where, as was the case in Bavaria, the prince was himself an enthusiastic collaborator. In these states, bureaucratic reformers tended to adopt administrative centralization and constitutional and legal reforms to address the problems posed by war and territorial changes – the integration of new territories, fiscal and debt problems, etc. As might be expected, the details varied from state to state, with much clearer evidence of surviving *ständisch* influences in Württemberg and Bavaria than in Baden, which had the widest and least corporatist franchise of any state in Germany before 1848. Baden, moreover, was the only one of these three states to complete a modern legal codification before 1848 (the *Badisches Landrecht* of 1809). Yet, despite these differences, there were certain clear parallels, whose origins lay in the events of 1801–6.

By contrast, the Prussian state's experiences were very different. In the crucial period after 1801, Prussian territory (and therefore its tax base) was cut in half by the Treaty of Tilsit (1807), a process that created unimaginable financial problems for the Prussian state. Those problems structured the reform policies adopted by men like Hardenberg to an extent that was probably unknown in the south, significant though fiscal problems were there as well. At this key point in the immediate aftermath of crushing military defeat in October 1806, there was much less incentive to develop institutional channels to secure acceptance of princely rule by the population for the simple reason that few if any members of that population had not previously been Prussian subjects. Certainly, there were aspects of the misleadingly-termed 'Prussian reform movement' that challenged dynastic loyalties; but that challenge proved to be much less powerful than was the case in the south – a fact that had more to do with the situation faced by the state than with the reforming determination of leading politicians.

Emphasis should also be placed on the enduring provincialism of the Prussian state – a fact that once again was certainly modified but nevertheless remained an essential feature of the state until 1866 and arguably until 1918. The *Allgemeines Landrecht* of 1794 was not implemented in all provinces as the primary source of law, and co-existed in some places with the common law, in others (notably large parts of the Rhineland) with the French Civil Code, and with a range of provincial and local legal systems. Meanwhile, Frederick William III's promise to introduce a constitution in 1815 remained unimplemented, while the Provincial Chambers (*Provinziallandtage*) established in 1823 entrenched provincialism at the heart of what participatory politics existed in Prussia before the 1840s. Nor were these provincialisms and regionalisms effectively counterbalanced by centripetal forces emanating from an all-powerful bureaucracy, as has on occasions been claimed. This was in the main because the Prussian state bureaucracy was relatively small (and getting smaller in relation to the population before 1850), and was kept that way for fiscal and political reasons. To say this is not to deny the real extent of potential bureaucratic power in Prussia after 1815; but it is very important to remember the other side of this coin, especially given the entrenchment of much of the field administration in provincial concerns. In proportion to the size of the population, the southern states were in general far more bureaucratized than Prussia, just as they were certainly more centralized,[6] and it was really against that background rather than the very different Prussian one that the origins of Hegel's famous paean to the bureaucracy as the 'universal estate' transcending social divisions are to be found.[7]

Finally, there was the 'third Germany' of states such as Hanover or Hesse-Kassel, which had generally either been ruled directly by the French or been incorporated into the kingdom of Westphalia. This created possibilities for a restoration of the *ancien régime* on a scale that exceeded that of almost any other state in Germany, with the conceivable exception of Mecklenburg. The details varied in important ways from state to state, but the main drift was towards a type of rampant restorationism to be carried through by noble-dominated bureaucracies cooperating with noble-dominated estates. The consequences were particularly striking in Hanover, where although a state-wide political assembly (the *Allgemeine Ständeversammlung*) was created in 1819, it co-existed with surviving provincial Estates, had decidedly little power *vis-à-vis* both the bureaucracy and those provincial Estates, and was in any case constructed in such a way that noble dominance was virtually certain. It was this constellation of forces, connecting deficient state-wide integration at an institutional level with the increasingly contested issue of noble rights and privileges, that determined the political history of the kingdom for the fifty years between the Congress of Vienna and the annexation by Prussia in the summer of 1866.

One further feature of this 'third Germany' is worthy of note here. In both Hanover and Hesse-Kassel, the restoration of privileges and other aspects of a pre-Napoleonic order (for instance, the absence of codified laws), went hand in hand with a decided tendency towards monarchical absolutism, which culminated in *coup d'états* in both states in the 1830s and again in the 1850s. These moves towards absolutism were in general justified by their proponents on the grounds that no prince was bound by his predecessor's agreement to a specific set of limitations on princely powers. This was, of course, the type of argument used by Charles X in France in the run-up to 1830. But in contrast to the French case, the Kings and Electors of Hanover and Hesse-Kassel tended to get away with it – though not without some difficulty (as in Hesse-Kassel, where the Elector was forced to abdicate in the early 1830s) – because the German Confederation refused to intervene on the side of their opponents. In the Hanoverian case, there was a clear convergence of monarchical-absolutist and noble designs both in 1837 and in 1855. In Hesse-Kassel, matters were rather different, in that the 1831 crisis was in large part triggered by the collapse of good relations between the Elector and the nobility – a pattern that continued until the 1850s. Yet the case of Hesse-Kassel only made explicit something that remained implicit until the late 1850s in Hanover: that monarchical absolutism, if pursued more than half-heartedly, was actually incompatible in the long run with aristocratic interests, because it necessarily involved bureaucratic intrusions into spheres of influence and privilege that nobles tended to believe were rightfully theirs.[8] This dilemma was arguably insoluble, but the main consequence of failing to solve it was to prevent the evolution of a form of moderate conservative/liberal politics of property-owners as the main bulwark of the political system. Unsurprisingly then, Hanover and Hesse-Kassel became the major strongholds of *kleindeutsch* nationalist politics after its revival in the summer of 1859, and were bastions of support for the newly-founded National Liberal party after 1866. Post-1848 liberal nationalists concluded that the only chance of breaking through the barriers posed at small-state level by intransigent princes, and by their reactionary allies, was through enlarging the sphere of effective political action beyond the state's boundaries.

Certain common themes emerge from these very different responses to the Napoleonic legacy during the Restoration. The first of these is that of state-building and integration. There were two principal phases of this – 1801–8 and 1815–23 – and the approach adopted depended greatly on what happened in the first of those phases. Nevertheless, even after 1820 states needed to address problems of integration. As Helmut Berding has cogently argued, the core problems of integration were the size of the gap between the original state and the new state that had to be integrated; confessional differences, especially between a new region and the dynasty or dominant grouping in the older parts of the state; and differences in legal and social culture. Where these problems overlapped – as, for example, in the Prussian Rhineland – the potential for serious political difficulties existed, which the state was ill-equipped to combat except by outright repression. Even the coincidence of two of them – for example, in the Bavarian Palatinate or the bishopric of Osnabrück – frequently converted the areas concerned into enduring sources of opposition to the prince's government, especially when, as in the case of the Palatinate, the prince had given the province a special legal status shortly after 1815.[9] This is one of a number of examples in which the willingness of Restoration princes to recognize a province's or a locality's particular 'historic' rights stored up potential for future problems.[10] Overwhelmingly, the type of moderately liberal opposition that came to the fore in the various March ministries after the princes backed down temporarily in 1848 was staffed by people whose origins lay in territories that had been recently acquired by their states – the Rhinelanders Ludolf Camphausen and David Hansemann in Prussia, the Osnabrücker Carl Bertram Stüve in Hanover, and so on.

Secondly, there is the well-known general tension in Napoleonic politics between 'backward-looking' and 'forward-looking' elements. In Germany, this found expression in a number of ways: for example, the tendency of reformers to convert pre-existing feudal social arrangements into apparently more modern-seeming capitalist ones without seriously disrupting the interests of many ex-seigneurs.[11] Where major resistance to emancipation arose, it was often the product of injured pride rather than injured interests. Of all aspects of Napoleonic rule, the sale of *biens nationaux* was probably least contentious, but that was largely because it fitted in so well with the interests of land-hungry princes and landowning élites who had identified Church lands as ripe for the picking well before the Napoleonic territorial revolution was under way.

Above all, however, Napoleonic policies offered a vision of a coherent, rationalized, centrally-directed state whose integration and strength rested on the unmediated relationship between subject-citizens and the prince – put more accurately, it meant that the only mediating functions of any significance were to be exercised by the state's own servants, who were to be accorded significant privileges and guarantees of at least some autonomy from the prince's arbitrary will in return for providing this service. (This was, of course, one of the major attractions of this vision of the modern, impersonal rationalized state to the bureaucratic collaborators mentioned earlier). This state-centred approach had the important consequence that key sections of the reforming bureaucracy tended to see parliamentary or quasi-parliamentary bodies as having decidedly limited rôles – for example, in advising the bureaucracy on policy-making in specific areas. Furthermore, the implementation of this vision was highly problematic, depending as it did on the cooperation of local power-élites who were often embedded into precisely the system of interests that the reforms were designed to combat. This factor is among the most significant in explaining the rather ambiguous outcomes of the Napoleonic period with regard to the liberalization of society and politics.

Thirdly, the implementation of this rationalizing vision was decidedly varied in terms of results. No German state succeeded in codifying its civil law between 1815 and 1848, an endeavour widely regarded as the principal keystone of any modern state-building project. Only one state (Saxony) managed this feat before 1866, and then only in 1863. In each of the three Germanies identified earlier, state-building had to co-exist with continuing regionalisms, provincialisms and localisms, sometimes – as in Prussia and Hanover – as a result of policies deliberately adopted by the prince, sometimes, as in much of the south, because of the survival of *ancien régime* residues in the economy – guilds, *Standesherren*, seigneurial dues, etc. Whatever its deficiencies as an analytical model, Hans-Ulrich Wehler's concept of 'defensive modernization' seems quite useful here, in that élites were attempting to modernize the state without provoking another 1789.[12] In the absence of anything remotely resembling a modern police force, some type of structure was essential within which population growth and mobility could be contained. Only Prussia really welcomed freedom of movement whole-heartedly before 1848, and even this was, as Hermann Beck has recently shown, conditional upon finding solutions to problems of poor relief that did not unduly burden landowning *Junkers*. In some southern states, notably Bavaria, restrictions on movement and domicile were actually strengthened (largely for reasons of social control) around 1830, and this tended to entrench the 'home-town' mentality, which was, in principle, at variance with the vision of the bureaucratic reformers.[13]

Fourthly, despite all such reservations and setbacks, it seems clear that state-building was working, at least in the loose sense of transforming identities, providing a new and larger focus for political activity beyond the locality. In many respects, the persisting regionalisms alluded to earlier were in fact new creations, consequences of the state-building and reforming processes that were supplanting earlier, more localist perspectives.[14] Yet this raised two central questions. The first – regarding which the Napoleonic tradition was once again highly ambiguous – concerned the relationship between this developing sense of statehood and dynastic interests. This was already problematic at the Congress of Vienna, which insisted both that the 'monarchical principle' be upheld and that every state should have a *ständisch* constitution. These two desiderata stood in a decidedly tense relationship with each other, despite their common origins in the desire to avoid a recourse to destructive violence on the Napoleonic model. Such tensions became extremely problematic when princes sought to argue that, in some senses, the state was their property, and that a return to the eighteenth-century patrimonial-absolutist order was needed, usually coupled with assertions about the divinely-ordained nature of their own sovereignties.[15]

This theme is too ramified to discuss fully here; but it does help to explain one of the key attributes of mid-nineteenth-century German liberalism – its statism and its concentration on a largely procedural version of the rule of law (*Rechtsstaat*), with a consequent tendency to downplay government–parliament relations as the primary focus of political interest. From the perspective of the 1830s or even later, the primary objective of many liberals, especially in northern and central Germany, was to secure the end of personalized, patrimonial visions of kingship. Not only was this yet to be won, at least in any secure sense, but the presence on German thrones of kings like Frederick William IV of Prussia or Ernst Augustus of Hanover did little to encourage optimism about future victory. This is precisely why the basic argument of German legal positivism – that the impersonal state holds sovereignty and the prince merely exercises it as an organ of the state – should first have been outlined in connection with the constitutional controversy that led to the celebrated case of the Göttingen Seven in 1837 (it was indeed articulated by one of the Seven).[16]

Another key question, as hinted earlier, concerns the very problematic relationship between state-building and the national question. The connection between developments emanating from France and the intensity with which German nationalism was articulated is clear throughout this period, as is made evident by a brief consideration of the years between 1813 and 1815, the early 1840s or the period after 1859. Put very simply, the stronger states like Bavaria became, the more difficult it would be to unite Germany as a nation-state, at least on a reasonably consensual basis that went further towards a centralized state than the post-1815 Confederation. In so far as the Napoleonic period had given a decisive spur to modern state-building, it had arguably helped to generate a powerful barrier to nation-state formation, especially when Metternich decided to accept and build on many of the most significant territorial changes in the run-up to the Congress of Vienna. As the nationalist politicians of 1848/49 discovered, this was all the more the case when all the primary instruments of state-power – the army, bureaucracy, legal systems, etc. – were in the hands of princes who were highly reluctant to relinquish them to a higher authority that existed only in name. And finally, the involvement of princes, especially the king of Bavaria, in generating a conscious 'state nationalism' after 1848[17] showed quite clearly that the rhetoric of the nation could have a range of different reference points, as for that matter did the conservative-monarchist 'For God and Fatherland' associations that sprang up in Prussia and Hesse-Kassel around 1848.[18]

There was, therefore, a clear ambiguity within the Napoleonic inheritance, to be sure expressed differently in different parts of Germany, but with some marked trends. By 1848, the feudal *Ständestaat* was effectively dead outside a few unusual backwaters such as Mecklenburg, partly because it simply could not cope with changing needs – transport, poor relief policy – but also because of a shift in the mentality of powerful elements within the state that certainly had pre-Napoleonic roots, but that developed very rapidly in the period after 1801. Even where the political methods adopted were consciously anti-Napoleonic – as, for instance, in the moderate so-called 'organic' or historical liberalism prevalent in the north and centre of Germany, with its emphasis on vibrant local government and justified local peculiarities – most intelligent commentators recognized that the military, fiscal and other political realities of the post-Napoleonic age simply could not be adequately addressed if anything even remotely approaching a full-scale restoration of the status quo ante was attempted.

Moreover, any such attempt to restore the pre-Napoleonic order was all but impossible with regard to the territorial changes, which were, as we have seen, the cause of many of the innovations of the 1800s and 1810s. In general terms, governments found increasingly that they could not live without parliaments or similar institutions. Even states like Prussia, which attempted to do so, found that this was impossible in the long run, as is evidenced by the connection between Hardenberg's State Debt Law of 1820 and the belated calling of the Prussian United Landtag in 1847.[19] Yet such bodies almost always tended to outrun the limited intentions of their initiators – a fact that produced so many of the characteristic controversies (for example, over the political disciplining of civil servants who served in parliaments) in this period. Consequently, many princes came to feel that they could not live with parliaments – a sentiment reinforced by the divine-right obscurantism to which many of the less politically far-sighted German rulers of this period felt drawn, and that played such an important role in the frequent constitutional conflicts in the German states of the early and middle nineteenth century.

As was seen above, the primary casualties of Napoleon's ambiguous legacy for political representation were those who sought to construct a sustainable moderate liberal–conservative politics of property-owners (which was arguably Napoleon's own aim, at least in the second half of his career). In a sense, both liberalism and conservatism emerged in extremely problematic forms, with both ideologies fundamentally unable to arrive at coherent views about the bureaucratic state and its proper role in the face of rapid social and political change.[20] These ambivalent attitudes became central to the political debates of the 1840s – a decade in which it was difficult to find any significant commentator ascribing solely positive features to the term 'bureaucracy'. Rather, the debates tended to focus the bureaucracies' habit of interfering unnecessarily in their citizens' associational activities and above all in the burgeoning sphere of local government, which was rapidly becoming the primary instrument of politicization, particularly in the west and south of Germany.[21] At this point – a key stage in the development of a form of politics in which liberalism in particular found it difficult to decide whether the (central) state or local participatory self-government should be the main focus of political activity[22] – the true legacy of the Napoleonic period and the Restoration began to take on a clearer form. There was nothing fortuitous about the fact that local oppositional activism should have been most powerfully articulated in those areas where the state had taken its centralizing mission most seriously. Opposition was after all in many ways a response to that centralizing mission, and the more successful that mission was, the more it threw up countervailing forces that challenged its legitimacy.

Problems of this sort were arguably inherent in the French revolution itself, combining as it did decidedly authoritarian, centralizing forms of government with a vision of progressive, participatory politics that had echoes in parts of Central Europe at least until 1848.[23] But the scale and speed of territorial re-ordering in Germany, followed by a 'restoration' that in most parts of Germany was in fact nothing of the sort, brought unprecedented problems of state-building, integration, legitimacy, public finance and confessional realignment. These problems arguably were different in nature (though not necessarily in scale or significance) from those to be found elsewhere in post-Napoleonic Europe, and they created a political legacy of the utmost importance for the rest of the nineteenth century and beyond. Neither conservatism nor liberalism found it easy (or indeed possible) to construct durable coalitions of interest that spanned the various social, regional and confessional cleavages that were built into the post-1815 order. Under these circumstances, the prospects for a moderate property-owning consensus (whether with a liberal or a conservative complexion) around the main pillars of any plausible nineteenth-century constitution were decidedly poor, and the probability of an eventual recourse to violence correspondingly greater.

Notes

1. For useful general treatments of this pre-revolutionary world, see J. J. Sheehan, *German History 1770–1866* (Oxford, 1989), Chs. 1–2; D. Blackbourn, *The Fontana History of Germany 1780–1918: The Long Nineteenth Century* (London, 1997), pp.1–44.

2. H. Best, *Die Männer von Bildung und Besitz. Struktur und Handeln parlamentarischer Führungsgruppen in Deutschland und Frankreich 1848/49* (Düsseldorf, 1990), esp. pp.416–67.

3. For cogent views on this subject and others addressed here, see J. Sperber, 'State and Civil Society in Prussia: Thoughts on a New Edition of Reinhart Koselleck's *Preussen zwischen Reform und Revolution*', *Journal of Modern History*, 57 (1985), pp.278–96.

4. Blackbourn, *Fontana History* is a good recent example.

5 These figures and those in the preceding paragraph are taken from H.-U. Wehler, *Deutsche Gesellschaftsgeschichte*, I (Munich, 1987), pp.362–6.

6. See the evidence in H.-J. Henning, *Die deutsche Beamtenschaft im 19. Jahrhundert* (Stuttgart, 1984), Ch.1.

7. See the stimulating remarks in J. E. Toews, *Hegelianism: The Path Toward Dialectical Humanism, 1805–1841* (Cambridge, 1980), pp.50–1.

8. Brief introductions to these questions may be found in G. W. Pedlow, *The Survival of the Hessian Nobility* (Princeton, NJ, 1988), Chs.2 and 7, and R. Oberschelp, *Politische Geschichte Niedersachsens 1803–1866* (Hildesheim, 1988), *passim*.

9. H. Berding, 'Staatliche Identität, nationale Integration und politischer Regionalismus', *Blätter für deutsche Landesgeschichte*, 121 (1985), pp.373–6; see also H. Gollwitzer, 'Die politische Landschaft in der deutschen Geschichte des 19./20. Jahrhunderts. Eine Skizze zum deutschen Regionalismus', *Zeitschrift für bayerische Landesgeschichte*, 27 (1964), pp.523–52.

10. A good example here is the campaign by elements within the new territories in Württemberg immediately after 1815 for the restoration of ancient rights (*das gute alte Recht*) that they had in fact never previously possessed; see W Kaschuba, 'Zwischen Deutscher Nation und Deutscher Provinz. Politische Horizonte und soziale Milieus im frühen Liberalismus', in D. Langewiesche (ed.), *Liberalismus im 19. Jahrhundert. Deutschland im europäischen Vergleich* (Göttingen, 1988), pp.92–5.

11. See especially H. Berding, *Napoleonische Herrschafts- und Gesellschaftspolitik im Königreich Westfalen 1807–1813* (Göttingen, 1973) and E. Fehrenbach, *Traditionale Gesellschaft und revolutionäres Recht. Die Einführung des Code Napoleon in den Rheinbundstaaten* (Göttingen, 1974).

12. This concept is advanced at length in Wehler, *Gesellschaftsgeschichte*, I, esp. pt. 2.

13. See H. Beck, 'The Social Policies of Prussian Officials: The Bureaucracy in a New Light', *Journal of Modern History*, 64 (1992), pp.263–98 and M. Walker, *German Hometowns: Community, State and General Estate, 1648–1871* (Ithaca, NY, 1971), Chs.9–11.

14. Compare the shifting application of the word 'particularism' from the immediate provincial level to that of the individual states between 1815 and 1848; see I. Veit-Brause, 'Partikularismus', in *Geschichtliche Grundbegriffe*, IV (Stuttgart, 1978), p.744. On particularism as the ideology of modernizing state bureaucracies with far from purely reactionary overtones, see T. Schieder, 'Partikularismus und nationales Bewußtsein im Denken des Vormärz', in W. Conze, *Staat und Gesellschaft im deutschen Vormärz 1815–1848* (Stuttgart, 1962), pp.9–38.

15. Such claims, which were particularly likely to arise in the 'third Germany', were bolstered after 1815 by the likes of Karl Ludwig von Haller, whose *Restauration der Staatswissenschaften* appeared in six volumes between 1816 and 1825.

16. The scholar in question was Wilhelm Eduard Albrecht (1800–1876), who is conventionally credited as being the founder of the German school of legal positivism, with its emphasis on the state as a 'person'

bearing sovereign powers and the monarch as merely an 'organ' of that person.

17. See M. Hanisch, *Für Fürst und Vaterland. Legitimitätsstiftung in Bayern zwischen Revolution 1848 und deutscher Einheit* (Munich, 1991) and more recently A. F. F. Green, 'Particular Fatherlands: Myth-Making, State-building and the German Question. Hanover, Saxony, Württemberg 1850–1866', Unpublished Ph.D. thesis, University of Cambridge, 1999.

18. W. Schwentker, *Konservative Vereine und Revolution in Preußen 1848/49: die Konstituierung des Konservatismus als Partei* (Düsseldorf, 1988); Pedlow, *Hessian Nobility*, p.241.

19. Briefly, the 1820 Law committed the Prussian state to state-wide consultation should new debts be proposed for supra-provincial spending, as became necessary with the onset of railway-building.

20. Liberal ambivalence about the state is the primary theme of J. J. Sheehan, *German Liberalism in the Nineteenth Century* (Chicago/ London, 1978). Conservative ambivalence, which tended to focus on the alleged 'levelling' of historical traditions and social differences by bureaucratic action is a persistent theme – see for example H. Beck, *The Origins of the Authoritarian Welfare State in Prussia: Conservatives, Bureaucracy and the Social Question, 1815–70* (Ann Arbor, MI, 1997).

21. See, for example, the emphasis placed on the 1831 Local Government Ordinance in Baden by P. Nolte, *Gemeindebürgertum und Liberalismus in Baden 1800–1850* (Göttingen, 1994). The classic contemporary statement of the tension between bureaucracy and local initiatives is R. Mohl, 'Ueber Bureaukratie', *Zeitschrift für die gesammten Staatswissenschaften*, 3 (1846), 330–64, esp. pp.341–2. On these debates in general, see H. Hattenhauer, *Geschichte des Beamtentums* (Cologne/Berlin/Bonn/Munich, 1980), pp.211–20.

22. See the classic article by R. Koch, 'Staat oder Gemeinde? Zu einem politischen Zielkonflikt in der bürgerlichen Bewegung des 19. Jahrhunderts', *Historische Zeitschrift*, 236 (1983), pp.73–96.

23. See, for example, J. Sperber, 'Echoes of the French Revolution in the Rhineland, 1830–1849', *Central European History*, 22 (1989), pp.200–17.

–6–

Napoleon and Germany: A Legacy in Foreign Policy[1]

Brendan Simms

I conclude my work with the year 1815, because everything which came after that belongs to ordinary history. Since that date the age was left to itself; it progresses because it cannot be held back; but led it will never be again . . . We have fallen upon a time when a thousand small calculations and small views on the one side, gross mistakes and feeble remedies on the other, form the history of the day. The sea still runs high, but it is only from the storm which has passed over. One may easily upset in such a sea – for the wind is more difficult to reckon than in a storm – but the spectacle is no longer imposing.

> – Metternich's diary entry of 18 October 1818, on the occasion of the anniversary of the battle of Leipzig.[2]

The storm of this fateful life has whistled past us and the most distinctive memories and miracles, which he brought with him, are deeply engraved in our consciousness.

> Rotteck and Welcker, *Staatslexikon*.[3]

In October 1817 the Prussian ambassador to Bavaria, General Zastrow, not for the first or the last time, bemoaned the continued presence of a large Bonapartist community in Munich. He listed nine offenders, among them one General Vaudoncourt, allegedly writing military history. There was also 'A certain Tasatte, who deals in paintings . . . [But] as he was previously secretary to [the Napoleonic marshal] Masséna his love of art is probably just a disguise . . . [there is] Popp, one-time police commissar in Strasburg, the Swiss Stoffel, formerly in Bonaparte's service, Bonain, a Sicilian, a colonel under Napoleon . . . All these [people] are still here.'[4] Some nine years later, the poet Heinrich Heine, in his prose epic *Ideen. Buch Le Grand*, created a poetic persona who thought back wistfully to his days in the Hofgarten at Düsseldorf, listening to tales of Napoleon's great victories to the musical accompaniment of Le Grand's drum;[5] the early Heine, who was such an incisive critic of German politics, showed himself distinctly susceptible to Bonapartist militarist pathos. Later on in the same work he referred to St Helena as 'the holy grave, to which the peoples of the orient and the occident journey to make their pilgrimage'. His fellow-writer and co-religionist, Heinrich Börne, was more sceptical of Napoleon, whom he condemned as a 'heartless chess-player, who has used us like wood and thrown us away as soon as he has won the game'.[6] But even he confessed to being captivated by a theatre performance on Napoleon's life and times at the Paris Odeon in January 1831: 'In the preceding overture the *Marseillaise* and *Ça ira* were played, melodies which have been sleeping in my heart since my earliest days as a child. Perhaps some forty years have passed since I last heard them, and I wept tears of joy.'[7]

No tears were being shed, of course, in the chancelleries of Europe. Already in late 1814, Frederick William III of Prussia was writing to his eldest son that he had 'nearly forgotten Napoleon Bonaparte', the 'Näppel' or 'Nöppel', as they called him.[8] In view of Bonaparte's imminent return from Elba, the Prussian monarch's insouciance seems rather premature. It was, in any case, untypical. Throughout 1814–15, and for many decades thereafter, European and particularly German governments – including the Prussian one – remained preoccupied with the memory of Napoleon. Even reading about the events of those years was enough to induce insomnia in Count Metternich, Austria's long-serving chief minister. 'I lay there', he confessed in 1820, 'with 1814 in my head and in my heart ... and I could not sleep till five in the morning.'[9]

'We stand at the grave of the fallen emperor and ask: what has remained of his life's work, what is the legacy he has left to posterity?'[10] The question posed by Rotteck and Welcker's *Staatslexikon* was easily answered in 1815. The profound modernizing reforms in Prussia and in southern and western Germany – peasant emancipation, secularization, and abolition of the guilds – were all directly or indirectly his legacy. So were the new constitutions in Bavaria, Württemberg, and a number of other states, even if these assemblies could also trace their origins back to long-standing traditions of corporate representation. Similarly, the unfulfilled promise of a Prussian constitution – rashly made during the hundred days in order to stimulate popular enthusiasm in the renewed struggle against France – was a Napoleonic legacy. In the newly Prussian Rhineland, the most visible legacy of Napoleon was his popular law code, which its inhabitants soon rechristened 'Rhenish Law' in defiance of unsuccessful Prussian attempts to impose their own more archaic corporate laws (The Allgemeines Landrecht of 1794). And, of course, the new German nationalism, which had had its apotheosis during the Wars of Liberation, was intimately connected to the stimulus of the French Revolutionary models on the one hand, and the experience of occupation and subjection on the other. The memory of 1813–14 was to sustain a critique of the *ancien régime* in Prussia – and elsewhere – for many decades to come.[11] All this is well known.

Less well known is the related but nonetheless distinct Napoleonic legacy in foreign policy.[12] After all, when Rotteck and Welcker posed their question about Napoleon's legacy, their first thought was of his failed hegemonic project,[13] unparalleled in conception since the fall of the Roman Empire. As Tim Blanning and Paul Schroeder have shown, the period after 1792 saw an unprecedented revolution in European international relations.[14] At first, this had been as much an opportunity as threat for the states of the *ancien régime*. Until 1805–6, Austria, Prussia and Russia were all net beneficiaries in territorial terms, at least. But thereafter, the Napoleonic experience – particularly in Germany – became increasingly traumatic. In the winter of 1805 Austria was humbled and reduced; in the summer of 1806, the Holy Roman Empire was finally destroyed; and some months later Prussia was so decisively beaten that only the Tsar's intervention saved her from complete extinction. For the next six years or so both German (ex-)great powers were forced into satellite status; fears of total dismemberment were stimulated by rumours of Franco-Russian partition plans, which Alexander's legendary meeting with Napoleon at Tilsit in 1807 did nothing to dispel. Even the smaller and middling German states – in territorial terms the biggest winners – found themselves locked into a French-dominated *Rheinbund* whose limitations on their sovereignty were as irksome as those of the *Reich* they had just helped to destroy. In short, Napoleon left behind a legacy of radical French hegemonic pretensions, which was all the more threatening for its ability to appeal to a wide variety of princely and dissident interests within Germany.

The territorial dispensation at Vienna in 1815 very much reflected this. In Europe as a whole, the system of barriers originally erected against Louis XIV's France was revised and renewed. The former Austrian Netherlands (Belgium) were united with Holland to form the northwestern bulwark; Piedmont-Sardinia was enlarged to block any possible French expansion into Italy. Russian designs on the whole of Poland were frustrated, albeit after some fairly tough negotiation. In Germany, the new arrangements amounted to nothing less than a geopolitical revolution. The smaller states obliterated during the revolutionary and Napoleonic period were not recreated. Indeed, to speak of a simple restoration in 1815 is misleading. It is well known that one of the keys to Metternich's German policy in 1813-1814 – which aimed at expelling Napoleon without at the same time letting in Russia – was the series of treaties concluded with former French satellites such as Baden, Bavaria and Württemberg, guaranteeing many of their territorial gains at the expense of the smaller states.[15] But what is less frequently commented upon is the great geopolitical reorientation of Austria and Prussia after 1815. The Habsburgs, once guardians of the gate against France in the west, surrendered Belgium and her south-western enclaves (*Vorderöesterreich*). In return they (re-)gained Lombardy-Venetia and Dalmatia. This transformed Austria from a primarily western and German power – albeit with strong eastern commitments – into a chiefly Italian and south-eastern power, albeit with strong German pretensions. Conversely, Prussia's late-eighteenth-century focus on northern and eastern Europe was reversed through the acquisition of the Rhineland, which made her Germany's main line of defence against France in the west.[16] This was to prove the most enduring Napoleonic legacy in foreign policy.[17]

The internal reorganization of Germany after 1815 was also a direct result of the Napoleonic legacy in foreign policy. Its main aim was the establishment of a central European order that would be too weak to threaten the balance of power itself, yet strong enough to act as a deterrent to any renewed French encroachments. A unitary German state as demanded by radical nationalists was never a viable proposition. But even the much looser bonds of the old *Reich* were no longer acceptable to the states of the Third Germany, determined to safeguard their precious new sovereignty; they resisted anything that smacked of hierarchy. The upshot was a new Confederal system, the German Confederation, or *Bund*, conceived as an equal association of sovereign states. The *Bund* had a triple task. First of all, it was charged with liquidating the subversive domestic legacy of Napoleon and the struggle to remove him, especially such radical student fraternities as the revolutionary *Burschenschaften*. Secondly, the Confederation was intended to regulate the peaceful coexistence of the German states; here it was the heir to the old *Reich*. Thirdly, and most importantly, however, article 11 of its constitution empowered the *Bund* to organize the collective security of Germany against external attack, more successfully, it was hoped, than the *Reich* had been able to do in the 1790s.

The core of this system of collective security was the new Confederal Military Constitution, heir to the old *Reichskriegsverfassung*. Prussia and Austria each supplied three of the ten corps, Bavaria one, with the other three being made up of contingents from the smaller states. Theoretically, this force was to be ready for action three weeks after mobilization. In wartime the Supreme Command was to be elected by the *Bundestag*, which met under Austrian presidency at Frankfurt.[18] At the same time, the *Bund* inaugurated an ambitious programme of fortress construction at Mainz, Landau, and Luxemburg, in the first instance, followed by Rastatt and Ulm. These fortresses were to be jointly funded and garrisoned by the member states. All of these measures were focused on the western border of the *Bund*, and thus against the danger of renewed French aggression.

None of this, of course, satisfied nationalist opinion. Writing in 1814, just after the disappointing first peace of Paris, Ernst Moritz Arndt observed:

> As far as the fate of our Fatherland is concerned, the dice have not fallen in accordance with the forces of light. We can only build it [the Fatherland] from within through courageous and loyal attitudes and through disseminating real hatred against all things foreign [lit. *Wälsch*]. There will be no lack of storms from without which will drive us more and more towards unity.[19]

These storms were not long in coming. In 1818, the last allied forces of occupation were withdrawn from France; from now on the task of bulwark against France in the west devolved entirely to the new Kingdom of the United Netherlands and the German *Bund*.[20] At around the same time, the new Bourbon government began to question the territorial settlement agreed at Vienna. French territorial revanchism, in fact, was an ideologically bipartisan consensus between old Bonapartists and the restoration regime.[21] As one veteran German nationalist, Joseph Görres, put it 'In Bourbon lilies there remain Napoleonic bees and wasps seeking honey.'[22] At the conference of Verona in 1823, French diplomats demanded a return to the natural borders on the Rhine. This deeply unsettling development was underlined by the ostentatious French intervention in Spain that same year, nominally to restore the monarchy but in reality to assert French power in the area. Throughout the 1820s French plans for the Rhineland varied between schemes for outright annexation and for a system of satellite states on the left bank.

Some Germans would have welcomed the revival of French power, and even the return of Bonaparte. Easily the largest Bonapartist constituency was to be found in the particularist states of the Third Germany, which had enormously benefited from Napoleon's policies and had only latterly turned against him; as one Prussian observer noted contemptuously, their sovereignty was a *Geschenk Napoleons* ('a present from Napoleon').[23] After 1815 their policy was driven by two contradictory and powerful considerations. On the one hand, they feared French expansionism and looked to the confederal institutions for protection; on the other hand, they wished to retain their Napoleonic gains, especially their sovereignty, and looked to both Russia and France to protect them against Austro-Prussian hegemony via the *Bund*.

The classic locus of post-1815 Bonapartism was Württemberg. Publishers such as Cotta in Stuttgart did a roaring trade in translations of Las Cases' *Mémorial de Sainte Hélène* and Ségur's history of the Russian campaign, to name only the most successful titles. A veritable flood of providentialist and millenarian publications appeared, which cast Napoleon in the role of 'The Lord's anointed', 'messiah' and 'martyr'.[24] Yet, as Otto-Heinrich Elias has pointed out, Bonapartism was no mere mood or literary movement; rather, as in France, it was also periodically a political phenomenon with imperatives towards political action.[25] For the King of Württemberg, William I, was surrounded by Bonapartist figures such as General von Theobald, the special envoy von Bismarck, and the Vice-President of the Military Council, General von Hügel, all of whom were veterans of Napoleon's campaigns. In particular, William was influenced by his *éminence grise* August von Trott, a former bureaucrat of the satellite kingdom of Westphalia and a firm Bonapartist.[26] For many, Bonapartism was a strictly foreign-policy rather than a domestic orientation: figures such as the Württembergian envoy to Karlsruhe, Frederick William von Bismarck, were conservative domestically, but remained champions of the Napoleonic alliance even after 1815.[27] The result was an activist south-German particularist policy, which borrowed heavily from the Rheinbundist past and looked to Russo-French protection against Austro-Prussian influence; William himself, formerly an opponent of the emperor, restyled himself as a kind of German Napoleon, and seems to have wanted to put himself at the head of a broader German movement. The resulting struggle against Austro-Prussian tutelage in the period 1818–1824 ended with the humiliation of Württemberg, especially after the two German great powers tarnished William's name with the Russians by accusing him of Bonapartism. As if to prove their charge, one Swabian statesman, Wintzingerode, complained that 'Under similar circumstances Napoleon would certainly have extended more protection to states of secondary rank.'[28]

In Bavaria, of course, there was no enthusiasm for the Württembergian variant of Bonapartism; but the Bavarians had their own fond and potent memories. The army in particular was rumoured to be a hotbed of

Bonapartist sentiment;[29] throughout the 1820s, military commissions repeatedly referred to the military genius of Napoleon.[30] As the Prussian ambassador in Munich observed of the Bavarians: 'I have not been able to observe any particular sympathy for Napoleon. But they secretly wish for a change of government (*revirement*) in France, which they regard as the only chance of further aggrandizement.'[31] Indeed, so fearful was this ambassador of the Napoleonic memory, that he saw in the appearance of mass-produced little statues of the Emperor in Munich not so much an opportunist commercial enterprise as a dastardly plot to keep old memories alive.[32]

One of the foci of Bavarian Francophilia was Napoleon's step-son, the Duke of Leuchtenberg.[33] Despite his blameless and discreet conduct, he was described by one observer as 'the focal point of Bonapartist-minded Frenchmen in Bavaria'.[34] Moreover, the complex system of diplomatic marriages arranged by Napoleon had also left a legacy in Württemberg. The daughter of the king, Katharina, had been married to Jérôme, brother of Napoleon. Unlike Napoleon's unwilling bride Marie Louise, Katharina refused to separate from her husband after the restoration, bore him a son and heir, and followed him into exile in first Austria and then Switzerland. To make matters worse, Jérôme showed none of the discretion of the Duke of Leuchtenberg, for during the hundred days he revealed his unrepentant Bonapartism by slipping away and joining Napoleon;[35] his role in the event of future upheavals could only be guessed at.

To German patriots and to Prussian and Austrian statesmen, the revived French hegemonic pretensions and the existence of a potentially large Francophile fifth column reactivated painful memories of Napoleon. The danger of a joint Franco-Russian revision of the Vienna settlement was reminiscent of Tilsit (1807), when Napoleon and Alexander had divided Europe between them into spheres of influence. Liberal and conservative particularist flirtations of the Third Germany with France put people in mind of the *Rheinbund*.[36] And the increasing, and often explicitly revolutionary, militancy of student radicals and other groups carried echoes of the short-lived Jacobin Republic of Mainz, and of other collaborationist ventures that had made common cause with the French invader.[37]

In this context, of course, the revolutions of 1830–32 in Paris, Belgium, Poland and various areas of Germany and Italy, and the threatened absorption of Belgium into France, bore an uncanny resemblance to the 1790s and were calculated to trigger both *ancien régime* and patriotic traumas. Thus, in early 1831, the *Karlsruher Zeitung*, a pro-government

Badenese newspaper, printed without comment a chronology of the events of 1789–93, and those leading up to 1831. The suggested parallel was clear: as in the 1790s, a possible French incorporation of Belgium might be the signal for greater things.[38] As Metternich observed (retrospectively) to the Austrian envoy in Paris: 'If we scrutinise the events of 1830, and the consequences which up to this moment have resulted from them, with a strict but impartial glance, we shall find it impossible to look upon them as anything else than a *recurrence of the Revolution* [his italics].'[39] Indeed, Metternich suggested elsewhere that 'The vast network of conspiracy, which has been weaving in France for some time back, bears the visible impress of Bonapartism.'[40] Nor were German anxieties assuaged by the plan to make the younger Duke of Leuchtenberg King of Belgium. As one Prussian diplomat noted, he was being pushed by 'some influential friends in Paris and Brussels, declared partisans of Napoleon Bonaparte';[41] when Leuchtenberg junior – at French insistence – renounced his candidature to the Belgian crown, this was welcomed by the Bavarian government, now under the Francophobe Ludwig I, with the observation that it would not be expedient to have a young relative of Napoleon on a throne in the neighbourhood of France.[42] *Ancien régime* paranoia was further fuelled by an extraordinary letter from Napoleon's brother Joseph Bonaparte, who suggested putting his nephew – the son of Napoleon and the Austrian princess Marie Louise – on the French throne.[43] Likewise, there was much alarm when the command of the French invasion force sent to repulse a Dutch counter-attack in Belgium was entrusted to an old Bonapartist soldier, Marschal Count Etienne Gérard.[44] Finally, Germans were not reassured by the growing official and unofficial 'cult' of Napoleon, as represented by Thiers, Hugo, Ségur and many others, that took root in the French July Monarchy after 1830.[45]

After 1815 the memory of Napoleon thus served to focus several distinct but related *ancien régime* traumas: French imperialism, pan-European revolutionary movements, and the threat of a charismatic usurper. This becomes strikingly clear in a revealing letter from Metternich written on the occasion of marriage plans between the Duke of Leuchtenberg and Queen Maria of Portugal:

> When transplanted into Portugal, and placed under the protection of Don Pedro, you will see that spectre of Bonapartism once more assume a body. Bonapartism represents a certain element in the universal disorder; it would be nothing were the social body less agitated than it is. It possesses the advantage of furnishing kings and presidents whom the Revolutionists put up for sale in the market-place . . . The

Duke of Leuchtenberg would, as King of Portugal, attract a portion of the sect to him; the young Louis Bonaparte is seeking to secure himself another section, for Bonapartism . . . extends from military despotism down to the Society of the Friends of the People.[46]

Twenty years later the rise of Napoleon III, predictably enough, provoked similar *angst*. In December 1851, the veteran Prussian conservative Leopold von Gerlach wrote to Bismarck: 'Since the coup of 2 December, Bonapartism, the most practical and therefore most dangerous tendency within the revolution, has begun to rear its mighty head'; he then added that it was easier for him 'instinctively to fear and hate Bonapartism, because I am older, because I saw it and experienced it, and fought against it with all right-thinking people since I was sixteen'.[47] The same fears were addressed in a later edition of the famous liberal *Staatslexikon* with much greater optimism: '"Napoleon was unique in history, a singular phenomenon", thus wrote Rotteck, who did not live to witness 2 December [the coup of Napoleon III in Paris]. Will this judgement remain valid today, when France is ruled if not by the son then at least by the nephew [of Napoleon I]?' Despite all the justified concern, the *Staatslexikon* felt that the answer was yes: 'We do not share the concerns of many honourable men about lasting victories of a new Napoleonism or Jacobinism at all.'[48]

Clearly, by mid-century the spectre of classical Bonapartism as a hegemonic threat had begun to recede; already shortly after 1815 fear of Napoleon became increasingly synonymous with traditional – 'hereditary' – fears of French expansionism.[49] Significantly, the news of Napoleon's death in 1821 produced little reaction in Germany;[50] yet his legacy at first remained as vibrant as ever. What Germans feared was not so much the increasingly remote grand Napoleonic Empire, as the legacy of the 'natural frontiers'. Strictly speaking, this concept dated from the Revolutionary Wars, not Napoleon; but it was now often indiscriminately – and unhistorically [51] – attributed to a whole rogues' gallery of Frenchmen, from Louis XIV, through the eighteenth-century *ancien régime*, the Revolutionary and Napoleonic period, and the Bourbon restoration right up to the Constitutional Monarchy of Louis Philippe after 1830.[52] As King Ludwig of Bavaria exclaimed in 1837: 'The behaviour of the French on the Rhine towards the end of the seventeenth century is terrible, but Germans forget it; they also forget the humiliations inflicted by Napoleon.'[53] Even if Ludwig was a child of the Palatinate, which had been ravaged by French troops in the late seventeenth century, the origins of his Francophobia lay in the specific trauma of Napoleon. As an impetuous teenager his first recorded political intervention had been a vain letter in 1805 imploring his father Max Joseph not to side with Napoleon against Austria.[54] Throughout 1814 he was preoccupied – reasonably enough as it turned out – by the prospect of Napoleon's returning from Elba and rallying the French people for another bid for hegemony.[55] After 1815, Ludwig remained obsessed with Bonaparte. In 1826, for example, he deliberately timed the laying of the foundations (*Grundsteinlegung*) of the *Königsbau* in Munich on the anniversary of Waterloo, much to the chagrin of the French representative; as one observer noted, Ludwig was so preoccupied with Napoleon that he seemed determined to commemorate even battles in which Bavarian troops had taken no part![56] Some five years later, Ludwig caused another upset by writing some Francophobic lyrics to Meyerbeer's music for the 'Bayerischer Schützenmarsch im Jänner 1814'.[57] Later still, he was to make the liberation from Napoleon and the founding of the *Bund* the centrepiece of his great monument 'Walhalla'.[58]

In short, the complex and protean Napoleonic legacy in foreign policy in Germany can be summarized under three separate headings. First of all, there was a generalized but profound fear of French expansionism, in particular of French designs on the Rhine frontier. This manifested itself most sharply at times of crisis, such as during the Revolutions of 1830, and in a more attenuated form in 1848; the memory of Napoleon formed a central and explicit part of these fears. Secondly, there was a fear of princely, revolutionary and other fifth columns within Germany that might cooperate with a resurgent France; here again 'Bonapartist' anxieties were central. Thirdly, the territorial and institutional dispensation of the treaty of Vienna, in particular the Prussian presence in the Rhineland, was intended to contain future Napoleons.

But the legacy in foreign policy did not end there. The continued threat of French revanchism served to drive German states together and explore ways of improving their confederal military bonds, especially after the upheavals of 1830 and 1840; Arndt's prediction of 1814 was thus realized. The geopolitical revolution of 1815, which put Prussia in the first line of defence against France, meant that the leadership of Germany devolved to her and not to Austria, her presidency of the *Bund* notwithstanding. At the same time, the continued French threats drove not only the emerging liberal nationalist public sphere but also the smaller and middling states of the Third Germany, periodically, into the Prussian camp. None of this would have been conceivable without the events of 1797–1815 and their aftershocks. Herein lies what was Napoleon's most decisive contribution to the unification of Germany under Prussian leadership. In this sense later German nationalists were perfectly justified in claiming Napoleon 'for Germany'. Well might Stefan George write that: 'The shame we incurred at your hands, your foot on our necks, was worth more to us than many empty victories.'[59]

Notes

1. In his article 'Die Deutschen und Napoleon im 20. Jahrhundert', *Historische Zeitschrift*, 252 (1991), pp.587–625, Roger Dufraisse announced a forthcoming study on 'Die Deutschen und Napoleon, 1795–1840', which has not yet appeared. His recent *L'Allemagne à l'époque napoléonienne. Questions d'histoire politique, économique et sociale* (Berlin, 1992) is a collection of previous essays.
2. *Memoirs of Prince Metternich 1815–1829* edited by R. Metternich, translated by Mrs Alexander Napier, Volume 3 (London, 1881), pp.338–9.
3. K. Welcker, *Das Staats-Lexikon: Enzyklopädie der sämtlichen Staatswissenschaften für alle Stände* (Leipzig, 1859), Vol. 3, p.162: 'Der Strom dieses verhängnisreichen Lebens ist an uns selbst vorübergerauscht, und die hervorragendsten Erscheinungen und Wunder, die er mit sich führte, stehen tief eingeprägt in unserer noch tiefen Erinnerung.'
4. A. Chroust (ed.), *Gesandtschaftsberichte aus München, 1814–1848. Dritte Abteilung. Die Berichte der preußischen Gesandten,* Vol. I (Munich, 1949), p.155: 'Ein gewisser Tasatte, der mit Gemälden handelt . . . Da er früher Sekretär Massenas gewesen war so wird seine Kunstlieberei wohl nur ein Vorwand sein . . . Popp, früher Polizei-Kommissar in Straßburg, Der Schweizel Stoffel, früher in Diensten Bonapartes, Bonain, ein Sizilianer, Oberst unter Napoleon . . . Diese alle sind noch hier.' In a similar vein, see De la Garde to Richelieu, 12 Feb. 1817, Munich, in Anton Chroust (ed.), *Gesandtschaftsberichte aus München 1814–1848. Abteilung I. Die Berichte der französischen Gesandten* (Munich, 1935), I, p.18; and Marquis de la Moussaye to Baron Pasquier, 14 Dec. 1821, Munich, in Chroust (ed.), *Französische Gesandtschaftsberichte*, I, pp.164–5. On the problem of Bonapartist refugees in Bavaria see S. Krauss, *Die politischen Beziehungen zwischen Bayern und Frankreich 1814/15–1840* (Munich, 1987), pp.147–9.

5. H. Heine, *Ideen. Buch Le Grand* (1827, Stuttgart, 1991), p.31. On literary Francophilia and hero-worship of Napoleon see H.-O. Sieburg, *Deutschland und Frankreich in der Geschichtsschreibung des neunzehnten Jahrhunderts* (Wiesbaden, 1954), pp.111, 275–8, *et passim*; and M. Schömann, *Napoleon in der deutschen Literatur* (Berlin and Leipzig, 1930), pp.19–23. Schömann describes Heine, p.23 as 'unter den Deutschen der glühendste Bewunderer und gläubigste Verherrlicher (wenn auch nicht zugleich der tiefste Kenner und umfassendste Deuter) des Kaisers'.

6. L. Börne, 33rd letter, in A. Estermann (ed.), *Ludwig Börne. Briefe aus Paris* (Frankfurt, 1986), p.154: 'herzloser Schachspieler, der uns wie Holz gebraucht und uns wegwirft, wenn er die Partei gewonnen'.

7. Börne, 25th letter, p.108: 'In der vorausgehenden Ouvertüre wurde der Marseiller Marsch und ça-ira gespielt, Melodien, die mir seit meiner frühesten Kinderjahren im Herzen schlummerten. Es sind vielleicht vierzig Jahre, daß ich sie nicht gehört, und ich weinte Tränen des Entzückens.'

8. See T. Stamm-Kuhlmann, *König in Preußens großer Zeit. Friedrich Wilhelm III, der Melancholiker auf dem Thron* (Berlin, 1992), p.403.

9. *Memoirs*, III, p.359; pp.588–9 regarding his reading the biography of Napoleon by O'Meara.

10. Welcker, *Staatslexikon*, p.172: 'Wir stehen an des gefallenen Kaisers Grab und Fragen: was ist übrig geblieben von seinem Wirken, welches ist sein der Nachwelt hinterlassenes Vermächtniß?'

11. See C. Clark, 'The Wars of Liberation in Prussian Memory: Reflections on the Memorialisation of War in Early Nineteenth-Century Germany', *Journal of Modern History*, 68 (1996), pp.550–76.

12. For example, there is nothing specifically on foreign policy in D. Groh, 'Cäsarismus, Napoleonismus, Bonapartismus, Führer, Chef, Imperialismus', in O. Brunner, W. Conze, and R. Koselleck (eds), *Geschichtliche Grundbegriffe. Historisches Lexikon zur politisch-sozialen Sprache in Deutschland* (Stuttgart, 1972), Bd.1, pp.726–71, esp. pp.739–43: 'Die Bonapartisten in Deutschland. Das Beispiel Heine's'.

13. Welcker, *Staatslexikon*, p.175.

14. P. Schroeder, *The Transformation of European Politics, 1763–1848* (Oxford, 1994); T. C. W. Blanning, *The Origins of the French Revolutionary Wars* (London, 1986); idem, 'The French Revolution and Europe', in C. Lucas (ed.), *Rewriting the French Revolution* (Oxford, 1991), pp.183–207.

15. See E. E. Kraehe, *Metternich's German Policy*, Vol. I. *The Contest*

with Napoleon, 1799–1814 (Princeton, NJ, 1963), *passim*.

16. The only general account that explicitly refers to this, even *en passant*, seems to be T. Nipperdey, *Deutsche Geschichte 1800–1866. Bürgerwelt und starker Staat* (Munich, 1983), p.91.

17. See B. Simms, *The Struggle for Mastery in Germany, 1780–1850* (Basingstoke, 1998), for a more detailed discussion.

18. J. Angelow, *Von Wien nach Königgrätz. Die Sicherheitspolitik des deutschen Bundes im europäischen Gleichgewicht 1815–1866* (Munich, 1996), pp.43–6.

19. Quoted in Sieburg, *Deutschland und Frankreich*, p.108: 'Was das Schicksal unseres Vaterlandes betrifft, so sind die Loose leider nicht so gefallen, wie die Guten es sich gedacht hatten. Wir können es nur von innen heraus durch tapfere und treue Gesinnung und durch Verbreitung echten Hasses alles Wälschen erbauen; von Außen her werden auch die Stürme nicht fehlen, die uns mehr und mehr zur Einheit zusammentreiben.'

20. For Austrian and Prussian fears and the need to organize Confederal institutions accordingly, see Metternich to Francis I, 7 Oct. 1818, Aachen, *Memoirs*, III, p. 180; Metternich, 'Abridged Summary of the Situation on November 1 1818', *Memoirs*, III, p.185; L. J. Baack, *Christian Bernstorff and Prussia. Diplomacy and Reform Conservatism* (New Brunswick, NJ, 1980).

21. Sieburg, *Deutschland und Frankreich*, p.27.

22. M. Rowe, 'German Civil Administrators and the Policies of the Napoleonic State in the Department of the Roer, 1798–1815', Unpublished Ph.D. thesis, University of Cambridge, 1996, p.349.

23. Küster to Hardenberg, 1 Jan. 1817, in Chroust (ed.), *Preußische Gesandtschaftsberichte*, I, p.98.

24. O.-H. Elias, 'Das Bild des Kaisers. Literarischer und politischer Bonapartismus in Württemberg', in *Baden und Württemberg im Zeitalter Napoleons. Ausstellung des Landes Baden-Württemberg unter der Schirmherrschaft des Ministerpräsidenten Dr. hc. Späth* vol. 2 (Stuttgart, 1987), p.723.

25. Ibid., p.725.

26. Ibid., p.727.

27. P. Burg, *Die Deutsche Trias in Idee und Wirklichkeit. Vom alten Reich zum deutschen Zollverein* (Wiesbaden and Stuttgart, 1989), p.168.

28. Ibid., pp.730–1.

29. See Küster to Frederick William III, 25 May 1815, Munich, in Chroust (ed.), *Preußische Gesandtschaftsberichte*, I, pp.22–3; Coulomb (*chargé d'affaires*) to Pasquier, 3 Sep. 1820, Munich, in Chroust (ed.),

Französische Gesandtschaftsberichte, I, p.140.

30. H. Gollwitzer, *Ludwig I von Bayern. Königtum im Vormärz. Eine politische Biographie* (Munich, 1986), p.427.

31. Zastrow to Hardenberg, 28 May 1817, Munich, in Chroust (ed.), *Preußische Gesandtschaftsberichte*, I, p.143: 'Ich habe zwar keine besondere Vorliebe für Napoleon hervorblicken sehen. Man wünscht aber im Geheimen ein Revirement in Frankreich, das man als das einzige Vergrößerungsmittel ansieht . . .' See also in a similar vein: Zastrow to Hardenberg, 12 July 1817, Munich, in Chroust (ed.), *Preußische Gesandtschaftsberichte*, pp.149–50; Count de la Garde (French envoy) to Richelieu, 26 Nov. 1818, Munich, in Chroust (ed.), *Französische Gesandtschaftsberichte*, I, pp.70–1.

32. Zastrow to Frederick William III, 19 Sep. 1819, Munich, Chroust (ed.), *Preußische Gesandtschaftsberichte*, I, pp.228–9.

33. Eugène de Beauharnais, Duke of Leuchtenberg: b. 3 Sep. 1781, Paris; d. 21 Feb. 1824, Munich. He was Josephine's son from her first marriage. See *Allgemeine Deutsche Biographie* 18 (1883), pp.475–9. He was succeeded by his son.

34. Küster report for Hardenberg, 1 Jan. 1817, 'Politisches Gemälde von Baiern', in Chroust (ed.), *Preußische Gesandtschaftsberichte*, I, p.90: '*Vereinigungspunkt der bonapartistisch gesinnten Franzosen in Baiern*'. See also in the same vein: Zastrow to Frederick William III, 30 Aug. 1820, Munich, Chroust (ed.), *Preußische Gesandtschaftsberichte*, I, pp.259–60; Dönhoff to Frederick William III, 27 Nov. 1838, Munich, in ibid, III, pp.82–3.

35. P. Sauer, *Napoleons Adler über Württemberg, Baden und Hohenzollern. Südwestdeutschland in der Rheinbundzeit* (Stuttgart/Berlin, Cologne/Mainz, 1987), pp.294–5.

36. For governmental particularism see Burg, *Deutsche Trias*, *passim*; for accusations of 'Rheinbundism' against South German liberals see E. Schunk, 'Vom nationalen Konstitutionalismus zum konstitutionellen Nationalismus. Der Einfluß der "Franzosenzeit" auf den pfälzischen Liberalismus zur Zeit des Hambacher Festes', *Zeitschrift für bayerische Landesgeschichte*, 51 (1988), p.468.

37. The best account of events in Mainz is T. C. W. Blanning, *Reform and Revolution in Mainz, 1743–1803* (Cambridge, 1974).

38. W. Gauer, 'Badische Staatsräson und Frühliberalismus um die Juliwende. Regierung, Presse und öffentliche Meinung in Baden 1830–32', *Zeitschrift für die Geschichte des Oberrheins* (N.F.), 45 (1932), p.379.

39. Metternich to Hügel, 22 Oct. 1833, Vienna, in *Memoirs*, 5, p.369.

40. Metternich, 'Historical Sketch of the Revolutionary Movements in Modena and the Papal States', Metternich, *Memoirs*, V, p.103. In the same vein see also: Metternich to Apponyi, 15 Feb. 1831, Vienna, ibid., pp.104–7. For similar parallels between 1830–31 and the Napoleonic experience see Gollwitzer, *Ludwig I*, p.299.

41. Küster to Frederick William, 17 Jan. 1831, Munich, in Chroust (ed.), *Preußische Gesandtschaftsberichte*, II, pp.182–3: 'quelques amis influens à Paris et Bruxelles, partisans déclarées comme eux de Napoleon Bonaparte'.

42. See Küster to Frederick William III, 8 Feb. 1831, Munich, in Chroust (ed.), *Preußische Gesandtschaftsberichte*, II, p.187.

43. Joseph Napoleon Bonaparte to Metternich, 9 Oct. 1830, Point Breye, in Metternich, *Memoirs*, 5, pp.107–8.

44. Angelow, *Von Wien nach Königgrätz*, p.91.

45. See Sieburg, *Frankreich und Deutschland*, pp.154ff. See also: J. Lucas-Dubreton, *Le culte de Napoleon, 1815–1848* (Paris, 1960).

46. Metternich to Apponyi, 11 Sep. 1834, Vienna, in *Memoirs*, 5, pp.422–3.

47. Leopold von Gerlach to Bismarck, 20 Dec. 1851, Charlottenburg, in H. Kohl (ed.), *Briefe des Generals Leopold von Gerlach an Otto von Bismarck* (Stuttgart and Berlin, 1912), p.5.

48. Welcker, *Staatslexikon*, III, pp.177–8.

49. On the theme 'Napoleon als Nationalfeind' (Kleist, Arndt, Körner, Schlegel, etc.), see Schömann, *Napoleon in der deutschen Literatur*, pp.3–15. For the daemonic view of Napoleon among German nationalists see M. Jeismann, *Das Vaterland der Feinde. Studien zum nationalen Feindbegriff und Selbstverständnis in Deutschland und Frankreich 1792–1918* (Stuttgart, 1992), pp.76–9.

50. For example, Zastrow to Frederick William III, 27 July 1821, Munich, in Chroust, *Preußische Gesandtschaftsberichte*, I, p.281.

51. See E. Buddruss, *Die französische Deutschlandpolitik, 1756–1789* (Mainz, 1995), *passim*.

52. See H. Schmidt, 'Napoleon in der deutschen Geschichtsschreibung', *Francia*, 14, (1980), pp.530–60.

53. Gollwitzer, *Ludwig I*, p. 637: 'Wie die Franzosen gegen Ende des 17. Jahrhunderts am Rhein gewütet, ist schauderhaft, aber Deutsche vergessen es; vergessen die Schmach von Napoleon angetan; (Straßburg, das Elsaß wurde Frankreich gelassen)'; see also p.168.

54. Ibid., p.66.

55. Ibid., p.169.

56. Küster to Frederick William III, 21 June 1826, Munich, Chroust (ed.),

Französische Gesandtschaftsberichte, II, pp.40–1. On Ludwig and Napoleon see also: Küster to Frederick William, 29 Oct. 1828, Munich, in Chroust (ed.), *Preußische Gesandtschaftsberichte*, 117–18; and Moussaye to Baron de Mas, 23 Nov. 1825, Munich, Chroust (ed.), *Französische Gesandtschaftsberichte*, II, p.7.

57. Küster to Frederick William, 25 Mar. 1831, in Chroust (ed.), *Preußische Gesandtschaftsberichte*, II.
58. Gollwitzer, *Ludwig I*, pp.649–50.
59. Cited in H.-O. Sieburg, 'Napoleon in der deutschen Geschichtsschreibung des 19. und 20. Jahrhunderts', *Geschichte in Wissenschaft und Unterricht*, 21 (1970), p.483.

Part II
The Legacy of Annexation

Map 3. The Polish Kingdom

7

The Polish Kingdom (1815–1830): Continuity or Change?

Andrzej Nieuwazny

Although Napoleon's defeat in Russia and the subsequent occupation of the Duchy of Warsaw by Russian troops in the winter and spring of 1813 brought an end to the Napoleonic era in Poland, the Polish army remained faithful to the French Emperor until his abdication in 1814. Even outside the army, Napoleon's defeat and abdication were not welcomed by most Poles, painfully aware that nothing could revive the Duchy of Warsaw. It fell to Tsar Alexander, the strongest of the victorious allies, to dictate the fate of the former Napoleonic satellite. The policy pursued by the Tsar with regard to Poland's constitution, representative and judicial systems, and army reveals some striking and surprising continuities with the Napoleonic era. Yet while the policy was meant to ease relations between the Tsar and his subjects in the Kingdom of Poland, it resulted eventually in the creation of severe tensions.

In September 1814 Napoleon's Polish supporters were given one last chance to demonstrate their loyalty during the funeral ceremonies for the fallen hero, Prince Poniatowski. The symbol of independent Poland and the only foreigner appointed to the rank of Marshal of the Empire, Poniatowski died while covering the retreat of the French at Leipzig on 19 October 1813. In 1817 his remains were consigned to their final resting place among the Polish kings in Wawel Cathedral in Cracow. Poniatowski's death was mourned not just because he was a patriotic hero, but also because it represented the end of an era. Henceforth, patriotic hopes would centre on Adam Czartoryski, former Russian Foreign Minister and a friend of the Tsar. Since at least as early as 1803 Czartoryski had been inclined to seek a Russian solution to the Polish question.[1] After 1814, fear of a renewed partition of Poland made this position more widely acceptable.

After the defeat of Napoleon, the Tsar was at pains to win over the Poles, while simultaneously preparing for the forthcoming peace congress in Vienna. Gradually Alexander modified the policy he adopted towards the occupied Duchy of Warsaw. Although he changed neither the provisional administrative structure – from March 1813 Russian-occupied Poland had been ruled by the so-called Supreme Provisional Council – nor the country's rôle as a gigantic barracks for the vast Russian army of occupation, the Tsar introduced sharp reductions in requisitioning and taxation. Moreover, he began to prepare reforms of the structures of the state from the perspective of its still uncertain links with Russia. In July 1814, the Tsar established the Civil Organization Committee (*Komitet Organizacji Cywilnej*) under the Speaker of the Senate, Ostrowski. This Committee was to work on projects concerning the new administrative system, a new law code to replace the Code Napoléon, and the position of the peasantry.

While preparing for the future negotiations with Prussia and Austria over the partition of Napoleon's heritage, Alexander chose not to disband the 35,000 Polish soldiers who had been captured in France, considering them a useful tool in any future struggle for power. Instead, these men were repatriated to Poland, granted, according to Fontainebleau (11 April 1814), 'their arms and baggage as proof of their great services'.

At the Congress of Vienna, the Polish problem emerged as the most divisive issue for the powers of the victorious coalition. Alexander's determination, combined with territorial concessions by Austria and Prussia, resulted in the creation of a satellite Polish state, comprising most of the former Duchy of Warsaw, linked by personal union with Russia.[2] On 18 May 1815 a treaty was signed in Vienna between Russia and Saxony, whereby the Saxon King, Frederick Augustus, renounced the title of Duke of Warsaw and all rights and claims regarding the Duchy. The Tsar then abolished the Supreme Provisional Council by decree, and set up a Provisional Council of State and a Provisional Government to lay the foundations of the Kingdom of Poland. This was ceremoniously proclaimed on 20 June 1815. For the next fifteen years the small Polish white eagle, located on the breast of the Romanovs' black eagle, would be the symbol of the new state. This symbol was in some senses prophetic, for from the moment the Kingdom was born it was seen as 'too much for the Russians, too little for the Poles'.[3]

The Polish Kingdom, which was granted a constitution, was conceived by the Tsar as a potential ally in his often awkward relations with the conservative Russian oligarchy. This group in turn viewed his plans for Poland with intense hostility. In addition, Alexander wanted Poland to be a 'shop window', displaying his liberalism and winning the sympathy of European public opinion. Yet the guarantee of the Poles' extensive political rights was also meant to calm the fears of the other powers that Russia's acquisition of Duchy's lands would make Russia too strong. Instead, although lying within the boundaries of the Russian Empire, the new Kingdom of Poland was to function as a laboratory for new laws and institutions, which might (but need not) be transplanted to Russia itself at a later date. Whether or not Alexander really wished to make Russia a constitutional state is still a matter for debate; but until 1830 the possibility certainly could not be ruled out. Thus, while on the one hand the Tsar's liberal experiments in the Kingdom of Poland were a means of strengthening his position both in Saint Petersburg and in Europe, on the other they threatened the interests of both domestic and foreign reactionaries. Certainly a constitutional Russia would give a very different character to the Holy Alliance from that envisaged by Metternich.[4]

The establishment of the Polish Kingdom demanded that decisions be taken regarding new institutions and the future of the legal system introduced by Napoleon. Although there were some proposals to reject the institutions and laws of the Napoleonic Duchy wholesale, the *Zasady dla konstytucji Królestwa Polskiego* (*The Priniciples of the Constitution of the Kingdom of Poland*) drew heavily on Napoleonic legislation, supplementing it with guarantees of personal liberties (looking back to the Constitution of 3 May 1791), and seeking to restrict and control executive power. The *Zasady* (*Principles*) became the cornerstone of the new constitution drawn up by Ostrowski's committee. The new constitution was proclaimed on 24 December 1815.[5] However, the Tsar had made some apparently minor, but extremely clever, amendments that enabled him to restrict or simply ignore certain clauses of the constitution.

Although those responsible for the 1815 constitution avoided mention of its links with the Napoleonic era, and, indeed, were much happier to point to the 3 May 1791 as its progenitor, the connections between the system introduced in 1807 and that introduced in 1815 are obvious. As one historian has remarked: 'the constitution of the Duchy was a building material that was used to make the constitution of the Kingdom. This material was processed, significantly improved (in some aspects it was worsened), but it was essentially based upon [the 1807 constitution], and whole passages were borrowed from it'. The constitution of 1815 not only acknowledged the basic liberties embodied in the 1807 constitution, but strengthened them: it was much less vague in its guarantee of the inviolability of personal freedom, and of property rights, in its defence of freedom of conscience and of the press, in maintaining the independence of the judiciary, and in requiring ministerial responsibility.[6]

As under the Duchy, the new constitution granted the hereditary monarch full executive powers, and the exclusive right of legislative initiative. The king alone controlled foreign policy, and appointed senators, judges and civil servants. The 1807 constitution had given Frederick Augustus the power to appoint a viceroy – a power he had not used. The 1815 constitution replaced the viceroy with a Governor General (*namiestnik*) appointed by the Tsar. This position was occupied from 1815 to 1826 by General Józef Zajączek.[7]

Another similarity with Napoleon's Duchy was that the Kingdom of Poland also had a two-chamber parliament – the *Sejm*. Formerly, this had consisted of a Senate composed of bishops, voivods and castellans, and of a Chamber of Representatives (*Izba Poselska*). From 1809 the lower chamber had consisted of members of the Council of State, 100 elected representatives of the gentry (*Szlachta*) and 66 deputies from the communes, elected by men satisfying the appropriate property, public and military service and educational requirements. Under the Kingdom the number of representatives of gentry and commoners fell to 77 and 51 respectively, but it is significant that the ratio in favour of the former was retained. The election law of 1 December 1815 differed little from that of the Duchy. However, it did distinguish between propertied and propertyless gentry, and deprived military men of their voting rights. It also increased the minimum age for voters, and some landowners were constitutionally guaranteed certain positions.

By 1820 the new voting system had enfranchised between 105,000 and 115,000 Poles out of a total population of 3.5 million. This represented 3.3 per cent of the population, compared with perhaps 3.7 per cent in the Duchy prior to 1809, but a mere 2.5 per cent in the period after the territorial expansion of 1809. The figures for the Kingdom of Poland compare favourably with those for Restoration France under Louis XVIII, where only 90,000 men were entitled to vote out of a population of 30 million (0.3 per cent of the population). Nevertheless, the relatively wide franchise in Poland did not prevent the gentry from continuing to dominate the *Sejm*. Indeed, the ratio of gentry actually increased: in 1809 they constituted 75 per cent; by 1811 this figure had risen to 81 per cent; under the Kingdom it grew to almost 83 per cent in 1818, and over 88 per cent by 1825.[8]

If the gentry remained paramount within the *Sejm*, the powers of the parliament widened. Under the Napoleonic system, it could deliberate only on civil and penal legal cases and issues of taxation and the budget. After 1815 the right to deliberate on constitutional amendments was granted to parliament, as was a certain limited control over the government. Although legislative initiative belonged purely to the king (i.e. the

Tsar), the *Sejm* itself could vote to introduce a bill for assemblies two years later.

Another Napoleonic body to survive (albeit in a significantly altered form) was the Council of State (*Rada Stanu*). While the so-called General Meeting (*Zgromadzenie Ogólne*) fulfilled the same basic role as the Duchy's Council, an Administrative Council (*Rada Administracyjna*) consisting of ministers and councillors appointed by the King, was also set up to advise the Governor General and Alexander himself. After General Zajączek died in 1826, the function of Governor General was abolished, and the Administrative Council became the supreme governmental body. Substantial change in the administrative system was also seen in substituting the principle of collective management – much more in keeping with Polish tradition – for that of individual management. Thus the ministers of the Duchy were replaced by governmental committees, although these were still headed by a minister. Similar reforms were introduced in provincial administration: the position of prefect was abolished, and departments were replaced by voivodships, each with a voivod at its head.[9]

In 1814–15 the Napoleonic Code also led to serious disagreement. When introduced in 1808 the Code generated serious objections among most gentry (*szlachta*), and in 1814 the more conservative and clerical aristocrats hoped to see it replaced with a legal system based on feudal rights and ancient Polish law with some Prussian and Austrian elements. Alternatively some called for the reintroduction of the old Lithuanian Statute (*Statut Litewski*), the most comprehensive code of ancient Polish and Lithuanian law. Behind these calls for the Statute lay a nationalist agenda, for it still remained in force in the nine western provinces of Russia that had been annexed during the partitions of Poland in the late eighteenth century. Both pro- and anti-Napoleonic Polish patriots still yearned for redemption of these lands, and the existence of a common legal system would provide the basis for further steps towards reunification. Adam Czartoryski in particular championed the Statute as the first stage towards the union. Meanwhile the Church was anxious to see the end of the 'godless' Napoleonic Code, which enshrined civil marriage.

The Napoleonic Code had its champions. Its major beneficiary – the bourgeoisie – was too weak to defend it on its own, but allies were at hand among the landowners. Although most had opposed the introduction of the Code in 1808, they soon began to realize the advantages and profits they could derive from the Napoleonic system. In particular they benefited from the fact that the Code refused to acknowledge traditional peasant rights to the lands they cultivated, or to recognize the common use of pasture and forests. True, the 1807 constitution had given the peasants personal freedom; but the decree of December 1808, that gave them the right to leave their villages, also demanded that all their lands be returned to the property-owner. This decree opened possibilities for the landowners who wished to remove their peasants. Moreover, if the peasants wanted to retain their homesteads, they had to accept the serfdom (*pańszczyzna*) imposed on them by the landowner. In effect the Code, although it did not make any actual provision for serfdom, through assuming freedom of economic relations implicitly enabled landowners to regulate the position of the peasantry for their own advantage. This practice continued after the establishment of the Kingdom. As a result, in central Poland the Napoleonic Code paradoxically served to strengthen feudal relations and underpin the feudal ownership of the land.

During the discussion surrounding legal reform in 1814–15, most civil servants and lawyers also supported the retention of the Napoleonic Code. For them French law seemed vastly more progressive and efficient than that of pre-partition Poland, and they were wont to stress that whatever the fiscal difficulties of the Duchy, the judicial system had functioned smoothly.[10] This group found other useful allies in the Tsar (who was concerned that Czartoryski's proposals to reintroduce the Statute might be used to precipitate reunification with Russia's western provinces), and among many influential figures in Saint Petersburg (who were also frightened at the possibility of any greater union between the former Duchy of Warsaw and lands taken by Russia during the partition).

With such powerful vested interests at work, it is no surprise that the Napoleonic legal system remained largely intact. Nevertheless, after 1815, the Code did undergo some modifications. Clerical opposition to civil marriage, for example, led to a major debate in the *Sejm* in 1818. In fact, the issue of civil marriage was more important in principle than in practice, since in the entire period 1808–18 only three civil ceremonies had taken place and only seven divorces had been decreed! Attempts to end civil marriage were blocked by the lower chamber, but the Minister of Religion and Education, Stanislaw Potocki, recognized the need to accommodate Polish tradition when interpreting the Napoleonic Code, which he nonetheless described as 'faultless . . . civil law'.[11] Eventually, because of pressure from the Church, those sections of the Code relating to marriage law were changed in 1825. However, despite some minor changes – for example, the alteration of regulations regarding mortgages in 1818 – the new legal code of the Kingdom of Poland continued to resemble the Napoleonic Code closely.

The fact that the Napoleonic Code was essentially retained was to have a major influence on the history of civil legislation in Russian Poland. No longer was the Napoleonic Code perceived as a foreign system imposed from outside. Instead, it came to be seen as distinctively Polish, and ever more appropriate for local conditions. Not only did it outlast the abolition of the Kingdom's administrative institutions after the failed insurrection of 1830–31, but it also largely survived the 1876 reform of the judicial system, when Russian civil law *procedures* were introduced in the place of the French. The adoption of Russian procedures did, of course, lead to some amendments; but civil law remained essentially Napoleonic, which alone distinguished Poland from the rest of the Russian Empire. Any suggestion that the system be changed was treated as an attack on 'national' law. Indeed, when Poland regained its independence, some lawyers suggested that the Code be extended to the areas formerly under Austrian and Prussian control, as well as to those lands acquired from Russia to the east of the former Kingdom's frontiers. By 1939, when Poland was once again invaded by German and Russian forces, no new civil code had been introduced. In central Poland the Code was not finally abolished until 1946.[12]

The 1815 constitution preserved the independence of the courts of justice that had been guaranteed under the Duchy. Moreover, except for a few minor details, the administration of the courts retained in practice the same structure as it had during the Napoleonic era. The only really significant change was that the Council of State ceased to be a Court of Cassation, this function being transferred to the Supreme Court for civil cases, and to the Court of Appeal – another Napoleonic innovation – for criminal cases.[13] This judicial system escaped change after Polish autonomy was dismantled following the 1830–31 revolution, and was only brought into line with that of Russia with the aforementioned procedural reforms of 1876.

This brief comparison of the institutions of the Duchy of Warsaw and the Kingdom of Poland reveals the strong lines of continuity between the two. This continuity was underlined by the fact that there was no attempt to purge the political élites of men connected with the Napoleonic regime; and no politically inspired emigration from Poland took place during the Restoration years. This was in large part due to the absence of alternatives. In the period 1807–30 the constitutional order guaranteed that power remained in the hands of the prosperous gentry (the so-called *szlachta*). Given the absence of a substantial bourgeoisie, Poland's rulers had little choice but to look to this group for support. The most important offices remained concentrated in the hands of a relatively small group of families. Especially in the earliest years after the Congress of Vienna,

Alexander was keen to appoint Poles to the Kingdom's highest offices. And this, coupled with the Tsar's very real efforts to win the loyalty of his new subjects, his readiness to defend liberal reforms and the fact that he had saved the former Duchy of Warsaw from further partitions, won him enormous popularity. Recognizing that he was not anxious to persecute the former servants of the Duchy, that group in their turn were happy to seek accommodation with their new ruler. Even the most zealous 'Napoleonists' were won over. Nevertheless, Alexander also showed some caution, sometimes inclining towards the selection of men with reactionary reputations or alternatively seeking out those of a more malleable disposition. Thus, while everyone expected him to make Adam Czartoryski Governor General, he chose instead General Zajączek. Czartoryski was rich, independent and well-connected; Zajączek was an embittered invalid who viewed his own nation with contempt. While Zajączek rapidly became a symbol of passive servility, Czartoryski observed in vitriolic fashion that 'Those who degraded themselves before Napoleon, are now used by Alexander.' As Marceli Handelsman has emphasized, the Tsar appointed ministers from a relatively narrow coterie related by blood and connection. In addition the tight-knit nature of this group enabled the government to adopt a firm line in arguments with the *Sejm*.[14]

The field in which the Napoleonic period left its strongest and most significant heritage was in matters military. The retention of a Polish army was the most important symbol of the Kingdom of Poland's special status within the Russian Empire. Adam Czartoryski's project for a constitution, drafted during the Congress of Vienna, provided for an army that would preserve its national character and emblems, and would defend the monarch and the frontiers of the Kingdom. It was envisaged that the army would be permanently quartered in Poland, and could be used by the king only within Europe; in other words, the Tsar could not deploy it elsewhere in his empire, and in particular could not use it to fight on his Asian frontiers. Such a definition of the role of the national armed forces came close to that in the 1791 constitution, as well as to that of the Duchy of Warsaw. In the end a similar set of measures was adopted for the Kingdom of Poland, even though no specific mention was made of defence of national frontiers or national existence. Nevertheless, the Kingdom's army did use its national emblems and, bar the commander-in-chief, was commanded overwhelmingly by Poles. As such it could be seen as a genuinely national force. This was underlined by the fact that while 45 per cent of officers came from the Kingdom itself, a further 36 per cent were drawn from Poles in the lands annexed by Russia, Austria and Prussia. Only 13 per cent came from lands located beyond the borders of the old Poland.[15]

Under Napoleon the Polish army had numbered almost 100,000 soldiers. This figure was reduced to a mere 30,000 under Alexander's rule. However, there was no attempt at a political purge. This was in part because, with the exception of a few generals who had 'disappointed' the French Emperor, there had been no open opposition to Napoleon during the Duchy of Warsaw. Thus it was impossible to make distinctions between officers on the basis of their loyalty or otherwise to the previous regime, and there were no other cadres from which to draw officers for the new royal army. During 1814–15 the so-called *Komitet Wojskowy* (Military Committee) consisting of the Duchy's generals and presided over by the Tsar's brother, the Grand Duke Constantine, decided on the fate of individual officers. But the most important figure in this committee, as far as such decisions were concerned, was General Jan Henry Dąbrowski, usually perceived as a faithful Napoleonic officer (although by 1814 possibly privately disillusioned with the French Emperor). The slimming down of the officer corps was facilitated by the fact that many had no wish to serve the Kingdom, and requested that they be discharged. Others simply wanted to retire, or were deemed inadequate by the Committee. Certainly large numbers of officers were constrained for one reason or another to quit their military careers. Yet, although on occasion personal prejudice does seem to have played a role, the Committee's decisions on future service do not appear to have been dictated by political considerations.[16]

The generally ambivalent attitude to Napoleon's legacy was revealed in the issue of decorations. In the years 1815–30 Polish servicemen were still entitled to wear military decorations received while campaigning for Napoleon, including those medals won fighting the Russians. Quite often, therefore, a soldier might wear French, Polish and Russian decorations. This reflected a sense of corporate military identity and pride that was independent of political changes.

As mentioned already, in 1814 the Tsar's brother, Constantine, was appointed as head both of the provisional Polish army and of the Military Committee. He was to remain commander-in-chief until the Polish insurrection of 1830. He was to use this position to increase his personal authority, so that he became the unofficial ruler of the whole country. By effectively detaching the War Committee (*Komisja Wojny*) from the civilian apparatus of state, he was soon able to enjoy almost unlimited military authority. He then extended his influence in other non-military fields by pressing for the appointment of retired or even still active army officers to high-ranking civilian posts. Even more significantly, Constantine barred the civilian authorities from any control over the military budget, which in itself amounted to almost half of all state expenditure.

Constantine's autocratic methods of running the army soon proved problematic. One particular problem lay in the use of corporal punishment. The different attitudes of the Napoleonic and Tsarist armies towards this issue typified the different spirit of the two systems. Corporal punishment for soldiers had quite simply not existed under the Duchy of Warsaw, but was energetically reintroduced along Russian lines after 1815. This was just one area where the different military styles of the Duchy and the Kingdom caused tensions for the officers and men of the Polish regiments, generating conflict and opposition to the post-Vienna order. On the whole the former Napoleonic generals, broken by the defeats of 1812–13, accepted the new order and, unlike the younger officers, proved loyal to the Tsar and unwilling to join the 1830 insurrection. Yet even the older generation seem not to have forgotten the dreams of independence that had flourished in 1807–12. The Austrian diplomat, Count Carl Ludwig Fickelmont, who after 1831 criticized the effects of Alexander's over-liberal policy towards the Poles, was especially scathing of the indulgence shown towards the Polish army: 'What spirit could enliven this old band? Until the very last moment they remained under Napoleonic banners, so is there any reason to believe their loyalty to their new monarch? These units served Napoleon, the heir of all revolutions, and they served him because they never stopped waging was against the three powers that partitioned Poland!'[17]

In some senses Fickelmont was mistaken, but he got one thing absolutely right: the Polish Kingdom was undoubtedly a continuation of the Duchy of Warsaw, inheriting a number of legal institutions and the Duchy's basic military establishment. However, the greatest legacy of the Napoleonic period was that it once again returned the Polish question to a central position in international affairs, while simultaneously reawakening hopes of the rebirth of a Polish state. As Jerzy Skowronek points out, the pejorative term 'Congress Poland' was not used in the period 1815–30 (the term did not become general until considerably later); instead people referred simply to the 'Kingdom of Poland' or plain 'Poland'. Indeed, if the last was considered misleading, it was not because of the Kingdom's position in a legal sense, or because it was not considered a genuine state, but simply because there were large areas of Poland that were not included within its frontiers. According to Skowronek, Poles were prepared to accept the 'doctrine of reduced liberty', but in return demanded that the compromise reached in 1815 should be fully honoured by the Tsar. Before 1830 Polish conspirators did not actually demand independence. Instead, they wanted simply to defend the 1815 settlement, and perhaps to extend the Kingdom to include the Lithuanian lands (a potentiality for which some provision had been made at the Congress of Vienna).[18]

But the Polish situation was a paradoxical one, reflecting the ambiguities both of the Napoleonic legacy and of the position of Tsar Alexander himself. After 1815, the bizarre situation existed in which the most autocratic monarch in Europe, on crossing the River Bug, became the ruler of a constutional state. As Prince Piotr Wiaziemski remarked: 'Will the Polish constitution soften the Russian despotism, or will Russian despotism snatch the Polish constitution in its claws?' In the end the peculiar legacy of Napoleonic institutions and practices in Poland would prove irreconcilable with the Tsarist regime to the east.[19] In part this was because both Grand Duke Constantine and the unofficial supervisor of the Polish government, the Russian senator, Prince Nikolai Novosiltzov, were ill-disposed to the Polish constitution and prone to disregard it. However, the real problem lay in the contradictions inherent within the institutions themselves.

While the Polish Kingdom inherited the *Sejm* it also inherited a long-standing tradition of parliamentary opposition. In 1807, when Napoleon drew up the constitution, the Polish representative assemblies were granted much wider powers than those permitted by other Napoleonic constitutions. These concessions were partly made to a strong parliamentary tradition that dated back to the fifteenth century; but they were also intended to encourage Polish support for the new order. By 1811 a relatively active opposition had developed within the *Sejm*, and, in accordance with Enlightenment traditions, its criticisms of government policy were printed and distributed widely across the Duchy. This vociferous opposition continued after 1815. Liberals in the *Sejm* actively condemned the Tsar's systematic violations of the constitution, most notably the removal of the military budget from civilian control, and the 1819 introduction of censorship. This opposition brought the *Sejm* into direct conflict with the Tsar himself. Before 1813 confrontation with the government was not considered to be a hostile act, perhaps because the opposition, although vocal, was not especially well-organized. However, after 1818 the Tsar began to consider any criticism from the *Sejm*, however justified on legal grounds, to be a personal attack, which had to be fiercely combated. A sharp contradiction had, therefore, developed between the letter and the spirit of the law. Between 1818 and 1820, when the *Sejm* actually rejected government proposals for legal changes, the situation deteriorated dramatically, and Alexander became more determined than ever to stamp out opposition. By the time the third *Sejm* was convened in 1825, a special amendment had been introduced ordering that parliamentary debates be held behind closed doors, and that major opponents of the government should not be allowed to take seats in the assembly.

The fate of the Kingdom of Poland's relatively liberal system was further undermined by events beyond its frontiers. The increasingly reactionary climate of restoration Europe (embodied by the Troppau Protocol of 1820 and the use of force against revolts in Italy and the Iberian peninsula), and the constant hostility of Russian élites to the Polish constitution meant that an increasingly unfavourable climate had developed by the early 1820s. The pressure exerted by the Poles to try to effect closer links between the Kingdom and Lithuania also contributed to bad blood that would sooner or later lead to open conflict. Finally, a generation of Poles too young to have been disheartened by the defeats of 1812–14 had reached maturity. Matters were not helped by the Tsar's response to the growing discontent in the Kingdom. Rather than seeking accommodation he greeted conspiracy and agitation with repression in both Vilnius and Warsaw, with the Tsarist police assuming an ever more active rôle. It became increasingly clear that the Tsar was eager to break the constitutional compromise of 1815.

It was in this atmosphere of repression and heightened tensions that the era of Napoleon came to be idealized. The French diplomat, Béchu de la Sensée, commented with surprise in August 1820 on the simultaneous admiration of young Poles for both the former French Emperor *and* the liberal theories of Benjamin Constant. As he remarked, the strange myth of Napoleon 'the liberal patron of freedom' had developed on the banks of the Vistula not only before the publication of Las Cases's *Memorial de Sainte Hélène*, but even before Napoleon had died.[20] Béchu was quick to see that liberalism and freedom did not mean the same thing on the Vistula as on the banks of the Seine. However, any hope that either liberalism or freedom might survive in a Russian-controlled Kingdom of Poland was to evaporate with the death of Alexander. The 1825 succession of Nicholas I, fiercely reactionary and absolutist, could only accelerate the end of the constitutional experiment, although it was not until the outbreak of military mutiny and open rebellion that the Tsar would be able to silence the *Sejm* once and for all.

Notes

1. W. H. Zawadzki, 'Russia and the Re-opening of the Polish Question, 1801–1814', *International History Review*, 7 (1985), pp.17–44.
2. For the Polish question at the Vienna Congress see *Historia Dyplomacji Polskiej* (Warsaw, 1982), Vol. 2, pp.116–25; H. Kissinger, *Le chemin de la paix* (Paris, 1972), pp.194–210; W. H. Zawadzki, 'Adam Czartoryski: An Advocate of Slavic Solidarity at the Congress of Vienna', *Oxford Slavonic Papers*, new series 10 (1977), pp.73–97.
3. The greatest part of the Warsaw archives dealing with the the Duchy of Warsaw, the Supreme Provisional Council and the period of transition was destroyed during the Warsaw insurrection of 1944. In consequence the following old works are still invaluable: J. Bojasinski, *Rządy Tymczasowe w Królestwie Polskim* (Warsaw, 1902); K. Bartoszewicz, *Utworzenie Krolestwa Kongresowego* (Cracow, 1916).
4. The fullest treatment of the Kingdom of Poland in English is F. W. Thakeray, *Antecedents of Revolution: Alexander I and the Polish Kingdom 1815–25* (Boulder, CO, 1980). On attempts to inroduce the constitutional system in Russia see S. Mironenko, *Samoderzhavie i reformy. Polticheskaia borba v Rossii v nachale XIX veka* (Moscow, 1989). An interesting paper on Alexander's motives for pursuing a liberal policy is J. Skowronek, 'Eksperyment liberalizmu parlamentarnego w Królestwie Polskim', *Przegląd Humanistyczny*, 39 (1995), pp.1–14.
5. S. Askenay, *Rosya-Polska 1815–1830* (Lwow, 1907), pp.66–8. The English text of the Constitution can be found in A. T. Pienkos, *The Imperfect Autocrat: Grand Duke Constantine Pavlovich and the Polish Congress Kingdom* (Boulder, CO, 1987), pp.152–72.
6. Bartoszewicz, *Utworzenie*, pp.222–3.
7. M. Senkowska-Gluck, 'Les institutions napoléoniennes dans l'histoire de la nation polonaise', in *L'Epoque napoléonienne et les Slaves* (Wroclaw, 1982), pp.51–4.
8. J. Skowronek, 'Skład społeczny i polityczny sejmów Ksiestwa Warszawskiego i Królestwa Kongresowego', *Przegląd Historyczny*, 52 (1961), pp.468–9, 476. T. Mencel, 'Prawo wyborcze w Księstwie Warszawskim i Królestwie Polskim (1807–1830) na tle porównawczym', in *Pamiętnik X Powszechnego Zjazdu Historyków Polskich w Lublinie* (Lublin, 1969), p.40. The most detailed anlysis is in idem, 'Udział spoleczeństwa w życiu politycznym Królestwa Polskiego w latach 1815–1830', *Przegląd Historyczny*, (1968), pp.629–61.

9. Senkowska-Gluck, 'Les institutions', pp.53–4.

10. H. Grynwaser, 'Le Code Napoléon dans la Duché de Varsowie', *Revue des Etudes Napoléoniennes*, 12 (1917), pp.129–70; T. Mencel, 'L'introduction du Code Napoléon dans la Duché de Varsovie 1808', *Czasopismo Prawno-Historyczne*, 2 (1949), pp.141–98; W. Sobociński, 'J. W. Bandtkie, obrońca Kodeksu Napoleona', *Rocznik Lubelski*, 3 (1960); idem, 'Quelques observations sur le bilan social de la Pologne en 1815: questions juridiques et sociales', *Acta Poloniae Historica*, 14 (1966), pp.105–16.

11. A. Wronski, 'Duchowieństwo katolickie a sprawa narodowa w Krolestwie Polskim w latach dwudziestych i trzydziestych XIX w.', *Studia z dziejów polskiej myśli politycznej*, 4 (1992), p.126.

12. K. Sojka-Zielińska, 'La reception du Code Napoléon en Pologne', in *Rapports au huitième Congrès International de Droit Comparé* (Warsaw, 1970), pp.210–20.

13. Napoleonic penal procedures had never been introduced to Poland, and the penal code introduced in 1818 had no origins in the French system.

14. M. Handelsman, 'Kryzys r. 1821 w Królestwie Polskim', *Kwartalnik Historyczyny* (1939), p.230.

15. M. Tarczyński, 'Le rôle de l'armée dans le développement social de Pologne dans les années 1807–1831', in *L'armée aux époques des grandes transformations sociales* (Warsaw, 1980), pp.43–4.

16. Dąbrowski served from 1797 to 1814, but by the time the Duchy of Warsaw collapsed he seems to have become secretly disillusioned with Napoleon.

17. M. Tarczyński, *Generalicja Powstania Listopadowego* (Warsaw, 1980), pp.25–48.

18. K. D. Fickelmont, *Lord Palmerston, l'Angleterre et le Continent*, Vol. II (Paris, 1852), p.81.

19. J. Skowronek, 'Idea niepodległości narodowej w polskiej myśli politycznej pierwszej połowy XIX w.', *Przegląd Humanistyczny*, (1989), pp.21–2.

20. P. Wiaziemski, *Z notatnikow i listow* (Cracow, 1985), pp.24–5.

8

The Napoleonic Legacy in the Rhineland and the Politics of Reform in Restoration Prussia

Michael Rowe

In 1837 the radical Rhenish publicist and opponent of the Prussians, Jakob Venedey, mused in his diary:

> Nothing is more a mystery to me than how committed liberals, and even republicans, can be enthusiastic about Napoleon, a man who stigmatized their views as 'ideology', who saw nothing noble in mankind, and whose achieve- ment as the greatest egotist of all time was, appropriately, only constructed upon the selfishness of others.[1]

Venedey personified the radical republican tradition in the Rhineland. Brought up in the spirit of Rousseau by a father who was a former member of the revolutionary club in Mainz, Jakob continued the family tradition of opposing authoritarian government by criticizing the Prussians after 1815.[2] The elevation of Napoleon to liberal icon in the Rhineland, commented upon by Venedey, requires explanation. At one level one might dismiss this phenomenon with the observation that Napoleon, and symbols of France generally, were simply seized upon by Rhinelanders throughout the nineteenth century as provocative material for the construction of a counter-culture in opposition to the Francophobe Prussians.[3] In what follows, I argue that support for much of the Napoleonic legacy in the region was constructed upon more substantial foundations than this.

The Rhineland's geographical location in the extreme west of German-speaking Europe dictated that it experienced the impact of the French Revolution relatively early. Exploitation and revolutionary extremism followed the French occupation of 1794.[4] The princes and archbishop-electors fled across the Rhine, abandoning local élites to their own devices. Those left behind suddenly found official responsibilities thrust upon them. Some successfully rose to the challenge, gaining experience in public affairs. They took the initiative in drawing up petitions, negotiating with French military commanders, bribing key officials, and extending loans or providing supplies out of their own funds to meet the quotas imposed on their communities by the revolutionary authorities. This education would continue under Napoleon, albeit it in the more orderly confines of the advisory councils, electoral colleges and chambers of commerce into which local notables were enticed.

The Napoleonic coup of 19 November 1799 saw the establishment of peace, security and stability on the left (west) bank of the Rhine, which was officially annexed to France in March 1801. Unlike in Italy, the preceding decade of revolutionary turmoil could not be blamed on Bonaparte personally; Napoleonic reforms, notably the law codes, simply consolidated earlier, revolutionary decrees. Instead, the new régime consciously portrayed itself as one of restoration. The resonance this theme struck locally is reflected in the language used in the addresses in support of Napoleon's assumption of the imperial title. 'Men and things have been put back in their place' stated one, whilst another declared that Napoleon sensed 'the necessity of returning to the principles and the foundations of social order which the experience of centuries have confirmed'.[5] The Napoleonic administration openly dismissed the earlier period of French rule as an anarchic interlude, whilst at the same time rehabilitating the *ancien régime* image of the electorates and principalities.[6] A record of solid achievement, including the restoration of international peace at Lunéville, the Concordat with the Papacy, the suppression of banditry, the abolition of revolutionary symbols and festivities, and the return of stolen relics and artistic objects, helped give official claims of restoration credibility. To quote the Freemasons of Aachen, Napoleon appeared the restorer of 'interrupted harmony'.[7] This applied also to local administration, including matters relating to personnel. Though talented radicals and republicans generally remained in their posts, they were now joined by many former servants of the *ancien régime*.[8] The government trumpeted such cases of *ralliement* – the 'rallying' of old élites to the new régime – as evidence for the restoration of legitimate order.[9]

Napoleonic rule rested essentially upon the immutable class of local notables, the so-called *masses de granit*, defined officially as the top six hundred property-tax payers per department. It was a politically inclusive though socially exclusive group defined by landed wealth, and consisted in the Rhineland mainly of an amalgamation of the new business élite and the old nobility.[10] The latter element remained peculiarly resilient in the northern part of the Rhineland, the area that would fall to Prussia after 1815. Its socio-economic position was hardly affected by the abolition of 'feudalism' and noble tithes. Its wealth, unlike that of its southern counterpart, was based directly on the ownership of land and the payment of money-rent by tenants, and not on feudal dues or employment in princely courts and cathedral chapters.[11] Rather, the northern nobility, like other landowners, benefited from the secularization and sale of the vast landed property of the Catholic Church.

The real losers in the Napoleonic period were the small craftsmen and merchants organized in guilds. Conflicts in Rhenish towns in the final years of the *ancien régime* often revolved around underlying socio-economic tensions between this group and the rising class of wealthy businessmen. Napoleonic rule saw that conflict decided in favour of the latter: the guilds were abolished, and legal restrictions obstructing the business élite removed. Though the territorial fragmentation of the *ancien régime* had represented less of a barrier to development than is often claimed, thanks in part to the putting-out system, the removal of the plethora of internal frontiers and other hindrances nevertheless contributed to future economic expansion.[12] Growing differentiation between the pinnacle of the economic élite, and the larger class of craftsmen, shopkeepers and guild members below, was reinforced by the sale of secularized church property, which accounted for a staggering 10 per cent of cultivatable land in the four departments into which the Rhineland was divided.[13] Napoleonic France, unlike some of its German satellites, made no attempt at selling this mass in modest parcels to encourage small farmers. Instead, most was purchased by the wealthy urbanized business élite.[14] The sale of secularized monasteries at knock-down prices encouraged industrial concentration, not social equality.[15] The composition of the economic élite itself changed little during the two decades of French rule. Probably less than 10 per cent could be considered 'new men'. Only those with capital stood to benefit from the opportunities of Napoleonic rule.[16]

The administrative, judicial and representative institutions introduced by Napoleon reflected the developing Rhenish social order. In practice, they proved less bureaucratic and centralized than in theory. Paris enjoyed diminished control over local appointments because of unofficial prior local pre-selection, which resulted in a lack of candidates; and bureaucratic discipline became unenforceable in circumstances where no one was willing to replace those sacked for misconduct. Municipal councils convened illegally to aid mayors in the administration, because this conformed with the old way of doing things, whilst elsewhere bilingual secretaries, over whom the government had no control, performed all the important duties. Even military conscription, often held up as the worst example of Napoleonic state-building and despotism, afforded local Rhenish administrators ample opportunities to exercise their patronage over clients through supplying them with substitutes. The elected departmental and district councils, which were dominated by the notables thanks to the plutocratic electoral arrangements, together with the newly created chambers of commerce, allowed the élite to present its grievances to the government.[17] Of particular significance, given its controversial position during the Prussian period, was the Napoleonic judiciary, one of the few 'French' institutions that was almost completely composed of native Rhinelanders. These, drawing on their heritage of exploiting the old imperial law to preserve their privileges, similarly used the new French law codes to temper Napoleonic despotism. This sustainable, flexible system eventually came under threat not from Rhinelanders, but from Napoleon himself during the final years of his reign. His increasingly autocratic methods and determination to enforce ever tighter centralized control – as manifested in the special police commissioners, special non-jury courts, stricter censorship, and other arbitrary measures – together with the unprecedented levies of conscripts in 1813, threatened to destroy the stable order established earlier in his reign. The allied invasion of January 1814 came just in time to preserve the best aspects of Napoleonic rule on the Rhine.

Many contemporaries mistook the collapse of Napoleonic hegemony as Germany's *Stunde Null*. The public debate over the future territorial and political settlement conducted in 1814 and 1815 wrongly assumed that things could be planned from the ground up.[18] The Rhineland, as 'vacant territory', assumed central importance in this debate – which combined territorial, constitutional and political issues – as it would inevitably serve as compensation for losses incurred by powers elsewhere. The inter-allied Central Administration, headed by the former leading light of the Prussian reform movement, the Freiherr vom Stein, assumed initial responsibility for the governance of territories vacated by the French. Stein emanated from the former imperial nobility, which had lost its quasi-sovereign status as a result of the Napoleonic reordering of Germany. He had many axes to grind. In particular, he loathed the newly sovereign states of the former Confederation of the Rhine, whose territorial accretions had been at the expense of nobles like himself. Under his stewardship, the blandly-named Central Administration became a highly political instrument that attempted to further the cause of German unity by establishing facts on the ground.[19] In this he received the support of other Prussian reformers, but was opposed by the Austrian chancellor,

Metternich, and all the smaller German states.

The 'Germanization' of Rhinelanders was one ingredient of the Central Administration's policy. This was in part to ensure that the Rhine would regain its status as a German river at the coming peace settlement. The policy also conformed with the hatred felt by Stein and many others for Germans who had 'collaborated' with Napoleon. 'Believe me', Stein once wrote, 'all who have served the enemy, and all without exception, can be used but not trusted.'[20] Justus Gruner, Governor General of the Middle Rhine (one of the two allied general governments into which the four Rhenish departments were grouped; the other was the General Government of the Lower Rhine, under Johann August Sack) and another important figure in the Prussian reform movement, was particularly enthusiastic in his encouragement of German patriotism.[21] To assist in this he enlisted the services of German nationalists, including Ernst Moritz Arndt and Joseph Görres. The latter, himself a native Rhinelander who had initially welcomed the French before turning against them, was particularly influential through his mouthpiece, the *Rheinischer Merkur*, the most important German newspaper from its inception in January 1814 until its suppression by the Prussian government two years later. A recurring theme in the *Merkur* was condemnation of bureaucracy as Napoleon's most pernicious legacy to Germany.[22] Görres's abuse extended to those Germans, including Rhinelanders, who had served within the French administration. 'Never before was hatred more justified than against the French and their collaborators', he concluded in one article.[23] Arndt, who travelled through the Rhineland in April to June 1814, was even less discriminating in his condemnation of the region's inhabitants. Its urban élites, he wrote, were 'depraved and poisoned', its youth 'on the whole feeble', and fifteen out of sixteen native officials pro-French.[24] The fact that notables in cities such as Aachen and Cologne spoke French better than what was considered to be good German was held up as further proof of their lack of national fibre.[25] Arndt in particular condemned cosmopolitan societies, such as Masonic lodges, for importing the French language onto German soil, thereby aiding and abetting Napoleonic hegemony.[26]

The German nationalist rhetoric had surprisingly little impact on the actual personnel policy pursued by either Gruner or Sack. Both were too preoccupied in supplying the needs of the allied forces marching through their general governments to risk an upheaval in the local administration. Despite some real misgivings,[27] they instead defended the authority of the local administration inherited from the French, sometimes with military force. Sack, following the principles of his friend and mentor

Stein, involved local property-owners in public affairs. He mobilized the business élite, as represented in the Napoleonic chambers of commerce, seeking their assistance in the alleviation of the serious fiscal position caused by the ongoing war and the consequent need for military supplies.[28] He also appointed special cantonal commissioners, again recruited from amongst the notables, to supervise local government.[29] Far from being in a position to be choosy, Sack encountered the problem of finding suitable individuals willing to shoulder public responsibilities. Few notables were willing to serve as either mayors or councillors, even in the bigger cities.[30] It was hardly surprising given these circumstances that the allied, and later the Prussian, authorities were extremely reluctant to dismiss local officials, no matter what their position with regard to Napoleon. The result was continuity at the local level. All that changed was the terminology: '*préfets*' became '*Gouvernementskommissaren*', '*sous-préfets*' '*Kreisdirektoren*', and '*maires*' '*Bürgermeister*'.

Other changes instituted by the governors-general at this time improved rather than threatened the French legacy. The abolition of such Napoleonic institutions as the dreaded special non-jury courts and special police commissioners, accretions of the later, autocratic years of French rule, together with tighter restrictions on the use of particularly harsh punishments such as branding, marked a return not to the *ancien régime*, but to the more liberal principles of the Consulate.[31] In later years, when Rhinelanders spoke of their liberal French institutions, they were in fact referring to a legacy they had inherited not directly from Napoleon, but via Prussian reformers. The latter's initial hostility to all things French gave way to recognition of some of the strengths of Napoleonic institutions. As early as June 1814 Sack expressed his support for the French jury system in a letter to his friend and ally, General Gneisenau, who was then commander of the Prussian forces on the Rhine. He even recommended its general introduction throughout Prussia.[32] In this he sought Gneisenau's support, for he counted upon resistance from conservative forces in Berlin, or the 'obscurantism' of the 'Hatzfeldt–Schuckmann–Wittgenstein clique', as he preferred to describe it in one of his letters to Stein.[33] Thus began half-a-century's institutionalized centre–periphery conflict between Berlin and the Rhineland over the Napoleonic legacy.

The Rhineland's *de jure* annexation to Prussia in April 1815 coincided with the rebound of conservative confidence within the monarchy following the initial shock of 1806 and subsequent reforms. Despite much progress, the monarchy's administrative and constitutional order remained unresolved, and the struggle between reformers and conservatives undecided.[34] The latter had formulated an ideological response to the reforms, providing intellectual justification for the preservation of a paternalistic nobility as a privileged estate and prop to the monarchical order. At the same time, conservatives condemned the nascent bourgeoisie as a rootless oligarchy of usurers and speculators, a despotism of money that threatened to dissolve the social order. The defeat of state-chancellor Karl August von Hardenberg's *Gendarmerie Edikt* of 1812 marked the limits of reform, and paved the way for the East-Elbian nobility's reconquest of local and central government.[35] The incorporation of the west came just too late to swing the balance back decisively in favour of reform; an opportunity for Prussia to modernize further was let slip. The subsequent conflict between Prussian conservatism and the monarchy's new Rhenish and Westphalian provinces became symptomatic of the *Sonderweg*, the failure of Germany's 'feudal' élite to step aside quietly and make way for the bourgeoisie.

Within weeks of the annexation, the Prussian government issued two important cabinet-orders: the first (30 April 1815) provided for wide-ranging reform of provincial and local government; the second (22 May 1815) promised the establishment of a representational body for the monarchy. This last initiative was couched in sufficiently vague terms – it variously mentioned 'representation of the people', and an 'assembly of representatives of the land' – to raise the hopes of conservatives, who favoured representation by estate, and reformers, who favoured legal equality. Constitutional and administrative reforms were inextricably linked.[36] Hardenberg remained determined to complete the modernization of the administration before embarking on constitutional reforms that might produce assemblies packed with his conservative opponents. As a result of these considerations, the constitutional commission, which had been planned to start work in September 1815, was postponed. Conflict over the future of the Rhineland's French institutions was quickly subsumed into this wider debate over the character of the new Prussia.

Prussian conservatives, as Görres recognized at an early stage, viewed the new provinces as centres of revolutionary contagion.[37] Ironically, they adopted the same strident nationalistic rhetoric as Görres and Arndt in attacking Napoleonic institutions. They similarly accused Rhinelanders of betraying their national character in favour of superficial French principles. East-Elbian officials of a conservative stamp posted to the west felt themselves duty-bound to 'root out all impure foreign filth in customs, language and dress',[38] and bring new values to 'that shallow, ignorant, quibbling lawyer-folk'.[39] They condemned the French system of local government as 'an institution of foreign rule', whilst justifying their own projects as an attempt to restore the 'old German autonomy of the communes', in accordance with the 'German character'. They blamed the large-scale sale of secularized property for destroying the hard-working and honest character of the Rhenish middle classes.[40] In Berlin, the Prussian privy-councillor and later minister of justice, Karl Albert von Kamptz, in his semi-official *Annalen der Preußischen innern Staats-Verwaltung*, condemned supposedly 'artificial' French judicial institutions, such as the jury system, as unsuitable for Germans. Rhinelanders, he admonished, should re-conform to 'German customs, German convictions and the German way of thinking'. The appointment of 'old Prussians' from the east, he hoped, would help propagate 'German practices and habits'.[41] The minister of the interior, Schuckmann, used similar arguments in early 1816 in support of his attempts retroactively to annul marriages conducted under French law unless they were confirmed in a religious ceremony. He wrote: 'we are dealing with a people who, under the rhetoric of liberal toleration, have been driven to and fro in the excrement of revolutionary immorality. It is therefore necessary that the new régime present itself as a strict, religious moral judge, rather than reinforce the previous indifference'.[42] Conservatives would employ similar rhetoric throughout the nineteenth century, the implication always being that Rhinelanders were the carriers of foreign contagion, be it French, Habsburg or Catholic.[43] Prussia derived its legitimacy on the Rhine as protector of Germany's western frontier against France. Unfortunately, Rhinelanders themselves hoped for defence only against French expansionism, not French institutions.

The condemnation of reform as an alien imposition was a continuation of the rhetoric employed within Prussia itself since the beginning of the Stein–Hardenberg reforms, which had been condemned by conservatives from the outset as the work of 'foreigners'.[44] These claims were not entirely without justification. Indeed, many of the reformers, including Sack, were natives of Cleves, the administrative centre of the old Prussian enclaves along the Rhine that Berlin had ceded to France in 1795. Many had served under Stein as the senior Prussian official in the area at the time of the French occupation. Most subsequently decided to emigrate, preferring to remain in Prussian service rather than become Frenchmen. Many later rose in the Prussian administration. In the mid-1820s ten out of the two dozen or so Prussian district governors, or *Regierungs-präsidenten*, originated from Cleves.[45] By that time Sack was serving as provincial governor (*Oberpräsident*) of Pomerania. Before his transfer in 1816, conservatives accused him of packing the provincial Rhenish administration with like-minded friends and numerous in-laws, or '*Säcken und Sackvettern'*, as one opponent contemptuously described them.[46] Amongst these in-laws was his wife's brother, Georg von Reimann, who served as district governor of Aachen from 1816 to 1834.[47] Another was Christoph Wilhelm Sethe, of whom more below.

The resulting institutionalized centre–periphery conflict would be brought into sharper relief following the central government's lurch towards reaction in 1819 in the aftermath of Kotzebue's assassination and the Carlsbad Decrees. There followed the persecution of the 'demagogues', those radicals and subversives attempting to overthrow the existing order in Germany. The Rhineland, according to the 429-page report produced by the special committee established at Mainz to investigate subversion, was a centre for the 'party, which works for the political reorganization of Germany', an elusive group whose members had been encouraged by Gruner and Gneisenau in particular, under the guise of 'Germanizing' the left bank.[48] In this hostile, anti-liberal climate, the western provincial governors saw themselves, more than before, as the guardians of earlier reform.[49] A renewed wave of suspicion followed the 1830 revolutions in neighbouring Belgium and France. On this occasion, Berlin commissioned secret policemen to spy on the provincial administration and the 'unreliable' local judiciary, as well as on known revolutionaries linked to 'the foreign party of movement'.[50]

Conservative East-Elbian attacks provoked indignation in the western provinces, especially when accompanied by the daily arrogance faced by civilians at the hands of Prussian soldiers on Rhenish streets.[51] Rhinelanders had their own fears and prejudices concerning the Prussians, or 'Litauer' as they called them.[52] Some of this hostility dated from the Seven Years War, and to Prussia's duplicitous policy in the 1790s, culminating in its betrayal of the *Reich* at Basle in 1795. Added to this was deeply ingrained popular terror of Prussian militarism.[53] The concentration of garrisons in the *Rheinprovinz*, even after Napoleon's defeat, hardly produced a situation conducive to dispelling some of these fears.[54] Nor were all Rhenish stereotypes entirely without justification. The East-Elbian nobility did enjoy wide scope for the exercise of arbitrary authority: the Prussian alternative to the Napoleonic codes, the *Allgemeines Landrecht* (ALR), permitted noble estate-owners to imprison their peasants for forty-eight hours without a court ruling. Nor did the lower courts have much effect in hindering more brutal behaviour on the eastern estates, reports of which occasionally filtered out to the west. Equally offensive for the majority of Rhinelanders were all the trappings that accompanied the privileged, noble culture of Prussia. The fact that the ALR devoted 152 paragraphs to offences against honour hardly recommended it to the 'new Prussians' of the west.[55]

Rhinelanders also considered Prussia economically backward, and therefore exploitative. This view was summed up in the banker Abraham Schaaffhausen's supposed exclamation upon hearing of the Rhineland's fate in 1815: 'Jesus, Mary and Joseph! We *have* married into a poor family.'[56] Accusations of Prussian exploitation, of tax revenues being siphoned off to subsidize the eastern provinces and of the burden being higher than under the French, of lucrative government posts going to East Elbians, of Rhinelanders being discriminated against when it came to state pensions for veterans, of the western provinces having to support excessively large garrisons, and so on, recurred in the decades following annexation.[57] These accusations of eastern exploitation took place in the context of the depressed economic climate of the Restoration. French reports at the time of the allied invasion speak of tens of thousands of unemployed workers in the Rhenish departments.[58] Prussian fiscal stringency and, more seriously, the disruption of Napoleonic trade patterns by new trade barriers erected by the Netherlands – now including Belgium – and France hit Rhenish exports. Prussia's liberal trade policy, meanwhile, opened the floodgates to a deluge of British imports.[59] The Continental System had nurtured industries that proved fragile when confronted with the cold breeze of competition blowing in from across the English Channel.[60] A series of poor harvests after 1815 completed the picture of economic woe.[61]

Expansion westwards brought with it Prussian fears not only of liberal pollution, but also of Catholic contamination. After 1815, Catholics made up two-fifths of the monarchy's previously overwhelmingly Protestant population. Subsequent confessional mistrust between the predominantly Catholic west and Protestant east provided an added ingredient to centre–periphery conflict. This was not a legacy solely of French rule, but dated in part from the eighteenth century, when Prussia was regarded by the Protestant minorities scattered in the Rhineland as a protector, and by Catholics as hostile. The major French contribution was the destruction of much of the Catholic Church's wealth and temporal power in the 1790s. In some respects, the Church emerged strengthened by this. At the grass-roots level in particular, the abolition of various feudal dues and tithes removed areas of conflict with the lay population. Furthermore, the dissolution of the Rhenish prince-bishoprics in the 1790s paved the way for the resurgence of Papal power in the nineteenth century. The impact of this dual legacy of traditional Catholic mistrust, and a Church that was more spiritual and Ultramontane, was not felt immediately after 1815. In practice, the Prussian authorities simply imposed the same restrictions on manifestations of public religiosity and baroque piety as had their predecessors.[62] The Organic Articles and Concordat inherited from Napoleon similarly remained in force, despite Papal protests. However, what was acceptable from the Catholic French was unacceptable from the Protestant Prussians. By 1819 Görres – himself a Catholic – was publicly condemning 'Protestant zealots' within the Prussian government for undermining the Catholic Church.[63] The first major breach occurred over mixed marriages, ignited by the cabinet-order of 17 August 1825, which decreed that children of mixed marriages should be raised in the religion of their fathers. This conflict escalated dramatically in the 1830s, culminating in the arrest of the Archbishop of Cologne by the Prussian authorities. This in turn led directly to the formation of a politically coherent 'Catholic party' – the forerunner of the Catholic Centre Party – at the 6th Rhenish diet of 1841.[64]

Johann Friedrich Benzenberg, the 'first Rhenish liberal', once wrote that Rhinelanders accepted rule from Berlin in order to remain German, not in order to become Prussian.[65] In practice, this formula meant protecting Napoleonic institutions, whilst at the same time wishing to preserve the essentially German culture and language of the region. The most important and fought-over of these institutions was the judiciary. Opposition to this particular Napoleonic legacy was led by, amongst others, Friedrich Karl von Savigny, the founder and spokesman of the new 'historical' school of law. Napoleonic institutions might be suited for France, he argued, where they marked the natural culmination of the revolutionary process; for Germany they represented a foreign implant heralding artificial change. Friedrich Leopold von Kircheisen, an official of the 'Prussian-Frederican' stamp who held the justice portfolio in Berlin from 1810 to 1825, agreed. He was determined that the ALR should be introduced immediately in the new western provinces.

Opposition to these plans initially emanated from amongst reformers within the Prussian administration rather than from Rhinelanders. Sack, supported by Hardenberg, successfully employed bureaucratic delaying tactics to block Kircheisen.[66] The minister made the tactical error of appointing Sack's brother-in-law, Sethe, as special commissioner charged with paving the way for the introduction of the ALR. Sethe reported in September 1815 that French judicial procedure was superior to the Prussian in criminal law.[67] Hardenberg thereupon suspended the extension of the ALR westwards, and set up yet another commission, the *Immediat-Justiz-Kommission* (IJK), to conduct further investigations. Manoeuvring with his customary skill, he outflanked Kircheisen by appointing Karl Friedrich Beyme as 'minister for the revision of legislation' with responsibility for the IJK. Beyme was both open to reform and enjoyed excellent relations with the king. The IJK consulted widely, not only taking soundings from jurists, but also accepting the complaints of ordinary Rhinelanders, who formed the habit of appealing to the commission against arbitrary policing by junior Prussian officials. Thus, the IJK connected abstract principles with the down-to-earth issues that affected the everyday lives of ordinary people.[68]

Not that Rhenish jurists were entirely absent from the debate. Alexander von Daniels in particular played an important role in determining the final shape of the IJK's report. Former students of the Napoleonic law school in Koblenz similarly agitated in favour of French law.[69] The IJK completed its work in 1818 and, despite condemnation from Kamptz and some last-minute manoeuvring by Kircheisen, presented a report recommending the preservation of the French judicial system in the Rhineland until the general revision of Prussian law.[70] This was enshrined in the cabinet-order of 19 November 1818. French law would remain in force in the Rhineland until 1 January 1900. The IJK had completed its work just in time. The following year (1819) witnessed the forced resignation of the remaining liberal ministers in the Prussian government, including Beyme, following their opposition to the Carlsbad Decrees.

The preservation of the Napoleonic law codes and legal procedure in turn made it difficult to replace other French institutions; hardly any Prussian law could be introduced in the Rhineland without modification.[71] There was little that could be done about this following the cabinet-order of 19 November 1818. A frontal attack against French law was now impossible; instead, its opponents resorted to salami tactics. One of the first manifestations of this was the cabinet-order of 6 March 1821, which directed that crimes against the state and infractions by public officials would come within the purview of ALR, even if committed in the Rhineland. Equally pernicious from the point of view of the principle of equality was the cabinet-order of 2 August 1822. This stated that army officers should only be questioned in military, not civilian, courts. If it were essential that an officer testify in a case in a civilian court, then he could only be questioned by one of the judges and not a lawyer, and his statement was then to be read out.[72] The cabinet-order of 17 April 1830 exempted privileged landowners from Napoleonic legislation concerning hunting rights.[73] Other conservative inroads included the cabinet-orders of 16 January 1836 and 21 January 1837, which exempted the Rhenish nobility from French legislation concerning succession and inheritance. These measures kept the controversy surrounding French law on the boil. The cabinet-orders of 1836 and 1837 provoked a particularly strong reaction in the Rhineland. Secret police reports singled out 'the judicial party and its particular adherents', together with senior provincial officials, for mobilizing public opinion against the measures. One report went so far as to accuse leading Rhenish judicial officials of being separatists, and accused the liberally-inclined provincial governor, Bodelschwingh, of spreading rumours against the Minister of Justice, Kamptz.[74] The Rhenish diet of 1837 demanded that all attempts to replace the French codes cease immediately, and that cabinet-orders infringing the principle of legal equality be repealed forthwith.[75]

The Prussian government utilized the Rhenish nobility – or rather ex-nobility, as it was following French rule – as a tool for undermining the principle of legal equality in the Rhineland, as can be seen in a couple of the cabinet-orders cited in the previous paragraph. Conservatives in Berlin saw a revived Rhenish nobility as a bridge between the region and the rest of the monarchy, and as a Trojan Horse that would pave the way for the integration of the west on the east's terms. Attempts by the Prussian government to recreate a privileged Rhenish nobility of birth aroused opposition from the rest of the Napoleonic class of notables. Even in the north, where they remained strongest, former nobles accounted for only approximately 6 per cent of the land, concentrated in the hands of about twenty families.[76] They had nonetheless become effective lobbyists, gaining especially valuable experience at the Congress of Vienna, where a united Rhenish 'nobility' first emerged out of the need to present a common front. In their subsequent efforts they enjoyed the support of powerful allies, including Stein and the Prussian Crown Prince.[77] Their opponents included most of the Prussian administration in the Rhineland, which publicly and provocatively refused to acknowledge any privileged titles abolished by the French.

Plans to recreate a Rhenish nobility as a separate, privileged estate, were quickly subsumed within the wider constitutional debate. As we have seen, Hardenberg postponed the convocation of the constitutional commission that was supposed to transform the vague declaration of 22 May 1815 into legislative fact. The actual composition of the planned commission now opened up a new front between reformers, who put forward schemes for representation that resembled Napoleonic arrangements, and the conservatives.[78] The latter demanded that the influence of the western provincial governors in constitutional matters should be curtailed, as they were clearly motivated by 'party spirit'. The conservatives then won the vital skirmish over the composition of the commission, paving the way for final victory, in the form of the diets *organized by estate* set up in each of the monarchy's provinces in 1823–4. Soon thereafter Berlin issued another cabinet-order (18 January 1826), re-establishing hereditary nobility in the Rhineland.[79] The conservative triumph was made complete by the creation of a special commission for estate affairs to supervise the provincial diets, whose members included the leading conservative personalities: the Crown Prince, his tutor Ancillon, and the ministers Schuckmann (interior) and Wittgenstein (police).[80] The principle of representation through estates was subsequently extended to the lower territorial division of the *Kreis*.[81] Karl Varnhagen von Ense's metaphor seems most appropriate in summing up the subsequent strains on the Prussian ship of state: 'The anchor has been dropped into the feudal system, but the sails on the high seas are filled with popular representation; it remains to be seen which is stronger, the anchor or the wind.'[82] Most of the stress, it might be observed, was born by the Rhenish mast, which stood in some danger of being carried away.

Apart from a serious riot in Aachen, the Prussian Rheinprovinz remained relatively quiet in 1830, when revolution swept France, Belgium and some of the smaller German states.[83] The year's events nevertheless gave new momentum to the reform movement in the Rhineland, and witnessed the coming of age of a new generation of liberal businessmen, led by David Hansemann, Ludolf Camphausen and Gustav Mevissen. Their activities, previously restricted to civic politics and commercial concerns, henceforth broadened to encompass matters provincial and national.[84] They now took over from reform-minded Prussian bureaucrats and Rhenish judicial officials as the main defenders of the Napoleonic legacy.[85] Hansemann led the way, responding to the 1830 revolutions with reflections on the state of the Rhineland and Prussia.[86] The most striking characteristic of Hansemann's political writings in these years is their confidence. History was clearly on the side of reform, for 'every epoch forces upon states a certain unique type of organization', and because institutions must keep step with social developments. Significantly, Hansemann rejected bureaucracy, be it reforming or conservative, as well as 'feudalism' as the future basis for the state. With respect to the latter, Hansemann wrote in his memorandum of December 1830:

> The Rhine-provinces . . . have not come over to Prussia in order to experiment in how far leftovers from the feudal age can co-exist with the culture of the new age, but in order to demonstrate how the latter will appear in the eastern provinces once freedom of trade and the liberation of the peasants has taken root.[87]

Hansemann's own vision was in part Napoleonic. The key element were the notables, the *masses de granit*. The lower, popular classes did not count: '[They] do not form a lasting political force within the state.'[88] He made a sharp distinction between what he termed 'general' rights, where he favoured equality, and 'political' rights, which should be determined by an individual's social 'weight'.[89] Hansemann even favoured a recreation of the 'majorats', or entailed estates, as a means of infusing the aristocracy with new blood from the *Mittelstand* in a Napoleonic-style amalgamation of new and old elements.[90] Only the exaggerated fear of the French and of revolution prevented the foundation of the Prussian state on such secure socio-political foundations, he argued, and had caused all the misguided policies since the restoration.[91] This newly assertive liberal critique of conservative Prussia set the tone for Rhenish politics during the *Vormärz* that followed the Restoration. It would climax in 1848, when Hansemann and his generation would be presented with a half-chance of putting their ideas into practice following the March revolution.[92]

It was Jacques Droz who identified Rhenish liberalism as it developed after 1830 as a synthesis of the three preceding historical episodes, each of which contributed its own ingredients: the Enlightenment, with its attack on feudalism; French rule, which contributed the principle of legal equality and the structures of the big state; and finally, the post-1814 transition, presided over by Prussian reform-bureaucrats, who encouraged participation and patriotism.[93] One can adopt this basic structure, while modifying some of the details in the light of more recent research. For the *ancien régime*, one might lay greater stress on the institutions of the Holy Roman Empire and the home towns, so long condemned in historiography as useless and decrepit, but now recognized as efficacious in conflict resolution and as tools to blunt the pretensions of the power state. For the French period, a distinction should be made between the 1790s – a period of upheaval, when local élites were abandoned by their princes and left to confront the challenges of occupation alone – and the early Napoleonic era. The latter witnessed the creation of new institutions, and the rallying of old élites. Representative councils, electoral colleges and chambers of commerce provided new fora for notables – a class defined by wealth and not hereditary privilege – to represent their interests and involve themselves in public affairs.

It was fortuitous that much of this legacy should be preserved from the despotism that marked the latter part of Napoleon's reign by the allied occupation of the Rhineland in 1814. Prussian reformers, led by Stein, Sack, Gruner and Gneisenau, were determined to stimulate patriotic sentiment amongst the inhabitants of the Rhine in their anti-Napoleonic crusade, but also quickly recognized some of the strengths of French institutions after seeing them at first hand. These institutions, shorn now of their late Napoleonic authoritarian accretions, soon became the focus of conflict in the ongoing reform debate in Prussia as a whole. The preservation of French law marked the most important victory for the reformers, for it made it difficult to attack the rest of the French legacy. Subsequent conservative attempts to attack this edifice piecemeal, especially through the cultivation of the native nobility, kept the political temperature on the boil in the 1820s and 1830s. By then a newly assertive generation of Rhenish liberals had emerged who took over from the reform bureaucrats and native lawyers as the main defenders of the Napoleonic legacy, thereby marking the transition from the Restoration to the *Vormärz*.

Notes

1. A. Kuhn, *Jakobiner im Rheinland. Der Kölner konstitutionelle Zirkel von 1798* (Stuttgart, 1976), p.161.
2. *Allgemeine Deutsche Biographie* (56 vols, Leipzig, 1875–1912), vol. 34, pp.600–4.
3. For use of French symbols in the Prussian Rhineland, see U. Schneider, *Politische Festkultur im 19. Jahrhundert. Die Rheinprovinz von der französischen Zeit bis zum Ende des Ersten Weltkrieges (1806–1918)* (Essen, 1995), pp.109–10, 272, 344, and J. Sperber, 'Echoes of the French Revolution in the Rhineland, 1830–1849', *Central European History*, 22 (1989), pp.200–17.
4. T. C. W. Blanning, *The French Revolution in Germany 1792–1802* (Oxford, 1983).
5. Archives Nationales, Paris (AN), F1cIII Roër 3, nos. 31–2.
6. H. Molitor, *Vom Untertan zum Administré. Studien zur französischen Herrschaft und zum Verhalten der Bevölkerung im Rhein-Mosel-Raum von den Revolutionskriegen bis zum Ende der Napoleonischen Zeit* (Wiesbaden, 1980), p.177.
7. Bibliothèque Nationale, Paris (BN) (Manuscrits), FM2533 dossier 2, no. 17.
8. S. Graumann, *Französische Verwaltung am Niederrhein. Das Roer-departement 1798–1814* (Essen, 1990), pp.106–7, 185, 203, 232; K.-G. Faber, 'Verwaltungs- und Justizbeamte auf dem linken Rheinufer

während der Französischen Herrschaft. Eine personengeschichtliche Studie', in *Aus Geschichte und Landeskunde. Forschungen und Darstellungen. Franz Steinbach zum 65. Geburtstag* (Bonn, 1960), pp.350–88.

9. See, for example, the ceremony marking the installation of the former *Bürgermeister*, Johann Jacob von Wittgenstein, as mayor of Cologne in 1803. Historisches Archiv der Stadt Köln, Cologne (HASK), Bestand 1123, Kastennr. 22, dossier 'Französische Ehrenlegion betreffend'.

10. R. Dufraisse, 'Les notables de la rive gauche du Rhin a l'époque napoléonienne', *Revue d'histoire moderne et contemporaine*, 17 (1970), pp.758–76.

11. C. Dipper, 'Der rheinische Adel zwischen Revolution und Restauration', in Helmuth Feigl and Willibald Rosner, *Vorträge und Diskussionen des elften Symposions des Niederösterreichischen Instituts für Landeskunde, Horn, 2–5. Juli 1990* (Vienna, 1991), pp.91–112; R. Dufraisse, 'De quelques conséquences économiques et sociales de la domination française sur les régions du Rhin inférieur 1794–1814', in P. Hüttenberger and H. Molitor (eds), *Franzosen und Deutsche am Rhein 1789–1918–1945* (Essen, 1989), pp.129–60.

12. R. Boch, *Grenzloses Wachstum? Das rheinische Wirtschaftsbürgertum und seine Industrialierungsdebatte 1814–1857* (Göttingen, 1991), pp.29–34. For a more positive assessment of the French contribution see H. Kisch, 'The Impact of the French Revolution on the Lower Rhine Textile Districts. Some Comments on Economic Development and Social Change', *Economic History Review*, 15 (1962–3), pp.304–27, and J. M. Diefendorf, *Businessmen and Politics in the Rhineland, 1789–1834*, (Princeton, NJ, 1980).

13. C. Dipper, 'Probleme einer Wirtschafts- und Sozialgeschichte der Säkularisation in Deutschland (1803–1813)', in A. von Reden-Dohna (ed.), *Deutschland und Italien im Zeitalter Napoleons. Deutsch–italienisches Historikertreffen in Mainz 29. Mai – 1 Juni 1975* (Wiesbaden, 1979), pp.134–5.

14. G. Clemens, 'Immobilienhändler und Spekulanten. Die sozial- und wirtschaftsgeschichtliche Bedeutung der Großkäufer bei den Nationalgüterversteigerungen in den rheinischen Departements (1803–1813)', Ph.D. thesis, University of Trier 1992, pp.70ff.

15. Kisch, 'Textile Districts', pp.311–12.

16. Dufraisse, 'Conséquences', pp.157–60. See also R. Dufraisse, '"Élites" anciennes et "élites" nouvelles dans les pays de la rive gauche du Rhin a l'époque napoléonienne', in idem (ed.), *L'Allemagne à*

l'époque napoléonienne: questions d'histoire politique, économique et sociale (Bonn and Berlin, 1992), pp.404–48.

17. I develop these arguments further in M. Rowe, 'German civil administrators and the politics of the Napoleonic state in the department of the Roer, 1798–1815', unpublished Ph.D. thesis, University of Cambridge, 1996.

18. I. Schlieper, 'Die Diskussion um die territoriale Neuordnung des Rheinlandes 1813–1815', unpublished Ph.D. thesis, University of Cologne, 1971, p.111.

19. P. von Kielmansegg, *Stein und die Zentralverwaltung 1813/14* (Stuttgart, 1964).

20. Stein to Vincke, 16 January 1814, in W. Hubatsch (ed.), *Freiherr vom Stein. Briefe und amtliche Schriften* (9 vols, Stuttgart, 1957–74), Vol. 4, p.463.

21. *Neue Deutsche Biographie* (Berlin, 1953–), Vol. 7, pp.227–9.

22. *Rheinischer Merkur*, 86 (13 July 1814) and 108 (26 August 1814).

23. Ibid., 41 (13 April 1814).

24. K.-G. Faber, *Die Rheinlande Zwischen Restauration und Revolution. Probleme der Rheinischen Geschichte von 1814 bis 1848 im Spiegel der Zeitgenössischen Publizistik* (Wiesbaden, 1966), p.27.

25. J. D. F. Neigebaur, *Statistik der preußischen Rhein-provinzen in den 3 Perioden ihrer Verwaltung: 1. Durch das General-Gouvernment vom Niederrhein. 2. Durch jenes vom Nieder- und Mittelrhein. 3. Nach ihrer jetzigen Begrenzung und wirklichen Vereinigung mit den Preußischen Staate. Aus offiziellen Quellen. Von einem preußischen Staatsbeamten,* (Cologne, 1817), pp.48, 56, 64. J. A. Boost, *Was waren die Rheinländer als Menschen und Bürger, und was ist aus ihnen geworden?* (Mainz, 1819), p.202.

26. E. M. Arndt, *Noch ein Wort über die Franzosen und über uns* (Leipzig, 1814), pp.29, 33.

27. Hauptstaatsarchiv, Düsseldorf (HStAD), Gen. Gouv. Nieder- und Mittel Rhein, 27, [no. 18].

28. Stadtarchiv, Aachen (StAA), Bestand RAII (Allgemeine Akten), 248, nos. 69–70.

29. Max Bär, *Die Behördenverfassung der Rheinprovinz seit 1815* (Bonn, 1919), p.77.

30. HStAD, Gen. Gouv. Nieder- und Mittel Rhein, 27 [nos. 13, 22, 28].

31. F. Vollheim, *Die provisorische Verwaltung am Nieder- und Mittelrhein während der Jahre 1814 bis 1816* (Bonn, 1912), pp.205–6.

32. Sack to Gneisenau, 21 June 1814. Wilhelm Steffens, *Briefwechsel Sacks mit Stein und Gneisenau (1807/17)* (Stettin, 1931), part 2, pp.81–2.

33. Sack to Stein, 27 January 1816. Ibid., p.116.
34. Debate over the character of the Prussian reforms has spawned an extensive literature. The positive assessment of the pre-war era has long given way to a more critical interpretation. The current debate centres essentially around the nature of the 'reform bureaucracy': was it sincere in its pursuit of liberal reform, but defeated by its stronger noble conservative opponents, or merely a faction within the governing class that strove to preserve its dominant position through defensive modernization from above? The classic statement of the former position remains R. Koselleck, *Preußen zwischen Reform und Revolution: Allgemeines Landrecht, Verwaltung und soziale Bewegung um 1791 bis 1848* (Stuttgart, 1967); a more polemical representation of the second thesis is H. Rosenberg, *Bureaucracy, Aristocracy and Autocracy. The Prussian Experience, 1660–1815* (Cambridge, MA, 1958). For a recent reassessment of conservative opponents of reform, and in particular, a re-evaluation of Hardenberg's position, see M. Levinger, 'Hardenberg, Wittgenstein, and the Constitutional Question in Prussia 1815–22', *German History* 8 (1990), pp.257–77.
35. R. M. Berdahl, *The Politics of the Prussian Nobility. The Development of a Conservative Ideology 1770–1848* (Princeton, NJ., 1988), pp.141–3.
36. Koselleck, *Reform und Revolution*, pp.221ff.
37. J. Görres, *Deutschland und die Revolution* (Koblenz, 1819), pp.37–8.
38. J. Koppe, *Die Stimme eines preußischen Staatsbürgers in den wichtigsten Angelegenheiten dieser Zeit* (Cologne, 1815), pp.29–30.
39. E. Landsberg (ed.), *Die Gutachten der Rheinischen Immediat-Justiz-Kommission und der Kampf um die rheinische Rechts- und Gerichtsverfassung 1814–1819* (Bonn, 1914), p.xli.
40. Koppe, *Stimme*, p.42.
41. *Annalen der Preußischen innern Staats-Verwaltung*, 1 (1817), part 1, pp.292–3, 297.
42. Landsberg, *Gutachten*, p.xxxviii.
43. One need look no further than Treitschke for an example of this. H. von Treitschke, *History of Germany in the Nineteenth Century*, translated by Eden Paul and Cedar Paul (7 vols, London, 1915–19), vol. 1, pp.31–2, 73, 138, 146, 149, 200–3.
44. Berdahl, *Prussian Nobility*, p.135.
45. H. Carl, *Okkupation und Regionalismus: die preußischen West-provinzen im Siebenjährigen Krieg* (Mainz, 1993), pp.414–15.

46. W. von Haxthausen to Gneisenau, 5 August 1815, in Steffens, *Briefwechsel*, part 1, p.52. Sack's habit of filling official positions in the Rhineland with his numerous relatives was one reason why Berlin transferred him, much against his will, to Pomerania in 1816. M. Koltes, *Das Rheinland zwischen Frankreich und Preußen. Studien zu Kontinuität und Wandel am Beginn der preußischen Herrschaft (1814–1822)* (Cologne, 1992), p.114.

47. Bär, *Behördenverfassung*, pp.83, 198.

48. A copy of the report, which was entitled 'Vorträge über das politische Treiben am Rhein, ins besondere, zu Bonn', survives in the Geheimes Staatsarchiv, Berlin (GStA), rep. 77, tit. 17, nr. 54, nos. 1–2, and rep. 77, tit. 17, nr. 55, vol. 1.

49. R. Schütz, *Preußen und die Rheinlande. Studien zur preußischen Integrationspolitik im Vormärz* (Wiesbaden, 1979), pp.55ff.

50. Secret police report of 3 September 1833. GStA, rep. 89, nr. 16157, nos. 2–4. See also General Müffling (commander of the VII army corps in Münster) to Pestel (provincial governor of the Rhineland), 3 February 1833, and Freiherr von Brenn (minister of the interior) to Pestel, 8 May 1833. J. Hansen (ed.), *Rheinische Briefe und Akten zur Geschichte der politischen Bewegung 1830–1850*, (2 vols, Essen a. d. Ruhr, 1919), vol. 1, pp.111–13, 114.

51. Neigebaur, *Statistik*, pp.182–4. For an English traveller's eyewitness account of conflict between Prussian troops and Rhinelanders see C. E. Dodd, *An Autumn near the Rhine; or Sketches of Courts, Society, Scenery, & c. in some of the German States bordering the Rhine* (London, 1818), pp.503–4. For conflict between the civilian administration and the military, see Vollheim, *Verwaltung*, pp.145–7, and Koltes, *Rheinland*, pp.26–7, 34–44.

52. J. Heyderhoff (ed.), *Benzenberg. Der Rheinländer und Preuße 1815–1823. Politische Briefe aus den Anfängen der Preußischen Verfassungsfrage* (Bonn, 1928), p.40.

53. Neigebaur, *Statistik*, pp.182–3.

54. For Prussian military deployments to the Rhineland see Bär, *Behördenverfassung*, pp.459–77.

55. Berdahl, *Prussian Nobility*, pp.74–5.

56. 'Jesses, Marja, Joseff! Do hirohde mer in a ärm Famillige!', to quote the original dialect. A. Bergengrün, *David Hansemann* (Berlin, 1901), p.26.

57. Some of these grievances were aired at the Rhenish provincial diet of 1832. Brenn to Pestel, 14 May 1832, in Hansen, *Briefe*, vol. 1, pp.107–9.

58. Ladoucette (prefect of the Roër department) to Savary (minister of police), 3 February 1814. AN, F78390, no. 412.

59. For a thorough account of Prussia's economic policy in the Rhineland in the first years after 1815, see Koltes, *Rheinland*, pp.333–58, 373–83.

60. J. A. Demian, *Geographisch-statistische Darstellung der deutschen Rheinlande nach dem Bestande von 1. August 1820*, (Koblenz, 1820), pp.54–60. For the Anglophobia this engendered see Dodd, *Autumn near the Rhine*, pp.469, 503, and J. D. F. Neigebaur, *Darstellung der Provisorischen Verwaltung am Rhein vom Jahr 1813 bis 1819 . . . . Mit einer Vorrede vom Dr. Luden* (Cologne, 1821), p.285.

61. Neigebaur, *Darstellung*, p.291.

62. H. Koss, *Quellen zur Geschichte des alten Bistums Aachen* (Aachen, 1932), pp.56, 61.

63. Görres, *Deutschland und die Revolution*, pp.73–9.

64. Hansen, *Briefe*, vol. 1, pp.284 n. 1, 285.

65. F. Petri, 'Preußen und das Rheinland', in W. Först (ed.), *Das Rheinland in Preußischer Zeit* (Cologne, 1965), pp.42–3.

66. Landsberg, *Gutachten*, pp.xix–xx, xxv.

67. Ibid., pp.xxx–xxxiii.

68. Ibid., p.lx.

69. L. Mallmann, *Französische Juristenausbildung im Rheinland 1794–1814. Die Rechtsschule von Koblenz* (Cologne, 1987), pp.151, 176–8.

70. Landsberg, *Gutachten*, pp.ci–cxvii, lx–lxi.

71. Solms-Laubach (provincial governor of Jülich-Kleve-Berg, one of the two provinces into which the Prussian Rhineland was initially divided) to Bülow (minister of finance) and Schuckmann (interior), 31 May 1816. GStA, rep. 77, tit. 50, nr. 50, nos. 4–12.

72. GStA, rep. 74 H II Niederrhein, nr. 2a, bd. 2, nos. 30–1.

73. Ibid., nos. 173–6.

74. Schnabel (*Landrat* and secret policeman) to Rochow (minister of the interior), 9 March 1836, 26 February 1837 and 6 April 1837. Hansen, *Briefe*, vol. 1, pp.136–7, 142–4, 144–7 respectively.

75. Deliberations of the fifth Rhenish *Landtag*, 14 June 1837. Ibid., pp.148–50.

76. Dipper, 'Adel', pp.98ff, and idem, 'Die Reichsritterschaft in napoleonischer Zeit', in E. Weis (ed.), *Reformen im rheinbündischen Deutschland* (Munich, 1984), pp.66–73.

77. F. Petri and G. Droege (eds), *Rheinische Geschichte* (4 vols, Düsseldorf, 1976–83), vol. 2, pp.489–93.

78. Schütz, *Preußen*, pp.168, 176, 182ff.
79. Dipper, 'Adel', pp.93–4, 98–106.
80. Berdahl, *Prussian Nobility*, pp.208–10.
81. GStA, rep. 74 H II Niederrhein, nr. 2a, bd. 2, nos. 99–102, 116–17.
82. Quoted from Berdahl, *Prussian Nobility*, p.202.
83. Hansen, *Briefe*, vol. 1, pp.14, 14 n 5.
84. Bergengrün, *Hansemann*, pp.57, 69, 75–6.
85. E. Fehrenbach, 'Rheinischer Liberalismus und gesellschaftliche Verfassung', in W. Schieder (ed.), *Liberalismus in der Gesellschaft des deutschen Vormärz* (Göttingen, 1983), pp.279–80.
86. In particular, Hansemann's memorandum of 31 December 1830 on the state of Prussia and its policies, reproduced in Hansen, *Briefe*, vol. 1, pp.12–78 and his book *Preußen und Frankreich*. This latter work created quite a stir and was widely read in the Rhineland, at least if government reports are to be believed. Hansen, *Briefe*, vol. 1, p.132.
87. Ibid., p.76.
88. Ibid., p.48.
89. Ibid., p.54.
90. This should be seen in the context of the Prussian government's policy in the period 1790 to 1840, when the conferment of patents of nobility on commoners was in constant decline. Berdahl, *Prussian Nobility*, pp.327–8.
91. Hansen, *Briefe*, vol. 1, pp.65–6.
92. Hansemann himself became Prussian Minister of Finance in the government set up after the revolution of March 1848, which was headed by the Cologne businessman, Ludolf Camphausen. Gustav Mevissen, meanwhile, was elected a deputy to the Frankfurt parliament.
93. J. Droz, *Le libéralisme Rhénan 1815–1848. Contribution à l'histoire du liberalisme allemand* (Paris, 1940), p.31.

–9–

The Restoration in Piedmont-Sardinia, 1814–1848: Variations on Reaction

Michael Broers

There is a bitter irony at the heart of the traditional historiography of the Restoration period. Especially marked in the case of Piedmontese history, it stems from the clichéd, but relevant maxim, that history is written by the winners. Thus, the ideological nuances among the various components of 'the party of movement' have been analysed and dissected in some detail, and with great care, while the Right – as quite distinct from the *Destra Storica*, that body of élitist but liberal politicians who dominated the state after unification – has traditionally been lumped together as 'reactionary'.[1] Of more importance, perhaps, its internal history has simply been neglected, and with it, the essence of the period itself, for it was the Right, not the 'party of movement', that dominated government and shaped the politics of the half-century between 1814 and 1848.

To explore the themes of reaction and conservatism in this context, then, represents an attempt to approach the history of the Restoration through what might be termed the 'normal', standard themes that form the subject of conventional political and administrative history. On first sight, this appears an odd form of 'revisionism'; but not on acquaintance with the peculiar preoccupations of the 'classic' historiography, the sole purpose of which was often to trace the emergence of the Risorgimento, and to look resolutely forward towards 1848 and beyond, thus failing to study the period on its own terms, or in the context of its own times. The result is a body of historiography that chronicles the wanderings of exiles – Garibaldi, Mazzini, the rebels of 1821 – and the development of theory – Cattaneo, Gioberti – while setting aside the dominant political forces of the period. This is the result of an understandable aversion to the ethos of a political culture so alien – and so opposed – to the values of the men who eventually overturned it; indeed, to examine it too closely might unsettle the creation of the official history – and the national myth – so necessary to the united state, which emerged only in 1859. The newness of the Italian nation rendered – and still renders – its recent history a sensitive issue filled with dangerous periods and areas of study, of which the Restoration is still, possibly, the most awkward, for even the Fascist era presented so singular a problem as to be considered unique, just as it was too recent and influential ever to be ignored.

There is a real need to reopen the history of the Restoration, despite its relative remoteness from the political world of the post-Risorgimento state. In part, this stems from the fragility of that state, from the need to push back the chronological limits of the problem of *stato civile–stato reale*, however unsettling some of the findings may prove. Another, truly pressing reason to uncover the internal history of the Savoyard state in these years is more concrete: it is simply that too little is known about that state and its ruling élite before 1848. This is an odd lacuna, given the importance of the subalpine *ceto dirigente*, the ruling élite, in the future Kingdom of Italy. The importance of the Napoleonic occupation for the future history of Italy is generally acknowledged. The mainland of the Kingdom of Piedmont-Sardinia was that part of Italy longest occupied by the French. Between 1802 and 1814, the Principality of Piedmont became five French departments, ruled directly from Paris, while the Duchy of Savoy and the County of Nice were annexed even earlier, in 1792. During this period, French law, administrative institutions and practices became firmly rooted in subalpine society, even if many other aspects of Napoleonic rule – conscription and the Concordat, in particular – remained widely disliked.[2] When the House of Savoy returned from its long exile in Sardinia in 1814, as part of the settlement achieved at the Congress of Vienna, it found itself at the head of a society much changed by the long experience of French imperial rule.

To neglect the history of the Savoyard monarchy in the decades after 1814 – and, therefore, to neglect the inner workings of reaction – is comparable to trying to write the history of nineteenth-century Germany without the *junkers*, or that of Spain without the Carlists. The seven years between the return to the exiled court from Sardinia in 1814 and the revolution of 1821 that made up the reign of Vittorio Emanuele I were marked by a very particular, intriguing brand of reactionary government. As in Spain, there was a concerted effort to return to the norms of the *ancien régime*, and the initial decrees of Vittorio Emanuele I are well known: the destitution of all officials who had served the French; the abolition of all Napoleonic legislation; the complete restoration of the judicial and administrative structures of the *ancien régime*. Equally well known is the chaos that ensued. However, in spite of these self-inflicted wounds, compounded by fear of Austrian expansionism and a series of poor harvests, the monarchy survived these years, and the revolutionaries of 1821 found no significant measure of popular support. The Savoyard state was far from successful or efficient, yet it did not go the way of the Kingdom of Naples, the Papal States or Spain, in these years or afterwards. Its survival, rather than the emergence of a reformist opposition, might be regarded as the historical problem most worthy of investigation for this period.

The resilience of the monarchy was based on three distinct, almost contradictory sources of strength. At the apex of the state, the *ceto dirigente* proved more cohesive and mutually forgiving within its ranks than the Court, and was able to curb the initial sting of the ferocious policy of reaction that sought to expunge all trace of Napoleonic rule – *La Palmaverde* – more than has often been allowed. The abhorrence of the Court-in-exile for any and all 'collaborators' was not matched by the more nuanced and discerning responses of those 'loyalists' such as Thaon di Revel, who had remained on their estates, in defiant but proximate opposition to the Napoleonic occupation. Revel, Cerutti, di Vallesa, and Alfieri di Sostegno were, on the one hand, the arch-reactionaries in the ministries of these years, their policy based on a belief in a complete return to the principles of the *ancien régime*. On the other, however, unlike most members of the Court-in-exile, they drew a clear distinction between 'honourable', pragmatic collaboration with the French, and that of a more ideological or even amicable character. Thus, they stood by their political opponent, Prospero Balbo (whose return to ministerial office was largely due to the influence of Thaon di Revel), in contrast to the general shunning of the Cavours, whose attendance at the court of Napoleon's sister Pauline Borghese was considered more treasonous than the conduct of Balbo, the Rector of the Napoleonic University of Turin. The distinction was, strictly, more social than political; but this division had little meaning for the Piedmontese élite.

What emerges in these years is a sense of cohesion within most of the élite, based on social and cultural ties that could transcend transient political differences, however important. This cohesion was defined within its own ranks, according to its own lights and experience, rather than by the king or by official policy. As a direct result, Balbo soon found his way back into the corridors of power, even if he saw most of his policies blocked by the same men who attended his salon and worked with him in the Royal Academy. Conversely, the Cavours remained social, as well as political outcasts, not only at Court, but in wider Torinese society. The return of Balbo to office in 1818 was the clearest sign that the restored monarchy was following the lead of its traditional servants, rather than coercing them into its policies.[3] In human terms, there was far more compromise at the centre of power, achieved far earlier, than might be imagined. This was not reflected at local or provincial level, where those who had served the French were kept both out of office and under police surveillance until the 1830s. The provincial municipalities had been the main strongholds of Piedmontese patriotism and, in this respect, the restored monarchy was probably correct to target them as sources of potential opposition.[4]

Compromise over men seldom ran to compromise over measures. The original judgement of liberal historians as to the ramshackle, often impotent nature of the régime before 1821 remains incontestable. The wholesale attempt to restore judicial norms already out of date in the late eighteenth century proved disastrous: by 1818, even Vittorio Emanuele was convinced of the need to reform and revise much of the legislation he had revived on his return.[5] The government proved incapable of coping with the subsistence crisis of 1816–17; its penchant for arbitrary financial behaviour towards its creditors led the British government to refuse loans to Turin in these years. The 'war scare' of the Hundred Days, in 1815, followed by the sack of Cagliari by the Barbary Corsairs in 1817, under-lined its military weakness, despite the large proportion of the budget lavished on the armed forces, and the keen interest taken by the king in military affairs. The conduct of government was, more often than not, a mixture of the inefficient and the arbitrary. Royal policy could fly in the face of the advice offered by ministers and magistrates. Indeed, had it not been for the retention of the French-created tax inspectorate and its system of policing, with the resurrection of the gendarmerie as the *carabinieri reali*, civil government might well have collapsed. Vittorio Emanuele inherited a well-policed, secure state far beyond the ability of the *ancien régime* to achieve. The French had destroyed organized banditry definitively by 1808, and introduced unprecedentedly high standards of policing and financial administration in the territories of the mainland. The new régime did not dissipate this part of the Napoleonic legacy, and its subsequent follies were afforded, in no small part, because of these firm, practical foundations. This was the second reason for the survival of the monarchy on its own terms: it had a respected police force to keep its territories well ordered, although the *carabinieri* were never as numerous or as well-equipped as their French predecessors. Good order was not always maintained, but its guardians were highly regarded.[6] By contrast, the army was weak, which, if a liability in foreign affairs, at least prevented the dynasty falling prey to its generals, as soon happened in Spain.

Impractical policies were not necessarily unpopular or resented by the masses. In this peculiar mixture of practical failure and political success lies the third source of the monarchy's resilience. In economic terms, it may have been hopeless to revive the *annona* (the system of state-subsidized grain stores reserved for charitable use); but in a period of acute shortage, such measures were popular. When the inevitable grain riots broke out, no discernible blame attached to the monarchy; in fact, quite the reverse was the case.

A similar approach is evident in the policy of devolving many responsibilities to the communal councils, less in the sphere of practical administration, than in dealing with local conflicts. In direct and deliberate contrast to the heavy-handed approach of the Napoleonic administration, the restored monarchy preferred to see local tensions diffused by local communities, without recourse to state violence. Above all, there was a determination on the part of the government to avoid the ruthless, militaristic character of Napoleonic policing. No community was to be subjected to military occupation or the taking of hostages, if at all possible, and garrison commanders who proved too aggressive in such cases were severely reproached. The result was widespread disorder, as rival communities clashed over communal lands and properties, forest and water rights, and their attendant boundaries. The revival of the public, collective aspects of baroque piety banned under the French – confraternities, the festivals of patron saints, the reopening of field chapels, and the refoundation of confraternities – brought the return of the disorder traditionally associated with them.[7] However, none of this made the king unpopular with anyone but his own family and the police.

A notable identity of interest between popular (or, more specifically, bourgeois) preoccupations and one of the more intransigent obsessions of the Court emerged in cases of *la police des familles*, of moral policing in a family context. The Court was obsessed – the word is not too strong – with the likelihood that French, secular rule had undermined the Catholic fabric of Piedmontese life. Although government ministers and local administrators often advised caution, the intense piety of the Court found a ready response among at least a section of the provincial propertied classes, as witnessed by a body of petitions from private individuals, usually wives and their fathers, against wayward husbands, most of whom had deserted their wives for other women during the French occupation. These wives and their families sought retribution through royal intervention, and they almost invariably received it. This 'revolution of the wife-swappers' ended in the arrest and incarceration of the husbands in state prisons, where they were kept alongside political subversives –

at the pleasure of their wronged wives, who were themselves constrained to lead chaste, Catholic lives. From the several cases explored in depth, it would appear that these incarcerations could last several years.[8] State intervention of this kind was almost unthinkable under the French, but came naturally to the Savoyard Court, following its own 'spiritual rebirth' in Sardinian exile. Clearly, this exaggerated aspect of reaction met the pressing needs of the petitioners. Whereas the interest taken in the Catholic revival by families such as the Cavours and other less unpopular aristocratic families may have been influenced – at least in part – by political opportunism,[9] there can be little doubt as to the genuine identity of outlook between the Court and these petitioners, or as to the popularity of its revival of baroque piety among the masses.

Set in the longer, wider perspective of social practices and mores, the popularity of these aspects of Savoyard reaction becomes less surprising. Many social aspects of the Napoleonic Civil Code had been received only with great reluctance in Piedmont, particularly its rulings on inheritance and its distaste for dowries.[10] At the higher levels of the magistracy, French legislation on divorce was interpreted in its most conservative sense, and petitions for it were rare; when offered the institution of juries for criminal cases by Napoleon in 1807, the *Cour d'Appel* of Turin – the highest tribunal in the ex-Piedmontese departments – refused the invitation. Even among those sections of the élite most committed to the Napoleonic régime, there were limits to the innovations they would accept. Clearly, there were deeply traditionalist currents in Piedmontese society at every level, which long predated Napoleonic rule, which survived it and which the restored monarchy was able to draw on. These examples reveal 'legitimacy' as a reciprocal process, the very nature of which indicates how a weak régime might transcend its faults and limitations. The basic assumptions of the restored monarchy mirrored those made by most sections of Piedmontese society. This identity of interest was made all the more clear to contemporaries by the proximity of French rule, which had remained alien in many important respects. Reaction had popular roots in subalpine society, and they cannot be ignored in any attempt to understand the durability of the restored régime.

Evident in all of this is a naive sense of purpose in the reign of Vittorio Emanuele. His approach to the restoration of his authority often had a very idealistic tone, exemplified in his unworldly initiative to lead an alliance of Italian princes in a crusade against the Barbary Corsairs, which was meant as a practical alternative to Metternich's proposal for a defensive league of Italian states under Austrian leadership.[11]

The period began not only with deep suspicions about the nature and extent of the 'impious' legacy of Napoleonic rule, but with an almost touching faith in the innate courage, loyalty and traditional piety of the Piedmontese and Savoyard masses. Nor was it wholly misplaced. This emphasis on Catholic piety, and on the desire of the monarch to identify with the needs of the popular classes, was probably the most striking of the transformations in the nature of the Savoyard monarchy wrought by the revolutionary conflagration. It was an aura not wholly in keeping with the secular, pragmatic traditions of the absolutism of the *ancien régime*, and many at the apex of the state did not feel at ease with these changes of style, or the policies they produced. Nevertheless, only in 1821, and then only half-heartedly, was the monarchy ever challenged from within. Weak in so many practical respects, the restored monarchy had a number of genuine, if rather intangible strengths.

This strength was underpinned by its foreign policy, the touchstone of dynastic loyalty. Vittorio Emanuele united the *ceto dirigente* around him in his determination to retain the independence of the realm from Austrian domination. His instrument at Vienna was Di Vallesa, a decided reactionary, while at home the reconstruction of the army was given to San Marzano, a prominent 'collaborator', who had worked alongside Di Vallesa in Vienna in the interests of the dynasty.[12] Suspicion of the Habsburgs was visceral within the Piedmontese aristocracy,[13] and it was matched by an atavistic hatred of the French among the peasantry, which long predated the Napoleonic occupation, but had not been extirpated during it.[14] In the early years of the Restoration there were tangible reasons to fear both these large neighbours, and they gave the monarchy an incalculable resilience in spite of all its failings. The history of the Restoration in Piedmont, at least prior to 1821, is in essence a singular testimony to the power and reality of dynastic loyalty as the pivot of political culture. The Piedmontese heartland of the Savoyard realm is a very real example of a 'nation before nationalism'.[15]

In his response to the events of 1821 – rather than in the revolution itself – Carlo Felice came very close to squandering this priceless heritage. The younger brother of Vittorio Emanuele I, Carlo Felice succeeded to the throne after the revolution of 1821 and reigned until his death ten years later. It would be difficult to classify his rule as anything other than reactionary. Nevertheless, it was fundamentally different from that of Vittorio Emanuele I in many respects, and shows, perhaps, that a reactionary regime could break with many fundamental traditions of the *ancien régime*.

The most important results of the revolution of 1821 had little to do with either the revolt itself or the constitutional demands of the rebels.

Rather, they emerged in the contrasting responses of Carlo Felice and the *ceto dirigente* to its aftermath. Carlo Felice conceived a distrust not only of the rebels, but of the whole ruling élite, so delicately reunited and reconstructed between 1814 and 1821. His desire to deal harshly with the rebels was probably thwarted by the ministers of Vittorio Emanuele who had served Carlo Alberto while regent. Their cohesion, as a social group, transcended their political differences, and their protection of the young army officers and students behind the revolt owed more to family and social ties than anything else. As a result, Thaon di Revel 'went down' with Prospero Balbo. The most striking result of the revolution of 1821 was not its rôle as the 'morning star' of the Piedmontese Risorgimento, but as the death knell of the *ceto dirigente* of the *ancien régime*. The withdrawal from public life that followed was more complete, and embraced more members of the traditional élite, than had occurred either under Napoleon or at the height of the *Palmaverde*. Unlike either of the previous régimes, Carlo Felice made no concerted effort to win any of them – liberal or reactionary – back to the fold. Perversely, the most reactionary régime of the period did more to break with the *ancien régime* than any other. Carlo Felice turned for his ministers to the peripheries of the state; his councils were filled with Savoyard and Ligurian nobles, who were usually in a clear majority over Piedmontese administrators. He spent little time in Turin.[16]

This break with the past reached beyond men to measures, most notably in the related spheres of diplomacy and defence. Here, the singular nature of the régime is clearest, and the break with tradition most obvious. The events of 1821 instilled in Carlo Felice a deep distrust of the military establishment, itself the institutional embodiment of the oldest families of the Piedmontese aristocracy.[17] This attitude, so akin to that of Francis I, led him into an alliance with the Habsburgs, less to defend his country from any French threat than to free him from dependence on his own nobility. The reign had begun with Carlo Felice's acceptance of Austrian help to quell the revolt, and he extended this to more systematic coop-eration with Metternich in Italian affairs.[18] Such a policy caused at least as much consternation among the reactionary families of the military aristocracy, as among radical unitarists. It was a genuine aberration in the history of the monarchy, and it corresponded to an unprecedented neglect of the army by a ruler of the house of Savoy, which was now shaped specifically to accommodate an alliance with Austria, and so became incapable of waging an offensive war, as was exposed in 1848–49. In his reliance on Austria, Carlo Felice brought his state into the 'Italian system' fostered by Metternich, following a similar policy to the Pope and the rulers of the central duchies. He deliberately sacrificed tradition to ideology, albeit the ideology of reaction. The paradoxes extended to internal affairs, for the reign actually saw several reforms of the administration of justice and of local government, which corresponded more closely to French norms than to those of the *ancien régime*. Nor was 'the black decade' devoid of economic progress, as what might be termed the 'peace dividend' created by reliance on Austria was reinvested in the improvement of communications and the fostering of the arts.[19]

All this took place in an ideological and political climate that bore the stamp of a régime devoted to the concept of 'throne and altar'. The army was staffed with Jesuit chaplains, an ill-disguised spy network, and the Church permeated every aspect of public affairs. The only members of the *ancien régime* élite to have any real influence on the régime were those associated with the *amicizia cattolica*, which was itself dissolved in 1828, seemingly to placate Russian opposition to its missionary work in the Balkans.[20] The 1820s remain among the least-studied periods of Piedmontese history, exactly because their avowedly reactionary ideology is so uncongenial to many historians. However, even in its outlines – and above all, in comparison to the reign of Vittorio Emanuele I and to the *ancien régime* – its complexities are evident. Carlo Felice certainly felt the need to free himself from the past more intensely than either his predecessor or his successor.

Although it has attracted far more attention from historians than the preceding reigns, the régime of Carlo Alberto, from 1831 to 1848, has only recently been rescued from basic misconceptions.[21] As Nada has rightly emphasized, the 'reactionary' credentials of the régime belong to an interpretation of its reforms that is too idealistic and is taken out of context.[22] The reforming absolutism of Carlo Alberto has suffered at the hands of many historians, in the same manner as many other, broadly similar régimes of the Restoration period. In fact, the nature of the reforms of the period 1831–1847 set the régime apart from its two predecessors, bringing it closer in character to the policies pursued by Consalvi in the Papal States and de' Medici in the Two Sicilies.[23]

The reforms of Carlo Alberto prior to the promulgation of the first constitution in Piedmontese history (the *Statuto* of 1848), broke definitively with both the arbitrary character of Vittorio Emanuele's reign and the dogmatic Catholicism of Carlo Felice's. Carlo Alberto's institutional reforms were modelled very closely on the Napoleonic example, but always interpreted in a conservative sense.[24] Yet, when set in the wider context of the *ancien régime*, there is much in the reign of Carlo Alberto that represents a return to older Savoyard traditions. The year 1831 saw the return of many of the great names of the 'robe nobility' to the apex of the state, although, by the 1840's, it was the sons of the men of the late *ancien régime* and the early Restoration who exercised ministerial office. It is also in this context that the singular nature of the rule of Carlo Felice becomes more obvious. This is equally true in the *volte face* that took place in foreign relations and defence; the return to an anti-Habsburg, expansionist policy by Carlo Alberto should be interpreted in a traditional, at least as much as in a liberal, light. Its practical effect was to rally to Carlo Alberto the *ceto dirigente* of the *ancien régime*.

If the régime of Carlo Alberto had any real claim to a 'liberal' character, it derives from the political climate it fostered, rather than the reforms it carried out. This is most evident, perhaps, in its general approach to local government. The concrete reforms in the sphere of local administration furthered the policies of centralization initiated by Carlo Felice, and were equally intent on clawing back control from the local élites, to whom it had been lost under Vittorio Emanuele. However, set beside this centralization was a willingness on the part of the régime to allow many notables of the Napoleonic period back into the administration of the municipalities. The late 1830s and, more markedly, the 1840s, saw men of this type emerge from the shadows of police surveillance and from the political wilderness.[25] They did not, as yet, enter a world of representative political institutions, and Carlo Alberto had no wish to see his reforms take such a course. However, the political world they had been ejected from in 1814 had not been a representative régime either. The concept of an 'administrative monarchy' was not enough for liberals by the 1830s and 1840s, as the manner in which the *Statuto* was wrung from Carlo Alberto reveals. Nevertheless, the creation of a Council of State and the promulgation of the Civil Code, together with a more professional, modern approach to administration, created a political climate in which the men of the Napoleonic period, and most moderate liberals, felt distinctly more secure – if still discontented – than under the previous régimes.

The strongest claim for those who would link the régime of Carlo Alberto to those of his two predecessors must rest on the opposition of all three rulers to any concession to demands for elective, representative institutions. This does not seem central enough, however, to subordinate the substantial differences of their approaches to government. Carlo Alberto was able to draw back into participation in public life two generations of men alienated by Vittorio Emanuele and, more comprehensively, by Carlo Felice. His major reforms show him able to think and work in terms very different from previous régimes, even if this did not extend to parliamentary government. It must be remembered that this aversion was not inspired solely by fear of the heritage of the French Revolution, but also – if not equally – in older fears for the unity and integrity of the state; indeed, it was its traditional centre – both human and geographic – he suspected most. For Carlo Alberto, the fact that the initial democratic agitation that led to the granting of the *Statuto* came from Liguria was probably as important as the demands themselves. Tradition guided the absolutism of Carlo Alberto and, to a lesser degree, that of Vittorio Emanuele; ideology drove that of Carlo Felice, who was as free of many Savoyard traditions as he was bound by Ultramontane Catholicism and a fear of modernity. The reign of Carlo Felice, perhaps more than any other reign in the history of Restoration Europe, illustrates what was new in the ideology of post-Napoleonic reaction, expressed especially in the need to jettison many aspects of traditional absolutism where it had become too secular and reforming in character. There is also an element of this in some of the policies of Vittorio Emanuele, which might be compared to the outlook of the French ultras in the same years: in a desire to devolve local government to its 'traditional' leaders, the minor nobility, the clergy and the representatives of (largely mythical) 'sturdy yeomanry': in the growing emphasis on the sacred character of monarchy; in the increasing, arbitrary interventions in the administration of justice. Vittorio Emanuele attempted to reach back to a much earlier absolutism, and emerged as the representative of a neo-medieval concept of Restoration monarchy. Carlo Alberto, by contrast, appeared as the saviour of the living tradition of Savoyard absolutism, perhaps all the more so in his ability to absorb the lessons of Napoleonic authoritarianism. With an irony that verges on the perverse, it is the rule of Carlo Felice that emerges as truly unique. Retrograde, yet devoid of traditionalism; artistically open, yet politically oppressive; absolutist, yet imbued with a suspicion of the instruments and executioners of oppression: Carlo Felice embodies the complexities and paradoxes of the ideology of reaction.

There are several wider insights that might usefully be drawn from the history of the Savoyard monarchy during this relatively neglected period. The inner cohesion of the Piedmontese *ceto dirigente* indicates its ability to surmount political differences within its ranks, in the interests of friendship and kinship. That is, the great Piedmontese families rallied to each other, first under the pressure of *La Palmaverde* of 1814, and again, in the face of the repression of the revolt in 1821. They were able to transform themselves from an élite of the type favoured by Mosca, into an élite closer to that outlined by Pareto; in the process, it is arguable that loyalty to their social group assumed at least an equal importance to their loyalty to the dynasty.[26] Conversely, when the period is examined from the standpoint of the Crown, as opposed to its servants or its opponents, the ideology of reaction emerges as a highly complex political phenomenon. Within it, two distinct strands seem to emerge, the first embodied by Vittorio Emanuele, traditionalist and backward-looking in character; the second belonging to Carlo Felice, which took as its foundation the explicitly eternal values of the Catholic revival, which made its ideology at once outside secular time and yet, concurrently, a response to its own times – that is, anything but backward-looking.

Notes

1. G. Candeloro, *Storia dell'Italia Moderna*, Vol. 2 (6 vols, Milan, 1956–70); D. Mack Smith, *The Making of Italy, 1796–1870* (London, 1968); S. J. Woolf, *A History of Italy, 1700–1866* (London, 1979) – three 'generations' of general histories that follow this tradition. In a Piedmontese context, the standard studies are A. Aspesi, *La Restaurazione in Piemonte 1814–1820* (Turin, 1960); A. Aquarone, 'La politica legislative della restaurazione nel Regno di Sardegna', *Bollettino Storico-Bibliografico Subalpino*, 57 (1959), pp.21–50; R. Romeo, *Dal Piemonte sabaudo all'Italia liberale* (Turin, 1963); and, more recently, N. Nada, 'Il Piemonte sabaudo dal 1814 al 1861', in *Storia d'Italia*, ed. G. Galasso, Vol. 8, ii, *Il Piemonte sabaudo* (Turin, 1993).
2. For a recent account in English, see M. Broers, *Napoleonic Imperialism and the Savoyard Monarchy, 1773–1821. State-building in Piedmont* (Lampeter, 1997).
3. G. P. Romagnani, *Prospero Balbo, intellettuale e uomo di Stato*, Vol. 2 (Turin, 1990).
4. M. Broers, 'Revolution as Vendetta: Patriotism in Piedmont, 1794–1821', *Historical Journal*, 33, 3 (1990), pp.573–96; idem, 'Revolution as Vendetta: Patriotism in Piedmont, 1801–1814', *Historical Journal*, 33, 4 (1990), pp.787–809.
5. I. Soffietti, 'Sulla storia dei principi dell'oralità, del contraddittorio e della pubblicità nel procedimento penale. Il periodo della Restaurazione nel Regno di Sardegna', *Rivista di Storia del Diritto Italiano*, 44 (1971), pp.125–241; G. S. Pene Vidari, 'Studi e prospettive recenti di storia giuridica sul Piemonte della Restaurazione', *Studi Piemontese*, 12 (1983), pp.32–87.

6. M. Broers, 'Policing Piedmont, 1789–1821: The "Well-Ordered Police State" in the Age of Revolution', *Criminal Justice History*, 17 (1994), pp.39–57.

7. For the single most important source for such incidents: Archivio di Stato, Turin (AST), Archivio di Corte, (AC), Serie Segretaria Interna, V (Miscellanea), Buon Governo e Polizia, 1814–1820. See also M. Broers, 'Sexual Politics and Political Ideology under the Savoyard Restoration, 1814–1821', *The English Historical Review*, 114 (1999), pp.607–35.

8. Broers, ' Sexual Politics'. See also AST, AC, Serie Segretaria Interna (Giuridico), Registri lettere, 1816–1820.

9. There is an extensive literature on the Cavour family in these years. The standard, general account is R. Romeo, *Cavour e il suo tempo*, Vol. 1 (Rome and Bari, 1969).

10. G. S. Vidari, 'Famiglia e diritto di fronte al "codice civile" ', in *Ville de Turin 1798–1814*, Vol. 2 (Turin, 1990); idem, ' Osservazioni sui rapporti patrimoniali fra conigui nel Piemonte del secolo viii;, *Rivista di Storia del Diritto Italiano*, 52 (1979); pp.19–66; idem, 'Rapporti patrimoniali fra conigui e successioni nel Piemonte prerivoluzionario', *Studi Piemontesi*, 17 (1988), pp.1–47. For an inter-regional context, see I. Fazio, ' Valori economici e valori simbolici: il declino della dote nell'Italia dell'Ottocento', *Quaderni Storici*, 79 (1992), pp.291–316.

11. AST, AC, Materie Politiche, Lettere dei Ministri, Rome: Mazzo 390, Registro I, 'Il Re di Sardegna, di Cipro e di Gerusalemine: Istruzione a Voi Conte Giuseppe Barbaroux per la Missione Straordinaria, alla quale vi abbiamo destinato presso la Santa Sede' , 14 February 1816.

12. L. Bulferetti, *Orientamenti della politica estera sabauda dal 1814 al 1819* (Rome, 1942); A. Segre, 'Il primo anno del Ministero Vallesa (1814–1815)', *Biblioteca di Storia Italiana Recente*, 10 (1928), pp.1–87. On the army, see S. Ales, *L'armata sarda della Restaurazione, 1814–1831* (Rome, 1987).

13. See especially W. Barberis, *Le armi del Principe* (Turin, 1988).

14. For its long history, see G. Quazza, 'Guerra civile in Piemonte, 1637–1642 (nuove ricerche)', *Bollettino Storico-Bibliografico Subalpino*, 57 & 58 (1959, 1960), pp.281–321. For its perpetuation in the eighteenth century, see M. H. de St Simon, *Histoire de la guerre des Alpes ou campagne de 1744 par les armées combinées d'Espagne et de France* (Amsterdam, 1770). On the 1790s, see M. Ruggiero, *La rivolta dei contadini piemontesi* (Turin, 1974).

15. For the standard exploration of this concept: J. A. Armstrong, *Nations*

before Nationalism (Chapel Hill, NC, 1982). This author has been deeply influenced by B. Anderson, *Imagined Communities: Reflections on the Origins and Spread of Nationalism* (London, 1983).

16. The best recent account of the reign is Nada, 'Il Piemonte Sabaudo', pp.163–75.

17. Ibid., pp.164–7.

18. For a good recent account of the diplomacy of the Italian states in these years, see D. Laven, 'Austria's Italian Policy Reconsidered: Revolution and Reform in Restoration Italy', *Modern Italy* 1, (3) (1997), pp.3–33.

19. Nada, 'Il Piemonte Sabaudo', pp.171–4.

20. C Bona, Le *'amicizie'. Società segrete e rinascita religiosa (1770–1830)* (Turin, 1962). It is indicative of the character of the reign, and the centrality of Catholicism – rather than 'conventional' politics – to understanding it that this probably remains the best published work on the 1820s. Its approach and terms of inquiry have yielded a deeper insight into the regime than most other approaches.

21. See the excellent N. Nada, *Dallo stato assoluto allo stato costituzionale. Storia del regno di Carlo Alberto dal 1831 al 1848* (Turin, 1980).

22. The earlier work of M. A. Benedetto, *Aspetti del movimento per le costituzioni in Piemonte durante il Risorgimento* (Turin, 1951) foreshadows Nada in seeing *Il Statuto* as part of a process.

23. See especially C. Ghisalberti, *Dall'antico regime al 1848. Le origini costituzionali dell'Italia moderna* (Bari, 1974).

24. G. S. Pene Vidari, 'L'istituzione del Consigli di Stato (18 agosto, 1831), *Studi Piemontesi*, 10 (1981), pp.337–45; idem, 'Un centocinquantenaio: il codice civile albertino', *Studi Piemontesi*, 16 (1987), pp.315–24.

25. M. Violardo, *Il notabilato piemontese da Napoleone a Carlo Alberto* (Turin, 1995).

26. Mosca and Pareto are generally regarded as two of the most influential thinkers on the nature of élites. Mosca defined élites according to what positions their members held and the degree of power they wielded. In contrast, Pareto saw the crucial characteristic of an élite in its social cohesion – its ability to remain a distinct, closely knit social group, whether it exercised power or not: G. Mosca, *The Ruling Class* (New York and London, 1939); idem, *Ciò che la storia potrebbe insegnare* (Milan, 1958 edn); V. Pareto, *The Rise and Fall of Élites* (Ottawa, 1968); idem, *Treatise on General Sociology* (New York, 1969), Ch. 11.

Part III
Political Opposition and 'Social Control'

The *Royaume du Midi* of 1815
Brian Fitzpatrick

The Hundred Days, the period of Napoleon Bonaparte's abortive attempt to regain control of France between 1 March and 22 June 1815, provoked a determined effort by a number of southern royalists to establish an independent jurisdiction in the Midi covering as much territory as possible south of a line from Bordeaux to Lyons. The so-called White Terror that afflicted the Midi in the wake of Bonaparte's defeat at Waterloo, which involved the intimidation and murder of known and alleged Bonapartist sympathizers, the extensive destruction of property and the rigging of elections to a new national parliament, was an integral part of a plan intended to place the Midi in the hands of a local faction that had fought against the values of Revolutionary France since 1789.[1]

The drive for self-government and separation from Paris was triggered by exasperation with the conciliatory approach adopted by Louis XVIII during the first months of the Bourbon restoration from July 1814. It was an approach that hard-line opponents of the Revolution and its political principles saw as a betrayal. Justification for the attempt to set up a separate *Royaume du Midi* came from the view, increasingly widespread in counter-revolutionary circles since the period of the emigration, that Louis XVIII was incapable of ruling France properly. The opportunity for a regional coup arose through the circumstances in which the southern departments of France came under Bonapartist rule in March and April 1815, and those in which they were retaken from the Bonapartists in June and July. The episode brought southern royalists into open conflict with the monarchy, and revealed clearly the restored Monarchy's appreciation of the value of the centralized Napoleonic state in the successful governance of post-Revolutionary France. Ironically, the ultra-royalist conspirators themselves found a number of elements of the Revolutionary and Napoleonic state so useful that they too were not slow to exploit them in their attempt to control the Midi. The extent of the resentment felt by self-proclaimed royalists at the moderate line taken by Paris was revealed in the reports of General Latour-Maubourg and police inspector Claude Eymard, both dispatched to the Midi as special investigators in the summer of 1814 by an already suspicious royal government.[2]

There was widespread indignation at the failure of the restored monarchy to punish leading Bonapartists and Revolutionaries. On the contrary, the king seemed to be rewarding them. The most infamous examples were Fouché, the ex-priest who had voted for the execution of Louis XVI, and Talleyrand, ex-bishop, revolutionary, and Imperial Senator, who had played a key rôle in the intrigues that had brought Louis to Paris in the spring and summer of 1814. The former was made Minister of Police, while the latter took the Ministry of Foreign Affairs.

It became clear, too, that property confiscated by the revolutionaries from individuals who had emigrated would not be restored to them by law. Instead, a scheme would be devised to compensate them. While many royalists whose property had been confiscated had been able to recover some or all of it by buying it back by proxy or by taking advantage of Napoleonic amnesties, there were still enough people with grievances to make the question of restoration or compensation a running sore during the reign of Louis XVIII, and it helped to undermine the king's efforts to bind France's wounds in 1814.

The royal policy of conciliation had other consequences at the local level. It meant keeping large numbers of mayors, deputy mayors, councillors, postmasters, tax officials, magistrates and guardians of the peace in post. Consequently there were few perks for the professed royalists who had suffered for the cause to a greater or lesser degree, and who now expected a recompense. Disenchanted royalists began ostentatiously to proclaim their loyalty to the king's brother, the Comte d'Artois, the future Charles X, and to edge the white emblems of the Bourbons with Artois green. Artois had been the embodiment of the most intransigent opposition to the Revolution since 1789, and in 1814 he continued to surround himself with counsellors who rejected the social and political compromises contained in Louis's *Charte constitutionnelle*.

In the Midi the majority of the disaffected royalists came from the lower-middle and popular classes, both urban and rural, and they remained largely leaderless during the First Restoration. Until Bonaparte's landing in March 1815 the country squires and minor noblemen who subsequently orchestrated the seizure of the Midi were largely content to pursue their personal ambitions via the restored monarchy's institutions. Some sought to reconstitute properties that had been confiscated, broken up and sold off when their owners had been declared émigrés or enemies of the people.

Others sought sinecures, honours or commissions in the royal army on the basis of their opposition to the Revolution.[3]

Following Bonaparte's landing on 1 March 1815, Louis-Antoine, Duc d'Angoulême, elder son of the Comte d'Artois, was made lieutenant-general of the 7th, 8th, 9th, 10th and 11th military districts, comprising some twenty-six southern departments, with the task of raising a force intended to defeat Bonaparte's supporters and rally the Midi south of Lyons to the royal cause. Angoulême had been reasonably well received in the south-west when the allies liberated the region in 1814. A force of about 10,000 volunteers was raised, mainly from the Toulouse and Nîmes areas of Languedoc. The royalist force camped near La Palud, a small village on the Rhône close to Pont-Saint-Esprit. The Bonapartists assembled a superior force and, to avoid the prospect of a pointless slaughter, Angoulême negotiated with the Bonapartist commander, General Gilly. The royalist surrender enabled Angoulême and his commanders to sail to Spain, while the volunteers were promised safe passage to their homes. However, attacks on groups of volunteers by Bonapartist supporters and subsequent imperial decrees that royalist volunteers should be disarmed and obliged to swear allegiance to the emperor, and that their officers should be subjected to police supervision, incited many royalists to take to the *maquis*.[4] Thus, the nucleus of an eventual southern royalist *état-major* was able to escape intact and to establish its headquarters at Figueras in Catalonia, while numerous disaffected volunteers remained on the run in the Midi. They were soon to become the backbone of a provincial royalist militia.

The principal coordinator of the southern royalists' enterprise was François Pons Louis de Villeneuve (1774–1842). A native of Saint Pons de l'Hérault, he accepted an appointment as a departmental general councillor under Napoleon, but was identified as a determined royalist by 1812. In 1814 he was appointed prefect of the Hautes-Pyrénées. Villeneuve was active in mobilizing opposition to Bonaparte in March and April 1815 and then accompanied Angoulême to Spain. Using his extensive special powers, Angoulême appointed Villeneuve *Administrateur général du Midi* and Villeneuve began planning the reconquest of the Midi from Toulouse to the Rhône.[5] His political papers, which were deposited in the Departmental Archives of the Gard in the late 1970s, reveal the extent of the southern royalists' intentions in 1815.[6]

During his enforced exile Villeneuve devoted much of his time to reading and reflecting about the state of France. Sixty pages of hand-written notes on Montlosier's *Monarchie française* reveal his conclusion that the monarchy had collapsed in 1789 because it had made the mistake of alienating the provincial aristocracy and so had deprived itself of essential regional support. The First Restoration, by retaining many of the Revolution's principles, had repeated the error. When Bonaparte dared to return, there were no obvious focal points or symbols of resistance in the provinces.[7]

Thus Villeneuve's project for a constitution proposed a very high level of decentralization. Provincial estates would have to be restored to act as a bulwark against the demands that centralized governments inevitably made. The provincial aristocracy, the natural leaders, would play a key, although not an exclusive, rôle in regional government. This prescription was put into effect without delay during the preparations for legislative elections in August 1815. In a memorandum to the Duc d'Angoulême he wrote of his electoral preparations in Toulouse: 'The electoral preparations here are progressing in the right direction. We have agreed the following proportions: Out of five deputies, two shall come from the old nobility, one from the new [meaning the imperial nobility], and two from the commercial bourgeoisie. This proportion seems to me to be reasonable. I shall take steps to ensure that it operates in all parts of the *gouvernement* [meaning the *Administration générale du Midi*]'.[8]

Villeneuve was by no means original or alone in his ambition to replace the *Charte constitutionnelle*. The restoration of provincial assemblies with powers to levy taxes was an aim held by a number of southern royalists. Joseph de Villèle, subsequently appointed president of the Haute Garonne's electoral college by the royalist *Administration générale du Midi*, had written and spoken against the Restoration's constitutional provisions in 1814;[9] another prominent southern royalist, Jules de Calvière, an *émigré* and subsequently prefect of the Gard appointed by Angoulême, observed in later years: 'Since 1814 I have argued with my Parisian political colleagues that, in accepting the *Charte*, Louis XVIII kept what he should have given away, namely local government, and gave away what he should have kept – the government of France'.[10]

A more strident attack on the 1814 settlement came from François Froment, a veteran counter-revolutionary from Nîmes. Berating the king's advisers for failing to put in place institutions and men able to counter the poisonous legacy of the Revolution, Froment referred to the *Charte* as a building without foundations, a tree without roots that the slightest breeze could topple. He argued that the national parliament's sessions should be restricted by law to specific periods each year 'as were those of our ancient parliaments'.[11]

Villeneuve also proposed to endow the country with appropriately named local administrative entities. In this regard, however, he was obliged to acknowledge the value of the Revolution's work. After all, the royalists' reconquest of the Midi was carried out *via* the *départements* and the administrative, police and military hierarchies associated with them. Thus his proposed local structures of *communes, baronnies, vicomtés* and *sénéchaussées* were in essence no more than the Revolution's *communes, cantons, arrondissements* and *départements*. However, his plan to establish a number of *grandes sénéchaussées*, each administered by a count, was indeed forward-looking, and would have to wait for the Fifth Republic's regional 'superprefects' for implementation. In one respect, Villeneuve's proposed units of local administration differed from those which emerged from the Revolution and the Empire. Instead of serving a 'national' or central government, they would be used to support provincial governments.

In his proposal to endow the Catholic Church with a suitable organization, Villeneuve again merely adopted the Revolution's solution of making religious jurisdictions coextensive with those of the civil administration. Thus bishoprics were to be coextensive with departments, archbishoprics with *grandes sénéchaussées*. In each case the bishop or archbishop would receive a salary equal to that of his civil counterpart.

Villeneuve was exercised by the strength of Protestantism in the Midi. He made copious notes on a biography of Bossuet written by a former bishop of Alès, monsignor Beausset. At one point Villeneuve observed that Calvinism was fundamentally hostile to the traditional monarchic constitution of France. Pointing to the civil and military privileges granted to the Protestants after the wars of religion, he concluded that the wars had been fought more about the nature of the state than about the truth of the old religion and the claims of the reformed faith.[12] The contemporary resonance could not be ignored: it was Benjamin Constant who drew up the *Acte additionnel* and it was the Protestant general Gilly who, having rallied to Bonaparte, accepted Angoulême's surrender at La Palud before taking up the position of military commander of Lower Languedoc during the Hundred Days. Even though a number of southern Protestants urged continued allegiance to Louis XVIII after Bonaparte's landing, many showed they were willing to give their support to the usurpation – largely because of the unease that royalists' taunts and threats had produced during the First Restoration. In Villeneuve's view the presence of a sizeable Protestant minority in parts of the Midi remained a serious threat to sound government. Protestant involvement in the Hundred Days gave the royalists an opportunity to tackle this perceived problem.

Circumstances played an important part in allowing the southern royalists to press ahead on their own terms. The court in exile was at

Ghent, far to the north. So, too, was the focus of allied military opposition to Bonaparte. The Midi was left to the devices of Angoulême's personnel.

As early as 3 June Villeneuve drew up decrees appointing prefects, sub-prefects and police commissars for the departments of the Midi,[13] and on 19 June, count Damas-Crux issued a decree from Toloza in the Basque region of Spain instructing special envoys, called royal commissars, to cross into France and begin the reconquest of the Midi. Commissars were instructed to form in each department a corps of gendarmes chosen from those elements of the population who were perfectly sound in their royalist opinions. Volunteers were to be paid twenty *sols* a day. Bonaparte's supporters were to be incarcerated, and a royalist administration accountable to Villeneuve alone was to be set up in each department.[14]

In the third week of June, the royal commissars entered the Midi and began their task. One of them, the marquis de la Rivière, was able to orchestrate the Marseilles insurrection of 24 June, the first royalist insurrection of the Midi, with the aid of irregulars he had organized in March, while René de Bernis, commissar for the Lozère and the Gard, had concentrated five hundred armed men at the small Rhône port of Beaucaire by early July.[15] Toulouse and Nîmes, key cities at either end of Languedoc, were in royalist hands by 17 July, and, to the east, Toulon was taken by 24 July. Toulouse became the headquarters of the *Administration générale du Midi*, and Angoulême and Villeneuve set up their headquarters there.

The royalist seizure of the Midi was carried out by means of royalist volunteers who were armed and formed into battalions by the commissars. In the *Toulousain*, these volunteers were called *verdets*; in Lower Languedoc they were known as *miquelets*. Their purpose was to terrorize the population into submitting to Angoulême's appointees, and to ensure that the writ of Angoulême's government ran unopposed.[16]

The royalist battalions were commanded by the gentry of the region. In Toulouse, Rigaud, Raymond, Villèle, MacCarthy and Limairac were involved. It was said that some 600 *verdets* were available to the local royalist committee.[17] In Lower Languedoc, Viscount Maurice de Rochemore, the Marquis d'Assas, the Marquis de Montcalm and Viscount Charles de Vogüé were the principal organizers.[18]

In Lower Languedoc, the nucleus of the *miquelet* battalions was the *Armée de Beaucaire*, assembled in the first days of July by the commissars René de Bernis and Jacques de Calvières, who had been appointed to establish a royalist administration in the Gard. Documents written by the commanders of the force show that an *Etat-major* of eleven senior officers and two battalions of 484 officers and men were in place by 5 July. The commanders then requisitioned 1,000 pairs of boots and 172 horses from '*communes insoumises*', that is to say villages deemed to be hostile to the royalists. These were almost exclusively Protestant villages. Funds were taken from the *receveur général des impôts*, from the postmaster and from the director of waterway taxes.[19]

The *verdets* and *miquelets* committed murder and carried out arbitrary arrests and requisitioning well into the autumn of 1815, even though Paris had begun to regain some control of the southern departments by the end of August.[20] Among their more celebrated victims were two military commanders who chose to take their orders from the Minister of War rather than from the local royalists. In Toulouse, General Ramel was murdered in August, and in Nîmes, General Lagarde was seriously wounded in a murder attempt in November. In both cases, the accused, known to be royalist militants, were acquitted as a shroud of secrecy was thrown over the incidents by the royalists.[21]

The violence of the *verdet* and *miquelet* battalions was not just a spontaneous act of revenge, and it is difficult to accept Guillaume de Bertier de Sauvigny's judgement that the White Terror was essentially a result of the breakdown of order, and *l'arbitrage anarchique des comités et chefs de bandes* ('the anarchic justice of gangs and gang leaders'), something akin to the *épuration* that took place in parts of France in 1944.[22] Certainly, the discipline and motivation of many volunteers were questionable and revealed the problematic relationship that existed between popular royalists and the ambitions of the royalist leaders. It was never a very harmonious relationship. However, the volunteers had a clear political function: to clear the way for the installation and consolidation of the civil administrators designated by Angoulême's government, and then to defend and police the *Administration générale*. This is why, in spite of the embarrassing excesses committed by a number of volunteer companies, the southern royalist leadership never failed to arrange a cover-up for royalists accused of violence.[23]

The royalist battalions were of particular value in determining the outcome of the legislative elections held in August. These were the elections that produced the celebrated *Chambre introuvable*. In Toulouse, even though the Paris government's choice for mayor, Malaret, had at last been able to take office and should have fulfilled the rôle of president of the Haute Garonne's electoral college, he was intimidated into hiding by the *verdets*. He was replaced by Villèle, appointed by Angoulême's prefect Limairac, who was also Villèle's brother-in-law. It was not surprising that the Haute Garonne returned on its list of five deputies the three royalists who had been intimately involved in setting up the *Administration générale du Midi* since March: Villèle, Limairac and Robert MacCarthy, members of the clandestine organization known as the *chevaliers de la foi*.[24]

In Nîmes, at the other end of Languedoc, similar tactics were employed. A threatening crowd surrounded the building in which the electoral college met, and sixty Protestant electors, about one-quarter of the electoral college, were prevented from taking part in the sessions. In the circumstances, four militant royalists were elected, including two of Angoulême's commissars, René de Bernis and Charles de Vogüé, as well as Jules de Calvière, Angoulême's prefectoral nominee in the Gard.[25]

As soon as the major centres of the Midi were taken over, the royal commissars put their own nominees in post. Thus, in Toulouse and Nîmes, the principal administrators were in place by 17 July. In the case of Nîmes, the commissar René de Bernis used his authority to create an entirely new position, that of *Commissaire général de police* for the entire department of the Gard. It was given to Antoine Vidal, a seasoned counter-revolutionary who had been active in fomenting the *Bagarre de Nîmes* of 1790, the first overt and violent rejection of the policies of the French revolution. Also in the Gard, Jules de Calvière, former émigré and commander of a royalist volunteer battalion, was installed as prefect, while the moderate Protestant mayor of Nîmes, David Daunant, was forced into hiding, and his position was given to the Marquis de Vallongues. The military command of the department was given to Jean de Barre, the commander-in-chief of the royalist *armée de Beaucaire*. In Toulouse, the royalist appointment to the *préfecture* of the Haute Garonne was Villèle, while his brother-in-law Limairac was appointed mayor of the city. The military command of the department was given to Adrien de Rougé, with General Ramel effectively placed in a subordinate rôle.

However, Louis XVIII entered Paris on 8 July. The royal government proceeded to make official appointments to *mairies* and *préfectures*. But the king's nominees, who arrived to take up their posts in the last week of July, were simply rejected by the Marquis de Villeneuve. A decree dated 20 July and signed by Angoulême stated that the king's nominees were not to be recognized as the king had not revoked Angoulême's special powers and clearly could not appreciate the success of the *Administration générale du Midi*.[26]

For about a week, until a royal ordinance annulling the powers of the special commissars was received in each *préfecture*, the royalists refused to recognize the authority of men who held the king's warrant. In Toulouse, Angoulême's prefect Limairac was finally obliged to vacate the *préfecture* in favour of Rémusat, while Villèle ceded the city hall to Malaret. In Nîmes, matters were handled in a manner more favourable to the royalists. Paris appointed the marquis d'Arbaud Jouques to replace Calvière as prefect. Jouques's arrival on 28 July provoked extensive rioting, and it was made plain to him that the real authority in the region was vested in the *Administration générale* at Toulouse. He was summoned to Toulouse by Villeneuve, whose letter makes it perfectly clear that he was resisting the royal ordinance of 19 July revoking the authority of Angoulême's officials.[27] When Jouques, who was himself a southerner, a native of Aix-en-Provence, returned to Nîmes on 16 August, he did so as a confirmed ultra-royalist. Thereafter he generally underwrote the policies of the department's royalists and defended the activities of the local *miquelets* until Decazes sacked him in 1817.

The southern royalists' enterprise collapsed when Angoulême obeyed a royal summons to Paris and left Toulouse on 3 August. On 7 August he signed a proclamation in Paris ending the *Administration générale du Midi* and instructing his nominees to vacate their positions. The proclamation was posted in Toulouse on 13 August, and its contents were known throughout the southern departments by 16 August.[28] While an ultra-royalist organization persisted in towns like Toulouse, Nîmes and Avignon, only the department of the Gard remained firmly in the grasp of the extremists, and they were unable to do more than control the department as a private fief thanks to the connivance of the prefect Jouques. The political conflict between the government and the ultra-royalists shifted to the Chamber of Deputies, where some three-quarters of the deputies, including those from the Midi, were distinctly counter-revolutionary in their outlook.

Philip Mansel has observed that Angoulême had built up a more or less independent kingdom of his own in the Midi: 'Out of provincial sentiment, royalist exaltation and general hatred for Talleyrand and Fouché, he might easily have built up a very serious threat indeed to his uncle's authority. As with so many crucial events within the Bourbon family circle, we do not know what made Angoulême change his mind when he returned to Paris in early August.'[29] But Mansel suggests elsewhere in the same book that while he was more sensible and restrained than his brother the Duc de Berry, Angoulême was no more brilliant,[30] and Bertier de Sauvigny observes that he was scrupulous in conforming to the will of the king, a quality suggested by his readiness to obey the royal summons and to terminate his jurisdiction in the south.[31]

A passage in Villèle's memoirs gives what is probably the most revealing insight into Angoulême's attitude to the governance of France.

According to Villèle, Angoulême had learnt to appreciate the value of the centralized, modern Napoleonic state before Napoleon's first abdication. Already in 1814, when a devoted royalist had tried to point out the architectural heritage the Estates of Languedoc had bequeathed to France, Angoulême apparently replied that the monarchy preferred departments to provinces.[32] Thus, the available evidence does not suggest that Angoulême had the qualities required to mastermind such an ambitious and disloyal conspiracy.

If Angoulême was an improbable conspirator and was, as some historians have suggested, essentially concerned to keep at bay the influence of the allies and of revolutionaries like Talleyrand and Fouché, both of whom were given positions in the cabinet formed in July 1815,[33] it is not difficult to accept that his enthusiasm and naïveté allowed him to be used by men whose ambitions went far beyond his own. During his tour of the Midi later that year he was fulsome in his praise of the ultra-royalist personnel still in place in the Gard, and his report on the political health of the department can only have been based on an uncritical acceptance of Arbaud Jouques's description of the situation. Certainly, Angoulême's glowing report contrasts starkly with the account given by Colonel Ross, an observer sent by the Foreign Office in London.[34]

There can be little doubt from his instructions in 1815 and his subsequent writings that the driving force behind the attempted coup in the Midi was the marquis de Villeneuve, and that he intended to achieve the greatest degree of autonomy possible for the southern departments. We have noted that Villeneuve paid close attention to organizing the elections according to a formula he had devised during the exile in Spain and that he was most concerned that the Midi be administered by local notables acceptable to himself and ratified by the Duc d'Angoulême. He clearly wanted no outside interference – hence his great satisfaction when Jules de Calvière, his appointee to the prefecture of the Gard, succeeded in limiting the perceived threat to local 'sovereignty' when the Austrian regiment of Stahremberg's *chasseurs* crossed the Rhône into the department. The *miquelet* battalions were prepared for a confrontation, but Calvière was able to persuade the Austrians that their assistance in the department was not required. Villeneuve notes, referring to Calvière: *il était du pays. Sa voix était connue et chérie* ('he was a local man. His voice was a cherished and familiar one').[35] At that very moment, Villeneuve was detaining the Paris appointee, the Marquis d'Arbaud Jouques, in Toulouse because he was not yet certain of Jouques's allegiance.[36]

Angoulême's summons to Paris on 3 August was a blow. It deprived

Villeneuve of the presence and moral authority of a prince of the blood. Yet Villeneuve persisted in seeking support for his administration. In a letter sent after Angoulême, Villeneuve exhorted the duke to return to Toulouse as quickly as possible, preferably having obtained a prolongation of his special powers, but failing that with some title that could be used to focus loyalty. Villeneuve outlined the need to obtain a separate budget for the royalists' administration in the south, a tenth of all taxes at most, at the least a twentieth of revenues raised in the Midi. 'That way Your Royal Highness will have between 400,000 and 500,000 Francs available each month, and money is the sinew, not only of war, but of all things.'[37]

In the same ledger there is a draft paper entitled 'Project for the organization of the finances of the *Gouvernement du Midi*'. Its opening sentence reads: 'If the government of His Royal Highness is to continue indefinitely . . .'. There follow expenditure estimates that include: Army pay – 30,000 per month; General Police – 12,000 per month; General Administration – 10,000 per month.[38] Such proposals strongly suggest that Villeneuve intended to establish a significantly independent jurisdiction under the patronage of Angoulême. Indeed, Villeneuve's comments in the manuscript notes he made for his memoirs are even more explicit. Concerning Angoulême's eventual submission to Paris, he writes:

> The service we could have offered to our provinces as such, and in consequence to the country as a whole was clear in my mind. But we faced the pedantry of Louis XVIII, the jealousy of the foreigners and the ambivalence of the new ministers. Two days longer and it is probable that we [Damas Crux, Villèle, Limairac and the Abbé Chièyre] would have decided to break with the Parisian system.[39]

Angoulême's obedience to the King left the southern royalists without an imposing figurehead and exposed them to the charge of treason if they persisted. Villeneuve became embittered because of the Restoration's refusal to operate a thoroughgoing counter-revolution. In 1816 he was appointed to the prefecture of the Cher, and was sacked in 1818 by the liberal Decazes. He remained out of public life until 1823, when Villèle offered him the prefecture of the Creuse, and then of the Corrèze. In a volume entitled *Charles X et Louis XIX en exil. Mémoires inédits du marquis de Villeneuve publiés par son petit fils* written between 1835 and 1842, the year of his death, but which was denied publication under an 1835 law forbidding public allegiance to a régime other than the July Monarchy, Villeneuve proclaims his loyalty to the Bourbons, but writes bitterly about Charles X, erstwhile hero of the more extreme royalists, who refused to acknowledge his talents and devotion. For Villeneuve, the reign of Charles X, Angoulême's father, was 'six years of exile at Tulle'. He concludes that he was punished because of his activities in 1815.[40]

In this respect, Villeneuve found himself in the same position as François Froment, a veteran counter-revolutionary from Nîmes, who had been forced to emigrate and who was then outspoken in his attack on the *Charte* and the king's ministers during the First Restoration. Froment felt so badly let down by the Second Restoration, even by the ultra-royalist Artois, the future Charles X, that he resorted to litigation in his disappointment and exasperation. It should not come as a surprise that he failed to obtain satisfaction.[41]

Men like Villeneuve and Froment had to be abandoned. They represented a narrow provincialism, a particularism and an *esprit frondeur* that had challenged the sovereignty of the monarchy over the centuries. In spite of their professions of loyalty, their actions expressed a remarkably disloyal 'we know best' attitude. Moreover, their appreciation of affairs of state was in many respects as limited as was that of the Parisian *sansculottes* during the First Republic.

On the other hand the hierarchical, streamlined and centralized administrative system bequeathed by the Revolution and Napoleon, with its prefects and sub-prefects, its rationalized police and military structures, strengthened the centre considerably and was, therefore, irresistible to a sovereign intent on ruling. In conjunction with the *Charte* of 1814, which made the King inviolable, and gave him the power to appoint and dismiss government ministers, the judiciary, and civil and military personnel, and to initiate legislation, the modern French state shaped by the Revolution and the Empire offered the monarch the prospect of greater effective control than any of his predecessors had enjoyed or could have hoped for. From what we know of his personality and the interest he took in the formulation of the *Charte*, Louis XVIII would not have countenanced losing such an opportunity.[42]

In the circumstances self-interested trimmers like Fouché and Talleyrand, *le crime et le vice*, in Châteaubriand's words, however distasteful their presence was, were deemed by the restored king to be more useful than those provincial royalists who sought to turn back the clock and who petulantly threatened to place their province under Spanish tutelage if they did not get their way.[43] Their pyrrhic victory was the failure of the Bourbon restoration in 1830, six years after the death of Louis XVIII, and six years into the far from conciliatory reign of his brother, Charles

X, the former Comte d'Artois, hero of the extreme royalists. But the southern royalists were essentially a *mouvement contre*; they were in many respects happier with a pretender or king in exile to legitimate their activities than with a monarch on the throne of France.

Notes

1. See D. P. Resnick, *The White Terror and the Political Reaction after Waterloo* (Cambridge, MA, 1966); G. Lewis, *The Second Vendée: The Continuity of Counter-Revolution in the Department of the Gard, 1789–1815* (Oxford, 1978).
2. Archives nationales (hereafter AN) F7 9049 and 124 AP.
3. Louis Pons de Villeneuve, soon to become General Administrator of the Midi, accepted the *préfecture* of the Hautes Pyrénées; the Marquis de Calvière-Vézénobres accepted a commission in one of the regiments of the *Mousquetaires du Roi*; Comte René de Bernis, appointed royalist commissar for the Lozère, was busy consolidating the family's property; as were Baron Jules de Calvière and the Marquis de Montcalm, who would become royal commissar for the Hérault.
4. Resnick, *White Terror*, pp. 2–4; AN F7 9049, reports of Baron Roggieri, prefect of the Gard, April–May 1815.
5. Bargeton (ed.), *Les Préfets du 11 Ventôse, an viii–1870* (Paris, 1981); D. Higgs, *Ultraroyalism in Toulouse from its Origins to 1830* (Baltimore MD, 1973).
6. Archives du Gard, Fonds de la Tour Saint-Chaptes. Villeneuve papers.
7. Villeneuve papers, Notes made during the Hundred Days.
8. Ibid., *Administration générale du Midi*. Villeneuve to Angoulême, 9 August 1815.
9. 'Observations sur la constitution de 1814', in J. de Villèle, *Mémoires et correspondance du Comte de Villèle*, Vol. 1 (Paris, 1888).
10. Archives du Gard, Fonds La Tour Saint Chaptes. Jules de Calvière to Roger de Larcy, 2 July 1837.
11. Ibid., Fonds légal 341, *Seconde note à Monsieur le Comte de Blacas*, 1815.
12. Villeneuve papers, Notes made during the Hundred Days. Notes on *La vie de Bossuet* by Mgr. Beausset.

13. Ibid., ledger entitled *Administration générale du Midi*.
14. Ibid. Located in a volume of notes and documents intended for memoirs; Archives du Gard, Chartrier de Salgas 72.
15. Resnick, *White Terror*, pp.7–14; Archives du Gard IMi137, Chartrier de Salgas 72, 103, reports on formation of royalist armed force, July 1815.
16. Archives municipales de Toulouse, 5S204, Fonds Rémusat. A.-L. de Rémusat, prefect, to the Duc de Richelieu, chief minister, 28 December, 1815; B. Fitzpatrick, *Catholic Royalism in the Department of the Gard, 1814–1852* (Cambridge, 1982), pp.37–44.
17. G. Bertier de Sauvigny, *Un type d'ultra royaliste. Le Comte Ferdinand de Bertier et l'énigme de la congrégation* (Paris, 1948), p.171; E. Daudet, *La terreur blanche* (Paris, 1906), pp.244–5.
18. Archives du Gard, Chartrier de Salgas 71, procès-verbal, 5 July 1815; AN F79051. Prefect of the Gard to Decazes, 19 December 1817.
19. Ibid., 71, 72 and 103. Reports and procès-verbaux, 1–11 July 1815.
20. See the reports of Colonel Ross in Foreign Office Papers 27 and 146, PRO, London.
21. Resnick, *White Terror*, pp. 31–7, 57–9; Fitzpatrick, *Catholic Royalism*, pp.42–3, 49–50.
22. G. Bertier de Sauvigny, *La Restauration* (Paris, 1955) p.118.
23. Fitzpatrick, *Catholic Royalism*, pp.47–59.
24. Bertier de Sauvigny, *Un type d'ultra royaliste*, pp.178–190.
25. Fitzpatrick, *Catholic Royalism*, pp.40–1.
26. Villeneuve papers, *Administration générale du Midi*, decree of 20 July 1815.
27. AN F79050. Villeneuve to Jouques, 1 August 1815.
28. Reproduced in L. de Santi, 'Notes et documents sur les intrigues royalistes dans le Midi de la France de 1792 à 1815', *Mémoires de l'Académie des Sciences de Toulouse*, Vol. 4, 1916, p. 85; Archives du Gard, F7 9050. Commissaire de police Vidal to the Minister of Police, 21 August 1815.
29. P. Mansel, *Louis XVIII* (London, 1981), p.264.
30. Ibid., pp.104–5.
31. Bertier de Sauvigny, *La Restauration*, p.62.
32. Villèle, *Mémoires et correspondance*, Vol. 1, pp.222, 248.
33. A. Nettement, *Histoire de la Restauration*, Vol. 3 (Paris, 1864), pp.218–19; H. Houssaye, *1815: la seconde abdication – la terreur blanche* (Paris, 1905), pp.475, 549; Resnick, *White terror*, pp.37–9, 117.

34. AN 239AP2. Angoulême to Vaublanc, minister of the interior, 13 November 1815; PRO London, FO 27/130 nr 20, 15 January 1815.
35. Villeneuve papers, *Administration générale du Midi.* Villeneuve to Angoulême, 9 August, 1815.
36. Ibid., Memorandum to Angoulême, 5 August 1815.
37. Ibid., Memorandum to Angoulême, 6 August 1815.
38. Ibid., Notes.
39. Ibid., Notes and drafts for memoirs, pp.171–6, 183–4.
40. Villeneuve, *Charles X et Louis XIX*, p.100.
41. Lewis, *Second Vendée*, pp.222–3.
42. Mansel, *Louis XVIII*, pp.179, 181–6; M. d'Audiffret-Pasquier (ed.), *Mémoires du Chancelier Pasquier*, (6 vols, Paris, 1893-5) Vol. 3, pp.406–7; Fitzpatrick, *Catholic Royalism*, pp.112–14, 136–9.
43. *Mémoires du Chancelier Pasquier*, Vol. 3, pp.406–7; Fitzpatrick, *Catholic Royalism*, pp.112–14, 136–9.

–11–

The 'Impossible Restoration': The Left and the Revolutionary and Napoleonic Legacies
Pamela Pilbeam

'An impossible restoration'. The settlement of 1814 has thus been dismissed by recent historians.[1] The aim of this chapter is to consider how close the régime came to permanence. In 1814 much of the institutional legacy of the Revolutionary and Napoleonic quarter-century was incorporated into the infrastructure of the Restoration régime without comment. That the right and left of the political community shared this inheritance has always attracted far less attention than their conflicts and the divisions within the left itself. This chapter focuses on the legacy, and, in particular, on how it was that royalists tacitly accepted such a panoply of revolutionary institutional change. The constitutional system, not a legacy of 1789, but inaugurated in 1814, was also accepted by royalists and their left-wing critics. Research into the *notables*, the ruling élites of the Empire and Restoration, underlines the high level of continuity between the two régimes, which survived the 1830 Revolution.

The notion that the Restoration was doomed to collapse was first enunciated by republicans and socialists in the 1830s, critical that a new monarchy was cobbled together after the 1830 revolution.[2] It was a convenient myth. If 1830 was a bourgeois revolution, this proved their theories that aristocratic power would give way to entrepreneurial.[3] The republicans in the Third Republic, anxious to clothe their own régime in authentic historical unanimity, were equally happy to dismiss the Restoration.[4] In reality, at the outset the whole of the political community of the Restoration – ultra-royalist, royalist and liberal – were prepared to work within institutions established in the Revolutionary years, to abide with each other as ruling élites within a constitutional régime.

In emphasizing the high level of consensus, it is important also to remember the differences. The terms, left and right, determined by seating arrangements in the revolutionary assemblies, were adopted as the common currency of Restoration politics. A virtual cascade of biographical dictionaries during the 1820s were unanimous in shuffling the ideas of the 400-odd deputies and associated peers into these categories,[5] although only the most sophisticated made subtle distinctions within the left and right.[6] The large number of these publications suggests that such categorization was important to Restoration politicians. Ultras routinely reviled the left as revolutionary and Jacobin,[7] while friendly observers described them variously as liberals, doctrinaires and constitutionalists. The left included those sympathetic to any of the kaleidoscopic array of régimes from 1789 to 1815, the experience of the Hundred Days having attached some Bonapartists, if not the former emperor, to that flank. The right embraced the majority of enthusiasts of the restored monarchy, who were usually called royalists, and, further to the right, a minority of ultra-royalists. Defended by skilful polemicists like Bonald and Maistre,[8] they shared an enthusiasm for the Bourbons, the Catholic Church and the traditional nobility.

Of course any student of post-revolutionary France would immediately remind us that party politics did not exist. Political groupings were fluid, and both left and right were habitually marked by crippling internal divisions. However, some common features identified individuals and families on the left. A man of the left would almost certainly have bought *biens nationaux*, confiscated property, mainly clerical, sold in the 1790s, which cemented his own, though not necessarily his family's, anti-clericalism. For example, Felix Hartmann, liberal deputy in Mulhouse in 1830, had acquired the Benedictine abbey in Munster for a cotton factory, while Nicholas Koechlin, another prominent local liberal and cotton manufacturer, bought the abbey of Masevaux for the same purpose.[9] A man of the left was also likely to be a member of the National Guard, and he might be a freemason or a Protestant, 1789 having launched many ambitious Protestants into government appointments.[10]

A left-winger's family would have held office at some stage between 1789 and 1814. He was likely to have held on to his job at the First Restoration, reverted to Napoleon in the Hundred Days, when some of his family would have joined the *fédérés*, a volunteer militia for the defence of the Empire, and to have been dismissed definitively at the Second Restoration in 1815. Typical was Etienne Hernoux, wealthy *négoçiant*, *lawyer* and landowner, whose father had been elected by the Third Estate in 1789. Hernoux was mayor of Dijon in the Empire and the Hundred Days, and imprisoned during the White Terror of 1815.[11] The son of a revolutionary enthusiast would be likely to join the *charbonnerie*, sometimes converting in the mid-1820s to Saint-Simonism. Etienne Cabet, son of a prosperous cooper who had been active in local politics in the 1790s in Dijon, trained as a *lawyer*, defending Hernoux in 1815, and became a member of the central committee of the *charbonnerie* in Paris; he was later to be the leader of the largest artisan socialist organization of the 1840s.[12] A left-winger would probably own, while not displaying, tricolour flags and emblems, and perhaps Bonapartist memorabilia. Hartmann had his new house built to the design of Napoleon's home in St Helena. It would be easy to repeat these examples of continuity of support for the ideas of 1789, tracing individuals and families through the revolutions of 1830, 1848, and even the rebellion against Louis-Napoleon's coup in December 1851, but behind the linkages lay considerable differences.

During the Restoration, 'left' could indicate monarchist, republican, Bonapartist, or social reformist, and possibly Saint-Simonian, sympathies, or a combination of several of these positions. Two examples will illustrate the varieties of the left. François Guizot was a leading liberal in the 1820s, even though the execution of his father – a revolutionary opponent of the Jacobins during the Terror – and the confiscation of his property made his own enthusiasm for aspects of the Revolution selective. Guizot welcomed the 1814 Restoration. 'Born a bourgeois and a Protestant, I am devoted to freedom of conscience, to equality before the law, to the great conquests of our social order. But my confidence in these conquests is complete and I did not consider that I had to view the Bourbons, the aristocracy and the catholic clergy as enemies to prove that my convictions were sound.'[13] In the 1840s, as Louis-Philippe's longest-serving minister, Guizot was an unbending conservative, refusing to countenance suffrage reform. In contrast, Voyer d'Argenson, one of the wealthiest men in France, a member of a distinguished *ancien régime* noble family, became an imperial prefect, and, elected to the Restoration Chamber, was a paymaster of the *charbonnerie* conspiracies, a democratic republican and an enthusiastic ally of Buonarroti, one of Babeuf's associates in the Conspiracy of the Equals of 1796.

The left lay low at the First Restoration. Guizot observed that in 1814 former republicans 'had no set beliefs ... they had lived through the Revolution, with its promises, excesses, defeat, and were fearful. The defeat of Napoleon, in whom they had believed, left them in total disarray.'[14] Republicans and Bonapartists attempted to melt away, and the restored king, Louis XVIII, believed that his best chance of remaining as king lay in compromise and conciliation. The thaw was brief. Napoleon's hundred-day return was succeeded by the wholesale dismissal of those bureaucrats and soldiers who had rejoined him, and their persecution during the White Terror, including the execution of Marshal Ney. This ensured that a vocal, aggrieved and ambitious body of men existed, who, in each department, formed a nucleus of those who resented the assertiveness of the ultras and the demands of the clergy. Hernoux, denied public office at the Second Restoration, was the leading liberal deputy in Dijon throughout the 1820s. Critics of the restored Bourbons emerged in parliament and the press. Radical dissent was voiced in numerous tiny rebellions between 1816 and 1822, focused in small opposition groups, secret because article 291 of the Napoleonic Code banned all organizations with more than twenty members.

The proclaimed axis of left-wing criticism that emerged after the White Terror was the constitutional charter of 1814 and (much vaguer and more tentatively-voiced) the revolutionary legacy. What was the revolutionary inheritance, and who were its beneficiaries? Only a tiny ultra fringe rejected the revolutionary and imperial concepts of the state and its institutions. The constitutional charter of 1814 confirmed the major features of former revolutionary institutions. The emperor was removed by the allied armies and a constitutional system was invented. The restoration of the elder branch of the Bourbons was far from a foregone conclusion among the allies who were responsible for presenting the Comte de Provence as king to a largely indifferent country. Very few dreamed of re-creating an *ancien régime* monarchy. Before the Revolution successive governments had attempted to standardize, and reform had been checked by powerful, wealthy interest groups such as the *parlementaires*, bent on their own 'reforming' agenda to defend their corporate interests.[15] At first the revolutionaries had tried to decentralize, but, as de Tocqueville observed, ultimately the Revolution was the greatest centralizer, and the Jacobins the principal defenders of Parisian dominance.[16] The ultras remained truer to their provincial roots in their championship of regional power after 1814.

The rationalization and centralization of administration, judiciary, codes of law and taxation, completed during the revolutionary decades, were not questioned in 1814. Often the changes recorded in the Constitutional Charter of 1814 were cosmetic; administrative and judicial structures, central and local, and accompanying codes of law, simply replaced 'imperial' with 'royal' in their names; imperial *lycées* likewise. Revolutionary fiscal systems were retained, and there was no serious expectation of reversing sales of church and noble lands from the 1790s. Napoleon's religious settlement was modified to make Catholicism the religion of the state.

Tacked on to this revolutionary and imperial superstructure was a floating pier of loosely-defined constitutionalism. In 1814 France became a constitutional monarchy, effectively for the first time. A tiny wealthy electorate of around 100,000 men, distinguished by being over thirty and paying at least 300 francs in direct taxes each year, elected a Chamber of Deputies from a cohort of about 15,000 potential candidates who were even older and richer (forty or more, with 1,000 francs tax qualification). A Chamber of Peers was also set up, the institutional heir of the Napoleonic Senate, most of whose members filled the benches of the new assembly. This new parliamentary system, spelled out in the 1814 constitution and revered by the left during the Restoration, was neither a revolutionary nor an imperial legacy. The political experimentation of the revolutionary years left no blueprint. Between 1789 and 1814 politics had teetered between oligarchy and dictatorship, with some lip-service to popular participation in the early 1790s. The few months of constitutional monarchy in 1791–2 had been little more than a charade. Napoleon was willing to surround himself with assemblies, but even keener to emasculate them. The constitutional régime of 1814 was invented with nods in the direction of the 1791 constitution, but with greater reliance on the example of Britain, where royalists and liberals had often spent considerable periods, the liberals by choice. Restoration liberals and their British counterparts knew each other well.[17]

The liberals were not the guardian angels of the constitution, despite their assertions. Even the ultras talked the language of constitutions, although claims that France had a constitution before 1789 were hard to substantiate.[18] Only a minority of ultras would have been comfortable with an absolutist régime in 1814; Louis XVIII did not number among them.[19] The constitution represented a consensus within the political élite. However, aspects of the new constitutional *Charte* gave a different and misleading impression. The preamble declared roundly that the *Charte* was a grant of royal grace (*octroyée*) that grew naturally out of pre-revolutionary *Chartes*, and hinted at the divine right of kings. But the main sections of the constitution, despite the archaic title *Charte constitutionnelle* (suggesting a counter-revolutionary attempt to reform pre-1789 defects)[20] were infused with the new philosophy of the state, in which the king had a contractual, not a feudal, relationship with the nation. There was ambiguity: the constitution said ministers were 'responsible', but failed to say to whom. The king was awarded dispensing and suspending powers in an emergency, but the constitution did not say who was to define the emergency; Parliament had the responsibility to vote legislation, but no direct control over the ministers who were responsible for proposing legislation. The left assumed that ministers would defer to the parliamentary majority.[21] Louis XVIII did so; but Charles X expected to govern, and to be able to ignore majority votes.

If the constitution failed to legislate on the balance of power between king, ministers and parliamentary assemblies, the definition of the electorate made it clear that the *pays légal* consisted of a tiny, wealthy élite. Liberals and royalists both accepted this: during the Restoration a democratic electorate was hinted at only by a small number of idio-syncratic ultras, who believed that monarchy could thrive on a popular vote.

The left was not the monopoly shareholder of the revolutionary legacy or of the new constitutional invention. The broad centre of Restoration politics, the 'royalists' of biographical dictionaries, took a positive pragmatic attitude to the creation of a constitutional monarchy, as did the elder Bourbon brother who became Louis XVIII in 1814. Louis was keen to limit the divisive damage of the White Terror, and speedily dissolved the ultra-dominated Chamber of Deputies elected in the wave of vengeance that accompanied the Second Restoration. Ultras were suspicious of the revolutionary inheritance; but they were a small minority, and divided amongst themselves. If the next Bourbon to be king, Charles X, had not been the leading ultra, and increasingly dominant in political matters after the murder in 1820 of his heir, the Duc de Berri, the ultras themselves would have been insignificant. Most of those who thought of themselves as royalist needed to make the Restoration constitution work.

However, although royalists and ultras accepted the centralized, rationalized, powerful state created by their predecessors, and were particularly charmed by the opportunity to tax efficiently, the ultras were keen, while observing the form, to change the spirit of the institutions. This was most noticeable with regard to the Church.[22] An evangelical campaign of young priests visited every commune, said prayers of atonement for the crimes of the Revolution and erected missionary crosses as a permanent reminder. Banned teaching orders returned, including the Jesuits. The lay University, *lycées* and faculties were taken over by clerics. A law introducing a death penalty for sacrilege was passed in 1825.[23] As ultra ascendancy increased, priests were required to use their pulpits as electioneering platforms for right-wing candidates to the Chamber of Deputies. The ultra archbishop of Paris, de Quelen, set the tone for the 1830 campaign from Notre-Dame in the following way: 'The lily banner, inseparable from the cross, will once more leave the field victorious . . . if we take care not to neglect our duty to use any means to obtain monarchical and religious elections. We have every reason to be interested in a cause so legitimate to the God of Clotilde and St Louis.'[24]

The reconstruction of the electoral system, launched after the murder of the Duc de Berri, was scarcely more subtle. The electoral principle as such was not attacked. Royalists and ultras accepted that some form of tax qualification was the least damaging for them as the basis for a ruling élite. They assumed that the richer an individual, the more royalist his politics. Hence the law of the double vote, 1820, gave a second vote in special departmental electoral colleges to the richest 25 per cent of the voters. Ultras hoped that this would replace the liberal with a right-wing majority.

In part because of this change, royalists and ultra-royalists were supreme in the 1824 Chamber, in which they clumsily pressed their advantage by passing the *Loi septennale*. This determined that in future the whole assembly would be renewed every seven years, instead of one-fifth of it annually. It was then decided that this legislation would be retrospective, and that elections could be avoided until 1831. These two attempts to manipulate the electoral system failed. The correlation of wealth and political opinion in the 1827 Chamber of Deputies was disastrously negative. There were more than twice as many 'left' and 'centre-left' deputies as 'right' or 'centre-right' amongst the richest members who paid more than 3,000 francs in tax annually.[25]

The undermining of the electoral system honed and brought together a left-wing liberal opposition. Persecution of critics, including death sentences for conspirators and increased press censorship, sharpened the perception that the constitution was under siege. Liberal suspicions were reinforced by 1825 legislation, backed by a state loan, indemnifying émigrés who had lost land during the Revolution. However, the most inept and cynical onslaught on the electoral system was the ill-conceived attempt, from 1822 onwards, to fix elections, by falsifying both electoral lists and the results of the elections themselves. Electoral lists shrank from around 110,000 names in 1817 to fewer than 79,000 in 1827 as prefects obeyed the instructions of successive ministers of the interior to exclude known liberals. In 1827 liberal critics, led by Guizot, Odilon Barrot and Duvergier de Hauranne, united in a new Parisian electoral committee, *Aide-toi, le ciel t'aidera*. Their headquarters were the leading liberal newspaper, the *Globe*.[26] Similar committees sprang up in the departments, centred on known liberal politicians, often lawyers. *Aide-toi* circumvented the law against associations because it was not a club; electoral organizations were not banned. It was not subversive; indeed, it was punctiliously legalistic. It issued series of short, simple pamphlets summarizing how a man could calculate whether he qualified to vote, what he had to show the prefect to prove his eligibility and how to proceed in the courts if still excluded. Further pamphlets explained how to make a legal challenge to falsified elections. *Aide-toi* took a leading rôle in the 1827 legislation that set up recognized procedures for revising electoral lists in the departments. The committees were in place to organize left-wing candidates for the election called by Villèle in November 1827 to try to rally royalists nervous of the growth of the left. Liberal candidates secured 180 seats out of 420, compared with fewer than 40 in 1824. Royalists were reduced to a similar number, and ultras were left with between 60 and 80 seats, tenuously holding the balance in a hung parliament. Although Charles X was able to appoint ministers to suit his ultra temperament after this election, subsequent by-elections soon put the liberals in a majority. In open defiance of the majority, Charles called and comprehensively lost another election in 1830, in which liberals secured control of the Chamber, with 274 seats.

This brief semblance of unity on the left was essentially the product of shared enemies. Above all it was the response to the policies of Charles X, and most notably his appointment in 1829 of an ultra government, completely incapable of establishing any broad basis of support within the country. Despite Charles X's fears, expressed in his speech opening parliament after a three-month delay in March 1830, liberals were not revolutionaries. They simply wanted to force Polignac out and oblige the King to govern within the constitutional *Charte*, respecting the views of the majority in the Chamber of Deputies, as had been the common practice of both Bourbons until the spring of 1829.

The divisions among the parliamentary liberals were only too apparent once Charles and Polignac had been removed and the liberal majority made Louis-Philippe, cousin of the deposed monarch, king. The more conservative element, led by Guizot and Casimir Perier, were happy to issue a modestly-revised constitution, taking away the King's power to make laws without parliament, but otherwise retaining a constitutional monarchy rather than a full parliamentary system. They became known as the *résistance*, because they were resistant to reform, particularly to the expansion of the electorate, for which the tax qualification had been lowered to 200 francs, giving an electorate of about 166,000. The *mouvement*, led by Jacques Laffitte and Odilon Barrot, and including for a time Cabet, pressed for a larger electorate and a more thoroughly parliamentary system. A minority of former liberals set up secret republican groups, the *Amis du Peuple* and the *Droits de l'homme*. Their aims were vaguely expressed, but the most radical hoped for a democratic electorate and a political system more sensitive to the problems of the unemployed, who were numerous in the early 1830s. Many republicans, encouraged by Buonarroti, liked to think of themselves as the heirs of the Jacobins. Cabet, who rapidly slid into republicanism, publicized what became a common view, that 1830 was *une révolution escamotée*, smuggled away from artisans who had been the chief defenders of the barricades in the Three Glorious Days.[27] The presence in Paris of the elderly Buonarroti, who had been part of Babeuf's Conspiracy of the Equals in 1796, which had talked of egalitarian redistribution of land following a revolution in the name of the 'people', added to the sustained political ferment that followed the apparent unity of radical opposition in 1830. The conflicts of the 1790s between constitutional monarchists, Girondins, Jacobins and Babouvists were being replayed in minor key. For much of the July Monarchy the *résistance* retained control, former liberals being transformed into staunch conservatives, as anxious to reinforce press censorship and restrictions on association as any Restoration royalist. While a dominant section of the Restoration left became the right, their former allies, including Cabet and Voyer d'Argenson, became ideological enemies.

The July Monarchy's motto, 'Liberty and Order', was a significant indicator of the attitude of Orleanist former liberals to the legacies of the revolutionary years. For them liberty was a quality for negotiation and purchase. `Order' was important to these heirs of 1789 because the upheavals of their own lifetimes appalled them. While they applauded the gains of the Revolution, the 1790s inculcated in them a profound and long-lasting antipathy to popular unrest, which was reinforced by the July Days, 1830, the risings of 1831 and 1834 in Lyons, the February revolution of 1848, and, above all, the June Days of 1848. This was the most profound legacy of the Revolution for men like Guizot. The search for order ran through the *régime censitaire*, the fortification of Paris, and the trials of errant journalists and aspirant republican politicians. The way in which the former liberals behaved in government after 1830 shows just how close their ideas were to those of Restoration royalists. What is fascinating, given the upheavals of the previous quarter-century, is that the Restoration almost survived. Cabet was right when he said that Charles X was not brought down by the liberal left, whose members could never agree to condemn Charles X's ordinances dissolving the new Assembly before it met, but by an artisan rising in central Paris, which the king lacked the military resources to control.

What gave the Restoration the greatest chance of success – the necessary condition whose contravention left Charles X vulnerable – was the continuity of personnel between empire and monarchy. One of the most colourful examples was Talleyrand, *grand chambellan* of Napoleon and in September 1815 of the king.[28] This was an honorific post; but former imperial officials kept their places wherever possible, and only a minority of émigrés gained office in 1814. Louis XVIII held on to 76 per cent of Napoleon's appointees. Prefects were key appointments, and here continuity was particularly striking; 45 out of 87 prefects were retained, not necessarily in the same department. Among the new prefects, 29 had held the same office in the Empire, and two-thirds had served Napoleon.[29] The main exception to this continuity was the army, where the Napoleonic regimental structure was replaced by regionally-based units. Over half the full complement of half a million men were retired, including the most politically-committed officers, who went home as *demi-soldes* (half-pay), and became centres of opposition in their localities.[30]

Although officials who reverted to Napoleon in the Hundred Days were subsequently excluded from employment until 1830, Louis XVIII was always circumspect. Just as the Imperial régime relied for a third of its officials on men who had held appointments under the *ancien régime*,[31] a substantial proportion of Restoration *fonctionnaires* had imperial pedigrees, even after the Hundred Days. Only one of the new prefects appointed at the Second Restoration had not served Napoleon. However, there were attempts to reconstruct a predominantly noble élite. Of the 164 prefects appointed after 1815, 118, or 70 per cent, were nobles with *ancien régime* titles.[32] The process accelerated with the growing influence of the Comte d'Artois, king from 1824. Charles X so convinced himself that the liberals represented a revolutionary threat that he began to make ultra mythology real, appointing young nobles as prefects for their quarterings of nobility rather than their legal and professional training.

The prefects of the late 1820s habitually claimed that their liberal critics were bourgeois, on the grounds that the satanic 1789 revolution had created bourgeois power. Liberals like Guizot gloried in 1789 as a bourgeois revolution because (in theory) traditional privilege had been replaced by careers open to talent. By the end of the century right-wing journalists such as Drumont blamed the decline of France on the ascent of the bourgeoisie.[33] Later right-wing historians refined this apocalyptic social analysis to link the emergence of a new bourgeois administrative élite with Napoleon.[34]

The truth was, as we have seen, somewhat less clearly differentiated. Reference to the personal files of prefects reveals that dynasties were the norm,[35] and a full list of first names is vital to avoid confusing successive generations of the same family. But dynasties were professional rather than political. Napoleonic, Restoration and Orleanist bureaucrats all liked to include in their *curriculum vitae* the fact that their ancestors had been *ancien régime parlementaires*, and preferably that their family had been in state service since time immemorial. A high proportion of Restoration officials had seen imperial service, and a not inconsiderable number went on to work for Louis-Philippe. Nau de Champlouis is a fine example. He came from the *noblesse de robe*: 'an old family which has served the state with honour since the fifteenth century'.[36] His father and grandfather were *avocats* in the Paris *parlement* and his own administrative career began in 1809. *Maître de requêtes* in 1821, he was a Martignac prefect in the Vosges in 1828, resigned in September 1829, and was elected local deputy in 1830. Restored to the prefecture of the Vosges in August 1830, he was promoted to Strasburg a year later.[37] A glance at such dynasties does more than underline the resilience of traditional élites; it reminds us that the ultra passion for the nobility was gloriously imprecise. A pre-1789 title might be old or recently purchased. Napoleon may well have added an imperial lustre to old nobles, or ennobled plebeians such as his senior army officers. New Bourbon ennoblements followed throughout the Restoration.

The most extensive administrative purge of the nineteenth century followed the 1830 Revolution.[38] Guizot replaced 83 per cent of the prefects. This was more a Bonapartist than a bourgeois revolution. Former imperial officials out of office since 1815 tended to seize power during the July Days, and Guizot rubber-stamped their self-appointment, even at prefectorial level. Often the long-term unemployed could not settle as bureaucrats, and were removed by Casimir Périer in March 1831. Although 1830 obviously provided opportunities for liberal critics of the deposed régime, Guizot's most successful nominees had recent administrative experience. Achille Chaper, successively prefect in the Tarn-et-Garonne, Gard, Côte-d'Or and Loire-Inférieure, had been mayor of his home town, Grenoble, for ten years.[39]

Although the elements of continuity within the ruling élite, or *notables*, were pronounced, and there can be no going back to simplistic social analyses that talked of a noble ruling class's being replaced by the bourgeoisie between 1789 and 1830,[40] one cannot deny that the new monarchy of 1830 was sold to the public as a 'bourgeois' régime. From December 1831 the hereditary peerage was abolished. In effect this only meant that future nominees to the upper chamber were life-peers. There was a legitimist withdrawal from national politics in 1830, an *émigration à l'intérieur*. However, research into the *notables* has shown that the abdication was cosmetic: legitimists, as Bourbon supporters were called after 1830, retained their power and rôle in local affairs in regions, like western France, where they were traditionally dominant.[41] The effects of 1789, the emigration of the revolutionary decades, had done little to dent their economic predominance. Some had even bought more land in the sale of *biens nationaux*.[42] France did not possess a consolidated body of *notables* after 1814 or 1830; but nor did she contain two distinct rival ruling élites of noble legitimists and bourgeois Orleanists. The very limited revision of the 1814 constitution after the 1830 Revolution is proof that a large measure of consensus existed.

Notes

1. R. Tombs, *France 1814–1914* (London, 1996), Ch. 17 'The Impossible Restoration, 1814–30', pp.329–52; P. Rosenvallon, 'Les Doctrinaires et la question du gouvernement représentative' in F. Furet and M. Ozouf (eds), *The French Revolution and the Creation of Modern Political Culture. Vol. 3: The Transformation of Political Culture 1789–1848* (Oxford, 1989); idem, *La Monarchie impossible: les chartes de 1814 et de 1830* (Paris, 1994); F. Furet, *La Révolution de Turgot à Jules Ferry, 1770–1880* (Paris, 1988), English trans. *Revolutionary France, 1770–1880* (Oxford, 1992).
2. L. Blanc, *Révolution Française. Histoire de Dix Ans* (5 vols, Paris, 1841–4).
3. K. Marx, *The Class Struggles in France 1848 to 1850* (Moscow n.d.), p.44.
4. G. Weill, *Histoire du parti républicain en France de 1814 à 1870* (Paris, 1900).
5. *Biographie des députés de la chambre septennale de 1824–30* (Paris, 1826); *Biographie des députés, session de 1828* (Paris, 1828); *Biographie des préfets depuis l'organisation des préfectures jusqu'à ce jour* (Paris, 1826); *Biographie impartiale des 221 députés* (Paris, 1831); *Biographie impartiale des 221 députés, précedée et suivie de quelques documents curieux* (Paris, 1830); *Biographie nouvelle et complète de la Chambre des Députés, contenant les députés nouvellement élus* (Paris, 1829); *Biographie spéciale des pairs et députés du royaume, session 1818–19* (Beauce, 1819); *Biographie Universelle* (Paris, 1823); J. G. Dentu and P. F. M. Massy, *Biographie*

des Députés de la Chambre Septennale (Paris, 1826); J. Dourille, *Biographie des députés de la nouvelle Chambre Septennale* (Paris, 1829); M. A. Lagarde, *Nouvelle biographie pittoresque des députés de la Chambre Septennale* (Paris, 1826); *Notice historique sur les membres de la Chambre des Députés, classés par ordre de département* (Paris, 1828); R. Raban, *Petite biographie des députés* (Paris, 1826); R. Raban, *Petite biographie des pairs* (Paris, 1826); H. Thabaud de Latouche, *et al.*, *Biographie pittoresque des députés, portraits, moeurs et coutumes* (Paris, 1820).

6. J. B. M. Braun, *Nouvelle biographie des députés ou statistique de la Chambre de 1814 à 1829* (Paris, 1830).

7. In 1820 de Serre, *garde des sceaux*, urged the procureurs to strive in the elections to oppose 'l'esprit de conservatisme à l'esprit de la révolution': 16 July 1820, Archives Nationales BB5.361.

8. L. de Bonald, *Théorie de l'éducation sociale et de l'administration publique* (1796); J. de Maistre, *Considerations sur la France* (Geneva, 1796), English trans. *Considerations on France*, ed. R. A. Lebrun (Cambridge, 1994).

9. P. Leuilliot, *L'Alsace au début du XIX siècle. Essai d'histoire politique, économique et religieuse 1815–30*, Vol.1 (1959), p.7.

10. B. Fitzpatrick, *Catholic Royalism in the Department of the Gard, 1814–52* (Cambridge, 1982).

11. E. Bourloton, G. Cogny and A. Robert, *Dictionnaire des Parlementaires Français* (5 vols, Paris, 1889–91), Vol. 3, p.146. His father was elected to the 1789 assembly and to the *conseil des anciens*. Etienne was one of the richest notables in the department, paying 4,504 francs in taxes in 1834: Liste Electorale Dijon, Archives municipales Dijon 4E.

12. P. M. Pilbeam, *Republicanism in Nineteenth-Century France 1814–71* (Basingstoke, 1995), p.167.

13. F. Guizot, *Mémoires pour servir à l'histoire de mon temps* (Paris, 1858), Vol. 1, p.27.

14. F. Guizot, *Des moyens de gouvernement et des moyens d'opposition dans l'état actuel de la France* (Paris, 1821).

15. G. Bossenga, *The Politics of Privilege. Old Regime and Revolution in Lille* (Cambridge, 1991); V. R. Gruder, 'A Mutation in Elite Political Culture: the French Notables and the Defense of Property and Participation, 1787', in T. C. W. Blanning (ed.), *The Rise and Fall of the French Revolution* (Chicago, 1996), pp.111–47.

16. A. de Tocqueville, *The Old Regime and the French Revolution*, trans. S. Gilbert (New York, 1955); I. Woloch, *Transformations of the French*

Civic Order, 1789–1820s. The New Regime (New York and London, 1994).

17. E. de Waresquiel, 'Les voyageurs français en Angleterre pendant la Restauration', unpublished paper, Modern French History Seminar, Institut Français, London, 13 February 1993.
18. De Maistre, *Considerations on France*, pp.68–70.
19. Tombs, *France*, p.336.
20. J. Roberts, *The Counter-Revolution in France, 1787–1830* (Basingstoke, 1990), p.82.
21. P. M. Pilbeam, *The Constitutional Monarchy in France 1815–48* (London, 1999).
22. M. Lyons, 'Fires of Expiation: Book-burnings and Catholic Missions in Restoration France', *French History* 10 (1996), pp.240–66.
23. M. Hartmann,'The Sacrilege Law of 1825 in France: A Study in Anti-Clericalism and Myth-Making', *Journal of Modern History* (1972), pp.21–37.
24. D. L. Rader, *The Journalists and the July Revolution in France* (The Hague, 1973), pp.208–9.
25. J. Oeschlin, *Le mouvement ultra-royaliste en France* (Paris, 1960), p.55.
26. S. Kent, *The Election of 1827 in France* (Cambridge, MA, 1975), pp.88–91; P. M. Pilbeam, *The 1830 Revolution in France* (Basingstoke, 1994), pp.27–9.
27. E. Cabet, *La Révolution de 1830 et la situation présente* (Paris, 1831).
28. P. Mansel, *The Court of France 1789–1830* (Cambridge, 1988), p.165.
29. A. Jardin and A. J. Tudesq, *Restoration and Reaction 1815–48* (Cambridge, 1983), p.13.
30. G. de Bertier de Sauvigny, *La Restauration* (Paris, 1955), p.76.
31. L. Bergeron and G. Chaussinand-Nogaret, *Les masses de granit* (Paris, 1979), p.32.
32. N. Richardson, *The French Prefectoral Corps, 1814–1830* (1966), pp.7–16.
33. E. Drumont, *La France juive* (Paris, 1888), p.16.
34. E. Beau de Lomenie, *Les responsabilités des dynasties bourgeoises* (Paris, 1964).
35. Archives Nationales F1bI – classified alphabetically.
36. P. Henry, *Histoire des préfets* (Paris, 1950), p.147.
37. Dossier personnel F1bI 168.1
38. D. H. Pinkney, *The French Revolution of 1830* (Princeton, NJ, 1972), p.294.
39. Dossier personnel F1BI157.17.

40. J. Lhomme, *La Grande Bourgeoisie au pouvoir 1830–1880* (Paris, 1960).
41. A. J. Tudesq, *Les conseillers généraux en France au temps de Guizot 1840–1848* (Paris, 1967); idem., *Les grands notables en France 1840–1849. Etude historique d'une psychologie sociale* (2 vols, Paris, 1964).
42. D. C. Higgs, *Nobles in Nineteenth-Century France. The Practice of Inegalitarianism* (Baltimore, MD, 1987).

National Colours and National Identity in Early Nineteenth-Century Germany

Andreas Fahrmeir

Thomas Nipperdey began his *German History* with the now famous opening sentence, 'In the beginning was Napoleon.'[1] Considering the extent of the change with which German governments had to come to terms in the period of Napoleonic dominance, this statement is not very much of an exaggeration. The annexation of the Rhine's left bank by France led to the 'mediatization' of all ecclesiastical territories, many Imperial Cities and a number of the smaller territories of the Holy Roman Empire in 1803. These were used to compensate the secular states that had possessed lands west of the Rhine, and these transfers of territory decisively altered the balance of power in the Empire, not least by eliminating those territories that had been most dependent on the Empire's legal order. In 1806, the Empire ceased to exist with the abdication of the Emperor. A new epoch of European history had begun.

The influence of Napoleonic France was twofold. First, while some of Napoleon's decisions regarding the distribution of territory in Germany were revoked after 1815, two key elements, the mediatization of the smaller territories and the destruction of the Holy Roman Empire, were never seriously challenged.

Second, even though the Holy Roman Empire was beginning to look like an international federation that contained territories of all shapes and sizes, it did have an influence on the internal development of German principalities. Certainly, its influence on domestic affairs was limited and exercised indirectly, for instance through the imperial courts, the Wetzlar *Reichskammergericht* and the Vienna *Reichshofrat*. Nevertheless, guild regulations were similar throughout the Empire, as was the structure of universities. Once the Empire had been swept away, the sovereign states that replaced it had a greater freedom of manoeuvre in these matters. Napoleonic France made sure that the old economic and social order was modified as soon as possible. It put pressure on the states organized in the French-dominated Confederation of the Rhine in 1806 to abandon the social order of the *ancien régime* and to become modern, 'bourgeois', societies. In addition, the French demands for soldiers and cash could hardly be met without a degree of modernization.

The level of actual change varied considerably between different types of territory even within the Confederation of the Rhine. Take Bavaria, elevated from an electorate to a kingdom in January 1806. Within limits, the King of Bavaria was able to choose which of the internal reforms urged on him by Napoleon he wished to adopt. So too were the sovereigns of states such as Hesse-Darmstadt, Württemberg, Nassau, or Baden. After 1815, these so-called *Rheinbundreformen* could be pursued further or abandoned.[2] The Napoleonic model states, such as the grand duchies of Berg and Frankfurt and the Kingdom of Westphalia, by contrast, were new creations, not expanded versions of territories that had existed for centuries.[3] Their rulers were appointed directly by Napoleon, and they were linked so closely to the new order that they could not survive his defeat. These states, in which reforms had gone furthest, were dissolved after 1813, either to be returned to their former rulers or to be handed over to new sovereigns.

Hitherto, the study of the reforms in German states during the Napoleonic era has focused primarily on attempts to create a 'bourgeois' society untrammelled by traditional restrictions on economic activity through the introduction of a civil code,[4] on administrative centralization, and on the steps towards constitutional government and parliamentary assemblies. Taking a longer view, the Napoleonic era was one in which a gradual process of modernization that was already well under way was accelerated dramatically;[5] but even at the end of Napoleon's rule its triumph was by no means uncontested or assured. The tug-of-war between modernizing and centralizing state governments and traditional corporations, for instance guilds and municipalities, over economic and political reforms had merely entered a new phase, in which both sides seemed to emerge victorious at times. In Prussia, economic reforms were comparatively radical: freedom of occupation was granted there in 1810, and freedom of movement of sorts was introduced in 1842.[6] In the southern German states, by contrast, reforming the economy proved to be far more difficult. In the case of freedom of movement, states were only able to reduce the control of municipalities over settlement and marriage when economic conditions were favourable; as soon as they deteriorated, some of the powers of municipalities, which financed poor relief, had to be restored.[7] Guilds experienced similar ups and downs until the foundation of the North German Confederation and the German Empire led to the introduction of Prussian laws in all German states with the exception of Bavaria.[8]

Yet the southern German states of Baden, Bavaria, Württemberg, Hesse-Darmstadt, and Nassau were ahead where political reforms were concerned. Constitutions and parliamentary assemblies were introduced in Bavaria in 1808, in Nassau in 1814, in Baden in 1816, in Württemberg in 1819,[9] and in Hesse-Darmstadt in 1820. It has frequently been argued that parliamentary assemblies were particularly necessary in these states, as they gave a sense of unity to a political élite that was not connected to its state by a long tradition.[10] While this is true, other states, not least Prussia, were also faced with the problem of assimilating considerable areas of formerly foreign territory. The Prussian government assumed, however, that the military and the administration would provide a sufficient connection. Parliamentary assemblies were not introduced because it was thought that they would delay economic modernization, even though their establishment had been promised.[11]

The different approaches to what was essentially the same problem of how to forge a number of previously unconnected territories into a viable modern state could also indicate that Prussia and the southern German states had significantly different goals. The southern states took the concept and potential of the Napoleonic nation state much more seriously than Prussia. Stuart Woolf has justly called 'the growing association of liberalism and standardizing administrative reforms as the method to forge a unified state identity . . . one of the most remarkable features' of the Napoleonic legacy.[12] There was indeed no compelling reason why German states should not attempt to follow this model.[13] However, it implied that they would have to become nation states (which is probably what Woolf means by 'unified state identity') in their own right, not remain traditional absolutist monarchies or become parts of a federal Germany. One way to trace such a programme of 'nationalization' is through the study of national symbols, and I should like to discuss this topic using 'national cockades' in nineteenth-century German states as an example.

The introduction of such 'national cockades' appears to have been closely linked to the new order in Germany. On 16 January 1806, the King of Bavaria issued the following royal proclamation:

> So that Bavarians can recognize themselves as brothers, and can receive the distinction in foreign countries to which they are entitled because of the strength of their allegiance to King and fatherland, We decree: that all servants of the state shall wear a blue and white cockade on their hats in addition to their uniform; and that all other Bavarian subjects, regardless of their rank,

shall be permitted to indicate the nation to which they belong by the national colours on their hat.[14]

This Bavarian proclamation on national cockades encapsulates the programme of national modernization and homogenization. The point of the proclamation was most probably not to introduce Bavarian colours, as it can hardly have been a secret what the colours of the freshly minted kingdom would be. Even though the Bavarian coat of arms offered other possibilities, including red, black and yellow, light blue and white were obvious choices because there was very little competition for them. Yellow and red were used by other states, the former in Austria, Saxony and the Thuringian states, the latter in Hesse-Kassel and Hesse-Darmstadt.[15] The proclamation also did not contain a detailed description of the form of the national cockade; the question whether white or blue should be on the outside was only settled definitively in 1879.[16] Its intention must, therefore, have been to enhance the status of the national colours of Bavaria in public awareness. The order that all male Bavarians should identify themselves publicly with the national colours, both at home and abroad, fits well into the framework of 'standardizing reforms'. The fact that the language of the proclamation is a curious mixture of traditional and modern formulations demonstrates the extent of the change that was in progress: nothing less than an absolutist, hierarchic state's attempting to transform itself into a national community. The cockade was to distinguish Bavarian 'subjects' (*Untertanen*) (not 'citizens') from foreigners so that they could be honoured for their 'loyalty' (*Anhänglichkeit*) to King and country. This sounds traditional, but is somewhat peculiar under the circumstances, as the existence of Bavaria in its present form depended precisely on her subjects' lack of enduring affection for and loyalty to their former rulers. By contrast, the notion that the cockade was to unite Bavarian subjects regardless of their rank was decidedly modern. Cockades were supposed to indicate the nationality of the bearer, and the colours blue and white were described as the 'national' colours (*Nationalfarbe*) of Bavaria – not the colours of the monarch or the kingdom. The exhortation to recognize fellow Bavarians as 'brothers' even contains an echo of the revolutionary demand for *fraternité*. The proclamation on national cockades thus suggested that Bavarian society was to be transformed from one in which different estates had their individual rights and duties to one in which all male citizens were equal. A national consciousness could also have the convenience of facilitating the mobilization of the population against enemies, even against France. It was perhaps not entirely coincidental that the decree introducing the Bavarian cockade bore the same date as a secret Franco-Bavarian agreement that prefigured the Confederation of the Rhine.[17]

The adoption of national cockades was indicative of the ambivalent relationship of Germany's monarchical states to the French revolution, with which cockades were by now closely associated. Cockades as such were not a particularly recent invention. Round pieces of cloth of a particular colour attached to items of clothing (primarily hats, as that gave them most prominence) had been used for various purposes for some time. In eighteenth-century England, for instance, they indicated allegiance to a political party, particularly on polling days,[18] as indeed they continue to do today. However, there does not seem to have been a very long tradition of 'national' cockades. In France, cockades in the colours of the commanding officers became part of military uniforms in the late seventeenth century. In 1767, the colour scheme was standardized; henceforth, the majority of soldiers wore a white cockade, while members of élite regiments were entitled to a black one. In 1782, the wearing of cockades was officially restricted to members of the armed forces. The outbreak of the revolution in France severed the connection between cockades and the army, because such symbols were now used primarily to indicate political convictions in France as well. By 1792, however, the French national cockade in red, white and blue had taken over. Red, white and blue cockades indicated French nationality as well as support for the ideals of the revolution, and had to be worn by Frenchmen and visiting foreigners alike. From September 1793, women were also required to wear them.[19]

Both the idea of a national cockade, and the design of the French national cockade, were products of the French Revolution. When they were transferred to German territories, however, the meaning of French revolutionary symbols changed somewhat. When they first appeared on the Rhine's left bank, they were consciously borrowed from France or even introduced by French occupation authorities. Whereas in France national cockades primarily represented support for the revolution, which entailed membership in the French nation state, outside the French borders such a 'national' identity had yet to be created. Variations of the French cockade were intended to infuse a sense of 'national' identity into the population of German regions that came under French control. Inhabitants of the Rhineland, for instance, were urged to wear a red, white and green cockade. But the attempt to create a Rhenish national identity from above failed dismally, and the lack of popular support for the occupation authorities had turned the tokens of liberty into symbols of the new ruling order imposed from above by 1794.[20] Far from being indicative of spontaneous popular feeling, national cockades came to be associated with a modern, but definitely post-revolutionary and state-centred order: in short, with nation-building from above. This was of course most acceptable to the states of the Confederation of the Rhine, which were in dire need of mechanisms that would secure the stability of their old and new territories. Cockades could therefore also be introduced in states that did not cooperate closely with France, and retained or introduced after 1815 in states that had not existed during the period of Napoleonic dominance: for instance, in Hesse-Kassel.[21]

Cockades appear to have been universally recognized as symbols of nationality. New national or supra-national symbols could, therefore, be designed by combining the colours of individual cockades. When Scharnhorst argued in an August 1808 memorandum that the war against Napoleon should be conducted as a German national war, he expressed this as follows: 'One should have only one cockade, the colours of the main nations in Germany, the Austrians and the Prussians, namely black, white and yellow.'[22] Crown Prince Ludwig of Bavaria, by contrast, preferred a German cockade in black, red and gold in 1813.[23] This colour scheme, which could be linked not only to the uniforms of the *Lützow'sches Freikorps*, but also, in some obscure way, to the Holy Roman Empire,[24] was open to a rather more federalist interpretation and was, therefore, more acceptable to rulers who took pride in their newly-acquired independence.

Whether national cockades actually made the national community, as it were, visible because they were worn by all male citizens must, however, remain an open question. The criminal codes of German states contained provisions that prohibited the wearing of the national cockade to convicted felons.[25] Clearly, the purpose of this was to humiliate criminals publicly, which would only work if the absence of the cockade singled them out. While it is possible that all honest men actually wore the national fashion accessory, the mere existence of such laws does not prove this. The Bavarian proclamation itself would appear to have been directed primarily at 'servants of the state', that is civil servants and soldiers, who may or may not have been a rôle model for others. But even linking soldiers and civil servants closely to 'their' state by asking them to identify publicly with its nationality, rather than with the regiment or branch of the civil service to which they belonged, and that their uniform was primarily designed to identify, was something of a revolution.

The territories of the Holy Roman Empire had placed few restrictions on the movement of persons from the service of one territory to that of another. In fact, everything suggests that those who held top bureaucratic or military positions in the Empire were members of a professional élite that was at the least imperial, if not European, in nature and outlook, and for which rank was far more important than nationality. This had profound effects on the composition of the bureaucratic and military élites. In France, for instance, ministers who tried to get the Crown out of its difficulties and those who contributed to them could be foreigners as easily as Frenchmen – Mazarin (Italian), John Law (British), or Jacques Necker (Swiss), for example. In fact, prohibitions against the employment of foreigners in high government posts seem to have been widely ignored, except in Britain.[26] In Germany the freedom to enter into the service of any monarch was an established right at least of the nobility. Prussian attempts to curb it in those territories received in compensation in 1805 had to be abandoned almost immediately.[27]

As a result, the senior ministers of German states were frequently not born in the state they served, which had the advantage of making them more dependent on their employer, as they lacked a local power base of their own. Metternich, Hardenberg or Stein come to mind, as does the chief administrator of Nassau-Weilburg, Hans von Gagern, who had been born in what was to become Hesse-Darmstadt. Count Montgelas, Bavarian Chief Minister at the time of the introduction of our cockades, happened to be born at Munich. But his family had no roots in Bavaria: his father's ancestors had served the Dukes of Savoy, and his father had worked for Austria before coming to Bavaria. Things were little different in the military. In 1789, a considerable part of the French officer corps was foreign-born, as were roughly 10 per cent of French troops. Even though foreigners attracted considerable suspicion in the early phases of the French Revolution,[28] the expansion of the French Empire under Napoleon saw to it that the supposedly effective French 'national' army was anything but homogenous in terms of nationality. A dictionary of French generals during the revolution and the empire not only lists 165 generals from states within the French sphere of influence, but also 19 generals from a state with which France was almost continually at war, namely the United Kingdom. In Prussia, this phenomenon was even more pronounced. One-third of the Prussian army's rank and file were non-Prussians at the accession of Frederick II, and the proportion rose slightly to 37 per cent in 1806.[29]

However, changes in French citizenship law introduced by Napoleon restricted the mobility of military personnel and civil servants. States could only employ foreigners in important positions if their native state had no claim on their emotions or their persons. Napoleon's 1811 naturalization edict challenged this assumption by stipulating that persons born on

French soil could not cast off their obligations to France even by naturalization abroad. If they served against their native country, they faced execution as traitors. French power being what it was at the time, this law could hardly be ignored. Hans von Gagern, born on the left bank of the Rhine, was no doubt one of many forced to give up a civil service position. This edict can be interpreted as nothing more than a strategic manoeuvre to force potential enemies to dismiss senior administrators or officers. Nevertheless, the introduction of national cockades elsewhere indicates that attempts to tie civil servants and soldiers more closely to the state that employed them were not restricted to France. Forcing civil servants to wear a national symbol in order to increase their national consciousness was also an attempt to turn professionals who happened to serve the Bavarian king to the best of their abilities, and might very likely serve the Prussian king the next month on the same terms, into Bavarian nationals or even nationalists.

This trend continued after 1815. Most German states stopped recruiting foreign soldiers, except as officers.[30] And some of the foreign officers wore their uniforms more as an indication of their political outlook than for any discernible practical purpose. In 1840s Hesse-Darmstadt, for instance, the Grand-Duke's Heir Presumptive was fond of putting on a Prussian uniform, while the Grand-Duke's younger brother preferred an Austrian one.[31] Certainly, things did not change from one day to the next: Hans von Gagern's career after 1815 is a case in point. He served as the Dutch and Frankfurt representative to the Germanic Diet before becoming a member of Hesse-Darmstadt's House of Assembly. Moreover, the situation in German states differed from that in other states because of the enormous fluctuation of frontiers up to 1815. Many civil servants were serving another state from the one they had worked for in 1789, even if they had not moved. Mobility of civil servants was also guaranteed by the Germanic Confederation's constitution, which permitted all citizens of German states to serve other German states without fear of sanctions.[32] However, this constitutional guarantee did not force German states to treat all applicants for public sector positions equally, and none appears to have done so; some constitutions clearly specified that preference should be given to state citizens.[33] This change in policy affected the lower ranks of the bureaucracy more than it did the higher ones. A recent study of Baden *Amtmänner* (district heads) has shown that virtually all those appointed after 1830 were born and educated in Baden.[34] A glance at the list of birthplaces of ministers of state listed in the *Minister-Ploetz*,[35] by contrast, suggests that foreign birth did not make appointment as a minister impossible at any time after 1815, but that prime ministers were now likely to be native-born citizens of the state they served. Whereas in 1815 both Austria and Prussia were governed by non-natives – Metternich and Hardenberg – both were the last non-native prime ministers in those states before German unification, if one exempts Duke Karl Friedrich August of Mecklenburg-Strelitz, the Prussian King's brother-in-law, who was Prussian chief minister between 1827 and 1837. (In 1867, immediately after the war of 1866, Friedrich Ferdinand von Beust, a native of Saxony, was appointed Imperial Chancellor in Vienna.) No foreign-born prime ministers were appointed in Baden, Württemberg, Hesse-Darmstadt, and Hesse-Kassel after 1820; in Bavaria and Hanover, the watershed was 1848.

There is some indication that the rising importance of the borders of German states in the nineteenth century was a conscious aim of policy. Contemporary observers feared that giving precedence to citizens in civil service appointments would create obstacles to German unification. Hans von Gagern remarked in the Hesse-Darmstadt legislative assembly in 1820 that 'this freedom to move across borders reminds us that we all belong to one great nation'.[36] But those who favoured individual states over 'German' nationalism could use this argument to advocate the opposite course of action: freedom of movement in Germany had to be restricted precisely because it would encourage a feeling of German national identity.[37]

This competition between a German and a particularist national identity added a particular twist to states' attempts to create nations at the state level. One effect of the period of Napoleonic dominance had been the rise of a pan-German nationalism that aimed at the liberation of 'Germany' from French domination. Both Prussia and Austria had sought to appeal to these nationalist sentiments during the 'wars of liberation' by hinting at their support of the notion of a German nation state of some sort. This had endowed nationalism focused on a German nation state with a certain degree of legitimacy. Even though plans for a close union of German states were quickly abandoned at the Vienna Congress, it was still thought necessary to conciliate nationalists in the opening speech of the Federal Diet in Frankfurt,[38] and it was impossible to suppress German nationalist sentiment entirely in practice.[39]

Moreover, because the Napoleonic reforms in Germany had (intentionally or not) started rather than completed a modernization of state, society and government, the conditions for carrying out the programme of turning German states into nation states were not favourable. Napoleon's ambition had been to rationalize 'Germany' sufficiently to make her a useful source of conscripts, but not to create potential rivals, and the policies of Austria and Prussia *vis-à-vis* the states of the 'Third Germany' were similar. Many of the states in Germany remained tiny. None could boast a contiguous territory without exclaves or enclaves; large parts of Prussia, Bavaria and Hesse-Darmstadt were entirely unconnected to the heartlands of these states. As states that had evolved from one dynasty, for instance, the two Hesses (-Darmstadt and -Kassel) shared the same colours, and it was difficult to come up with recognizably different national cockades for all of them. This was particularly noticeable in the so-called 'Smaller Saxon Courts' that had been members of the Confederation of the Rhine, but whose territorial distribution appeared to have escaped rationalization completely: Saxe-Coburg (Gotha), Saxe-Gotha (Altenburg), Saxe-Hildburghausen, Saxe-Meiningen, Saxe-Weimar, and Saxony. Saxe-Coburg-Gotha and Saxe-Meiningen actually had exactly the same green-white cockade.[40] In such circumstances, the politics of 'nationalization' made much less sense and was pursued with much less vigour than in, say, Bavaria. The Nassau colours, for instance, were blue and orange-yellow (as were those of Brunswick and the province of Lower Austria).[41] But the only surviving contemporary official document in the Hessisches Hauptstaatsarchiv Wiesbaden that specifies the colours of the Nassau flag is an instruction from the customs official at Caub issued in 1840 concerning the flags ships had to use on the Rhine.[42] The German national movement copied some of the individual states' methods and created a cockade of its own in black, red and gold that competed with those of the individual states (even though the Reuß and Waldeck flags had the same colours,[43] they were hardly serious competition for the 'German' flag).

Even after many decades of research on German nationalism, it remains difficult to estimate the level of support for national unification in the period of Napoleonic dominance or its aftermath. Helga Schulz has recently tried an original approach based on the analysis of the titles of journals published in German states around 1800. She has discovered two waves of what she calls 'semantic fields': journals with a title referring either to *Bürger*, *Mensch*, or *Nation* – burgher/citizen, man or nation, the semantic arsenal, so to speak, of the revolution – remained relatively few, and the peak of the publication of such titles lay between 1790 and 1799; by 1810 their number had declined drastically. Thereafter, editors preferred words such as *Volk* and/or *Vaterland*, people and fatherland, on their title pages.[44] But these results also illustrate the problems that research into this topic inevitably faces: all these terms can refer equally well to individual states or to Germany, or indeed to something in between. It is, therefore, not quite clear what the significance of the change is precisely, other than an indication of an increasing distaste for revolutionary vocabulary. For instance, when Karl von Rotteck delivered a speech in praise of the new Baden constitution in 1818, he remarked that it had 'created a Baden people' (*Volk*), and there is no reason to suspect that he meant any other people when he closed his speech with the exhortation, 'May heaven bless [. . .] the *free people*.'[45]

This ambiguous relationship between the states and Germany remained difficult to resolve; it was to remain one of the most significant legacies of the Napoleonic era. In the Holy Roman Empire, the relationship between the territories and the Empire had been much less problematic. The Empire was so venerable and yet so flexible and unobtrusive that no state felt compelled or able to challenge it, and no German national movement sought to construct a centralized German state. The destruction of the Holy Roman Empire under Napoleon changed this in various ways. The experience of French quasi-occupation gave rise to a small but influential group of radical nationalists who longed to turn Germany into a great power able to rival France. At the same time, the incomplete rationalization of the political order of Germany allowed at least some states to attempt to travel the road to independent nation status, without offering a permanent solution to the 'German question'.

Under these circumstances, it is hardly surprising that the national symbols remained contested. The unofficial German national flag in black, red and gold meant different things to different people. In 1848, one pamphlet felt that it was necessary to respond to the charge that its three-colour-combination (most state cockades only had two) made it too similar to the French tricolour.[46] It was therefore suspected that this flag represented 'French freedom' rather than 'German freedom',[47] which indicates that at least some of those who wore German cockades in the decades after 1815 viewed them first and foremost as a symbol of political freedom. However, it would be mistaken to interpret the German cockade, as one recent discussion of the 1832 Hambach Festival has done, solely along those lines: as something opposed to the 'complicated' colour schemes of noble coats of arms, and signifying an abstract belief in unity and freedom.[48] It was a direct counterpart of the national cockades of the individual states (which had even simpler colour schemes), and it indicated a belief in the preponderance of the German over the 'particularist' nationality. What made the 1832 Hambach Festival so dangerous in the eyes of German governments, for instance, was not that large numbers of cockades in black, red and gold were sold at the festival. What was particularly frightening was that by all accounts blue and white ones could scarcely be found at a celebration of the Bavarian constitution. This marked the oppositional character of the event even more than the speeches, which could probably be heard by only a few of the participants. Accordingly, persons who returned to Mainz from the festival wearing a German cockade rather than one of the officially recognized ones were arrested by the troops guarding the federal fortress,[49] and the German cockade was prohibited shortly afterwards.[50]

When state governments succumbed to the wave of revolutionary feeling in March 1848, the Germanic Confederation declared black, red and gold, supposedly the colours of the Holy Roman Empire, to be the colours of the Germanic Confederation, which had previously possessed only a coat of arms.[51] In May 1848, Frederick William IV of Prussia ordered the army to wear the German cockade along with the Prussian one,[52] and in August 1848 the National Assembly ordered all German troops to honour the German colours. This apparently unconditional surrender of state nationalism in Prussia and the smaller states would seem to indicate that the states' attempts at creating a national consciousness had failed. However, the state of affairs was considerably more complex. In the Rhineland, for example, the black-white Prussian flag, which had hardly been used there before 1848, now became the emblem of the region's Protestant minority, whereas Catholics adopted black-red-gold.[53] The prospect of German unity could create at least as much dissent as particularism.[54]

After the shock of revolution had passed, German states reinforced their attempts to create a national consciousness by adding a cultural dimension to the project. It has been documented, for instance, how many traditions we think of as typically Bavarian were created during those years.[55] But the German national flag nevertheless did not disappear from public view. After the revolution had been suppressed, Austria adopted the position that the Germanic Confederation had never ceased to exist and should be formally re-established. Black, red and gold had been declared the colours of the Germanic Confederation by an act of the Federal Diet in March 1848, which was, according to this interpretation, still legally valid, and had not subsequently been revoked. Nevertheless, the use of the German colours remained prohibited in Northern Germany, particularly in Prussia.[56] Careful observers might have noted that this did not bode well for Prussia's future relationship with the Confederation. As alienation between Northern and Southern German states increased, the southern states appear to have lost any remaining unease regarding the colours of 1848 and used them ever more demonstratively. In 1862, Württemberg officially permitted the use of the German colours, and in the same year Baden insisted that German flags were to be displayed when the bridge across the Rhine at Kehl was officially opened. When the Austrian Emperor Franz Joseph's birthday was celebrated in Frankfurt in 1863, they were to be found everywhere.[57] Thus it was logical that the troops of those states allied with Austria in 1866 who fought against Prussia in the name of the Germanic Confederation wore black, red and gold armbands. Some distinguishing mark was apparently necessary because the Confederation's military reforms of the 1850s had rendered the uniforms of German states all but indistinguishable; but the choice of colours surely indicated what was at stake.[58] The Prussian victory in this war saw to it that black, red and gold were suppressed for good, and their significance was quickly forgotten.

When the German Constituent National Assembly discussed the adoption of black, red and gold as the national flag on 2 July 1919, several members noted that these had been the colours of the Lützow Free Corps and the 1848 National Assembly. One speaker mentioned that they had been used by the 'enemies of Prussia' in 1866; none recalled that they had been the official colours of the Germanic Confederation.[59] The individual states' colours reigned almost supreme until 1919; the Wilhelmine Empire never developed national symbols strong enough to replace them. The article on 'cockades' in the *Encyclopaedia Britannica*'s 1910 edition stated simply that national cockades existed in all 'nations', for instance in Bavaria and Prussia, without so much as mentioning a German one.[60] Indeed, when a unit of the German army re-captured a fortress in Hungary in 1915, the soldiers, who happened to be Bavarians, unfurled a white and blue flag, and took the trouble to pick blue and white flowers for bouquets.[61] Thus, while the aim of turning at least some German states into modern nation states within the framework of the territorial order imposed by the Vienna settlement had not been achieved, the legacy of the national colours adopted during the Napoleonic period was of long duration.

Notes

1. T. Nipperdey, *Germany from Napoleon to Bismarck 1800–1866*, trans. D. Nolan (Dublin, 1996), p.1.
2. For the Bavarian reforms see the detailed documentation in M. Schimke (ed.), *Regierungsakten des Kurfürstentums und Königreichs*

Bayern 1799–1815 (Munich, 1996). Recent surveys of these reforms can be found in Nipperdey, *Germany*, pp.54–64, in J. J. Sheehan, *German History 1770–1866* (Oxford, 1989), pp.251ff., and in H.-U. Wehler, *Deutsche Gesellschaftsgeschichte. Erster Band: Vom Feudalismus des Alten Reiches bis zur defensiven Modernisierung der Reformära 1700–1815* (2nd edn, Munich, 1989). A. Schulz, *Herrschaft durch Verwaltung: Die Rheinbundreformen in Hessen-Darmstadt unter Napoleon (1803–1815)* (Stuttgart, 1991) is an excellent monograph on the reforms in the states of the Confederation of the Rhine.

3. Cf. K. Rob (ed.), *Regierungsakten des Großherzogtums Berg 1806–1813* (Munich, 1992); idem (ed.), *Regierungsakten des Primatialstaats und des Großherzogtums Frankfurt 1806–1813* (Munich, 1995); idem (ed.), *Regierungsakten des Königreichs Westphalen 1807–1813* (Munich, 1992); C. Schmidt, *Le Grand-Duché de Berg (1806–1813). Étude sur la domination française en Allemagne sous Napoléon Ier* (Paris, 1905).

4. E. Fehrenbach, *Traditionale Gesellschaft und revolutionäres Recht: Die Einführung des Code Napoléon in den Rheinbundstaaten* (Göttingen, 1974).

5. J. Kocka, *Weder Stand noch Klasse. Unterschichten um 1800* (Bonn, 1990), p.25.

6. The most recent summary of Prussian developments can be found in O. Büsch (ed.), *Handbuch der preußischen Geschichte. Band II: Das 19. Jahrhundert und große Themen der Geschichte Preußens* (Berlin, 1992).

7. K.-J. Matz, *Pauperismus und Bevölkerung: Die gesetzlichen Ehebeschränkungen in den süddeutschen Staaten während des 19. Jahrhunderts* (Stuttgart, 1980).

8. G. E. Krug, *Die Entwicklung ökonomischer Freiheitsrechte in Deutschland im Wandel von Staat, Wirtschaft und Gesellschaft vom Ancien Régime bis zur Reichsgründung (1776–1871)* (Frankfurt/Main, 1995).

9. J. Gerner, *Vorgeschichte und Entstehung der württembergischen Verfassung im Spiegel der Quellen (1815–1819)* (Stuttgart, 1989).

10. H. von Treitschke, *Deutsche Geschichte im neunzehnten Jahrhundert*, Vol. 2 (6th edn, Leipzig, 1906), p.296; H.-U. Wehler, *Deutsche Gesellschaftsgeschichte. Zweiter Band: Von der Reformära bis zur industriellen und politischen «Deutschen Doppelrevolution» 1815–1845/49* (2nd edn, Munich, 1989), pp.381f.; Nipperdey, *Germany*, pp.238f.

11. R. Koselleck, *Preußen zwischen Reform und Revolution: Allgemeines Landrecht, Verwaltung und soziale Bewegung von 1791 bis 1848* (2nd edn, Stuttgart, 1975), pp.163–216.

12. S. J. Woolf, 'The Construction of a European World-View in the Revolutionary-Napoleonic Years', *Past and Present*, 137 (1992), p.101.

13. H. Schulze, *Staat und Nation in der europäischen Geschichte* (Munich, 1994), p.105.

14. *Königlich-Baierisches Regierungsblatt* (1806), p.25.

15. Descriptions of the flags of those German states that survived the wars of unification can be found in H. G. Ströhl, *Landesfarben und Kokarden: Ein Vademekum für Maler, Graphiker, Fahnenfabrikanten und Dekorateure* (Berlin, 1910).

16. Ibid., p.17.

17. H.-P. Ullmann, 'Baden 1800–1830', in *Handbuch der Baden-Württembergischen Geschichte*, vol. 3 (Stuttgart, 1992), p.29.

18. See, for example, G. Rudé, *Wilkes and Liberty: A Social Study of 1763 to 1774* (Oxford, 1962), pp.40, 60, 64.

19. P. Berthelot, 'Cocarde', in *La grande encyclopédie: Inventaire raisonné des sciences, des lettres et des arts*, vol. 11 (Paris, [1850]), pp.756f.

20. O. Dotzenrod, 'Republikanische Feste im Rheinland zur Zeit der Französischen Revolution', in D. Düding, P. Friedemann, and P. Münch (eds), *Öffentliche Festkultur: Politische Feste in Deutschland von der Aufklärung bis zum Ersten Weltkrieg* (Reinbek bei Hamburg, 1988), pp.46–66.

21. For their existence in Prussia see *Gesetz-Sammlung für die Königlich Preußischen Staaten* (1825), p.192; Hessisches Staatsarchiv Marburg, 16/II 14/20, Report from Hanau, 16 July 1847.

22. F. vom Stein, *Briefe und amtliche Schriften, Band II/2* (Stuttgart, 1960), p.823.

23. V. Valentin, *Das Hambacher Nationalfest* (Mainz, 1982), p.34.

24. Cf. V. von Zuccalmaglio, *Die deutsche Kokarde: Ein politischer Katechismus für das deutsche Volk* (Koblenz, 1848), p.3; *Protokolle der deutschen Bundesversammlung* (1848), 137, p.234.

25. *Gesetz-Sammlung für die Königlich Preußischen Staaten* (1825), p.192. In Hesse-Kassel, someone convicted of a criminal offence abroad argued unsuccessfully in 1847 that, as he had not been deprived of the right to wear the Electoral Hessian cockade by the sentence of a foreign court, this punishment did not give him a criminal record in the Electorate: Regierung Hanau to Ministry of

the Interior, 16 July 1847 and reply, 27 July 1847, Hessisches Staatsarchiv Marburg 16/II 14/20.

26. The laws prohibiting the employment of foreigners in public offices were 12 and 13 Will. III, c. 3; 1 Geo. I, c. 4.

27. F. Keinemann, 'Freizügigkeit und Dienstzwang: Erwägung eines Verbots für den Adel in den preußischen Entschädigungslanden, auszuwandern oder in fremde Dienste zu treten. 1805', *Historisches Jahrbuch* 93 (1973), pp.104–10.

28. G. Noiriel, *La tyrannie du national: Le droit d'asyle en Europe, 1793–1993* (Paris, 1991), pp.35f.

29. P. Paret, 'Conscription and the End of the Old Regime in France and Prussia', in W. Treue (ed.), *Geschichte als Aufgabe: Festschrift für Otto Büsch zu seinem 60. Geburtstag* (Berlin, 1988), pp.159f.; S. J. Woolf, *Napoleon's Integration of Europe* (London, 1991), p.171.

30. See, for example, Hessisches Staatsarchiv Marburg 16/II 14/10 I and II; *Sammlung von Gesetzen, Verordnungen, Ausschreiben und sonstigen allgemeinen Verfügungen für die kurhessischen Staaten* (1832), p.183; (1834), pp.113ff.

31. V. Valentin, *Geschichte der deutschen Revolution von 1848–49* (2 vols, Berlin, 1930–33), Vol. 1, p.172.

32. E. R. Huber (ed.), *Dokumente zur deutschen Verfassungsgeschichte. Band 1: Deutsche Verfassungsdokumente 1803–1850* (Stuttgart, 1961), p.90.

33. Ibid., pp.176, 44; *Königlich-Baierisches Regierungsblatt* (1816), p.547.

34. J. Eibach, *Der Staat vor Ort: Amtmänner und Bürger im 19. Jahrhundert am Beispiel Badens* (Frankfurt/Main, 1994), p.36; cf. E. Treichel, *Der Primat der Bürokratie: bürokratischer Staat und bürokratische Elite im Herzogtum Nassau 1806-1866* (Stuttgart, 1991), pp.523–9, 542–63.

35. B. Spuler, *Regenten und Regierungen der Welt, Teil II, Band 3* (2nd edn, Würzburg, 1962).

36. *Verhandlungen der 2. Kammer der Landstände des Großherzogtums Hessen* (1820/21) II, Beilage LXXXVIII, p.69.

37. Ibid., VI, CLXII, p.17.

38. *Protokolle der deutschen Bundesversammlung* (1816), p.38.

39. D. Düding, *Organisierter gesellschaftlicher Nationalismus in Deutschland (1808–1847): Bedeutung und Funktion der Turner- und Sängervereine für die deutsche Nationalbewegung* (Munich, 1984).

40. Ströhl, *Landesfarben*, p.46.

41. Ibid., p.10.

42. Hessisches Hauptstaatsarchiv Wiesbaden, 253/13, Ausschreiben des Rheinzollbeamten in Caub, 31 January 1840. I am most grateful to Herr Seeger for this information.
43. Ströhl, *Landesfarben*, p.43; H. Hattenhauer, *Deutsche National-symbole: Zeichen und Bedeutung* (Munich, 1984), pp.19f.
44. H. Schulz, 'Mythos und Aufklärung: Frühformen des Nationalismus in Deutschland', *Historische Zeitschrift*, 263 (1996), pp.53–60.
45. K. von Rotteck, 'Zur Feier der neu verkündeten ständischen Verfassung für das Großherzogtum Baden', in P. Wende (ed.), *Politische Reden 1792–1867* (Frankfurt/Main, 1990), p.137. For Bavaria cf. E. Schunk, 'Vom nationalen Konstitutionalismus zum konstitutionellen Nationalismus: Der Einfluß der "Franzosenzeit" auf den pfälzischen Liberalismus zur Zeit des Hambacher Festes', *Zeitschrift für bayerische Landesgeschichte*, 51 (1988), p.451.
46. In 1847, a Prussian official investigating a supposed disturbance in the Düsseldorf district merely enquired whether the Marseillaise had been sung and 'three-coloured flags' had been on display, leaving it open whether he was actually on the lookout for red-white-blue or black-red-gold: U. Schneider, *Politische Festkultur im 19. Jahrhundert: Die Rheinprovinz von der französischen Zeit bis zum Ende des Ersten Weltkrieges (1806–1918)* (Essen, 1995), p.109.
47. Zuccalmaglio, *Kokarde*, p.3.
48. C. Foerster, 'Das Hambacher Fest von 1832: Volksfest und National-fest einer oppositionellen Massenbewegung', in Düding, Friedemann, Münch (eds), *Festkultur*, p.120.
49. Valentin, *Hambacher Nationalfest*, pp.100, 111.
50. R. D. Billinger, Jr., *Metternich and the German Question: States' Rights and Federal Duties, 1820–1834* (Cranbury, NJ, 1991), p.122.
51. *Protokolle der deutschen Bundesversammlung* (1848), 137, p.234.
52. I. Mieck, 'Preußen von 1807 bis 1850: Reformen, Restauration und Revolution', in Büsch (ed.), *Handbuch*, p.242.
53. Schneider, *Festkultur*, pp.128f.
54. J. Sperber, 'Festivals of National Unity in the German Revolution of 1848–1849', *Past and Present*, 136 (1992), pp.132, 138.
55. M. Hanisch, *Für Fürst und Vaterland: Legitimitätsstiftung in Bayern zwischen Revolution 1848 und deutscher Einheit* (Munich, 1991); A. F. F. Green, 'Particularist State-Building and the German Question: Hanover, Saxony, and Württemberg 1850–1866', unpublished Ph.D. thesis, University of Cambridge, 1998.
56. B. Gubben, *Schwarz, Rot und Gold: Biographie einer Fahne* (Berlin, 1991), pp.215f.

57. Ibid., p.217.
58. P. Wacker, 'Die Herzoglich Nassauischen Truppen: Teil 1', *Zeitschrift für Heereskunde*, 45 (1981), pp.101–8, here p.103.
59. E. Hilkron (ed.), *Die Deutsche Nationalversammlung im Jahre 1919 in ihrer Arbeit für den Ausbau des neuen deutschen Volksstaates*, Vol. 5 (Berlin, 1920), pp.3005, 2995f.
60. 'Cockade', in *Encyclopaedia Britannica*, Vol. 6 (11th edition, Cambridge, 1910), p.622.
61. H. H. Herwig, *The First World War: Germany and Austria-Hungary 1914–1918* (London, 1997), p.142.

–13–

The Napoleonic Moment in Prussian Church Policy

Christopher Clark

On Easter Sunday 1802, Napoleon Bonaparte published the text of a Convention between the French government and Pope Pius VII. Known as the Concordat of 1801, the convention opened with an acknowledgement by the French Republic that 'the holy, apostolic and Roman religion is the religion of the great majority of French citizens'. There followed a list of conditions that had been agreed between the two parties 'both for the good of religion and for the maintenance of domestic tranquillity'. Among these was the stipulation (art. 1) that the Catholic religion would be 'freely exercised in France' within the limits imposed by the need to maintain public order, and confirmation (art. 4) that the Pope retained the power of canonical investiture 'following the forms established with respect to France before the change of government'. Under article 6, bishops were required, before taking office, to 'render directly, between the hands of the First Consul, the oath of fealty that was in use before the change of government'. For its part, the government undertook (art. 11) to provide bishops and priests working in dioceses and parishes with an 'appropriate remuneration'.[1]

The Concordat marked a dramatic departure both from the confessional arrangements of the *ancien régime* and from the confessional practice of the Revolution. On the one hand, the massive secularization of Church lands and other property during the revolutionary era was confirmed as irreversible. On the other, the clerical democracy enshrined in the now virtually defunct civil constitution of the clergy (1790) was expunged without trace. Notwithstanding the 'Organic Articles' unilaterally appended to the Concordat by the French government, which further strengthened the hand of the state *vis-à-vis* Rome, the new settlement conceded an important if circumscribed authority over French Catholics to the Pope, who had not been a signatory to the old civil constitution. Most importantly, it secured for the Church a permanent place in the life of the state. The Concordat was to prove among the most durable monuments of the Napoleonic era. It survived the Bourbon Restoration despite the titular re-establishment of the catholic faith as the 'religion of state'[2] and remained the foundation document in French Church-State relations until well into the Third Republic (1905); in Alsace-Lorraine it remains in force to this day.

These arrangements were of the greatest importance for Catholic Church affairs in those parts of Europe that had come under the direct control or indirect influence of Napoleonic France. In the Rhineland, the Organic Articles remained in force as part of the legacy of Napoleonic law, even after 1815, when the Rhenish territories fell to Protestant Prussia.[3] The Italian Concordat, drawn up in 1802/03 but only fully ratified by an imperial decree of 1805, was in some respects more favourable to the Church than the French original, but followed the earlier model in formally establishing the Catholic religion as the 'religion of state', extending the influence of the government over the appointment of bishops, curtailing Papal powers of appointment in Venetia and the Legations, and loosening Church control over the management of charities. Like the French Concordat, it was supplemented by additional 'articles' that further consolidated the authority of the state; and as in France – a measure particularly resented by Rome – a Cabinet Minister was appointed with responsibility for religious affairs.[4] In Bavaria, likewise, the government negotiated a concordat in 1806/09 and then abandoned it, only to resume negotiations in 1815 and ratify an agreement in June 1817. Here, as in France, the new agreement confirmed the state's power to appoint bishops; in many other respects it made extensive concessions to Church requirements. The state agreed, for example, to ban books identified as undesirable by the Church authorities and formally forbade insults against the Catholic Church; the Concordat even promised that bishoprics, cathedral chapters and seminaries would be provided with adequate landed property to assure their economic independence, a measure that amounted to a partial reversal of the wholesale secularizations of the Napoleonic era. But here, as in France, the provisions of the Concordat were modified by territorial law, most importantly the Religious Edict of 1818, which drew extensively on the Organic Articles and contradicted a number of the concessions made in the concordat. In the Netherlands, likewise, the government unilaterally reinstated the Organic Articles and other pieces of Napoleonic confessional legislation in 1816/18, much to the chagrin of the Belgian Catholics; a Concordat was eventually signed in 1827.

The Restoration era saw the ratification of concordats in a range of

European states of Catholic or mixed faith, including Tuscany (1817), Piedmont (1817), the Kingdom of the Two Sicilies (1821), Hanover (1826), Lucca (1826), the Netherlands (1827) and the Swiss Cantons (1828).[5] These agreements varied considerably in their detail, but the establishment of Concordats and the conclusion, in many other states, of contractual agreements with Rome at a sub-constitutional level[6] testified to the enhancement of papal authority over the hierarchy that was a consequence of the settlement of 1801 and to the economic and structural damage wrought by secularization upon the national churches.[7] One of the most striking characteristics of the Napoleonic concordat was that under article 4 it granted the pope the power to invest new bishops and depose old ones, a power that had never been conceded to Rome by the authorities of the Gallican Church.[8] Throughout central and western Europe, the new 'post-Napoleonic' agreements between Church and state embodied an intertwining of papal jurisdictional primacy with the ecclesiastical sovereignty of the state.

These aspects of the Napoleonic legacy in European Church policy are well known and have been the subject of extensive research. Here, I propose to juxtapose the Church of the Concordat with another, Protestant, ecclesiastical invention of the early nineteenth century: the Church of the Prussian Union, founded in 1817 by King Frederick William III and gradually elaborated during the 1820s. I will be suggesting that, for all the many differences in genesis, context, timing and confessional substance, the Church of the Prussian Union and the Church of the Concordat were European Church establishments of a new type, which embodied novel ways of thinking about the rôle of religion in the legitimation of state power.

Why did Napoleon execute such a reversal in French ecclesiastical policy in 1801? One thing is sure: not because of his personal adherence to the doctrines of the Catholic Church. According to Christopher Herold's classic study, *Mind of Napoleon* (1955), the First Consul and later Emperor was 'privately a Voltairean deist throughout his life'.[9] At the age of seventeen he wrote an essay in which, drawing on themes from Rousseau's *Contrat Social*, he condemned rigorist forms of piety as a menace to the state on the grounds that excessive fidelity to the Gospels was likely to nourish political subversion.[10] He does not appear to have attended the services of the constitutional Church in or after 1790. Many of his remarks on religion suggest a largely instrumental conception of its rôle within the polity: he is reported to have announced to the priests of Milan in 1800 after the Battle of Marengo (14 June) that 'the Roman Catholic is the only religion that can make a stable community happy and establish the foundations of good government'.[11] He observed on various occasions that religion contributed to social peace by reassuring the disadvantaged that the iniquities of this world would be made good in the next. He remarked famously to the Council of State in 1806 that he saw in religion not the mystery of the incarnation, but the mystery of the social order.[12]

Why then did Napoleon break with the anticlerical policy of his revolutionary predecessors to restore the Church, through negotiation with the Holy See, to a permanent place within the life of the French state? The answer most historians have given is that the Concordat was an act of sheer *raison d'état* generated by the political exigencies of the day. Years of harassment and discrimination at varying levels of intensity since 1790 had left the French Church deeply divided between the adherents of the demoralized 'constitutional' Church, and the adherents of the proscribed 'refractory Church' whose opposition to revolutionary secularizing measures had placed it at the centre of a formidable movement of Catholic revival. From the mid-1790s, there was an explosive resurgence of devotional practices, driven especially by female piety and militancy: bells were ringing again in the Hérault despite laws against them, crucifixes, medallions and confraternities were reappearing, and Corpus Christi processions could again be seen in many areas.[13] The consequence was a stand-off between two parallel Churches. The expanding scale and energy of revival made it imperative to find a settlement that would assist the authorities in 'stifling religion as a vehicle of protest'.[14]

Moreover, Napoleon was acutely aware of the rôle played by religious allegiances in the counter-revolutionary insurgency still tying French troops down in the western provinces. Indeed, he appears to have believed that the refractory clergy in France were being led and coordinated by fifty émigré bishops in the pay of England: 'their influence must be destroyed and for this I require the authority of the pope'.[15]

During the Italian campaign, he had had ample opportunity to observe the loyalty that bound many Italian communities to their traditional faith and observance. The revolt of the Calabrian Sanfedisti, who succeeded briefly in gaining control of the Neapolitan Republic in 1799, illustrated the dangers of allowing local patriotisms to feed off religious resentments.[16] And the First Consul was also aware of the indignation aroused in the occupied Rhineland and Belgium by impious acts on the part of the French troops. Unless some means could be found to neutralize the religious disputes that were besetting the French at home and abroad, the chances of drawing Spain and the Italian states into an alliance against England were likely to remain slim. If Bonaparte saw negotiation with Rome as the way out of these difficulties, this also reflected his consistent inclination to over-estimate the power and influence of the pope. One of his earliest decrees as First Consul on 30 December 1799 ordered funeral honours for Pius VI, who had died in captivity at Valence, as 'a man who had occupied one of the greatest offices in the world'.[17] In August 1816, while in exile on St Helena, Napoleon remarked to Las Casas: 'I did not despair, sooner or later, by some means or another, of obtaining for myself the direction of that Pope, and from that time, what an influence! What a lever of opinion on the rest of the world!'[18]

Lastly, there was an imperial – or imperialist – dimension to Napoleon's confessional policy. In a much-quoted retrospective defence of his decision to negotiate with Rome, Napoleon declared that 'by making myself a Catholic, I was victorious in the war of the Vendée, by making myself a Muslim I established myself in Egypt, in making myself ultramontane, I won hearts in Italy [he is referring here to the Concordat granted to Italy in 1805]. If I were to govern a people of Jews, I would re-establish the Temple of Solomon.'[19]

Unlike Frederick the Great's similar but purely speculative reflections half a century earlier, these claims should be understood literally: a letter from Napoleon to the Divan of Cairo during the Egyptian campaign of 1798–9 opened with the rather extraordinary greeting (extraordinary at least in the mouth of a late-eighteenth-century European from Catholic Corsica): 'There is no other God but God and Mahomet is his prophet!' The First Consul even went so far as to sue for credit points by portraying himself as a Muslim who, in despoiling the papacy, had advanced the cause of Islam. In communications with his Muslim interlocutors he adopted the rhetoric of a Mahdi, bringing promises of millennarian political and spiritual renewal. Domestic and external pressures and the flexibility imposed by imperial over-expansion thus intertwined to strengthen the case for confessional conciliation by the state, much as they did for the British administrations in Catholic Quebec, on Malta and Gozo, or in the Orthodox Ionian Islands.[20] In short, to borrow Portalis's paraphrase of Napoleon: 'Good order and public safety [did] not permit us to leave the institutions of the Church to their own devices.'

Confining ourselves now to the rather narrower horizon of Prussian Church policy in the Restoration era, we might well ask what aspects of the Prussian Union – if any – justify comparison with the Concordat. A first objection to such a comparison might well arise from the question of religious belief broached above. Unlike Napoleon, Frederick William was a believing Christian who went to church. In 1808, during his exile in East Prussia (after the catastrophic defeats of Jena and Auerstedt), he experienced an religious awakening of sorts, brought on by the preaching of Pastor Borowski in Königsberg. The duress of exile and the struggle and exaltation of the Wars of Liberation appear to have awakened in him the faith in a providential God, whose hand could be seen in the restoration of Prussian fortunes.

But if we leave aside for a moment the question of personal religious conviction, we find that the two men, and their two policies, were less far apart in some ways than we may suppose. As a young man, Frederick William had declared in his confession of faith that he held the Church to be the 'best pillar of the state' and 'the best means of promoting the peace and welfare of civil society'.[21] In this endorsement of the social functionality of religion, as in his later zest for the rationalization of religious practice, Frederick William remained a child of the Enlightenment. He was staunchly anti-Catholic, but accepted with equanimity the conversion of his daughter Charlotte to the Russian Orthodox Church. And of course the same relative indifference to confessional boundaries could be observed in his project for a Union of the Lutheran and Calvinist Churches in Prussia. Originally launched as a titular merging of the two Protestant confessions in Prussia – the Lutheran and the Calvinist – the Prussian Union eventually came to encompass the entire spectrum of Protestant observance. A new syncretic liturgy was provided, which incorporated elements of both Calvinist and Lutheran practice. A long and growing list of further stipulations governed orders of service – including the length of sermons, vestments, the number and disposition of candles and crucifixes and so on. By 1830, the great majority of Protestant communities had accepted Frederick William's compromise.

If we turn to the context of the Prussian Union and the problems it was intended to address, we find a number of analogies with the 'Napoleonic Moment' of 1801. In the first place, the instruments with which Prussian Church policy was executed in the Restoration era were themselves in large part the fruit of the transformations wrought in the Prussian state structure by the 'impact of Napoleon'. It is true that responsibility for Church affairs had been transferred to state bodies in the provinces acquired as a consequence of the Polish partitions of 1772, 1793 and 1795. Similar arrangements were made for the territories acquired by way of compensation from France in 1803, and extended in the following year to East Prussia. In most of these areas, it was the War and Domain Chambers that came to exercise the supervisory and consistorial powers formerly held by Church bodies. But it was only in the 'reform era', in the context of the restructuring that followed the comprehensive defeat of Prussia by France in 1806/07, that the entire Prussian Church administration was unified under the control of the central state administration. Responsibility for the administration of Church affairs initially fell to the 'Section for Worship and Public Instruction', one of six sections within the reformed Ministry of the Interior.[22] The task of this body was to be the 'promotion of true religiosity without coercion or mystical fanaticism; freedom of conscience and tolerance without public provocation'.[23] However, on 3 November 1817, scarcely one month after his proclamation of the Church Union, Frederick William announced in a Cabinet Order that the 'dignity and importance of religious, educational and school affairs made it advisable to entrust these to a separate minister.'[24] The result was the foundation of the Ministry of Religion, Education and Public Health, whose more commonly used title, *Kultusministerium*, recalled the *Ministère des Cultes* established in France under Portalis in 1804.

Moreover, the territorial settlement of 1815 – itself a consequence of the threat Napoleon had posed to the German states – had brought a large area of the Rhineland under Prussian control. This appears to have influenced the preparations for Union in two ways. It is reasonable, in the first place, to assume that the very substantial increase in the number of Catholic Prussian subjects strengthened, in Frederick William's view, the case for Church reform, since it raised question about the confessional 'balance of power' within the population and the need for a solidarity among Protestants commensurate with the relative homogeneity of the Catholic Church in the Prussian territories. Frederick William did not seek publicly to legitimate his unionist project in these terms – the danger of playing into the hands of those opponents of union who saw it as a 'Catholicizing' measure militated against an overt appeal to such reasoning; but an awareness of the enhanced weight of the Catholic Church within the kingdom was latent in state confessional policy after 1815 and, indeed, concerns over this issue were to explode after 1830 in the controversy over mixed marriages. In the context of the eastern provinces, however, Frederick William did articulate a clear connection between liturgical and ecclesiastical reform and the need to consolidate the confessional identity of the Protestant diaspora: 'the restoration of the Liturgy', he wrote to Interior Minister Schuckmann in September 1816, 'will help to bolster the man on the land in [Prussian] Lithuania, who is particularly exposed to the temptations of Catholic proselytizing activity'.[25]

A second problem posed by the acquisition of the Rhenish territories concerned the constitutional arrangements of the Calvinist Protestants of that region. The reformist aspirations of the Rhenish Calvinists – in which traditional Calvinist constitutional traditions were blended with the democratic principles endorsed by the former French administration – eventually brought them into direct conflict with the neo-absolutist practice of the Prussian government. The negotiations turned on the powers, permanence, and representative character of district and provincial synods. The central concern for those who defended a presbyterial-synodal constitution was that the autonomy of the Church should be protected against unilateral intervention from the state. The presbyteries and district and provincial synods were to be, in the words of one Rhenish manifesto: 'the executive, disciplinary and administrative organs of the Church, from which there can be no appeal to a state authority'.[26] The government seemed willing at first to make concessions; but the provincial synod that ultimately emerged met only once and was accorded a purely advisory rôle. The consequence was a Church-constitutional conflict that lasted over two decades.[27] In the event, the presbyterial-democratic aspirations of the Rhenish ecclesiastical liberals and their ideological allies in Brandenburg were quashed under the Prussian Union, just as the Concordat expunged the clerical democracy installed in 1790.

There was also the need, for Frederick William in the 1810s and 1820s as for Napoleon in 1800, to forestall the potentially anarchic effects of religious revival. Frederick William had an instinctively neo-absolutist aversion to the proliferation of sects. Throughout the 1820s, Altenstein, chief of the new *Kultusministerium* and one of Frederick William's most dependable allies, kept a close eye on sectarian developments both within and beyond the borders of the kingdom, assembling dossiers on specific sectarian movements – of particular interest were the Swiss valley sects of Hasli, Grindelwald and Lauterbrunn, whose adherents were said to pray naked in the belief that clothes were a sign of sin and shame. The ministry assembled lists of sectarian publications, subsidized the publication of counter-sectarian texts and closely monitored religious groups and associations of all kinds.[28] It is clear that Frederick William expected the edifying and accessible rituals and symbolic culture of the Prussian Union to arrest the centrifugal pull of sectarian formations, just as Napoleon saw the need for an ecclesiastical compromise that would prevent provincial Catholic revivalism from deepening the chasm between refractories and constitutionals within the French Church. Indeed, one finds at the heart of the unionist project an obsessive concern with uniformity that is recognizably 'post-Napoleonic': the simplification and homogenization of vestments at the altar as on the field of battle, liturgical conformity down to the most minute detail, even modular *Normkirchen* designed to be built from prefabricated parts and available in different sizes to suit villages and towns.[29] Indeed, Frederick William appears to have seen the restoration of religious life in the kingdom as inextricably connected with the elimination of ecclesiastical pluralism: 'If every mindless priest wants to come to market with his unwashed ideas . . .', he told his confidant and collaborator Rulemann Friedrich Eylert, 'What will – or can – come of it? . . . I say: *Jus*, right, the Law. The right law for the Church is its harmony, its internal agreement, its community. That is what makes the Church a true Church.'[30]

The Union of 1817 and the measures that followed in later years were thus part of that process of territorial integration that preoccupied monarchs and governments in all the post-Napoleonic German states where the acquisition of new provinces had created a pluralism of traditions and loyalties. The unity of religious practice was to provide a foundation for the spirited, state-oriented sense of commitment that the reformers aimed to stimulate within the population. For Frederick William in particular, these domestic imperatives were reinforced – as, on a more ambitious scale, they were for Napoleon – by external factors. The Prussian monarch's German commitments required that he pose as the foremost Protestant prince of the German Confederation. In this connection it should be borne in mind that Church unions took place – in very different political circumstances and generally without government coercion – in many of the other Protestant states of the confederation, including Nassau, the Palatinate, Baden, Waldeck, Rhine-Hessen and elsewhere. Particularly important was the case of Nassau, where an independent Church synod proclaimed a union of the two confessions on 6 August 1817, thereby pipping the Prussians at the post, offending Frederick William's sense of prestige, and prompting an acceleration of preparations for the Union in Berlin.[31]

To the situational analogies we have considered one could add affinities of substance: in France the Concordat brought a stabilization and levelling of clerical status as well as bestowing upon clerical personnel some of the majesty of the state, to the extent that one spoke of parish priests as 'mayors in black'. Bishops enjoyed enhanced powers within the diocese – they were given the right to appoint parish and chapel priests, for example, which they had not enjoyed under the *ancien régime* – and increasingly felt themselves to be officials of the central administration.[32] In Prussia, the Union was part of a package of reforms that abolished or relativized the autonomy of the various pre-modern forms of patronage that interposed mediating instances – local landowners, city magistrates – between the parish and the state authority. One of the most important consequences of the Union was the consolidation – in the face of vigorous resistance from some quarters – of the state's right to appoint and dismiss clergy in districts where Church patronage had formerly been in private hands. Herein lies one reason for the enthusiasm with which a majority of the greater and lesser clergy welcomed the union: the clergy emerged more secure in their status from the reforms than they had been under the old Church regiment, precisely because their tenure and status were now tied to the enduring structures of the state, rather than to the whims of a local *Kirchenpatron*. The unionist project was also welcomed by those elements within the higher clergy who saw it as paving the way towards the emergence of a better-trained and more professional clerical corps.[33] It would be mistaken to suggest that the Union brought about the wholesale professionalization of the Prussian clergy – the rural clergy in particular remained economically dependent upon the locality and thus continued to be compromised in their independence by indebtedness and other obligations to local worthies until after the revolutions of 1848/9. But a start had been made: the training and examination of candidates was better and more uniformly regulated; the social and educational gap between the greater and lesser clergy was narrowed; an 'Agenda Fund' was established by the monarch for the purpose of repairing and improving Churches and supplying liturgical equipment to impoverished parishes; and the state began to use its clerical personnel systematically for the collection of information on matters, such as the provision of schooling to Jewish children of school age, for example, that pertained to the administrative competence of the *Kultusministerium*.

We can, moreover, discern echoes of Napoleon's reinforcement of episcopal office in Frederick William's Cabinet Order of January 1823 ordering the establishment of a united episcopacy as a mediating authority between the state and the parish. The decision was highly controversial in the anti-episcopalian climate of Prussian Protestantism in the 1820s, and surely out of tune with the Calvinist tradition of the Hohenzollern court. Moreover, taken together with the erection of crucifixes in churches, and the introduction of a sung liturgy, the creation of a Prussian episcopacy nourished potentially damaging suspicions that Frederick William was a crypto-Catholic. Such rumours were understandable, but ungrounded; as the King's biographer Thomas Stamm-Kuhlmann has shown, the key to Frederick William's ecclesiastical innovations did not lie in a predilection for Catholicism, but in an acute sensitivity to the sensual and dramatic elements of communal worship and an instinctive awareness of the public's need for accessible and edifying images, texts and rituals. There is little doubt that the appointment of bishops provided a focus for public interest and veneration that did much to raise the profile of the United Church. A contemporary memoir records that the visitations of Bishop

Bernhard Dräseke, appointed in 1832, 'became triumphal processions, such as Luther had once held or a miraculous holy man of ancient times. Whoever could not find a place in the closely-packed churches ringed with dense crowds from which to hear him, wanted at least to see him. People kissed his robe, raised up their children to show them the man of God.'[34]

Like the Concordat, the Union was a *majoritarian* Church, a Church that aimed not at the preservation of distinctions in observance and tradition, but at capturing the middle ground. Justifying the compromise of 1801, Napoleon explained to the Council of State: 'My policy is to govern men as the great majority of them wish to be governed. That is how to recognize the sovereignty of the people.'[35] Frederick William set out to design a Church that would answer the needs of the great majority of his Protestant subjects, Lutheran and Calvinist. That, in his view, was how to recognize 'freedom of conscience'. As Klaus Wappler has pointed out, the king attached crucial importance to the notion – illusory in some respects – that entry into the Union was voluntary. This assumption legitimated the state's unilateral action in unifying the two confessions and rendered the sanction of a representative body unnecessary.[36] It was impossible for Frederick William to imagine that there could be legitimate grounds for dissent from such a benevolent dispensation. Hence his disbelief and incomprehension when, in the 1830s, a movement of anti-unionist 'Old Lutherans' emerged that challenged the right of the state to intervene unilaterally in liturgical and sacramental practice and asserted the continuing autonomy of a Lutheran Church in Prussia. When reports reached him that Silesian Old Lutherans, weary of the administration's efforts to bully them into the Union, were leaving the country to settle in North America and Australia, he is reported to have responded with unfeigned bewilderment: 'Unheard of, in a country where freedom of religion and of conscience prevail.'[37]

Lastly, both the Union and the Concordat served, among other things, to place the person of the sovereign in the foreground. Napoleon addressed this problem with his customary brio: incorporation of the Pope into the rituals surrounding the rite of his coronation; a festival of *Saint-Napoléon* on his birthday to replace the feast of the Assumption; and hubristic plans to install the Pope permanently in Paris, where he could function as Napoleon's 'lever on world opinion'. A particularly striking example of the instrumentalization of religion to bestow legitimacy upon the secular ruler was the new imperial catechism, organized in the conventional question-and-answer format and designed to link piety with devotion to the person of the emperor in the minds of children. No passage better illustrates the self-consciousness of this strategy than the grounds on which youthful readers were urged to feel a strong personal attachment to the sovereign: 'for it is he whom God has raised up in difficult times to re-establish the public observance of the holy religion of our fathers, and to be its protector ... He has become the anointed of the Lord through the consecration that he has received from the sovereign pontiff, head of the Universal Church.'[38]

In Prussia, as one would expect, policies were conceived and executed in a less extravagant register, but the central place of the sovereign was no less apparent. Frederick William was himself effectively the 'pope' of his new United Church – there were no rivals for *that* position. The opening words of the Proclamation of the Union, issued and published by the monarch on 27 September 1817, made it clear that the new arrangement was to be understood as the accomplishment of a long-standing Hohenzollern policy: 'My blessed forefathers now resting with God, Elector Johann Sigismund, Elector Georg Wilhelm, the Great Elector, King Frederick I and King Frederick William I had already concerned themselves ... with the amalgamation of the two separated Protestant Churches, the Lutheran and the Reformed, into one Evangelical Christian Church in their territories.' Equally striking was the frequent use of the first person singular and the unequivocal emphasis on the monarch's personal agency in launching the process of unification: 'Just as I Myself ... shall be celebrating the forthcoming anniversary of the Reformation by the unification of the formerly Lutheran and Reformed congregations of the Court and Garrison Church at Potsdam, so I hope that this My Own example will exercise a beneficent influence on all the Protestant communities in My lands and will find general emulation in spirit and in truth.'[39] The new United liturgy, a romantic historicizing construct cobbled together from German, Swedish, Huguenot, and Anglican prayerbooks, was largely the King's own work, in whose defence he even published a quasi-anonymous pamphlet. Pastors who loyally entered the Church of the Union and adopted the new liturgy without complaint were rewarded with personal tokens of the monarch's favour: copies of the new liturgy, for example, personally signed by Frederick William, or silver medallions of thanks designed by Schinkel, with an image of Mother Church embracing her two Protestant (i.e. Lutheran and Reformed) sons.[40] The new state Church was intimately associated, both in fact and in the public eye, with the person of the sovereign.

What are we to make of all this? The aim of the juxtaposition explored in this chapter has not been to suggest that the Union was in any straightforward sense 'modelled' on the *église concordataire*, but to employ a more dialectical and less one-sidely 'casual' approach than the notion of 'influence' will allow in order to identify and interpret the affinities between two institutions that arose from related necessities and reflected new ways of structuring the relationship between state and society. Hence the reference in the title to a 'Napoleonic moment' that encompassed not only Napoleonic reforms and expansion and the subsequent influence of these on Church–State relations in Europe, but also the unstable and transitional state of affairs that gave rise to and helped to shape them in the first place.

Both the Concordat and the Union have been seen as episodes in the history of 'late absolutism'. This view reflects a widespread historiographical emphasis on the continuities between the enlightened 'bureaucratic absolutism' of the later eighteenth century and the reform era of the early nineteenth. 'The guiding aims of the eighteenth century,' one historian of this era has observed of the German state, 'determined the basic outlines of the nineteenth.'[41] Napoleon's settlement with the Church of France, another rhas suggested, 'stood within a long tradition of ecclesiastical statism (*Staatskirchentum*) that reaches back to the Reformation'.[42] The very text of the Concordat appeared to bear out this continuity, with its repeated invocations of usages 'before the change of government'. In fact, in confessional as in other areas of policy, a period of profound structural and political transformation separated the world of Louis XVI from the devastated landscape of French – and European – Catholicism in the post-Napoleonic era.[43] As Derek Beales has pointed out, even the reforms of the most radical ecclesiastical statist of the eighteenth century, Joseph II, appear modest in comparison with the damage wrought by the suppressions implemented in France during 1792.[44] Frederick William likewise portrayed his Prussian Union as the 'restoration' of a historical Prussian *Landesherrliches Kirchenregiment*. But no such regiment had ever existed; only a spectrum of diverse usages varying from province to province and sometimes from parish to parish, and subject to the authority of a bewildering array of patrons. Nor did the Prussian state of the pre-Napoleonic era possess the constitutional instruments to establish such a Church or to impose conformity to its usages. The advent of ecclesiastical 'big government' in Prussia represented a departure from the practice of earlier reigns; indeed it inaugurated an era of aggressive confessional statism that was arguably unprecedented in Prussian history.[45]

In quintessentially nineteenth-century fashion, the Church of the Prussian Union combined ecclesiastical innovation on a grand scale with a romantic deference to history and tradition as the ultimate foundations of legitimacy. Much ideological energy was invested in imbuing the new

Church of the Union with a sense of rootedness in history. Hence the emphasis in government propaganda on the continuities with traditional usage, the insistence that the 'New Order of Service' (*neue Agende*) as it was widely known, be termed the 'renewed Order of Service' (*erneuerte Agende*), and the commissioning of neo-medieval, Russian-inspired liturgical music for use in support of the new service. It was a conception of 'tradition' that explicitly repudiated the ecclesiastical and liturgical pluralism – and the confessional neutralism – of the eighteenth century. The same extravagant invention of tradition can be seen at work in the language and arguments of those 'Old Lutherans' whose opposition to the Union coalesced after 1830 into a concerted movement of ecclesiastical dissent.

Far from being the last laugh of eighteenth-century absolutism, then, these foundations – the Union and the Concordat in equal measure – were Church–State organisms of a new type. They did not entail, as Marx wishfully diagnosed in an influential essay of 1844, the banishment of religion out of the state into society. Nor did they bring about the enslavement of the Church by the state, as the critics of both the Concordat and the Union have sometimes claimed.[46] Rather, they inaugurated an era of symbiosis and dependency, in which state and clerical competences were blended. It was an era characterized on the one hand by the enhancement of the state's supervisory control over the institutions of the Church, and on the other by a revival of clerically sanctioned religion – marked in both France and Prussia by a rise in the number of candidates for clerical office and the proliferation of missionary and other voluntaristic initiatives.[47] In the French context, Jacques Lafon has written of a *ménage à trois* installed by the priests and the state for the purpose of better controlling those who are at once the faithful and the subjects'.[48] For the Prussian case, Hans-Dietrich Loock has highlighted the utopian element in the plan to create a new order that would overcome the Church–State divide, at once disciplining the Church and sacralizing the state, and thereby moving one step closer to the realization of God's kingdom on earth.[49] Having survived an age of enlightenment, indifference, anticlericalism, secularization, and even dechristianization, the new Churches, purged of those elements that could compromise their utility as administrative partners, gained an apparently permanent place within the state. As for the stronger and relatively centralized monarchical executives that emerged in Prussia and France after 1815: in a post-revolutionary world, their quest for popular legitimacy was more urgent than ever. They abandoned the enlightened principle of confessional neutrality in order not to forgo the benefits of institutional religion as a well-spring of legitimation for the secular authority.

Notes

1. The full French text of the Concordat and the Organic Articles, from which the present citations are made, may be found in E. Walder, *Staat und Kirche in Frankreich, Vol. 2, Vom Kultus der Vernunft zur Napoleonischen Staatskirche* (Berne, 1953), pp.87–109.
2. Article 6 of the Charter of 1814 declared that 'the apostolic Roman Catholic religion is the religion of state'. Louis XVIII initially planned to annul the Concordat of 1801 and replace it with the Concordat of 1516; protracted negotiations from 1814 between the French state and the papacy produced a new accord (June 1817) under which the Concordat was declared to have 'ceased to be in effect' and the Organic Articles abolished 'as far as they are contrary to the doctrine and laws of the Church'. This agreement was ratified and published by the Holy See, but not by the French government, which subsequently reneged on the convention and published in its place a law stipulating that the existing laws and regulations on ecclesiastical matters (including the Organic Articles) would be maintained. Subsequent negotiations with the Curia failed to generate a new compromise, so the Concordat remained in effect. An outline of these developments may be found in G. Bertier de Sauvigny, *The Bourbon Restoration*, trans. L. M. Case (Philadelphia, 1966), pp.66, 77, 300–5).
3. R. Aubert, J. Beckmann, P. Corish and R. Lill, *The Church Between Revolution and Restoration*, trans. P. Becker (London, 1981), p.136.
4. O. Chadwick, *The Popes and the European Revolution* (Oxford, 1981), p.491.
5. Aubert *et al.*, *The Church between Revolution and Restoration*, p.135.
6. See K. Schatz, *Zwischen Säkularisation und Zweitem Vatikanum. Der Weg des deutschen Katholizismus im 19. Und 20. Jahrhundert* (Frankfurt/Main, 1986), pp.46–8.
7. On the economic and ideological impact of secularization, see e.g. D. Stutzer, *Die Säkularisation 1803. Der Sturm auf Bayerns Kirchen und Klöster* (Rosenheim, 1978); H.C. Mempel, *Die Vermögenssäkularisation 1803/10. Verlauf und Folgen der Kirchengutversteigerung in verschiedenen deutschen Territorien* (2 vols, Munich, 1979); M. Müller, *Säkularisation und Grundbesitz. Zur Sozialgeschichte des Saar–Mosel* Raumes 1794–1813 (Boppard am Rhein, 1980).
8. Chadwick, *The Popes*, p.485.
9. C. Herold, *The Mind of Napolean: A Selection from His Written and Spoken Words,* ed. and trans. J. Christopher Herold (New York, 1955), p.106.

10. J. McManners, *The French Revolution and the Church* (London, 1969), p.140.

11. Cited in Chadwick, *The Popes*, p.484.

12. M. Lyons, *Napoleon Bonaparte and the Legacy of the French Revolution* (London, 1994), p.85.

13. H. McLeod, *Religion and the People of Western Europe 1789–1970* (Oxford, 1981), p.5; Aubert et al. (eds), *The Church Between Revolution and Restoration*, pp.68–9; G. Ellis, *Napoleon* (London, 1997), pp.59–60.

14. O. Hufton, 'The Reconstruction of a Church 1796–1801', in G. Lewis and C. Lucas (eds), *Beyond the Terror. Essays in French Regional and Social History, 1794–1815* (Cambridge, 1983), p.52; McManners, *The French Revolution and the Church*, pp.123–5; G. Ellis, 'Religion according to Napoleon. The Limitations of Pragmatism', in N. Aston (ed.), *Religious Change in Europe 1650–1914* (Oxford, 1997), pp.242–3; cf. Lyons, *Napoleon Bonaparte*, pp.81–2.

15. Lyons, *Napoleon Bonaparte*, p.83.

16. See T. C. W. Blanning, 'The Role of Religion in European Counter-revolution 1789–1815', in D. Beales and G. Best (eds), *History, Society and the Churches. Essays in Honour of Owen Chadwick* (Cambridge, 1985), pp.203–7.

17. McManners, *The French Revolution and the Church*, p.141.

18. Ellis, 'Religion according to Napoleon', p.255.

19. Cited in Lyons, *Napoleon Bonaparte*, p.82.

20. On British confessional policy in Quebec and the Mediterranean, see C. A. Bayly, *The Imperial Meridian. The British Empire and the World 1780–1830* (London, 1989), pp.94, 199–200.

21. Cited in G. Ruhbach, 'Die Religionspolitik Friedrich Wilhelms III. Von Preußen', in B. Moeller and G. Ruhbach, *Bleibendes im Wandel der Kirchengeschichte. Kirchenhistorische Studien* (Tübingen, 1973), p.310.

22. J. F. G. Goeters, 'Die Reorganisation der staatlichen und kirchlichen Verwaltung in den Stein-Hardenbergschen Reformen: Verwaltungs-union der kirchenregimentlichen Organe', in J. F. G. Goeters and R. Mau (eds), *Die Geschichte der Evangelischen Kirche der Union, Vol. 1, Die Anfänge der Union unter landesherrlichem Kirchen-regiment (1817–1850)* (Leipzig, 1992), pp.55–8).

23. Cited in T. Stamm-Kuhlmann, *König in Preußens großer Zeit. Friedrich Wilhelm III. Der Melancholiker auf dem Thron* (Berlin, 1992), p.457.

24. K. Wappler, 'Karl von Altenstein und das Ministerium der geistlichen,

Unterrichts- und Medizinalangelegenheiten', in Goeters and Mau (eds), *Die Anfänge der Union*, pp.115–25.

25. Cf. Frederick William to Schuckmann, Töplitz, 23 September 1816, GstA, Rep. 76 III, Sekt. 1, Abt. XIV, Nr. 5, fol. 115.

26. Manifesto drawn up in Duisburg in 1817, cited in W. H. Neuser, 'Die Entstehung der Rheinisch-Westfälischen Kirchenordnung', in Goeters and Mau (eds), *Die Anfänge der Union*, p.247.

27. Cf. J. van Norden, *Kirche und Staat im Preußischen Rheinland 1815– 1838. Die Genese der Rheinisch-Westfälischen Kirchenordnung vom 5.3.1835*. (Cologne, 1991), who has – somewhat hyperbolically – compared this conflict with the Kirchenkampf of the German Churches under the Nazi régime.

28. On anti-sectarian measures and the monitoring of sectarian activity, see the documents in GstA Rep. 76 III, Sekt. 1, Abt. XIIIa, Nr. 5, vol. 1.

29. H. N. Franz-Duhme and U. Röper-Vogt (eds), *Schinkels Vorstadt-kirchen. Kirchenbau und Gemeindegründung unter Friedrich Wilhelm III. in Berlin* (Berlin, 1991), pp.30–60.

30. R. F. v. Eylert, *Charakter-Züge und historische Fragmente aus dem Leben des Königs von Preußen Friedrich Wilhelm III* (3 vols, Magdeburg, 1844–6), Vol. 3, p.304.

31. K. Wappler, 'Reformationsjubiläum und Kirchenunion', in Goeters and Mau (eds), *Die Anfänge der Union*, p.101.

32. Aubert et al., *The Church Between Revolution and Restoration*, p.59; G. Lefebvre, *Napoleon, Vol. 1, From 18 Brumaire to Tilsit 1799– 1807*, trans. H. F. Stockhold (London, 1969), p.138.

33. H.-D. Loock, 'Die preußische Union, der Streit um die Kirchen-verfassung 1808–1817 und die Reaktion der brandenburgischen Landpfarrer', in A. M. Birke and K. Kluxen (eds), *Kirche, Staat und Gesellschaft im 19. Jahrhundert. Ein deutsch–englischer Vergleich* (Munich, 1984), pp.45–65.

34. Stamm-Kuhlmann, *König in Preußens großer Zeit*, p.486.

35. Cited in Lyons, *Napoleon Bonaparte*, p.82.

36. Wappler, 'Reformationsjubiläum und Kirchenunion'.

37. Eylert, *Charakter-Züge*, Vol. 3, p.320.

38. V. Bindel, *Histoire religieuse de Napoléon, Vol. 2, L'Église imperiale* (Paris, 1940), pp.19–20.

39. The full text, with a facsimile of the original, is given in Goeters and Mau (eds), *Die Anfänge der Union*, pp.89–92.

40. Eylert, *Charakter-Züge*, Vol. 3, p.353; Altenstein to Schröder, Berlin, 11 November 1819, GstA Berlin, Rep. 76 III, Sekt. 3, Abt. XVII, Nr.

5, vol. 1, B1. 33; C. M. Clark, 'Confessional Policy and the Limits of State Action: Frederick William III and the Prussian Church Union 1817–1840', *Historical Journal*, 39 (1996), p.989.

41. W. K. Blessing, *Staat und Kirche in der Gesellschaft. Institutionelle Autorität und mentaler Wandel in Bayern während des 19. Jahrhunderts* (Göttingen, 1982), p.23.

42. C. Dipper, 'Kirche, Revolution und Kirchengeschichte. Einleitende Bemerkungen', in P. Hüttenberger and H.-G. Molitor (eds), *Franzosen und Deutsche am Rhein 1789–1918–1945* (Essen, 1989), p.263. On the emergence of the modern state in general as a 'process of secularization', see E.-W. Böckenförde, 'Die Entstehung des Staates als Vorgang der Säkularisation', in H.-H. Schrey (ed.), *Säkularisierung* (Darmstadt, 1981), pp.67–89.

43. In support of this view see Lyons, *Napoleon Bonaparte*, pp.295–6.

44. D. Beales, 'Joseph II and the Monasteries of Austria and Hungary', in Aston (ed.), *Religious Change in Europe 1650–1914*, p.162.

45. See C. M. Clark, *The Politics of Conversion. Missionary Protestantism and the Jews in Prussia 1728–1941* (Oxford, 1995), pp.124–75; idem, 'The Politics of Revival. Pietists, Aristocrats and the State Church in Early Nineteenth Century Prussia', in L. E. Jones and J. Retallack (eds), *Between Reform, Reaction and Resistance. Studies in the History of German Conservatism from 1789 to 1945* (Providence and Oxford, 1993), pp.31–60.

46. For a survey of critiques of the Concordat along these lines, see J. Laspougeas, 'Concordat de 1801' in J. Tulard, *Dictionnaire Napoléon* (Paris, 1987), pp.451–6; for a similar assessment of the Union as the degradation of the Church to a 'pliable tool of the state', see G. Besier, *Preußische Kirchenpolitik in der Bismarckära* (Berlin, 1980), p.9.

47. On candidates for clerical office, see, for France, Bertier de Sauvigny, *Bourbon Restoration*, p.308; on the oversupply of theological candidates for Protestant clerical office in Prussia during the Restoration era, see K. F. W. Dieterici, *Geschichtliche und statische Nachrichten über die Universitäten im preußischen Staate* (Berlin, 1838; repr. Aalen, 1982), p.108. Interestingly enough, the missionary revival met with an ambivalent response from the authorities in both countries. The revival of evangelization in the French parishes – especially after the jubilee of 1803 – was closely watched by the police but also aided and sometimes subsidized by the civil authorities. After his disagreement with Pius VII in 1809, Napoleon suppressed this activity on the grounds that 'itinerant and vagabond priests could

become agents in the papal cause'. The revival resumed after the fall of Napoleon. In Prussia the proliferation of voluntarist groups with missionary objectives met with an official welcome and extensive government support. But there was also concern about the possibility that such formations might provide shelter for political or sectarian dissidents; the authorities thus kept all missionary associations under close watch and a number were dissolved during the Restoration era on suspicion of sectarian affiliations: Aubert el al. (eds), *The Church Between Revolution and Restoration*, p.69; Clark, *Politics of Conversion*, pp.212–34; C. Langlois and T. Tackett, 'A l'Épreuve de la Revolution (1770–1830)', in F. Lebrun (ed.), *Histoire des catholiques en France du xvé siècle à nos jours* (Paris, 1980), pp.284–6.

48. J. Lafon, *Les prêtres, les fidèles et l'état. Le ménage à trois du xixè Siècle* (Paris, 1987), p.364.
49. Loock, 'Die preußische Union', pp.63–4.

Cultures of Interdiction: The Politics of Censorship in Italy from Napoleon to the Restoration[1]

John A. Davis

Political censorship was the most distinctive and despised feature of the legitimist autocracies that the Congress of Vienna restored in Italy after 1814, for which it provided the principal weapon in the struggle against the ideas that had caused the Revolution and brought decades of political turmoil and anarchy to Europe. But it was also the means by which the legitimist rulers sought actively to impose controls over every sphere of ideological, cultural and religious life that were premised on the alliance between throne and altar and aspired to be total. Ironically, it was the Revolution and Napoleon that had provided the political and administrative means to pursue these goals.

Censorship and Restoration autocracy were inseparable, directing the struggles for political change against the constraints on the freedoms of speech and association. Virtually all the key as well as many of the less well-known figures in the political struggles of the Risorgimento were writers, publicists or journalists – even Garibaldi, the personification of action over thought, eventually found time to write anticlerical novels. Mazzini's stirring manifesto announcing the constitution of Young Italy (July 1831) appealed to the opponents of autocracy to throw off the clandestinity of the secret societies and propagate openly the cause of the Italian revolution. By the mid-1840s even those deeply opposed to revolutionary political change came to believe that censorship had dangerously alienated growing sections of the propertied and educated classes from the rulers. In his appeal to the revolutionaries in 1846 to abandon force in favour of moral persuasion, the Piedmontese nobleman Massimo d'Azeglio described public opinion as a 'conspiracy in open daylight'.[2] Following the revolutions of 1848, constitutional government survived only in the Kingdom of Sardinia, and left Piedmont with probably the most liberal press regulations in continental Europe in the 1850s. In the other Italian states the collapse of the liberal revolutions entailed the immediate resumption of the unbending régime of censorship.

Censorship was co-terminous with the history of the Restoration régimes, and it was the faltering of censorship in the 1840s that provided the first clear signals that the autocracies were entering into crisis. The first sign of political change came when Leopold II of Tuscany gave permission in 1839 for a meeting of an Italian Congress of Scientists to take place at Pisa. The Milanese journalist Francesco Predari, whose memoirs are one of the principal sources for the historian of censorship in this period, believed that it was Carlo Alberto's later decision to host the sixth meeting of the same Congress of Scientists in Turin in 1846, however, that signalled to the whole of Italy that the Piedmontese ruler wanted to improve relations with the moderate liberals.[3]

Censorship remained in force in Piedmont until the eve of the revolution; but the régime broke first in the Papal States when the newly elected Pope Pius IX agreed to relax censorship in March 1847. This decision marked the beginning of the revolutions of 1848. The Papal government hoped to create a moderate, pro-government press; but the flood of subversive pamphlets simply increased, and demonstrated that the Papal government had effectively lost control. In May 1847 Leopoldo II of Tuscany followed Pius IX's lead and relaxed censorship, and was immediately forced to make deeper political concessions.[4]

The collapse of the censorship régimes has often been interpreted as an inevitable consequence of the irresistible rise of new forms of 'public opinion'. What Massimo d'Azeglio described as a 'conspiracy in open daylight', historians now attribute to the emergence of new forms of 'public' opinion that reveal the presence of a self-conscious new middle class, pressing to obtain the public and political rôles enjoyed by their counterparts in other European states.[5]

The politics of censorship have, however, received relatively little attention from historians and, in reality, seem to retrace only imperfectly the fracture lines between autocracy and civil society. The forces undermining censorship were more complex than the polarity between autocracy and progressive public opinion allows, while public opinion may have been a weaker force than contemporaries chose to believe. Nor was censorship easily circumvented, although, once the battle was won, Risorgimento liberals took great pleasure in underlining the absurdity of the measures imposed by the censors in ways that were intended to heap further discredit and ridicule on the autocracies. In retrospect censorship created a sort of freemasonry of conspiracy, and the statistician Cesare

Correnti would later boast how 'moral statistics' had implicitly challenged the secrecy of absolutism: '. . . our revered master Gian Domenico Romagnosi had begun to make us realize how this statistical weapon was less worn out and blunt than the lamentations and the denunciations of the poets . . . Numbers told their secrets to those who knew how to read the code: they were the true language of mutes.'[6]

For how many that code was intelligible before censorship ended remains questionable, and the assumption that there was widespread if concealed mobilization against censorship before the mid-1840s risks underestimating the degree to which Restoration censorship, at least down to the early 1840s, drew on consent. It also neglects the reasons why the Restoration autocracies began to unravel in the 1840s. There was certainly no clear correlation in terms of time and place between the rise of public opinion and the collapse of censorship. In the Italian states that were most prone to political insecurity and revolution – the Papal States and the central Duchies – both the middle class and cultural life were narrow and fragmented. In Milan, by contrast, censorship did not prevent the development of what was without question the most vibrant cultural life of any Italian city, moving with relative freedom between aristocratic salons, journalism and the boxes of La Scala. Austrian censorship, although ever-present, was generally considered before 1848 to be both more rational and less irksome than in other Italian states.

As Kent Robert Greenfield long ago pointed out, the relationship between intellectuals, culture and politics in the Risorgimento was complex. Censorship did not prevent advocates of new ideas or issues of public welfare communicating with one another, but this did not mean either that they were political revolutionaries or even necessarily opposed fundamentally to the continuation of Austrian rule.[7] Nor did the removal of censorship in 1848 result in the formulation of more coherent political programmes, or serve to broaden the liberal movement. Indeed, if anything, the events of the revolution served to strengthen the more conservative instincts of the Lombard commercial and landowning classes.[8]

Any simple formula linking the rise of public opinion to the collapse of autocracy becomes particularly problematic in Piedmont. Before 1848 it was generally agreed that Turin was so uninviting and tedious that even tourists and foreign representatives chose to avoid it, preferring if possible to stay in neighbouring cities.[9] This had less to do with censorship than with the suffocating domination of the legitimist aristocracy and the Church. Yet after the revolutions Turin became one of the most progressive havens in continental Europe for the freedom of speech and association.

To attribute this about-turn to the sudden emergence of a fully fledged and progressive 'public opinion' is to overlook an alternative and more easily documented interpretation. The moves after 1846 to relax censorship and negotiate with the moderate liberals came from within the autocracy, and were explicitly if cautiously motivated by the desire to create a new political base for the monarchy. That meant creating 'public opinion' where it did not exist, not because it was stifled by censorship but because those like Cavour who became its protagonists were members of a tiny social, political and intellectual minority. Only through the cultural infusion provided after 1849 by the exiles from the other Italian states would Turin come to have a more vigorous 'public opinion'.

If measures of change in the 1840s came from within the autocracies themselves, this was not because the Italian rulers had become either enlightened or liberal. It had more to do with the political contradictions that the Restoration autocracies had inherited from the Napoleonic reorganization of their states. Indeed, the rise and fall of censorship in Restoration Italy retraces the history of the bureaucratic autocracies that were Napoleon's principal political legacy to the Italian rulers.

The Restoration did not invent censorship, which was as old if not older than the *ancien régime*. Between the Council of Trent (1545–63) and the revolutions of 1848–9 there were probably no more than three occasions when Italians were free of censorship: the first during the short-lived Jacobin Republics of 1796–99; the second during the revolutions of 1820–21 in southern Italy and Piedmont (those of 1831 in central Italy were too ephemeral to count); and the third the revolutions of 1848/9 that left the Kingdom of Sardinia as the first and only constitutional régime that respected freedom of speech.[10]

Before 1789 censorship in the Italian states had followed the objectives common to other European Catholic states. The apparatus of ecclesiastical censorship had taken shape to enforce Counter-Reformation orthodoxy and coexisted with forms of secular censorship. In the course of the eighteenth century the secular rulers had looked to extend their jurisdictions. Secular censors tolerated and promoted works like Pietro Giannone's *Civil History of the Kingdom of Naples* or Cesare Beccaria's *On Crimes and Punishments* that challenged the temporal power of the Pope, even when these had been placed on the Index. This, however, did not mean that secular censorship was more relaxed than ecclesiastical. In Naples, Charles III's minister Tanucci ruled that possession of Voltaire's *Dictionary* was punishable by two years of imprisonment (or two years of 'relegation' in the case of a nobleman), since: 'We do not consider it advisable to place in the hands and mouths of the common people ideas that criticize our rulers.'[11]

The tensions between secular rulers and the ecclesiastical authorities did make possible the debates and publications that constituted the era of enlightened reformism in Italy. But, even before 1789, relations between the reformers and the Italian princes had become strained, and, as the revolution in France took its course, the Italian princes mended their quarrels with the Church in ways that anticipated the alliance between throne and altar that would constitute the political foundation of the Restoration after 1815.[12]

Albeit short-lived, the Italian republics that sprang up in the wake of the invading French armies between 1796 and 1799 offered the first moment of free speech in modern Italy, and the first occasion for open discussion of censorship itself. Between 1796 and 1799 forty periodicals were launched in Milan alone, with another twenty in Genoa (where previously only a single official *Gazetta* had been published).[13]

This enthusiasm for freedom of speech was at variance with the politics of the Directory, which had reintroduced 'preventive censorship' in France. Yet even before Paris intervened, the Milan patriots found themselves confronting difficult choices. How much freedom should they give their political opponents? How could freedom of expression be combined with the need to educate the people in republican principles and values? In Milan, the republican ex-priest Francesco Saverio Salfi was in a small minority when he argued that attempts to silence the opponents of republics in Milan would simply encourage them to use other and possibly more dangerous means to disseminate their views. But even Salfi supported creating an *Academy of the Theatre* that would train republican actors and also monitor performances to ensure that they were free of counter-revolutionary propaganda. The Cisalpine Republic set up a committee of Theatre Commissioners to ensure that plays should 'inspire hatred for the government of tyrants as well as republican pride and courage among the oppressed' and conform to 'proper republican values as well as good taste'. For the first time castrati were banned from the stage, entry to theatres was made free of charge on certain days, and every town was obliged to organize productions of plays recommended by the commissioners.[14] In Naples, Eleanora Fonseca Pimentel argued that the theatre was the best means for reaching the illiterate masses and overcoming their hostility to the republican régime. The Interior Minister, Francesco Conforti, shared her views, but argued that it was important to maintain vigilant censorship: 'Since the theatre may as easily portray vice as virtue . . . it should be the subject of rigorous scrutiny by the public authorities, who should ensure that the people are not incited by sentiments other than those of patriotism, virtue and sound morality'.[15]

These debates were overridden even before the fall of the republics, and in Milan in 1798 the Directory ordered the closure of all political clubs and journals and required that all printing presses be placed under police surveillance.[16] The political resettlement of the peninsula after the defeat of the Austrians at Marengo (14 June 1800) assumed more authoritarian tones, and Napoleon insisted that French censorship laws and regulations be established immediately in all the Italian satellites and annexed territories. The French constitution of Year VIII made no mention of the freedom of the press, and in January 1800 Napoleon had banned all but thirteen journals in the Department of the Seine. In Milan the French authorities created a *Magistratura di Revisione* with responsibility for 'preventive censorship' (meaning submission prior to publication or performance) of all 'theatrical works and periodical publications whether national or foreign . . .'. The censors were instructed to be alert to any 'information bearing directly or indirectly on the system of government or on any person who holds public or judicial office'. These measures were warmly welcomed by Count Melzi d'Eril, whom Napoleon had nominated as Vice President of the Italian Republic, and it was indicative of continuities with both the past and the future that the censors appointed by Melzi d'Eril included two who had formerly worked for the Austrians: both would keep their jobs after the Restoration of 1814.[17]

When in 1805 the Italian Republic became the Kingdom of Italy Napoleon instructed his viceroy, Eugène Beauharnais, to change the title of the *Magistratura di revisione* to that of the Office for the Freedom of the Press. This Orwellian linguistic turn went hand in hand with the abolition of preventive censorship coupled with the threat of severe penalties against any publication guilty of 'disrespect to the government'. What this might mean was evident when the editor of the Treviso *Monitore* was imprisoned for publishing an article on *pellagra*, the debilitating disease that was endemic throughout rural Lombardy and the Veneto, but whose existence the government refused to acknowledge.[18]

Nowhere in Napoleonic Italy did freedom of speech exist; while everywhere political censorship was invasive. Agents of the later legitimist régimes readily acknowledged that the French reforms made the enforcement of censorship much more effective than under the *ancien régime*. Censorship and police surveillance were an integral part of the system of bureaucratic autocracy that replaced the devolved structures of the *ancien régime* principalities. But there were many continuities with the past, and in reality the battle against ideas hostile to the régime was waged by disorganized armies of *sbirri*, spies, and priests, whose activities were directed, but hardly coordinated, by a variety of different masters, each exercising wide discretionary powers and competing amongst themselves behind the cloak of secrecy. The French rulers also established separate administration for ecclesiastical censorship, reversing the eighteenth-century trend where, in Lombardy, Maria Theresia placed ecclesiastical censorship under secular authority. Secular censors were often clerics, however, because of their specialist training and skills. Distinctions between secular and ecclesiastical censorship remained blurred, therefore, while the essentially discretionary powers exercised by the censors placed the whole régime effectively outside the Napoleonic 'rule of law'.

The Napoleonic rulers also attempted to create an 'official' press that would function as an arm of political and dynastic propaganda. In 1805 Napoleon reprimanded Eugène Beauharnais for failing to ensure that there were 'good' newspapers in Milan, and ordered him to remedy the situation at once: 'Providing of course that the publication of any work opposed to the government shall not be permitted.'[19] The French authorities actively encouraged the publication of 'non-political' journals dealing with scientific, literary or artistic matters. These measures were part of the broader 'modernizing' politics of the Napoleonic enterprise that saw the Italian states endowed with an impressive structure of professional and technical academies, offering training in civil and military engineering, veterinary science and medicine.

While public administration provided some new career opportunities at a variety of levels, demand far outstripped supply and the relationship between the administrative autocracy and the emergence of a new professional middle class in Italy remained full of tension and contrad-iction. The autocratic exclusiveness that stood at the heart of these 'administrative bureaucracies' contradicted the broader promise of careers open to talent and political modernization, and from this grew demands for constitutional reform and the secret societies.[20]

It was only in the final years of French rule in Italy that political opposition began to take shape. Hitherto, the Napoleonic satellites in Italy had been remarkably successful in winning the support of intellectuals (despite important exceptions like Ugo Foscolo). Vincenzo Cuoco's admiration for Napoleon became a political template for the generation that had experienced the Jacobin republics of 1796–9. Although he has participated in the Neapolitan republican government, Cuoco's experience of the popular counter-revolution that had overwhelmed it in 1799 made him, during his exile in Milan, a committed advocate of enlightened authoritarian government as the only safe premise for political and cultural modernization.[21]

For many, the collapse of Napoleon's empire strengthened rather than weakened admiration for Napoleon. Looking back from the experience of the Restoration in the 1820s, the Milanese exile Giuseppe Pecchio made an impassioned defence of the profound institutional, economic and cultural changes that he believed French administration had brought to northern Italy. It was the admiration for Napoleon in Italy that provoked Mme de Staël's famous charge that the Italians did not understand the real meaning of liberalism, and were unable to distinguish between autocracy and open government.[22]

In other words, even amongst Italian liberals it was widely believed that censorship and other forms of authoritarian government were needed to protect Italy's small progressive élites from the forces of aristocratic, clerical and popular reaction. Although the Italian constitutional movement was a child of the Napoleonic occupation of the peninsula, the continuing admiration for the emperor's authoritarian brand of modernization was more than a cultural or ideological preference. It reflected the narrowness and insecurity of the new forces in Italian society, whose commitment to progress was hedged around by the threat of violent popular unrest and uncompromising clerical and aristocratic opposition to change. The Napoleonic experience had demonstrated that the Italian states lacked the social base for that broader régime of notables that in metropolitan France served to mask the sharper profile of autocracy. Of the Italian states, only in Austrian Lombardy was there real evidence of the emergence of comparable new social groups in the first half of the nineteenth century; but even there opposition to Austrian rule came primarily from the old landowning patriciate, who had been deprived of their control over local government, first by Napoleon and then again in 1814 by the restored Habsburg administration.[23]

The Restoration of the Italian legitimist rulers after 1814 marked an ideological break with the Napoleonic régimes, but there was almost uninterrupted administrative and institutional continuity. Even the most reactionary of the Restoration rulers was reluctant to weaken the administrative apparatus bequeathed by the emperor, and, except in the small number of states – Sardinia, Modena, the Papal States – that opted uncompromisingly to resituate themselves somewhere in time before the events of 1789, the Restoration rulers initially attempted to maintain the form of open autocracy experimented by the French.

The censorship regulations established by the French were retained, although in Lombardy and Tuscany separate ecclesiastical censorship was abolished. In the Kingdom of Sardinia Vittorio Emanuele I's *Instructions to the Revisers of Printed Works* (25 June 1816) reiterated the Napoleonic regulations and required that all printed materials be submitted for approval and amendments prior to publication. A Commission of Revisers was also reconstituted in the Habsburg Kingdom of Lombardy-Venetia. Printers and booksellers were obliged to obtain licences from the police authorities, and, in 1817, owners of print-works were obliged to post deposits of 500 florins with the police. In the Tuscan Grand Duchy nothing could be published without the prior approval of the Council of Regency in Florence. In Naples, the Bourbons confirmed the system of censorship introduced by the French and extended its operations to Sicily. In Naples and Milan, in particular, the restored Bourbon and Habsburg governments tried to continue Napoleonic practice by maintaining an 'official' press and attempting to win the support of intellectuals. In Milan, the poet Ugo Foscolo was asked to edit a government journal that would 'encourage public opinion to support the Austrian system of government'. Foscolo declined, but the government promoted various official newspapers like the *Gazzetta di Milano* that carried official proclamations and bulletins.[24]

The legitimist governments rejected in principle the Napoleonic model of the bureaucratic state, yet retained the Napoleonic institutions and, before the revolutions of 1820–21, even attempted their own strategy of 'amalgamation'. Yet this proved contradictory and unworkable, not least because even in the wealthiest states the new bureaucracies established by the French far exceeded available resources. To sustain them required massive increases in taxation, which even before the collapse of the Napoleonic satellites provoked widespread popular revolts. But when the Restoration rulers tried to solve the problem by reducing the size of the bureaucracies, they ended up alienating the administrative and professional groups that had rallied to the Napoleonic régimes. Popular grievances over taxation, white-collar unemployment and the grievances of patricians, whom both the Revolution and the Restoration had displaced from their former rôle in government, combined to fuel the revolutions of 1820–21.

The revolutions of 1820–21 pushed the legitimist rulers to embark on an uncompromising ideological crusade, and throughout Italy censorship was now deployed in earnest against modernity in all its forms. In Naples, the Minister of Police gave clear expression to the new political climate when he ascribed the troubles of the past to 'indulgence':

As a result of that indulgence, the fanaticism of innovation was spread by books. These were the source of the poison that masqueraded under the guise of reform, regeneration, progress and freedom. In this way the spirit of revolution brought desolation to our people, undid morality and destroyed religion . . . Everyone knows that there has never been nor ever will be any open attempt to subvert a legitimate government by force unless this had been prepared carefully over time. But the generality of people are not predisposed to such actions by meeting in clubs, in private houses or even in special meetings. This operation of preparation has always been and always will be the purpose of books and printed writings, as to which there can be no shadow of a doubt since we all have before our eyes the tearful memories of what has befallen us in recent years . . .[25]

Gregory XVI's encyclical *Mirar Vos* of 1832 took the campaign further, and in the aftermath of the upheavals of 1831 in the Papal States uttered an absolute condemnation of liberalism, described 'freedom of conscience' as utter 'madness' and compared the freedom of the press to a 'moral scourge'.[26]

The former emperor was a prime target, and in 1822 the Tuscan censors banned G. B. Niccolini's play *Nabucco* because the title role was seen as an allusion to Napoleon.[27] Verdi later played skillfully on the ambiguities of allusion when he dedicated his *Nabucco* (1842) to the Austrian Emperor, leaving his audience to work out whether this was more than a formal and tactical acknowledgment.[28] In Lombardy the censors banned any reference or allusion direct or indirect in any form to the previous régime. Ugo Foscolo's play *Ajax* was banned because it 'insinuates a spirit of freedom that is directed against Austria': ironically, the same play had been banned by the Napoleonic censors, who deemed it critical of the emperor.[29]

Except in Tuscany, which provided a home for Vieusseux's *Antologia* and thereby gained a reputation for toleration that was not entirely deserved, censorship regulations everywhere became more severe and more comprehensive in the 1820s. In the Kingdom of the Two Sicilies new Commissions of Scrutiny were established in Naples and Palermo, with greatly extended powers. As well as books, the new laws covered printed matter of all kinds, including invitations to private parties, posters, leaflets and theatre programmes. The scope of ecclesiastical censorship, which had already been considerably broadened under the terms of the Concordat of 1818, was further extended to cover all publications relating to religious matters and morality. Yet another Commission of Censors, with members appointed by the Minister of the Interior, the Minister for Education, the Minister of Police and the Cardinal Archbishop of Naples, was set up in 1825. In an attempt to prevent news of the July Revolution in France reaching the Kingdom, additional regulations in 1830 subjected all books and printed matter in transit through the Kingdom to seizure and censorship.[30]

Contemporaries generally agreed that the Austrian authorities in the Kingdom of Lombardy-Venetia operated the least obscurantist and the most consistent censorship in Italy. As well as being the centre of the most thriving book trade in Italy, Milan produced the largest number of periodicals of any Italian capital during the bleakest years of the Restoration, and the launching of Carlo Tenca's *Rivista Europea* and Carlo Cattaneo's *Politecnico* in the early 1840s restored the city's place as undisputed capital of Italian journalism. But censorship was nonetheless a reality, and no public discussion of political affairs was tolerated. As well as Milan the Imperial Department of Censorship had offices in Venice and the provincial capitals of Lombardy-Venetia. Their instructions were precise, and in addition to reviewing all materials submitted for publication and other kinds of printed matter, the censors were obliged to check all 'illustrated papers, geographical maps, allegorical writings, music sheets, pictures, and drawings – including those on the lids of snuff boxes.'[31] Lists of banned books were carefully updated and circulated regularly to the censors and to other government officials. In the 1830s the list included 950 titles, amongst which were the works of Rousseau, Voltaire, Diderot, Condorcet, Beccaria, D'Holbach, Bolingbroke, Mirabeau, Condillac, Mably, Melchiorre Gioia, Machiavelli, Alfieri, Foscolo, and the leading Neapolitan republicans of 1799. The authorities were also alert to seize texts hostile to religion, and especially non-Catholic texts. There was a veritable mania for tracking down translations of Protestant bibles carried by zealous travellers or deliberately smuggled from Switzerland. The Austrian police in 1836 reported that an Englishwoman, Lady Childers, was an agent of the 'well-known British Bible Society' and had distributed printed pamphlets attacking 'the dogma of our Sacred Catholic Apostolic and Roman Church' during her journey through the Tyrol.[32] The Austrian censors worked conscientiously. In contrast to 113 titles that were seized throughout the kingdom in 1821, in 1839 the Parma customs officials alone impounded 750 titles.[33]

Despite the severity of the Austrian regulations and the energy with which they were applied, Francesco Predari could barely believe the contrast when he moved from Milan to Turin in 1842. In Turin, he wrote, cultural life was still controlled by the Jesuits, and

... the press is in the grip of the most arbitrary, capricious and uninformed Censorship exercised by both the secular and the ecclesiastical authorities, which not only renders impossible any form of free manifestation of thought but places even the exposition of the most orthodox doctrine at risk should this fail to conform to the personal opinions of the ecclesiastical censor.

Works banned from public libraries in Piedmont in the 1840s included the works of Grotius, Montesquieu, Gibbon, Pascal, Melchiorre Gioia and the historian Botta, those of the naturalist Bory de St Vincent, which hinted at the possibility of 'the plurality of races', and Libri's *History of Mathematics*, which made open reference to Galileo.

Predari described the ways in which copy had to be edited to meet the requirements of the censors:

> ... 'political' interests must always be replaced by 'civil' interest, 'Italy' by the 'fatherland', 'nation' or 'country'; the term 'constitutional government' could not be used even in reference to Britain or France; the words 'liberal' and 'liberalism' were prohibited in any and every context; 'revolution' must be replaced with 'upheaval', 'anarchy' or 'the rule of violence'.

To add to Predari's difficulties the censor found both words in the title of Predari's proposed new journal – the *Antologia Italiana* – unacceptable.[34] But the sensitivity of the Piedmontese authorities stretched well beyond politics and religion. In 1841, for example, they refused to allow an essay on cooking to appear in the family domestic science journal *L'Amico della Famiglia*, since it had been written by a cook and, if it expressed views at variance with those of the head of a household, might give rise to insubordination.[35] Censorship was most effectively enforced through control at the point of production, and Marino Berengo has shown that despite the rapid expansion of the Milanese book trade during the Restoration period, few printers were willing to risk their livelihood by defying the authorities. That this was true more generally can be seen from a case in Tuscany. In 1822, the censor Padre Bernadini protested to the governor of Livorno, a city with a large number of printing works and a reputation for political dissent, that a book entitled *The Private Grief of Napoleon Bonaparte while on the Island of Elba* (which he rated as 'extremely dangerous') had been published illegally in the city. The reply from the governor's office illustrated how well informed the authorities were. It pointed out that the book could not have been printed in Livorno because no printer in the city used that particular type-face, while the book was printed on paper that 'is not known to any of our printers' and 'had a loose binding with thick thread and is an unwaxed cover' that did not conform to the style used by the Livorno binders. The official also added a more general but equally important consideration:

It seems quite impossible that the printing works owned by the Vignozzi brothers should have clandestinely printed this book. In terms of the trade and traffic that they conduct and the number of men they employ, theirs is the foremost printing works in Tuscany and has made the Vignozzi very wealthy. They run their affairs absolutely correctly and submit everything as they are required by the censors, since they are keen to avoid anything that might prevent them carrying on their lucrative business. The only printer in Livorno who might be suspect is Glauco Masi because of his political views, his frequent travels and his technical skills, and if an illegal edition promised a good financial return the printer Meucci might also be prepared to take a risk.[36]

If it was possible to control printers at home, it was much more difficult to prevent books or pamphlets printed abroad finding their way into Italy. Mazzini, for example, showed great ingenuity furnishing Milanese artisans with copies of *Young Italy*, hiding them in barrels of soda, empty wine flasks or trunks with false bottoms. This carried high risks for all those involved once the materials entered Italy. However, in the case of *Young Italy* the costs of producing and distributing the broadsheet proved to be a much greater obstacle than censorship.[37]

High levels of illiteracy raised even more powerful barriers to communication by the written word, although the Restoration police did deploy armies of spies and informers to monitor popular street theatre and tavern conversations. As in the Napoleonic period, all Italian states devoted special attention to theatrical performances and audiences. Scripts were subject not only to the censorship laws governing the press and printed matter, but also to the regulations governing theatres. All forms of improvisation were prohibited, and, in addition, permission for public performances had to be obtained from the police, who sent agents to all productions. In Tuscany the censors refused to consider any play that dealt with matters relating to 'History or events concerning the Church'. Nor could there be any allusion to the Old Testament or the Church in any form of dance sequence. Needless to say, the censors would not approve any play deemed to contain 'an evil theme that may weaken respect for Religion or the Throne, that incites ideas contrary to either, contains material of bad taste or presents crimes or other terrible deeds like assassinations, premeditated murders, suicides or such similar subjects'.[38]

Italian theatre audiences in the 1820s had to put up with somewhat narrow perspectives on the human condition. But that narrowness was also a reflection of the tastes of the still mainly aristocratic patrons who made up the respectable corps of theatre audiences. Until the end of the 1830s, the censorship imposed by the Restoration governments does not seem to have been out of line with the dominant ethos of the day. The principal theatres were royal theatres, and were supervised in most cases closely by the ruler in person – from the choice of costumes and staging to the organization of subscriptions and the leasing of boxes. Theatre audiences were socially exclusive, and the theatre was still the place where the aristocracy and nobility went to be seen. Indeed Carlo III of Naples had claimed in the previous century that he had built the San Carlo theatre to keep a watch on the Neapolitan nobility. A senior Habsburg official echoed the same sentiment when he argued that La Scala should be kept open after the supposed Milan conspiracy was discovered in 1821 'because it attracts to a place open to observation during the hours of darkness a large part of the educated population'. In Rome the authorities believed that the theatre kept people's minds off mischief.

The aristocratic ethos of the audience and the commercial interests of the impresarios, musicians and librettists – like those of the printers and publishers – conspired to subject the theatres to self-censorship as well as that imposed externally. Moreover, John Rosselli has argued persuasively that it is an exaggeration to believe that opera became a vehicle of nationalist aspirations before the 1840s: '. . . [O]nly in recent years have Italian writers come to admit that Rossini favoured the old régime, that Bellini and Donizetti were apolitical but eager to please the audience and that even Verdi was not quite the full-time nationalist he was once made out to be.'[39]

In Lombardy-Venetia, Tuscany and the Kingdom of Naples the 1830s saw a gradual abandonment of the exclusive cultural and political interdiction attempted in the previous decade. If this was an acknowledgment that the war against modernity could not be won, it was also motivated by the self-interest of the dynastic rulers. It was this that led the rulers of the largest of the Italian states, the Neapolitan Bourbons, after the revolutions of 1820–21 to attempt import substitution and the creation of strategic new industries (ship-building, engineering, textiles) behind a high tariff régime. The strategy was riddled with contradiction, brought Naples into direct conflict with Great Britain, and collapsed in confusion in the early 1840s. In Piedmont, Carlo Alberto's reforms began very much later, but took a different path that led the monarchy not into conflict but into the political alliance with the progressive Piedmontese élites that took shape around the constitution of 1848.[40]

Dynastic self-interest and the desire to promote growth threatened the censorship régime, since greater commercial freedom implied greater freedom of information. But other political contradictions were also undermining Restoration censorship, especially the tensions between the secular and religious authorities. In even in the most reactionary states the works of intransigent champions of Papal supremacy like Joseph de Maistre or Padre Gioacchino Ventura, who argued that Concordats were a greater infringement on the sovereignty of the Pope than were constitutions on secular rulers, were banned.[41] In Naples the secular controls over religious publications that had been abolished in the Napoleonic period were quickly reintroduced after the Restoration. In Tuscany this gave rise to endless feuds between the government and the ecclesiastical authorities. In 1831, for example, the Bishop of Forlì was severely reprimanded for circulating instructions calling for prayers against the cholera that had recently broken out in Italy, which the authorities considered to be 'an alarmist publicity'.[42] But even in reactionary Piedmont relations were hardly smoother.[43]

As social unrest and political tensions increased in the 1840s, doubts about the effectiveness and utility of censorship also increased. In January 1844 the Neapolitan Council of Ministers held a lengthy debate on the politics of censorship following a request from the Minister of Police for increased powers in the light of growing political unrest. This request was challenged by the President of the Council, the Marchese Ceva Grimaldi, who pointed out that, despite the draconian powers already available to the police, the Kingdom was 'inundated with pernicious books . . . which our printers openly publish, so that I myself, the President of the Council of Ministers, can purchase openly from any *bancarella* outside my house copies of books by banned authors like Vincenzo Cuoco and Pietro Colletta'.[44]

Ceva Grimaldi identified two problems. First, responsibility for imposing censorship was divided between too many competing authorities, with counter-productive results. Second, the police were too ignorant and uneducated to enforce censorship, and should have a more limited role. The Minister of Police defended his service by denouncing the inefficiency of the censors of the Interior Ministry, citing as an example the censors' approval of a book entitled *Lettere di un Italiano* that was full of 'patriotic, erotic and amorous expressions', as well as the novels of 'Wolter [sic] Scott, which are redolent with malicious anti-Catholicism'.[45]

The inter-departmental rivalries revealed by the debate indicate that the model of bureaucratic administration implanted by the Napoleonic rulers was far from realized. But Ceva Grimaldi had also raised a more fundamental consideration when he claimed that the censorship regulations were not obeyed because they were excessive and were seen to be out of line with those of other 'civilized nations'.

> To treat this matter with due seriousness while adding some degree of liberality we should examine more closely the measures currently in force in Austria, Prussia and also in France. In this manner, our own regulations will be seen to be in line with the conditions of our times and by reflecting the example of the measures adopted in other European civilized nations they will lose the taint of odium which currently attaches to them.[46]

Concern not only to reach, but indeed to create, broader public support spread rapidly within the autocratic régimes in other Italian states in the 1840s. This was precisely why the Papal Chief of Police urged Pius IX to relax censorship in December 1846, and why Count Bettino Ricasoli begged Leopoldo of Tuscany to follow suit in 1847. In fact this had been happening selectively in Tuscany from a much earlier date, and the censors frequently permitted publications that elsewhere would have been banned, provided that they carried fictional places of origin.[47]

Censorship was becoming counter-productive because it exposed the rulers to foreign intervention in ways that were humiliating. As individual rulers began to seek greater autonomy, censorship became an instrument of foreign policy through which Vienna and Rome attempted to regulate the internal affairs of the other rules. Protest from the Vatican in 1833, for example, led to the closure of Vieusseux's *Antologia* in Florence. The publication in Turin of the prison memoirs of Silvio Pellico in 1832 caused an even greater uproar. Pellico had been imprisoned by the Austrians in the notorious Speilberg prison for his part in the alleged conspiracy in Milan in 1821. His memoirs were a quietist tract of religious introspection and repentance, which he had published only after being urged to do so by Count Cesare Balbo, by the chief censor to the Archbishop of Turin and by the royal political censor, Count Pralormo. All believed the book to be exemplary for its religious sentiments; but when published it was immediately received throughout Europe as a denunciation of Austrian despotism, despite Pellico's publicly disclaiming such intent. Vienna protested and demanded that the censors be given exemplary punishment. Prince Metternich later confessed that Pellico's memoirs 'did not contain one single word of truth . . . but their effect was more terrible for Austria than a lost battle'.[48]

To avoid such humiliating foreign intervention the censors began to advise authors how to avoid external protest. The Tuscan practice of using fictional places of publication was copied in Piedmont and, as early as 1843, the Turin censor (with the King's approval) agreed to allow Cesare Balbo's *Hopes of Italy* – which argued that there could be no political stability in Italy while Austria ruled Lombardy and Venetia – to circulate provided that it was published in Paris. The Austrian government again protested vigorously, and the Austrian governor of Lombardy advised Vienna that the book appeared to have the approval of 'His Royal Highness the King of Sardinia'. On this occasion Turin stood firm, but in Florence the government was forced to comply with Austrian demands, even though the Tuscan censor found nothing unreasonable in Balbo's tract.

The internal contradictions of autocracy and growing friction between ambitions of dynastic autonomy and the realities of Austrian power combined to drag the politics of cultural interdiction into confusion on the eve of the revolutions of 1848. Seen through the eyes of the censors it becomes clear that the crisis had roots more complex than the miraculous rise, fully formed like Pallas Athene, of 'public opinion'. On the contrary, the persistence of censorship in the Italian states before the 1840s points to the overwhelming cultural and political predominance of the old nobility and the Church. The Napoleonic strategy of masking the contours of autocracy in a broader régime of notables remained difficult to realize in Italy because of the relative absence of new classes down to – and beyond – 1848. The Restoration looked for a solution through alliance with Austria, the legitimist nobility and the Church; but these allies ultimately risked compromising the autonomy of the dynastic rulers. The crumbling of the edifice of censorship was as much a result of attempts by the rulers to broaden their political base, as of pressures exerted by more independent, but still weak and uncertain, forces of public opinion. It is not surprising, therefore, that public opinion would first become a force in Piedmont, where its birth was carefully nurtured around the cause of the House of Savoy. Only on that fragile basis was it possible to move tentatively in the 1850s towards a political alignment capable of resolving the contradictions embedded in Napoleon's autocratic legacy in Italy.

Notes

1. This chapter forms part of a fuller account of censorship in Italy from the French Revolution to the First World War that is to appear in R. Goldstein (ed.), *Political Censorship in Nineteenth-Century Europe* (Westport, CT, forthcoming) and as *La censura politica nell'Italia dell'ottocento* (Naples, forthcoming).

2. Massimo D'Azeglio, *Gli ultimi casi di Romagna* (1846); on Mazzini see R. Sarti, *Mazzini. A Life for the Religion of Politics* (Westport, CT, 1997) and V. Castronovo and N. Tranfaglia, *La stampa italiana del Risorgimento* (Bari, 1976).

3. F. Predari, *I primi vagiti della libertà italiana in Piemonte* (Milan, 1861), pp.126–8.

4. G. Porizo, *Le origini della libertà della stampa in Italia 1846–1852* (Milan, 1980), pp.8–33.

5. See A. Lyttelton, 'The Middle Classes in Liberal Italy', in J. A. Davis and P. Ginsborg (eds), *Society and Politics in the Age of the Risorgimento. Essays in Honour of Denis Mack Smith* (Cambridge, 1991); M. Meriggi, 'La borghesia italiana', in J. Kocka (ed.), *Borghesie europee dell'ottocento* (Venice, 1988); A. M. Banti, *Storia della borghesia italiana: l'età liberale* (Rome, 1996).

6. Quoted in S. Patriarca, *Numbers and Nationhood* (Cambridge, 1996), p.43.

7. K. R. Greenfield, *Economics and Liberalism in the Risorgimento. A Study of Nationalism in Lombardy 1814–1848* (Baltimore, MD, 1934; 2nd edition 1964).

8. For the conservative backlash of the Lombard aristocracy after 1848, see M. Meriggi, *Il Regno Lombardo-Veneto* (Turin, 1987), Ch.7.

9. R. Romeo, *Cavour e il suo tempo,* Vol. III (Bari and Rome, 1984); H. Marraro (ed.), *L'unificazione italiana vista dai diplomatici statunitensi,* Vol. 1 (Rome, 1963).

10. See C. Capra, 'Il giornalismo nell'età rivoluzionaria e napoleonica', in V. Castronovo and N. Tranfaglia (eds), *La stampa Italiana dal '500 all'800* (Bari, 1976), pp.374–537; A. Galante Garrone, 'I giornali della Restaurazione', in Castronovo and Tranfaglia (eds), *La stampa italiana del Risorgimento*, pp.3–225; F. Della Peruta, 'Il giornalismo dal 1847 all'Unità', ibid., pp.249–519.

11. C. Rotondo, 'La censura ecclesiastica e la cultura', in *Storia d'Italia, Documenti*, Vol.5, Part 2, (Turin, 1987), p.1492; G. Ricuperati, 'Giornali e società nell'Italia dell'antico regime 1668–1789', in Castronovo and Tranfaglia (eds), *La stampa italiana dal '500 all'800*, pp.1–353.

12. Capra 'Il giornalismo'; A. M. Rao Esuli, *L'emigrazione politica italiana in Francia 1792–1802* (Naples, 1992), pp.210–15.

13. Capra, 'Il giornalismo', p.408.

14. C. A. Vianello Teatri, *Spettacoli, musiche a Milano nei secoli scorsi* (Milan, 1941), pp.349–59.

15. B. Croce, *I teatri di Napoli dal Rinascimento alla fine del secolo*

decimottavo (Bari, 1947), p.275.

16. Capra, 'Il giornalismo', p.408.

17. Ibid., p.489.

18. Ibid., p.490.

19. Ibid.

20. For a contemporary account of this term see L. Blanch, 'Il Regno di Napoli dal 1801 al 1806', in *Scritti Storici*, Vol. 1, ed. B. Croce (Bari, 1945); R. Feola, *La monarchia amministrativa* (Naples, 1975); A. M. Rao and P. Villani, *Napoli 1799–1815. Dalla repubblica alla monarchia amministrativa* (Naples, 1995).

21. On Cuoco see A. De Francesco, *Vincenzo Cuoco. Una vita politica* (Bari, 1997).

22. See R. Romano, *L'economia politica del Risorgimento italiano* (Turin 1994); M. Isabella, 'At the Origins of the Italian Risorgimento. The Revolutionary Activities and Politico-Economic Thought of Giuseppe Pecchio', unpublished Ph.D. thesis, University of Cambridge, 1997; and idem, 'Una scienza dell'amor patrio: Public Economy, Freedom and Civilization in Giuseppe Pecchio's works (1827–1830)', *Journal of Modern Italian Studies* 4 (1999), pp.157–83.

23. M. Meriggi, *Amministrazione e classi sociali nel Lombardo-Veneto (1814–1848)* (Bologna, 1983); R. J. Rath, *The Provisional Austrian Régime in Lombardy-Venetia, 1814–1815* (Austin, TX, 1969); D. Laven, 'Aspects of the Habsburg Administration of Venetia, 1815–35', unpublished Ph.D. thesis, University of Cambridge, 1990.

24. Galante Garrone, 'I giornali', p.20.

25. Archivio di Stato di Napoli (ASN); Ministero di Polizia, 1 Ripartimento, fascio 2921: 'Revisione de' libri, opuscoli, fogli volanti e periodici di attribuzione della polizia', Min Polizia Generale a S.M. il Re (n.d.).

26. Porizo, *Le origini*, p.30.

27. C. Di Stefano, *La censura teatrale in Italia (1600–1962)* (Rocca San Casciano, 1964), pp.70–1.

28. J. Rosselli, *The Opera Industry in Italy from Cimarosa to Verdi: The Role of the Impresario* (Cambridge, 1984), p.162; M. J. Philips-Matz, *Verdi: A Biography* (Oxford, 1994).

29. Di Stefano, *La censura teatrale*, p.83.

30. ASN Min. Polizia f. 2192.

31. G. Berti, *Censura e circolazione delle idee nel Veneto della Restaurazione* (Venice, 1989), p.8; Laven, 'Habsburg Administration', pp.240–307.

32. *Carte segrete della polizia austriaca in Italia dal 4 giugno 1814 al*

22 marzo 1848 (Capolago, 3 vols, 1851) Vol. III p.617 (10 giugno 1836).

33. Berti, *Censura*, pp.15–40.
34. Predari, *I primi vagiti*, p.21.
35. Galante Garrone, 'I giornali', p.61.
36. Cited in F. Ghidetti, 'Tipografi, stampatori e censura a Livorno dal 1815 al 1835', in *Risorgimento* (1989) 61 (i), p.36.
37. Galante Garrone, 'I giornali'; Sarti, *Mazzini*.
38. Di Stefano, *La censura teatrale*.
39. Rosselli, *The Opera Industry*, p.162.
40. For the comparison, see J. A. Davis, 'From "rivoluzione mancata" to "modernizazzione difficile": Italy's Path to the Twentieth Century' in P. Ciocca and G. Toniolo (eds), *Storia economica d'Italia* (Bari, forthcoming).
41. A. Manno, *Anedotti documentati sulla censura in Piemonte dalla Restaurazione alla Costituzione,* Vol. 1 (Turin, 1907), p.110.
42. A. De Rubertis, *Studi sulla censura in Toscana* (Pisa, 1936), p.55.
43. A. Manno, *Anedotti documentati*, p.115.
44. ASN. Min. Polizia f.2921 'Lavoro del Marchese Ceva Grimaldi per una legge sulla revisione e censura dei libri, stampe ecc. . . .', 4 gennaio 1844.
45. Ibid.
46. Ibid.
47. De Rubertis, *Studi sulla censura*, p.322.
48. Ibid., p.328.

–15–

'The Best Way to Keep the Peace in a Country'. Napoleon's Gendarmes and Their Legacy.[1]

Clive Emsley

On 14 May 1814 Vittorio Emanuele I returned to Turin for the first time since becoming head of the house of Savoy twelve years earlier. Encouraged by a clutch of *ancien régime* courtiers and ministers he was determined to destroy everything French. Yet, just two months after his restoration, his *Regie Patenti* of 13 July established the *carabinieri reali* – in all but name, a copy of the imperial gendarmerie. In the months that followed the restored régime in the Papal States followed suit, establishing the *carabinieri pontifici* on the French gendarmerie model; similar bodies were also being developed in the German lands and elsewhere.

Over the last twenty-five years there has been considerable research into the history of policing, yet this has always tended to focus on either state-civilian forces, such as the London Metropolitan Police or the men of the Prefect of Police in Paris, or on municipal-civilian police, forces that were sometimes subject to some form of state inspection and/or supervision, but that were recruited by, and responsible to, local government.[2] There has been no serious academic study of gendarmerie forces, a style of state policing described by Napoleon as 'the best way to keep the peace in a country, and it is a surveillance half civil, half military'.[3] Yet this style became common across much of continental Europe during the nineteenth century, and a variant of it could also be found on John Bull's other island, as well as other parts of the British Empire. This chapter explores two principal questions with reference to the gendarmeries. First, how the system was developed during the Napoleonic régime as a military-civil force for the maintenance of order and for the enforcement of conscription legislation; and second, what made gendarmeries attractive to the rulers of so many European states during the nineteenth century.

In Prairial year VI, General Etienne Radet, a battle-scarred veteran of the *ancien régime* army recovering from wounds received fighting for the Republic, reluctantly assumed command of the 24th Division of *gendarmerie nationale*. There were four companies in the command, based respectively in the departments of the Gard, the Hérault, the Bouches-du-Rhône, and the Vaucluse; and the whole region was infested with brigands. Radet was appalled by what he found in his division. There was little discipline, and many of his men had grown rather too fond of wine; those men who were doing their duty were exhausted, their horses were worn out, their barracks were poor, and their pay was late. 'This corps also makes war,' he thundered in a letter to a superior four months after taking command, 'and you know what kind of war. Each day it is in combat; in a month, I have lost nine men killed and five wounded . . .'.[4]

Radet's command might have been in rather worse shape than most of the other divisions of *gendarmerie nationale* as the Directory limped towards the coup of Brumaire; but nowhere was it in particularly good order. The *gendarmerie* had been established in 1791 out of the remnant of the military police of the *ancien régime*, the *maréchaussée*, which had patrolled the main roads and sought, in spite of its small numbers of 3,500 men, to maintain the safety and security of provincial France. While the courts of summary justice operated by the *maréchaussée* drew adverse comment and were abolished in September 1790, few had sought the abolition of the institution as a whole. The new *gendarmerie nationale* was to be a much bigger body than its predecessor; but, almost from its formation, it found itself under pressure and weakened. The demands of war led to a considerable depletion of the numbers deployed in the countryside for the maintenance of order and the protection of the main roads; able-bodied men were needed at the battle fronts, and gendarmes, as men who had already served in line regiments – usually cavalry regiments – were of particular value. Those who remained had to contend with low pay, which was often late and, when it came in *assignats*, virtually worthless. Their uniforms became worn and threadbare; their horses died from exhaustion and old age; and the gendarmes were neither reimbursed not given replacements. In many companies morale plummeted.

Following his appointment in the turbulent South-East, Radet made an impressive start at whipping his division into shape. Then in Vendémiaire year VIII he had a meeting which was to be of major significance for the future. General Bonaparte, recently returned from his ill-fated Egyptian expedition, had yet more bad luck when some of the brigands in Radet's jurisdiction pillaged his baggage. The two generals dined together, and appear to have got on well. 'I did not miss the opportunity of serving my division . . .' recalled Radet. 'I explained the situation of our men, requested his help in getting arms, and showed him all our needs.'[5] Five months after the coup of Brumaire, Radet was summoned to Paris and charged with preparing a reorganization of the entire gendarmerie.

Radet's deliberations resulted in the *Arrêté* of 12 thermidor year IX (31 July 1801), which established the structure of the gendarmerie for the Napoleonic period. The corps was to consist of 15,600 men. The smallest unit on the ground was to be the brigade of six men commanded by an NCO – a *maréchal des logis* or a *brigadier* – and stationed in a small barracks in a town or village on a main road. The majority of brigades were mounted (1,750, as opposed to 750 on foot); but it had long been recognized that it was more sensible to deploy men on foot in mountainous regions or where the ground was broken and criss-crossed with rivers. The brigades were organized into companies, one for each department, commanded by a *chef d'escadron* or captain; and four companies made up a legion (a term much more in keeping with republican, and later imperial, aspirations). The appointment to the companies was to be supervised by a departmental council made up of the prefect and two gendarmerie officers; the officers themselves were appointed by the First Consul, and later the emperor. The command of the entire corps was to be in the hands of a headquarters, comprising a general of division, who was to be the *Premier Inspecteur Général*, and two generals of brigade. Radet seemed the obvious choice for the principal post; but at this point he had a serious difference of opinion with the First Consul,[6] and the senior post went to General Adrien-Jeannot Bon de Moncey. Radet was given one of the two subordinate posts, and packed off to Corsica; the other subordinate post went to General Louis Wirion, who had established the gendarmerie in the Belgian departments and on the left bank of the Rhine, and reorganized the companies engaged in the Vendéen conflict.

Moncey, created a marshal in 1804 and subsequently Duc de Conegliano, was a prickly individual who regularly clashed with Fouché and others at the Ministry of General Police, particularly over maintaining the independence of his command and the autonomy of his men on the ground. Gendarmes could be summoned to provide *main-forte* for civilian functionaries seeking to carry out their duties; Moncey was quick to protest about any instance where civilian functionaries appeared to have taken advantage of this situation or seemed to have called on gendarmes simply to provide themselves with a bit of military swank and glamour. He was similarly incensed, as were the men in his command, when local officials took the part of local people against gendarmes, something which occurred particularly in confrontations or disorders over the enforcement of conscription. But if Moncey supported his men in confrontation with others, he expected them to behave like an élite. When mail coaches or tax convoys were attacked by brigands, and when some of the property or money was taken in spite of a gendarmerie escort, the members of that escort were promptly suspended, and their behaviour during the attack was investigated: '. . . a gendarme should die rather than yield to brigands, whatever their number', he declared in May 1807 when announcing such an investigation following an attack on the tax receipts of Bergerac.[7] The man who distinguished himself significantly by his courage in such an attack, or in a campaign against brigands, could expect praise and sometimes a reward – possibly a promotion, a money payment, or an engraved carbine or sabre.

The imperial gendarmerie was generally recruited from soldiers, usually NCOs who had served with the colours in several campaigns and who had good conduct records. The principal exceptions were men who were drafted from line regiments into gendarmerie companies when these were first established in some of the new departments of, first, the Republic, and, then, the Empire; this was the case, for example, with the first Piedmontese companies in the year X. Many French gendarmes were serving in the department of their birth, and it appears that men used the gendarmerie as a way of returning to their *pays natal* after years of campaigning. On 20 Fructidor year XI, for example, the colonel of the 3rd Chasseurs forwarded the names of four men in his regiment who sought appointment to the gendarmerie; all specified the department in which they wished to serve, and three out of the four requested their department of birth. A year later the colonel of the 12th Chasseurs forwarded a list of volunteers to the minister of war with the comment, 'they wish, citizen minister, to be employed, if it is possible, in their [native] department.'[8] Such men may have lost their patrimony because of their time away; they may have grown attached to the hierarchical, disciplined military way of life; either way the gendarmerie provided a route home with the prestige of a smart uniform and the promise of a pension. Concerns that local men might have more sympathy with local communities than with the demands of the state does not appear to have concerned gendarmerie commanders; moreover they recognized the value of having men who could speak the local *patois* or language. As the empire extended, so local men began to be recruited into the Belgian, Dutch, German, Italian, and Swiss departmental companies; the ratio of local men allowed in these companies appears to have varied from region to region, and in some instances local men were difficult to find, which probably meant that the ratios were not met; but the intention shows again that the value of men with local knowledge was recognized.

In the same way that questions were not posed about men's serving in the department of their birth, so, after the initial years of reorganization during the Revolution, no one queried the military nature of the corps. In December 1790 Robespierre had expressed concerns about the military nature of the old *maréchaussée* and what this might mean for liberty.[9] But within three years the *levée en masse* had, technically at least, created an army of the people. *La Grande Nation* was a military nation; the Napoleonic state was a state constantly at war. In addition to combating brigands – and the term brigand was a broad one, embracing highwaymen, smugglers, royalist rebels, sometimes (in the case of the Tyrol and the Kingdom of Naples) proto-nationalist rebels, and sometimes a combination of two or more of these – the gendarmerie also had duties that related specifically to the army and the military requirements of the régime. Its military ethos consequently remained, and tended to overshadow the 'half-civilan' element of which Napoleon was to write.

The gendarme's day-to-day tasks were divided into *service ordinaire* and *service extraordinaire*. The former involved patrolling the main roads, visiting fairs, markets, and village festivals, and liaising with the men of neighbouring brigades. A *journal de service* was carried, and had to be signed by mayors or other village functionaries on every routine or special patrol so as to verify that a brigade was carrying out its duties. Extraordinary service meant being called upon to provide *main-forte*, guarding tax receipts or ammunition convoys, or supervising troops on the march.

Throughout the Empire an enormous amount of the time of the brigades was taken up with enforcing conscription legislation. Officers were required to assist the sub-prefects in conducting the ballots, while the brigades were responsible for providing escorts for the conscripts *en route* to their muster points and squads for the pursuit of draft-dodgers and deserters. It was as a result of these tasks that the gendarmes clashed with the local communities, particularly in the more remote areas, where the peasantry had little inclination to see their fit young men dragged off to fight in wars about which they knew little and probably cared less. The gendarmerie had been developed in the early days of the Revolution, with its keenest advocates stressing that it would be of immense value in the villages by standing above local faction and partisanship;[10] yet in its rôle as the emperor's principal recruiting sergeant it appears in many instances to have united communities against the demands of the state. As Isser Woloch has stressed, the Napoleonic conscription system worked, and it grew in efficiency as the Empire progressed;[11] and while a statistical estimate is impossible given the fragmentary nature of the sources, it appears that violent hostility to the gendarmes over recruiting issues declined alongside the system's increasing efficiency.

The demands that the Napoleonic wars made on the gendarmerie did not stop at conscription. It was responsible for the supervision of prisoners of war, and the emperor was constantly calling for men to be detached from the departmental brigades for service in newly annexed territories or with the armies. At the beginning of 1807, for example, the gendarmerie company of the Ardennes had 23 men on detachment out of a complement of 103, and its neighbour in the Moselle had 39 on detachment out of a complement of 114 (see Table 1). Concerned prefects wrote to the ministry of police about their under-strength gendarmerie companies, and when in February 1813 Napoleon demanded 750 gendarmes to reinforce his heavy cavalry regiments, Moncey felt compelled to point out that there were already 4,373 men on detachment – the total establishment of the corps, forty legions across the whole Empire, was then set at 26,000 men.[12]

Table 1: Men on detachment from the companies of the Ardennes and the Moselle, 1 January 1807

	Ardennes	Moselle
Grande Armée	4	6
Army in Holland	3	2
Army on coasts	–	2
Army at Boulogne	1	–
Elite Legion	4	2
Dept of Meuthe	3	4
Dept of Bas Rhin	2	–
Dept of Mont Tonnère	–	2
Bitche	–	11
Luxembourg	3	4
St. Quentin	1	–
Verdun	1	2
Fulde (Prussia)	2	2
Mainz	3	–

Source: A.G. X^{f}92, Gendarmerie, revues d'inspection, an X-1870.

Under-strength or not, the Napoleonic gendarmerie generally did its job. Major-General Lord Blayney, captured by the French during the Peninsular War, recalled seeing parties of gendarmes, two or three strong, guarding large bodies of conscripts, draft-dodgers or prisoners as he was moved into France. 'The gend'armerie, indeed, forms the most efficient military police in Europe,' he wrote, 'and is so well established, that not only the roads are safe, but the people are also kept in complete political subjection.'[13] By the fall of the Empire, brigandage within France itself had been greatly reduced from the situation at the end of the Directory; brigandage was also less serious in the Low Countries and Piedmont, where French administration, and gendarmes, had been active for more than a decade. Of course, as in the case of the success of the system of the conscription legislation, the gendarmerie cannot take all the credit, and it would be difficult to separate its rôle from that of other groups and institutions; but, equally, it would be wrong to ignore its significance.

The success of the corps was not lost on the restored Bourbons. From the end of 1815 until the summer of 1816 the gendarmerie was purged of men who had demonstrated an excess of zeal for the usurper, especially during the Hundred Days.[14] But like many of the other institutions reorganized during the Revolutionary and Napoleonic years, the gendarmerie was maintained. There was some discussion of reviving the name *maréchaussée*;[15] after all its precursor had appeared a relatively successful *ancien régime* institution. But, above all the Bourbons recognized a value in maintaining a military police presence in the countryside. An Ordinance of 29 October 1820 was the charter of the Restoration gendarmerie. It consolidated changes and practices developed since the close of the *ancien régime* and settled the structure of the institution until the reforms of Napoleon III. Two élite companies were to be based in Paris; but the bulk of the corps, 14,000 men, were deployed in the provinces, one company to each department. The general passivity of the provinces during the 1820s, and the pressing desire to reduce the military budget, brought about a reduction of 1,400 men in December 1828.

With their colourful uniforms and the royal flag flying over their small barracks, the gendarmes were a physical manifestation of the state in the countryside. Their regular two-man patrols along the main roads, into the towns and villages, the markets and fairs, were demonstrations of state authority. But the presence of the gendarmerie brigades was also a demonstration of the state's insistence that it had a responsibility for the protection of its citizens. On their patrols the gendarmes looked for the kinds of people who were feared as dangerous or as threats to order. They arrested deserters, vagrants, beggars, disturbers of the peace, and people without passports, as well as those suspected of crimes and those caught in the act or with warrants against them (see Table 2). They acted also as direct representatives of the state enforcing its regulations; most notably, following the St Cyr Law of 1818, they continued their involvement with conscription and the pursuit of *réfractaires*; and they could be punished severely by their superiors if their activities smacked of arbitrariness and thus brought the state into disrepute. In February 1821, for example, the *brigadier* of Lavoûte-Chilhac (Haute-Loire) thought he had spotted a deserter, and arrested him; the local community was agitated, but did not seek to impede him. Unfortunately for the *brigadier*, he had got the wrong man, and his company commander thought it necessary to reprimand him for his over-eagerness. Similarly, one of the gendarmes in the same brigade was reprimanded and imprisoned for a day for firing his carbine unnecessarily when in pursuit of the same deserter. The legion commander considered it worthwhile to remind his men that their guns were only for defence.[16]

The gendarmes also provided the central government with additional sets of eyes and ears in the provinces. The commanders sent monthly reports to Paris on the state of commerce in their department, on public opinion, and chronicling any incidents of particular note. At times they told the government what it wanted to hear: 'The death of Bonnaparte [*sic*] has had no great impact.'[17] At times they emphasized a more personal agenda, notably the important, but hard-pressed, rôle of the gendarmerie, and the lack of support that it received from local mayors and the part-time police of the communes.[18] But overall the gendarmerie reports from the Restoration period contained little to concern the government; the corps itself, and perhaps also the bureaucrats in Paris, were inclined to put this down to the vigilance of their patrols.

Just as the efficiency and effectiveness of the Napoleonic regime, and of the gendarmerie, were not lost on the Bourbons, so it was with other rulers of Europe. Indeed, when many of them had met Napoleon, they must also have seen his gendarmes. The élite legion was incorporated into the Old Guard in 1804; its infantry battalion guarded the imperial palaces, while its two mounted squadrons followed Napoleon on his travels.

While the subject has been little explored, it seems that in continental Europe during the eighteenth century there were a variety of different kinds of organization deployed for the protection of property and/or the preservation of the peace. Many towns employed some sort of watch; in rural districts different systems had been developed for protecting the fields. Most Italian states had motley collections of *sbirri*, often little better

Table 2: Monthly arrests by the Gendarmerie Company of Finistère, 1817

Offence	Jan.	Feb.	March	April	May	June	July	August	Sept.	Oct.	Nov.	Dec.	Total
Murder	–	2	1	9	6	2	–	1	–	1	2	–	24
Theft	10	22	6	16	44	17	29	28	19	24	6	9	230
Arson	–	–	–	–	1	–	–	–	–	1	–	–	2
Other crimes	5	1	–	4	4	7	3	8	6	4	4	2	48
Strangers without passports	1	5	1	3	6	4	1	1	2	–	–	4	28
Disturbing the public peace	2	–	1	–	–	–	–	–	–	–	–	–	3
Beggars, vagrants, etc.	2	3	5	2	4	11	7	5	5	5	9	3	61
Arrested on warrant	14	32	34	16	42	43	32	32	11	7	20	14	297
Soldiers	8	4	6	10	10	7	3	3	1	1	1	2	56
Sailors	6	5	–	2	7	9	10	3	5	6	2	1	96
Total	48	74	54	62	124	100	85	81	49	49	44	35	805

Source: A.N.F[7] 3997, Rapports de Gendarmerie, Finistère, 1817 à 1825.

than the offenders against whom they might be deployed, and notorious for their indiscipline and violence. In Naples and Tuscany at least, in the last quarter of the eighteenth century, there were plans to reform the system.[19] The princes of the principal German states had begun to establish police organizations for their main towns and cities. These were similar to that in Paris under the *ancien régime*'s *lieutenant général de police de la ville*; their duties covered the broad, *ancien régime* definition of 'police' as the general administration of affairs, covering everything from street lighting to markets, as well as crime and public order; but they were increasingly perceived as a preventive authority intended to preserve the state against internal enemies. In the 1780s Count Pergen, Joseph II's chief of police, even went so far as to propose that a force similar to the *maréchaussée* be established for the Habsburg lands; but his plan came to nothing. When confronted by instances of serious disorder, or by a large number of beggars or vagrants, the first and last resort of most *ancien régime* rulers was the use of troops.[20]

Societies are never static, partly because the ideas and contexts within which they exist are never static. The period of the Enlightenment witnessed the development of new ideas about crime and punishment. Whether or not these shifting perceptions are best slotted into Whiggish notions of progress, Norbert Elias's concept of a civilizing process, or a bleak Foucauldian vision of new forms of discipline and power, is immaterial, at least for recognizing the existence of the new ideas. Cesare Beccaria's *On Crimes and Punishment*, first published in 1764, did not change men's minds; but it focused much of their thinking. There were only a few who articulated the demand for what might be considered as modern police institutions at the end of the eighteenth century, yet the logic of the arguments presented by Beccaria, and others, moved in this direction. Impartial justice required impartial enforcement of the law, and the certainty of punishment following a crime required that some kind of force be developed and deployed to ensure the certainty of capture after an offence had been committed.

Fears during the French revolutionary period gave a boost to the kinds of policing that concentrated on the preservation of the state against internal enemies. The Revolutionary and Napoleonic wars brought serious internal disruption across Europe. Napoleon's continental system was profitable for some; but it also upset many local economies, forcing people into penury and on to the roads as beggars. The British response to the blockade, and the Europeans' demands for British goods, provided new opportunities for smugglers. The French presence as an occupying power or a protector occasionally provoked proto-nationalist disorders, often tinged with a ferociously anti-French and pre-Concordat Catholicism. The scale and duration of the Revolutionary and Napoleonic wars meant enormous demand for soldiers, and led to armies criss-crossing the continent for a quarter of a century. Recruitment of soldiers, often through conscription, led to draft-dodgers hiding in the countryside. Armies lost men through desertion; they also left stragglers in their wake. Beggars on the roads, smugglers, draft-dodgers, deserters, and soldiers themselves, all fostered fears of 'brigands'.

Exposure to Napoleonic France through both war and the subsequent Napoleonic redrawing of state boundaries also provided exposure to the Napoleonic model of government and administration. Where the Empire was extended the gendarmerie was established as part and parcel of the imperial administration; its rôle was to bring order, tranquillity and what the French bureaucracy understood as the rule of law – one of the benefits of being 'French'.[21] Where Napoleon redrew frontiers and put allied monarchs under his protection he also encouraged them to reform and reorganize their government along French lines. Maximilian Joseph of Bavaria, for example, was encouraged to give his subjects a constitution in 1808. Section five of the sixth article of this constitution promised to create a gendarmerie 'for policing purposes' [*zur Handhabung der Polizei*], and the constitution concluded with a rousing postscript: 'People of our kingdom! Security, your common welfare, is our aim.'[22] It was another four years before the force was actually created; but this kind of declaration was indicative of the major shift away from the old corporate society and of the attempts by German princes, or more often their ministers, to whittle away at the old administrative, fiscal, and judicial independence of the nobles and gentry, and to create both unity in their territories and a common political identity. The gendarmeries need to be seen as part and parcel of these reforms. In addition to the perceived need for a coercive force to maintain order, to pursue criminals and vagabonds, and to prevent crime, the gendarmes, theoretically at least, provided an equal 'security' to all a prince's subjects. Hostility to things French in the aftermath of Napoleon's fall may have led to a disassociation of the gendarmeries from their roots, but did not lead to their abolition. In Württemburg in March 1823, for example, the title 'gendarmerie' was suppressed. The *Landjäger-korps*, as the force was now to be known, was tied more closely to the civilian authorities than previously; but it was still recruited from former soldiers with good conduct records aged between twenty-five and forty, and it still carried out the same duties, based on the French pattern. The major difference between the German gendarmes and the French was the way in which they were deployed.

Primarily, it appears, because of expense, the German forces were much smaller. The men were usually deployed singly, and required to find their own lodgings within their individual juridictions; costs thus fell largely on the men themselves, and there could be hardship, especially if a man was transferred.[23]

The Prussian reformers, who had little love for Napoleon, nevertheless sought to employ many ideas drawn from the French administration. The *Gendarmerie Edikt* of 1812 was a good example of this. Like their French counterparts, the new Prussian gendarmes were expected to mount patrols for the prevention of crime, to ensure safe passage on the roads, and to watch out for deserters and suspicious persons – notably vagrants. But the structure of the new corps was not outlined until two-thirds of the way through the edict. First came the plan for a major reorganization of local government across the kingdom, with state functionaries replacing the old feudal structures. The reformers reckoned without the concerted hostility of the *Junkers*, who, while intensely loyal to their king, saw the new structure as an attack on their way of life and particularly on the concept of *Herrschaft*, by which they took paternal responsibility for their peasants and administered their estates. As a result of this opposition, together with the financial stringency required after the massive upheavals and military effort of the war years, the new administrative structure was never set up. The gendarmerie was created, although on a far smaller scale than the original plan envisaged; instead of 9,000, the reductions implemented in 1820 resulted in a force of just over 1,300 NCOs and men, generally deployed, as elsewhere in Germany, not in small brigades but individually.[24]

There were other governments in Restoration Europe that considered that the gendarmeries created for departments outside France's frontiers of 1792 had proved their worth. In the wake of Napoleon's fall, William of Orange found himself King of the Netherlands, with centralized powers largely established by the French, of which his predecessors, as stadt-holders, could only have dreamt. William largely maintained the structures left by the French; and he also rapidly saw the value of re-creating a gendarmerie. Such a force was of particular use in his Belgian territories, newly united with the Netherlands, where French gendarmes had been deployed since 1795. The *Koninklijke Marechaussee* was recruited from both Belgians and Dutch, but with a high percentage of Belgian officers. After the revolution of 1830 the independent Belgian state opted to establish a *gendarmerie nationale* of its own to police the rural districts. The Dutch kept their *Marechaussee*, initially in their remaining southern provinces, where the population was predominantly Catholic, and, it was feared, likely to secede with the Belgians; but in emergencies, and subsequently permanently, the corps was spread across the rest of the country.[25]

There were also Restoration governments that regarded things French with suspicion, and that were even more susceptible to the pressure of vested interests and the old order. The gendarmerie introduced into Spain by Joseph Bonaparte never had the opportunity of settling in as an ordinary police institution, and was swept out of the country with the French. A proposal to establish a gendarmerie-type body in July 1820 was rapidly withdrawn; it had the potential for annoying too many interests.[26] Reformers under Fernando VII had far less clout than those in Restoration Prussia. Following Napoleon's fall several Italian provinces and states saw such corps completely abolished. The reasons why the Habsburg government decided against recreating a gendarmerie in Venetia are not entirely clear, especially given the fact that it decided to maintain such a body in neighbouring Lombardy.[27] In Naples and many of the smaller Italian states, the reason seems to have been partly at least a distaste for all things French, although it may also have been due to doubts about their efficacy. In much of Naples under the Napoleonic régime the gendarmerie had never been able to risk deployment in small barracks along the main roads because of the scale of brigandage; Neapolitan gendarmes under Joseph Bonaparte and King Joachim Murat appear usually to have acted in concert with the army.

But in Piedmont and the Papal States, in spite of their rulers' hostility to Napoleon, the restored rulers saw distinct advantages in developing gendarmeries. Not only had the imperial gendarmerie demonstrated an effectiveness against brigandage, in complete contrast to the old *sbirri*; but a gendarmerie appeared also to provide a means of establishing and cementing a new relationship between ruler and ruled. The *carabinieri* of Piedmont could profess links with the *ancien régime* partly through the long military traditions of the Savoyard monarchy but also, particularly, by claiming a lineage from the men of a military unit first established in 1791 to combat brigandage, who were subsequently deployed as light troops during the Revolutionary wars.[28] Brigandage remained a problem, with several *carabinieri* being killed in clashes with brigands during the Restoration period; but it was less serious than before. Moreover, Vittorio Emanuele and his ministers did not see the new force simply as a body organized to fight brigands and pursue other offenders. The new Piedmontese *carabinieri* and, even more explicit, those of the Papal States were intended to be very different from the old *sbirri*. The new *carabinieri* were to be moral forces whose impartial protection of the population and whose respectful behaviour towards the public – even when inspecting passports and travel papers – were intended to foster a new paternal relationship between ruler and ruled and a new respect for, and loyalty towards, the state.[29]

Of course, after a decade or more of war and occupation, many of the men best equipped to serve in these forces were Napoleonic veterans who had imbibed some liberal notions, not the least of which was the idea of a career open to talent. For many of these men it was galling to find themselves subordinate to commanders with little or no experience, but who possessed the fortune of birth. During the Piedmontese revolution of 1821 several *carabinieri* with Napoleonic backgrounds, like other military personnel, sided with the rebels; a few others appear to have been ambivalent, but the majority of the corps remained loyal to the existing régime.[30] The experience of 1821 prompted the Savoyard monarchy to attempt to tighten up on the men recruited and to require a new oath of allegiance that forbade membership of any political or masonic societies.[31]

Unlike the gendarmeries in Restoration Germany, those in Italy appear generally to have followed the French system of deployment in small brigades. But like the German corps, post-war financial retrenchment helped keep the Italian corps small and, often, under strength. In Piedmont there were complaints that some men lived in poor conditions and did not receive their pay on time. Such problems may have led to discontent and some corruption.[32] Most men appear, more or less, to have carried out the tasks required of them, though there were occasional complaints of individuals who were idle or simply not up to the job.[33] As might be expected with any institution, there were some who cut corners, or who bickered with their comrades, their superiors and/or their inferiors. Good officers and NCOs nipped such problems in the bud; but occasionally such clashes could result in gendarmes' having resort to their weapons to settle matters.[34]

The arguments for maintaining, or re-establishing, the gendarmerie corps were not always clearly articulated. The situation of Europe in the immediate aftermath of the Napoleonic adventure in itself provides an explanation on one level. Peace did not bring internal tranquillity. Demobilized soldiers were, after all, returning to labour markets in economies often as disrupted by peace as they had been by war and the blockade. The first years of peace witnessed poor harvests, which prompted disorders and drove more of the poor on to the roads, with the consequent fears of disorder and brigandage. In addition, the restored régimes were still fearful of the revolutionary ideologies that had convulsed Europe for a quarter of a century and that, in spite of defeat on the battlefield, had not ceased to excite minds. The gendarmerie model as developed under Napoleon offered at least part of a solution to each of these problems. Permanent squads of élite troops stationed in small numbers in the provinces could act as the eyes and ears of the state and the first line of defence against brigandage and disorder. They could also ensure that the state got what it demanded in taxes and conscripts.

But on a different level of analysis, the gendarmeries also fitted well with the reforming and integrationist programmes of the princes and ministers of several early nineteenth-century states both before and after Napoleon's fall. Such states had acquired new territories either during the Napoleonic regime itself (as in the case of Baden, Bavaria and Württemburg), or immediately following its collapse. There was a need to forge a unity and an identity in the newly expanded states, but also in those that had been wrenched from an *ancien régime* into the Napoleonic Empire, and then wrenched back to restored rulers. Gendarmes provided one way of demonstrating the presence of the state to the peasants, and to others, in both old possessions and newly acquired territories. Moreover, while it was not always possible for the reformers to dispense entirely with all the old judicial and administrative structures, the gendarmeries were precursors of the new. They contributed towards the reformist jurists' aspirations to equal and impartial justice for all and the reformist ministers' aspirations for a state within which loyalty was based on consent from below and a paternalist, rational bureaucracy administering from above. Rational bureaucracy required information to facilitate policy decisions; gendarmes constituted another source of such information, with their monthly and annual reports on the situation within their jurisdictions – reports that did not just focus on crime and order, but also discussed agriculture, commerce, and public opinion.

Notes

1. My thanks to the Leverhulme Trust for financial assistance, which has provided me with time to develop my research into the European gendarmeries. The issues discussed in this essay can be followed up in detail in Clive Emsley, *Gendarmes and the State in Nineteenth-Century Europe* (Oxford, 1999).

2. For the different varieties of police in nineteenth-century Europe see Clive Emsley, 'A Typology of Nineteenth-Century Police', *Crime, histoire et sociétés/Crime, History and Societies*, 3 (1999), pp.29–44.

3. *Correspondance de Napoléon 1er*, Vol. 12. no. 10243, au roi de Naples, 16 mai 1806.

4. Etienne Amadée Combier, (ed.), *Mémoires du général Radet d'après ses papiers personnels et les archives de l'état* (Saint-Cloud, 1892), p.112.

5. Combier (ed.), *Mémoires du général Radet*, p.131.

6. Ibid., p.148.

7. Archives Nationales Af IV 1156, Report to emperor, 13 May 1807.

8. A[rchives de la] G[uerre, Vincennes], Xf 246 Gendarmerie, recrutement An XI – 1806.

9. *Archives Parlementaires (1re série)*, xxi, 244–7.

10. A.-C. Guichard, *Manuel de la Gendarmerie Nationale* (Paris, 1791), pp.137–9.

11. I. Woloch, 'Napoleonic Conscription: State Power and Civil Society,' *Past and Present*, 111 (1986), pp.101–29; idem, *The New Regime. Transformation of the French Civic Order, 1789–1820s* (New York, 1994), Ch. 13; for violent confrontations between gendarmes and local communities over conscription and deserters, see A. Forrest, *Conscripts and Deserters. The Army and French Society during the Revolution and Empire* (New York, 1989), especially pp.220–1 and 232–5.

12. A.N. AFIV 1158, Report to emperor, 13 Feb. 1813. For letters about the problems of under-strength companies see, *inter alia*, Ernest d'Hautrive (ed.), *La Police Secrète de Premier Empire* (5 vols, Paris, 1922–64), Vol. 5, pp.510 and 590.

13. Major General Lord Blayney, *Narrative of a Forced Journey through Spain and France as a Prisoner of War in the Years 1810 to 1814* (2 vols, London, 1814) Vol. 1, p.486.

14. A.G. Xf 10 and Xf 11, Decisions ministerielles rendues sur les rapports du jury d'organisation de la gendarmerie.

15. A.G.MR 1957, Liasse 'gendarmerie, 1814 à 1830', Rapport sur la dénomination de maréchaussée à substituer à celle de gendarmerie, n. d.

16. A.N. F7 4143, monthly report from Rhône Company, Feb. 1821. The commander of the 19th Legion (Rhône, Saône-et-Loire, Loire, and Haute-Loire) appears to have mistakenly inserted his report on the Haute-Loire in the report of the company commander of the Rhône.

17. A.N. F7 4009, monthly report from the Gers Company, July 1820.
18. See, *inter alia*, A.N. F7 3947, annual report from the Cantal Company, 1818; F7 3997, monthly reports from the Finistère Company, Aug., Nov., Dec. 1821 and July 1823; F7 4144, monthly reports from Rhône Company, Jan. 1826, Jan., Feb., Mar., 1827, and Jan. 1828.
19. G. Alessi, *Giustizia e polizia. Il controlo di una capitale, Napoli 1719–1803* (Naples, 1992); C. Mangio, *La polizia toscana: organizzazione e criteri d'intervento, 1765–1808* (Milan, 1988); and for the *sbirri*, see S. C. Hughes, 'Fear and Loathing in Bologna and Rome. The Papal Police in Perspective', *Journal of Social History*, 21 (1987), pp.97–116.
20. See, *inter alia*, R. Axtmann, '"Police" and the Formation of the Modern State. Legal and Ideological Assumptions on State Capacity in the Austrian Lands of the Habsburg Empire, 1500–1800', *German History*, 10 (1992), pp.39–61; P. P. Bernard, *From the Enlightenment to the Police State: The Public Life of Johann Anton Pergen* (Urbana, IL, 1991), especially Ch. 5; W. Obenaus, *Die Entwicklung der preußischen Sicherheitspolizei bis Zum Ende der Reaktionszeit* (Berlin, 1940); F. Walter, 'Die Organisierung der staatlichen Polizei unter Kaiser Joseph II', *Mitteilungen des Vereins für Geschichte des Stadt Wien*, 7 (1927), pp.22–53.
21. See, for example, Moncey's *Supplément à l'ordre général du 5 frimaire an XI, specialement adressé aux brigades de la gendarmerie placées dan le ci-devant Piémont*.
22. P. Wegelin, 'Die Bayerische Konstitution von 1808', in W. Näf and E. Walder (eds), *Schweizer Beiträger zur Allgemeinen Geschichte* (Berne, 1958), pp.154–206. (The constitution itself is reprinted on pp.143–53.) For the creation of the gendarmerie in Bavaria, as well as in the other two major states of southern Germany whose frontiers were remade by Napoleon, see B. Wirsing, 'Die Geschichte der Gendarmeriekorps und deren Vorläuferorganisationen in Baden, Württemberg und Bayern, 1750–1850', unpublished Ph.D. thesis, University of Konstanz, 1991, Ch. 3 and Ch. 4.
23. W. Wannenwetsch, *Das Württembergische Landjägerkorps und die reichseinheitliche Gendarmerie in Württemberg mit einer Rückschau auf die Anfänge der Landespolizei* (Stuttgart, 1986), p.29.
24. R. Koselleck, *Preußen zwischen Reform und Revolution: Allgemeines Landrecht, Verwaltung und Soziale Bewegung von 1791 bis 1848* (Stuttgart, 1963), pp.460–1.
25. L. Van Outrive, Y. Cartuyvels and P. Ponsaers, *Les Polices en Belgique: Histoire socio-politique du système policier de 1794 à nos*

jours (Brussels, 1991), pp.18 and 29–30; W. van den Hoek, *De Geschiedenis van het Wapen der Koninklijke Marechausee* (Apeldoorn, 1963).

26. E-M. Ruiz 'Las Fuerzas de Seguridad y Orden Publico en la Primera Mitad del Siglo XIX', *Cuadernos de Historia*, 4 (1973), pp. 149–52.

27. D. Laven, 'Law and Order in Habsburg Venetia, 1814–1835', *Historical Journal*, 39 (1996), pp.387–9.

28. M. Ruggiero, *Storia del Piemonte* (Turin, 1979), p.768.

29. S. C. Hughes, *Crime, Disorder and the Risorgimento. The Politics of Policing in Bologna* (Cambridge, 1994), pp.38–40.

30. P. Di Terlizzi, *Quando frammenti di storia si ricompongono. Alle radici culturali e formative dell'Arma dei Carabinieri* (Bari, 1991), pp.31–84.

31. *Regolamento Generale del Corpo dei Carabinieri*, 16 Oct. 1822.

32. Archivio di Stato di Torino, Sezione Riunite, Categoria: Guerra. Segretaria di Guerra e Marina. Registro: Corrispondenza col Ministro di Polizia e Carabinieri Reale, 1819–1822: 5 Apr. 1821, Sindaco of Brusasco: Registro 1 bis, Divisione: Registro della Corrispondenza per Reggimenti Provinciali e Milizie, Oct. 1816, charges of harassment, corruption and extortion. My thanks to Mike Broers for this reference.

33. See, for example, the complaints about several of the Prussian gendarmes in the Krefeld district during the silk-workers' dispute of 1823, Heinrich Rösen, 'Der Aufstand der Krefelder "Seidenfabrikarbeiter" 1823 und die Bildung einer "Sicherheitswache": Ein Dokumentation', *Die Heimat: Zeitschrift für Niederrheinische Heimatpflege*, 36 (1965), p.41.

34. In an incident which, but for its appallingly tragic nature, smacks of comic-book Latin passions, *carabiniere* Giuseppe Papadore killed two women as a result of his 'excessive and frantic jealousy'. When his comrades came to arrest him he killed one, wounded two more, one mortally, and then shot himself. The officers investigating the case, which occurred at Sampierdarena (Genoa) in October 1818, concluded that *brigadier* Stefano Moresco, Papadore's NCO, might have prevented the tragedy had he been firmer at the outset. Archivio del Museo Storico dell'Arma dei Carabinieri, Rome, Morto in Servizio, Scheda 9 (Rovere, Bartolomeo) and Scheda 10 (Sbarbaro, Andrea).

Index

Index

Index

Index

Index

Catholic Church, 3, 14–15, 41, 139, 171, 184–6, 188, 217, 225, 230
censorship, 33, 38, 41, 242
citizenship, 205–206
Consulate, 134, 217
Directory, 241–2
elections and electorate, 4, 31, 36–43 *passim*, 118, 175, 186–7, 189
expansionism, 101–102
Fifth Republic, 171
gendarmerie, 4, 30, 258
imperial legacy, 178
July Monarchy, 104, 177, 191
liberals, 33, 36, 39, 41–2, 187–92
local government, 42, 170–71
Ministère des Cultes, 223
national colours, 168, 209
National Guard, 184
nobility, 14–15, 170, 183–5, 192
notables, 4, 30, 176 193–4
Police, 4, 169, 172–3, 176, 178
prefects, 30, 33, 36, 42, 192–3
Protestants, 171, 173–4, 184–5
representative institutions, 173, 175, 187–90
republicans, 185
Revolutions,
    1830, 41, 43, 88, 137, 142, 183, 185, 191, 193–4
    1848–9, 191
Third Republic, 218
see also Charte, French Revolution, Napoleon
France Méridionale, 43
Francesco IV of Modena, 10
Francis I of Austria, 6, 9–10, 12, 14, 158, 199
Francis Joseph, 49, 210
Franco, 65
Frankfurt, 101, 200
    Federal Diet, 207, 210
    Parliament (1848–9), 83
Frederick Augustus of Saxony, 116, 118
Frederick II of Prussia, 205, 221
Frederick William III of Prussia, 98, 219, 221–8 *passim*, 226
    religious beliefs, 221–2
    head of Church of the Prussian Union, 228

Frederick William IV of Prussia, 87, 91, 210
freemasonry, 14, 130, 133, 184, 238
French Revolution, 3, 7, 19, 93, 143, 167–70, 185–6, 192
    and Catholic Church, 217
    and Germany, 83, 143
    and Italy, 51
    Terror, 185
Froment, François, 170, 178

Gagern, Hans von, 205–207
Galileo, 248
Gallicanism, 41, 219
Garay, Martin de, 75
Gard, 36, 169, 172, 174–6, 193, 258
Garibaldi, Giuseppe, 49, 151, 237
Gazzetta di Milano, 245
gendarmerie, 257, 260
    and conscription, 262
    and French Revolution, 261
    and Napoleonic administration, 267
    and territories annexed by Napoleon, 260
    and state power in the countryside, 263, 271
    Bavaria, 267
    Belgium, 259, 268
    France, 4, 10, 30, 36, 258, 263–4
    Germany, 267–8
    Italy, 269
    Kingdom of Naples, 269
    Lombardy, 269
    not retained in Venetia, 13
    not retained in Kingdom of the Two Sicilies, 13
    Papal States, 269
    Prussia, 13, 135, 268
    Sardinia-Piedmont, 13, 154, 260, 269
    Spain, 269
    used in war, 262
    Württemberg, 267
Gendarmerie Edikt, see Prussia
Gentz, Friedrich, 12
Genoa, 18, 241
George, Stefan, 107
Gerlach, 105
German Confederation, 12, 17, 92, 206

Index

nobility, 88
representative institutions, 87
Hansemann, 89, 142–3
Hardenberg, Karl August von, 9, 86, 92, 135–6, 139, 141, 205, 207
Hartmann, Felix, 184–5
Hasli, 224
Hatzfeldt-Schuckmann-Wittgenstein clique, 134
Haussez, 36–8
Haute-Garonne, 38, 42, 170, 173
Haute-Loire, 264
Hegel, 87
Heine, Heinrich, 97–8
Hérault, 220, 258
Hernoux, Étienne, 184, 186
Herold, Christopher, 219
Herrschaft, 83, 85, 268
Hesse-Darmstadt, 200–201, 205–208
constitution, 201
national colours, 202
Hesse-Kassel, 87–8, 92, 207
law codes, 88
national colours, 202
Hofer, Andreas, 6
Hohenzollern dynasty,
Calvinist tradition, 226
see also Prussia
Holbach, 247
Holy Alliance, 44, 117
Holy Roman Empire, 83, 85, 99–100, 133, 137, 143, 199, 204–5, 209
House of Savoy, 152, 205, 253, 257
and Italian Unification, 49
see also Sardinia-Piedmont
Hügel, 102
Hugo, 104
Huguenots, 228, *see also* Protestantism
Hundred Days, *see* Napoleon
Hungary, 211

Iguanza, Pedro, 71
illiteracy, 40, 249
Imaz José, 77
Immediat-Justiz Kommission, 139–40
Infantando, 69, 72–3
Inquisition, 66–7, 68, 74
Ionian Islands, 221,
Ireland, 257

Isère, 36
Italy, 49–64 *passim*, 151–64 *passim*, 237–56 *passim*
ancien régime, 50–60 *passim*, 240–41
bourgeoisie, 243
Catholic Church, 15, 54, 59, 251, 253
censorship, 13, 53, 237–56 *passim*
constitutions, 62 note 9
Concordat, 218
democrats, 50, 57
French invasion and occupation, 5, 51, 57, 130, 220, 241, 243
frontier changes, 18
gendarmerie, 269
Jacobins, 53, 240, 243
law codes, 52
liberals, 57–60, 244
nobility, 15, 51–52, 54–5, 58, 244, 253
notables, 244
police, 243
popular revolts, 245
prefects, 55
representative institutions, 56
Restoration, 241, 244
Revolutions, 126
1820–21, 14, 151–3, 157–8, 161, 240, 250, 270
1848–9, 237–8, 240, 245, 253
Unification, 49
see also Kingdom of Lombardy-Venetia, Kingdom of the Two Sicilies, Papal States, *Risorgimento*, Sardinia-Piedmont
Italian congress of Scientists, 238

Jacobins, 14, 184–6, 191
and Italy, 53, 240, 243
Jena, battle (1806), 9, 221
Jérôme Bonaparte, *see* Bonapart, Jérôme
Jesuits, 41, 68, 74, 78, 159, 188, 247
Jews, 221, 226
John, Michael, 11, 18
Joseph Bonaparte, *see* Bonaparte, Joseph
Joseph II, Holy Roman Emperor, 1, 229, 266
Jouques d'Arbaud, 175–6
journals, 208, 242
Journal de Grenoble, 37
Journal de Rouen, 39

Index

Index

Murat, Joachim, 9–10, 14, 17, 269
Muret, 38
Muslims, 241

Nabucco, see also Verdi *and* G. B.
   Niccolini
Nada, Narcisso, 159
Naples, 9, 16–18, 66, 240–46 *passim*
   and Revolution of 1820, 14
   censorship, 251
   nobility, 250
   sbirri, 266
see also Kingdom of the Two Sicilies *and*
   Neapolitan Republic
Napoleon, 97–8, 167
   administrative centralization,
      modernization, and state building,
      1–2, 4, 18, 31, 42–3, 54–5, 89, 92–3,
      132, 139, 152, 167, 176, 178, 200,
      207, 243, 251, 267
   and Alexander I, 99
   and army, 205
   and Catholic Church, 219–221, 224,
      226, 228–9, 237
      Concordat, 3, 5, 13, 130, 139, 152,
         218, 219–227 *passim*, 267
   and conscription, 261
   and consensus, 19
   and Continental System, 266
   and education, 3
   and Egypt, 221, 258
   and élites, 130, 142–3, 158, 193
   and Eugène Beauharnais, 243
   and gendarmerie, 259, 262, 271
   and German states, 11, 66, 83–6, 89,
      92–3, 100–102, 129–30, 133–4, 139,
      143, 199–200, 207–208, 223, 267
   and Habsburg Empire, 106
   and Holy Roman Empire, 209
   and Italy, 50–55, 57, 66, 130, 152, 156,
      220, 240, 242–3, 245
   and law codes, 3, 4, 39, 66, 98, 117,
      120–21, 140, 144, 156, 186, 200
   and local government, 2, 4
   and Metternich, 99
   and Netherlands, 66
   and Poland, 66, 115–20, *passim*
   and representative government, 30
   and Russia, 115
   and Spain, 65–6, 69, 72
   and Talleyrand, 192
   and Vendée, 221
   authoritarianism, 8, 29, 52, 132, 144,
      155, 244
   Brumaire coup d'état, 2, 9, 130, 259
   exile to Saint Helena, 185
   expansionist ambitions and bellicose
      nature, 3, 99, 261, 266
   fall from power, 49–50, 115, 167,
      244–5, 268
   First Consul, 220
   Hundred Days, 33, 98, 103, 154,
      167–71, 184–5, 192, 263
   impact outside Empire, 9
   Jacobinism, 6–7, 53
   marriage to Marie Louise, 103
   military abilities, 3, 103
   Naturalization Edict (1811), 205
   nicknames, 98
   personality cult, 5
   plebiscites, 5
   Protestant support, 171
   religious views, 219–21, 224
   resistance and opposition, 2, 72, 92,
      100, 143, 152, 157, 243, 261, 266
Napoleon III, 105
Nassau, 86, 200–201, 208
   constitution, 201
   national colours, 208
Nassau-Weilburg, 205
national and state colours and cockades
   Austria, 202, 204
   Baden, 210
   Bavaria, 201–204, 208, 211
   Brunswick, 208
   France, 168, 209
   German Confederation, 210–11
   Germany, 208–209,210–11
   Hesse-Darmstadt, 202, 208
   Hesse-Kassel, 202–203, 208
   Nassau, 208
   Prussia, 204, 210–11
   Reuß, 208
   Saxe-Coburg-Gotha, 204
   Saxe-Meiningen, 204
   Saxony, 202
   Thuringia, 202
   Waldeck, 208

Index

Index

Index

Index